THE CAMBRIDGE GUIDE TO THE ARTS IN BRITAIN
VOLUME 3   RENAISSANCE AND REFORMATION

The Cambridge Guide to the Arts in Britain

The Cambridge Guide to the Arts in Britain

edited by
BORIS FORD

VOLUME 3
RENAISSANCE AND REFORMATION

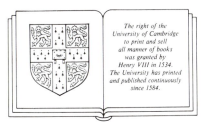

The right of the
University of Cambridge
to print and sell
all manner of books
was granted by
Henry VIII in 1534.
The University has printed
and published continuously
since 1584.

CAMBRIDGE UNIVERSITY PRESS
CAMBRIDGE
NEW YORK   NEW ROCHELLE   MELBOURNE   SYDNEY

Published by the Press Syndicate of the University of Cambridge
The Pitt Building, Trumpington Street, Cambridge CB2 1RP
32 East 57th Street, New York, NY 10022, USA
10 Stamford Road, Oakleigh, Melbourne 3166, Australia

© Boris Ford 1989

First published 1989

Printed in Great Britain by William Clowes, Beccles

British Library cataloguing in publication data

The Cambridge Guide to the Arts in Britain.
  Vol. 3: Renaissance and Reformation
  I. Ford, Boris
  700′.941

Library of Congress Cataloguing in Publication Data
(Revised for volume 3)

The Cambridge guide to the arts in Britain.
  Includes bibliographies and indexes.
  Contents – v. 2. The Middle Ages, 1100–1500
  – v. 3. Renaissance and Reformation.
  1. Arts, British.   I. Ford, Boris.
  NX543.C36   700′.942   87-11671
  ISBN 0 521 30975 1 (v. 2)

ISBN 0 521 30976 X

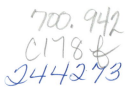

Contents

Notes on Contributors

Malcolm Airs is Conservation Officer for South Oxfordshire District Council. He was formerly Architectural Editor of the *Survey of London*. His publications include *The Making of the English Country House, 1500–1640*, and *Tudor and Jacobean* in the *Buildings of Britain* series.

Dominic Baker-Smith is Professor of English at the University of Amsterdam. He has published on many aspects of Renaissance literature and intellectual history, and is currently completing a study of Thomas More's *Utopia*.

Philippa Glanville was curator of the Tudor and Stuart Department at the Museum of London before moving to the Victoria and Albert Museum, where she is the specialist on early English silver. She is the author of *London in Maps, Tudor London, Silver in England*, and *Silver in Tudor and Early Stuart England*, the first catalogue of the national collection of early English silver.

Maurice Howard is Lecturer in History of Art at the University of Sussex, where he teaches on the visual arts of the Renaissance and the seventeenth century. He is the author of *The Early Tudor Country House*, and *Architecture and Politics 1490–1550*.

Michael Leslie is Lecturer in English Literature at the University of Sheffield. He is an editor of *Word & Image: a Journal of Verbal/Visual Enquiry*, and the author of *Spenser's 'fierce warres and faithfull loves': Martial and Chivalric Symbolism in 'The Faerie Queene'*.

Nigel Llewellyn is Lecturer in History of Art at the University of Sussex. He is the author of a forthcoming book on English Renaissance Tombs, and is collaborating with Maurice Howard on a broader study of Elizabethan visual culture.

Eric Mercer was, until he retired, on the staff of the Royal Commission on Historical Monuments (England). His principal publications are *English Art 1533–1625, Social History of European Furniture, English Vernacular Houses*, and *History of the Architecture of Shropshire* (forthcoming) for the Victoria County Histories.

John Milsom is Lecturer in Music at Christ Church and at Oriel College, Oxford. He is writing a study of foreign influence on Tudor music, preparing a new collected edition of Tallis's Latin-texted works, and compiling a catalogue of the music manuscripts at Christ Church, Oxford.

John Steane, formerly a grammar school headmaster, is a Keeper of Environmental Records at the Oxfordshire Country Museum. He is the author of *The Northamptonshire Landscape*, *The Archaeology of Medieval England and Wales*, and *Peopling Past Landscapes* (with B. Dix).

Derek Traversi, who is Professor Emeritus of English Literature at Swarthmore College, Pennsylvania, was successively British Council Representative in Uruguay, Chile, Iran, Spain and Italy, 1948–70. He is the author of *An Approach to Shakespeare* and three other volumes of Shakespearean criticism; *The Literary Imagination: Studies in Dante, Chaucer and Shakespeare*; and books on Chaucer and T. S. Eliot.

General Introduction

BORIS FORD

If English literature is, by common consent, pre-eminent in the world, the same would not often be claimed for Britain's arts as a whole. Indeed, the British people sometimes strike foreigners, and even themselves, as rather more philistine than artistic. And yet, viewed historically, Britain's achievements in the visual and applied arts and in architecture and music, as well as in drama and literature, must be at least the equal, as a whole, of any other country.

The Cambridge Guide to the Arts in Britain, to give it its full title, is not devoted, volume by volume, to the separate arts, but to all the arts in each successive age. Histories of the independent arts are legion. But being of their nature self-centred, they provide a very poor impression of the cultural richness and vitality of an age. Moreover, these separate histories obscure the ebb and flow of artistic creation from one age to the next.

When the arts in Britain are viewed collectively, it can be seen how often they reinforce each other, treating similar themes and speaking in a similar tone of voice. Also it is striking how one age may find its major cultural expression in music and drama, and the next in architecture or the applied arts: while in a later age there may be an almost total absence of important composers compared with a proliferation of major novelists. Or an age may provide scope for a great range of anonymous craftsmen. These contrasts in the degree to which the individual arts have flourished are not fortuitous, but are bound up with the social aspirations and characteristics of the age, with its beliefs and preoccupations and manners, which may favour expression in one art rather than another.

The Cambridge Guide is planned to reveal these changes and the resulting character of the arts and the balance between them. Thus these volumes do not consist of a sequence of mini-surveys, packed with facts and dates. Rather, they are designed to help readers find their bearings in relation to the arts and culture of an age: identifying major landmarks and lines of strength, analysing changes of taste and fashion and critical assumptions. And these are necessarily related to the demands of patrons and the tastes of the various overlapping publics.

These volumes are addressed to readers of all kinds: to general readers as well as to specialists. But virtually every reader is bound to be a non-specialist in relation to many of the arts under discussion, and so the chapters on the individual arts do not presuppose specialist knowledge. On the other hand, these volumes are not elementary nor naive; they assume a measure of familiarity with the arts, and above all a wish to understand and appreciate the artistic achievements of successive ages in Britain.

Renaissance and Reformation

The arts in the Tudor and Elizabethan ages, which are the subject of this third volume of *The Cambridge Guide*, are very hard to describe in a single all-embracing phrase. If the sixteenth century saw 'the arrival of that international movement known as the Renaissance', and with it a new awareness of classical civilisation, the individual arts in Britain were affected in very differing and inconsistent ways by these developments. Thus architecture, in a period of very rich building activity, pursued a course almost wholly independent of the continent. On the other hand, poetry and drama were greatly influenced by classical ideas of rhetoric and by Italian models; and the English madrigal was an Italian importation.

The other characteristic of Tudor and Elizabethan art is that much of it, especially in the visual arts, was produced for explicitly social purposes, often for the aggrandisement of the crown and the nobles, and with small concern for its aesthetic appeal. Yet the social–religious function of a great deal of the music, and the political function of much of the drama, did not prevent Byrd and Shakespeare and many of their contemporaries from creating superlative 'works of art'. And today we rightly think of the Elizabethan age as one of Britain's richest periods of art.

Each of the nine volumes in this series contains five kinds of material:

The Cultural and Social Setting

This major introductory survey provides a map of the cultural landscape, and an examination of the historical and social developments which affected the arts (both the 'high' and popular arts):

(a) The shape and pattern of society; its organisation, beliefs, ideals, scepticisms.

(b) How the concerns of society were embodied or reflected in the individual arts, and in the practical arts and crafts; the notion and 'function' of art at that time.

(c) The character and preoccupations of the separate arts, and of patrons and audiences. Why particular arts tended to flourish and others to decline in this age.

(d) The organisation and economic situation of the arts.

Studies in the Individual Arts

These studies of individual artists and themes do not aim to provide an all-inclusive survey of each art, but a guide to distinctive achievements and developments. Thus the amount of space devoted to the individual arts differs considerably from volume to volume, though it is interesting that literature is very strong in almost every volume.

In this section, one chapter focuses on a single town, Shrewsbury, and on a particular house, Hardwick Hall, as microcosms of the period.

Appendix

Bibliographies and brief biographies, for further reading and reference.

Illustrations

The volumes are generously illustrated, though it has been decided not to include pictures of individual artists.

Index

This is the key to making good use of each volume. Many chapters naturally refer to the same historical developments and works of art. These have not been cross-referenced in the texts, because material common to various chapters has been fully noted in the Index. So the Index is the place from which to explore and take full advantage of the interdisciplinary character of the volume: which is its distinctive strength.

Where the contributors to these volumes have been obliged to use specialist terms, they have for the most part explained these in the text. But they have also assumed that readers will use their dictionaries. The following are among the most useful dictionaries in relation to these volumes: *The Oxford Illustrated Dictionary*, *The Penguin Dictionary of Architecture*, *The Penguin Dictionary of Art & Artists*, and *The Penguin Dictionary of Music*.

In conclusion I am greatly indebted to Professor Donald Mitchell and Dr Joseph Rykwert for their generous and detailed advice during the preliminary stages of this project; and to the staff of the Cambridge University Press, especially Sarah Stanton and Ann Stonehouse, for their sympathetic collaboration and unfailing patience.

Part I
The Cultural and Social Setting

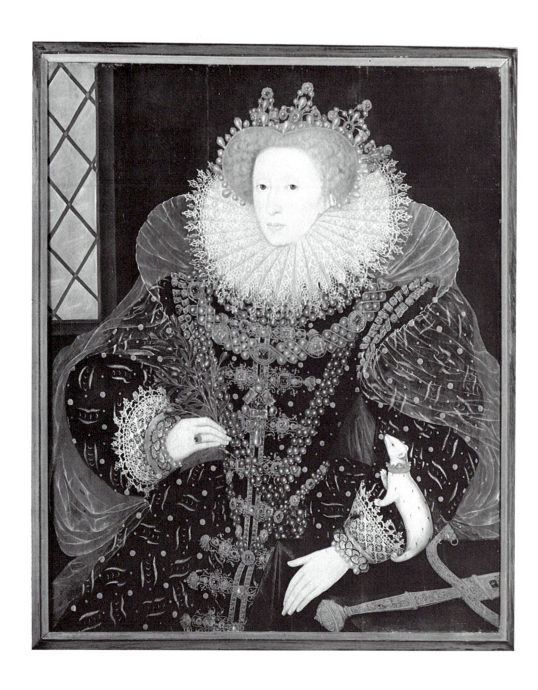

The 'Ermine' Portrait of Elizabeth I (1585), attributed to William Segar.

Renaissance and Reformation

DOMINIC BAKER-SMITH

Introduction

On 23 September 1586 a small skirmish took place outside the town of Zutphen in the eastern Netherlands. Zutphen, an old Hanseatic port on the river Ijssel, was held by a Spanish garrison against the Anglo-Dutch army of the Earl of Leicester. On that late autumn day a Spanish supply train creaked its way towards Zutphen in an attempt to relieve the defending forces until, just outside the town, it came under attack from a hastily mustered English force. It was not a very serious military operation: the supply train lumbered on to Zutphen but the English, who were probably glad of a little action after a frustrating summer campaign, ventured under the cover of fog rather too close to the defenders' positions. Among the casualties was Leicester's nephew, Sir Philip Sidney (1554–86); his thigh shattered by an arquebus shot, he died of gangrene just under four weeks later. Without that notable death the insignificant skirmish would soon have been forgotten, but as it is the event and its aftermath have a great deal to tell us about the character of Renaissance England.

Sidney's body was brought back to England with great solemnity and in February buried at St Paul's with a costly funeral that virtually bankrupted his father-in-law, Sir Francis Walsingham. Since Walsingham played a central part in the process leading to the execution of Mary, Queen of Scots, only days before Sidney's funeral, it is reasonable to see in this expensive ceremony a great deal more than family pride. The dead Sidney was a powerful propaganda instrument for those who wished to nudge Elizabeth into an anti-Spanish crusade. A Sidney myth was promoted not only by the impressive funeral procession but also by the engraving of it prepared by the Dutchman Theodoor de Brij, and by the novel publication of volumes of commemorative Latin verse by the universities of Oxford and Cambridge. In all these steps Sidney's mourners followed continental precedents; even the funeral shows marked resemblances to that of William the Silent at Delft in 1584; and it was no accident that the university volumes were dedicated to the Earl of Leicester, Governor-General in the Netherlands and longstanding advocate of direct action against Spain. The whole affair provides an illustration of the practical use given to the arts in Tudor England.

If there is one theme which stands out in the commemorative poems which lament Sidney's passing it is his combination of practical ability with achievement in the academic arts. This is true of the English elegies written in his honour as much as the Latin, and in one memorable phrase Sir Walter Raleigh hails him as 'Scipio, Cicero and Petrarch of our time'. The Scipio allusion is not so surprising since behind it lies the heroic figure of Scipio the Younger, Roman conqueror of Carthage and a friend of scholars. In Petrarch's Latin epic, *Africa*, Scipio is presented as the ideal leader, a brilliant general and a generous patron of poetry, a point which was emphasised in the gloss to *October* in Spenser's *The Shepheardes Calender*. Many contemporaries called Sidney a second Scipio because he so aptly combined a military and political role with the active support of literature. But to call him, as Raleigh does, 'Cicero and Petrarch of our time' is to go beyond conventional praise of an aristocratic patron and point to him as a literary performer in his own right. Cicero (106–43 BC), as the great exponent of oratory or persuasive public speaking, represents the political life, while Petrarch (1304–74), lover of Laura and master practitioner of the sonnet, stands for the tradition of love poetry which Sidney exploited with such originality in his *Astrophel and Stella*. In a special sense the tributes to Sidney, with their stress on cultural as well as military skills, celebrate the fulfilment of an educational revolution among the governing class. It was a revolution which had profound implications for the arts.

The first factor for change in sixteenth-century England was the arrival of that international movement known as the Renaissance. But what exactly was reborn? It is always important to remember that the very terms the 'Middle Ages' and the 'Renaissance' which we adopt instinctively were coined by the Italian humanists who were architects of the revival of classical culture. It is dangerously easy to overlook the evaluation built into them: that the 'Middle Ages' are what stand between the period of rebirth and the grandeur of classical antiquity, a hiatus of barbarism and Gothic ignorance. In fact the whole complex movement of ideas which we recognise as the Renaissance originated in fourteenth-century Italy as a protest against the narrow specialisation of the medieval university curriculum. But, of course, the classics were studied in the Middle Ages. Scholars like Poggio Bracciolini (1380–1459), who spent four years in England, might scour the old monastic libraries and discover forgotten texts, but the greater part of the Latin literature known to us was available to the Middle Ages.

The new element, which we can see quite clearly in Petrarch, is an awareness of classical civilisation as a coherent whole, a manner of responding to the world, which could be invoked to expose the inadequacies of the contemporary scene. There is a medieval classicism, conveniently illustrated by John of Salisbury, Thomas à Becket's secretary who died as Bishop of Chartres in 1180; this may reveal as great an intimacy with Latin literature as that of any Renaissance scholar, but the texts are treated rather like Roman buildings, as useful sources of raw material to be incorporated into a post-classical structure. In the same spirit, medieval depictions of the classical gods show them as contemporary figures, Mars dressed in the armour of a knight or Venus in the costume of a fashionable lady. So an immediate feature of Renaissance classicism is its retrieval of classical forms: the imitation of a Roman literary style, the recovery of artistic techniques, and eventually the adoption of architectural orders.

If such a retrieval of forms is to be creative, to answer a felt need, then it must presuppose some comprehension of the concerns and aspirations behind the work that is imitated. In its most positive sense, then, Renaissance humanism strains to recover the mental experience of antiquity, and to do this primarily by way of the arts of language. 'Humanism' is a problematic term which is frequently used as though it conveyed some specific programme of ideas or beliefs about human nature. In fact the term originated in the nineteenth century and derives from the *studia humanitatis*, the curriculum offered by Italian teachers of the arts of language, which comprised grammar, rhetoric, poetry, history and moral philosophy, all studied with close reference to the standard authors of the ancient world. Close adherence to this residual definition of humanism is a valuable antidote to the inflated and anachronistic use of the word which still befogs discussion. But it does leave something out. We can get a better sense of what that is if we consider humanism in relation to the arts of language as these are described in the rhetorical world of Cicero.

The tradition of rhetoric

When all is said and done, Cicero probably had a more profound influence on the culture of the Renaissance than any other single figure from the Ancient World. The rediscovery of Plato, as Latin translations became available and the ability to read Greek spread, might seem more dramatic, but it was the influence of Cicero that decided how the experience of classical literature was received. Cicero was the spokesman of the rhetorical tradition, and it was the rhetorical tradition that humanism set out to revive. The great flowering of medieval civilisation which marks the twelfth and thirteenth centuries was dominated by the need to organise and codify; under the influence of Aristotle's logical writings, the *Organon* which had only recently become available from Arabic sources, a new philosophical Latin was created which was the language of scholasticism. By its nature it aimed to be objective and universal, an accurate medium for definition.

But Cicero, in the spirit of rhetoric, saw language as a persuasive medium, designed to tap the emotions and operate on a personal level. To Petrarch, scholasticism, for all its analytic precision, did not provoke a personal response and thus failed to activate the will. Rhetoric is, in the final analysis, about language as a means to action; so when, at the very end of the tradition which we are considering, Milton in the *Areopagitica* (1644) describes Edmund Spenser (1552–99) as 'a better teacher than Scotus or Aquinas' he is not being so much anti-Catholic as anti-scholastic. Spenser *moves* the reader, and moving may stimulate action; the philosopher merely promotes contemplation of an idea. It is this concern with moving that is the critical

feature of humanism, and even in its decay, when humanism shrinks into
pedantry, the association is maintained.

So the cluster of interests that make up the humanist curriculum can be
summarised under the *studia humanitatis*. A glance at a Latin dictionary
under 'humanitas' can make clear how much the word gained its currency
from Cicero, together with a semantic range which extended from human
nature to benevolence, from good manners to cultural refinement. The ideal
of the English gentleman is in direct line of descent from Cicero's ideal of the
orator as the cultivated man of affairs. This is no accident. The very books
that were devised in the course of the Renaissance to instruct a new
governing class were grounded in the Ciceronian concept of the orator. And,
of course, it was this class that provided the patrons of the arts.

At the outset, then, it is important to recognise that in this period,
literature and the other liberal arts were not regarded for themselves alone, as
from a purely aesthetic standpoint; their value lay in their effects within the
sphere of social action – moral or political. The pleasure we derive from the
arts of Renaissance England today may sometimes have little to do with their
original function, but our enjoyment can be enhanced if we are alert to the
factors which shaped them. Petrarch's devotion to *bonae literae* goes beyond
what we understand by *belles lettres*; it takes for granted that literary study is
a route to moral maturity, and a more effective one than the abstractions
represented by Scotus or Aquinas. While Petrarch is still sufficiently medieval
to regard the active life with suspicion, his immediate pupils such as
Leonardo Bruni and Coluccio Salutati found within the Florentine republic
scope for a reappraisal of political action as an expression of 'humanitas'. In
this they gave a fuller expression to Cicero's sense of rhetoric as the art of
persuasion: language, the unique property of man, may be used to incite
other men to acts which will fulfil their nature as moral and political beings.
The rediscovery in 1421 of the complete text of the *De Oratore*, together with
the *Orator* and *Brutus*, served to confirm the rhetorical basis of this
Ciceronian humanism.

The *De Oratore* (Of the Nature of the Orator) had a profound significance
for the Renaissance, in the literary arts, in the visual arts (though this was
not felt in England until the seventeenth century), but most strikingly in
ideas about education. After all, in so far as there was a concept of the omni-
competent 'Renaissance man', it came from Cicero's description of his ideal
orator in *De Oratore*.

Two elements in that work have a bearing on the broader developments
that we are concerned with in the arts. First of all there is Cicero's
moderately sceptical view of human nature. The important decisions in life,
he concludes, are not based simply on rational judgement; instead a whole
range of subjective factors which he terms *affectiones* come into play. These
'affections', as they become in Tudor English, represent those feelings or
inclinations which may not respond to rational analysis but which may be
fired by an appeal to the emotions. In an age which did not possess our
psychological vocabulary we can recognise in the affections that kind of
response which we would label as subjective or subconscious. The skilled
orator surpasses the merely rational philosopher by playing on the subjective

responses as well as the rational ones; he appeals to the whole range of the personality, seeking not rational assent (which may have no further outcome) but a movement of the will, which may result in action. This becomes, in essence, the familiar Renaissance justification of the arts, and we meet it in Sir Philip Sidney's *A Defence of Poetry*.

The second element in the *De Oratore* that has particular relevance is its insistence on the comprehensive attainments of the orator. Cicero's attack on the separation of dialectic, or the art of reasoning, from rhetoric promotes an idea of general culture which contrasts sharply with a specialist view of education, such as that found in the medieval universities. Cardinal Newman's ideal of a liberal education (which, as he noted, was the education for a gentleman) represented a nineteenth-century version of the *studia humanitatis* as devised by the Renaissance educators out of hints provided by Cicero. It was a model which dominated English education into the 1960s, marked by preference for a broad flexibility rather than specialised skills. As Cicero remarked of the orator. 'All things whatsoever that can fall under the discussion of human beings must be aptly dealt with by him.'

Thus the orator should combine skill in the persuasive use of language with insight into the psychological forces which underlie human behaviour, a knowledge gained from literary studies and history as well as observation. While the abstract specialist, the scholastic philosopher for example, remains shut within a mental world, the orator uses his communicative powers to bridge the gulf between ideal conception and actual performance. Indeed we could say that this anxiety to relate ideal worlds and actuality through the persuasive resources of the arts is one of the dominant features of the Renaissance. When Leon Battista Alberti (1404–72) set out in his *De Pictura* to raise the status of the painter from craftsman to artist it was to Cicero's orator that he turned for a model: the painter too is a rhetorician, a persuader.

It was this common appeal to the classical tradition of rhetoric which led to talk of painting and poetry as sister arts, poetry being in effect 'a speaking Picture' and painting 'a silent Poesie'. The persuasive power of the arts, recognised by Sidney in *A Defence*, was aptly summarised by Franciscus Junius, Dutch secretary to the Earl of Arundel, in his *The Painting of the Ancients* (1638); painting and poetry, he asserts, 'doe hold the raines [i.e. reins] of our hearts, leading and guiding our Passions by that beguiling power they have wheresoever they list'. Now it is true that the kind of painting which Alberti has in mind is not really applicable to Britain until the seventeenth century, but Junius is describing that power to move auditor, reader or viewer which was generally accepted as the social justification of the arts, and it is no surprise to find his arguments illustrated by rhetorical texts from Cicero or Quintilian.

The same approach could be applied to music. In *Of the Laws of Ecclesiastical Polity* (1594–7) Richard Hooker defends the liturgical use of music against Puritan attacks by appealing to

an admirable facility which music hath to express and represent unto the mind, more inwardly than any other sensible mean, the very standing, rising and falling, the very steps and inflections every way, the turns and varieties of all passions whereunto the mind is subject; yea so to imitate them, that whether it resemble unto us the state wherein our minds already are, or a clean contrary, we are not more contentedly by the one confirmed, than changed and led away by the other.

(V, xxviii, 1)

Perhaps we should see Junius' allusion to 'the raines of our hearts' as the key: a horse's bridle, used to check and direct its animal energies, was conventionally used in the Renaissance as a symbol of temperance, the virtue of self-mastery. This association echoes Plato's parable of the charioteer in the *Phaedrus* who must rein back his black horse and curb its wantonness: the idea of psychological and social control is never far from the arts in Renaissance England. They are invariably associated with the assimilation of memorable or 'infectious' images which will qualify the percipient's behaviour, loyalties and values; individual response is constantly referred outwards to prescribed schemes of political, moral or religious conduct. Self-expression was not a concept that signified much to the pre-Romantic mind, and in Tudor England the raw energies of the individual were lured by the arts to imitate ideal or socially approved types. When the clergyman George Gifford wrote his eye-witness account, *The Manner of Sir Philip Sidney's Death*, he was careful to transform personal details into the time-honoured ritual of the good death. This was not hypocrisy; it was a way of interpreting experience, giving it order and making it exemplary. In a similar way the icon-like quality which strikes us in Tudor portraits comes from the same urge to assimilate the individual to a general category or type.

The domestication of humanism

The reception of Renaissance ideas and practices in England was not a hasty affair. Chaucer wrote of 'Frauceys Petrark, the laureate poete', suitably punning on the name of the poet's mistress Laura, and his ironic handling of chivalric themes anticipates the spirit of a later generation which his immediate followers did not share. For the most part those who developed a taste for classical letters were clerics who visited Italy either as diplomats or as aspiring lawyers at the great legal universities of Padua and Bologna.

The first notable patron of these new interests was Humphrey, Duke of Gloucester (1391–1447), who employed Italian scholars in his household and bequeathed a rich collection of manuscripts, including works by Petrarch, Salutati and Giovanni Boccaccio, to Oxford University. Thanks to his lead a generation of English scholars made their way to Italy and a cluster of them studied under the humanist Guarino of Verona. Among these was the extraordinary aristocrat John Tiptoft, Earl of Worcester (1427?–70), a resolute Yorkist whose practice of impaling the bodies of his victims earned him the title 'butcher of England'; yet his English version of Buonaccorso's *A Declamation of Nobleness* is one of the earliest translations of a humanist text. More typical, however, were ecclesiastics like Robert Flemmyng, Dean of Lincoln (d. 1483), and John Free who died as bishop-elect of Bath and Wells in Rome in 1465. Both these men made their mark at the Papal Court, and Free can be judged the first Englishman to match the elegant Latinity of the Italians.

In such cases one can see that humanistic skills were an exotic extra, added
to administrative and legal abilities; but with the growing international
influence of humanism there was an increasing demand for such skills in the
centres of power. A classical education became a qualification for
administrative office: the usual Latin term for ambassador was, after all,
orator. Less than a hundred years after John Free's death William Cecil was
to pack Queen Elizabeth's first Council with former Greek pupils of John
Cheke at Cambridge. Classical education had arrived.

It was in the generation after Free that the domestication of humanism
gained pace, a stage associated with three names, William Grocyn
(1446?–1519), Thomas Linacre (1460?–1524) and John Colet (1467?–1519).
All three studied in Italy and brought back an interest in Greek studies;
indeed, Grocyn may have been the first Englishman to teach Greek. Linacre
was tutor to Prince Arthur and in later years to the Princess Mary, but his
most notable contribution was to the development of medical studies. Colet,
who became Dean of St Paul's in 1504, was the most influential and the most
irascible of the three. Quite apart from his Italian experience which attracted
him towards Platonism (he corresponded with Marsilio Ficino, the greatest
Platonist of the age), Colet represented, as the son of a successful London
merchant, an urban mercantile attitude which was impatient with many
inherited forms. His Oxford lectures on St Paul, delivered in 1497 after his
return from Italy, abandoned the scholastic practice of glossing the text and
offered instead a continuous exposition which aimed to lay bare the 'spiritual
sense'. This appeal to a simplified and strictly practical exegesis, which Colet
associates with the early centuries of the church, is close to that developed by
Erasmus, whom he first met at Oxford in 1499.

As a preacher, too, Colet had a talent for striking a subversive note: his
1511 address to the Canterbury Convocation – summoned to extirpate heresy
– was founded on the argument that the greatest heresy is the corruption of
the clergy. When in 1549 one 'W.S.', probably Sir Thomas Smith, wrote *A
Discourse of the Common Weal* he could still allude to 'Doctor Collettes
Sermon' when dealing with reform of the clergy. Two years later, when
Henry VIII was about to invade France, Colet preached at court on the
incompatibility of war and Christian love. The most lasting work of Colet,
funded by his inherited wealth, was St Paul's School which he set up under
highly qualified and highly paid masters to promote knowledge of Latin and
Greek, 'and good authors such as have the very Roman eloquence joined with
wisdom, especially Christian authors that wrote their wisdom with clean and
chaste Latin'. Significantly he placed the school under the surveillance of
laymen, in this case his father's guild, the Mercers.

Colet's critical spirit was commemorated after his death by Erasmus
(1466–1536), who introduces him under the pseudonym Gratianus Pullus
(colt) in the colloquy *A Pilgrimage* (1526) to make the characteristic remark
that Thomas à Becket would rather see the poor fed than his shrine encrusted
with gems. It was, of course a prophetic touch; ten years later, after Henry
VIII's break with Rome, the shrine was stripped, and Erasmus' satire found
its place among a number of writings which were translated and printed
under the direction of Thomas Cromwell to educate public opinion.

It is clear that Colet was by temperament a puritan; he would not have married men as vergers in his cathedral, for one thing. But his humanist background led him to look behind the accumulated layers of inherited conceptions and seek out the primitive model or source. Just as a manuscript tradition might be traced back through generations of scribal error to the original text, so social institutions and their accompanying customs might be exposed to critical assessment. Just how far Colet was a formative influence on Erasmus can never be settled, but the kind of return *ad fontes* which is represented by Erasmus' critical text of the New Testament, first published in 1516, can be seen as the logical fulfilment of his reforming endeavours. A less obvious expression of this critical spirit can be found in another book which appeared in the same year, More's *Utopia*.

Thomas More (1478–1535), the first English humanist to win European recognition, is a representative figure. Born the son of a judge and raised in the same mercantile and city ambiance as Colet, he served briefly as a page in Cardinal Morton's household before going to Oxford, probably to round off his classical studies rather than enter the Arts course. After two years he entered the Inns of Court, first at New Inn and then in 1496 at Lincoln's Inn. The Inns were virtually unique in Europe as schools of national (i.e. common) law and they provided an entry to the most influential of Tudor professions. More's lifetime coincided with their greatest influence: between 1484 and 1559 all twenty-two Speakers of the Commons were common-lawyers. Such training as the Inns could offer did not limit its recipients to practising the law but equipped them to enter the expanding managerial class or even the royal service. More's father, Sir John, was successful enough, rising to be a Justice of the King's Bench, and the education that he devised for his son was aimed to qualify him for important office. From the reign of Edward IV to the later years of Henry VIII the common law was the route to social advancement, so More's appointment as Chancellor in 1529 marked a high point in its history. Not only was he the first layman to hold the office, he was also the first common lawyer. By the late 1540s Oxford and Cambridge had adjusted to new educational patterns and it was increasingly to their graduates that the government turned for trained administrators. That is in itself a sign of the impact of humanism.

The advance of More's legal career does not seem to have hindered his literary activities, at least in early years. During 1501 he was called to the bar and appointed Reader at Furnivall's Inn, but he also collaborated with William Lily, the future high master of Colet's school, in Latin translations from the *Greek Anthology* and gave a course of lectures on St Augustine's *City of God* in Grocyn's church of St Lawrence Jewry. If we disregard his religious writings, then More's secular works display a typically humanistic concern with the moral life and politics. Though he never travelled to Italy his close friendship with Grocyn, Linacre and Colet gave him a first hand knowledge of Italian authors such as Giovanni Pico della Mirandola, whose biography he translated in 1505. The evidence suggests that works by Italians, at first those in Latin but later vernacular ones as well, were widely available; the book list of the Bridgettine Monastery of Syon in Isleworth, a house More knew well, records a surprisingly rich collection of humanistic titles.

While More was aware of Italian discussion on such themes as the importance of political activity and the best mode of government, it is clear that he was influenced by Colet's radicalism. The political vein in his humanism is evident in the Latin epigrams which were first printed in 1518 but which had been composed over many years. They have been described as the best book of Latin epigrams published in the century and they were the basis for More's contemporary reputation. What stands out is the number of poems on tyranny, a theme which is the underlying concern of *The History of Richard III*, a book which More never completed and which remained unpublished in his lifetime.

Utopia or, to give it its proper title, *The Best State of a Commonwealth*, sets up a contrast between the corrupt political practice of Europe, where a ruler is insulated against reality by self-seeking flatterers and the austerely rational democracy of the Utopians. In the argument between the much travelled Raphael, who has been to *Utopia*, and More's own persona within the fiction about the question of getting involved in politics or keeping one's hands clean, no obvious preference emerges. The reader is landed with the question in a way which is typical of much Tudor writing. More did get involved, of course, and the whole logic of his career demanded that he should; within a year of the publication of *Utopia* he was sworn into the King's Council.

This step, which was to lead to his appointment as Lord Chancellor in succession to Cardinal Wolsey (1475–1530), and indirectly to his disgrace and death, was taken with open eyes. More's instinctive sense of irony led easily to satire, a literary form that he developed together with Erasmus in order to expose the inertia of contemporary institutions, ecclesiastical and secular. It is easy to overestimate the intentions behind works like *Utopia* and *The Praise of Folly* which Erasmus completed in 1509 and dedicated to More. The common target of Erasmus' considerable satirical output, as of More's ironical attacks, was custom, the dead weight of precedent. The primary function of *Utopia* and *The Praise of Folly* was not to offer alternative ways of conducting affairs (despite the literalism of many later readers of *Utopia*) but to shake loose the grip of inherited forms: social and religious habits in which outward signs or ritual might displace genuine commitment. *Utopia* marks Tudor humanism at its most radical.

New directions in education

When, at the conclusion of that work, the fictional More disowns the uncompromising attitude of Raphael, who sees all political action as participation in madness, he voices the view of common sense. Such a view required that the ideals of Italian humanism be adapted to local circumstances, above all to those of a feudal monarchy. The social history of humanism in Tudor England after More is one of adaptation and assimilation. As such it is inseparable from the restructuring of education, especially the preparation of the governing classes for new roles. The introduction of humanist texts and interests was largely a matter of private initiative and had little effect on the schools or universities; even in the case of a man like Thomas More, his formation in good letters was dependent on personal contact and residence in London. Yet he had spent a brief spell in Oxford and may have had some contact with Bishop Waynflete's new foundation, Magdalen College (1458).

This College represented several innovations which looked to the future: not only did it give special emphasis to college teaching, thus providing a degree of independence from the official syllabus of university lectures, but it laid stress on grammar and moral philosophy, topics closely linked with humanism. To support this Wayneflete established a grammar school which soon became a centre for new methods of teaching Latin. A further innovation which was to prove of great importance in the following century was the provision of places for undergraduate commoners, that is the sons of nobles or distinguished persons who could benefit from study in the College while paying their own expenses. This arrangement was developed further in later foundations such as Brasenose (1512), where by 1552 some forty per cent of the membership was drawn from this category.

For cultural purposes the importance of this innovation can hardly be overestimated. While the traditional student halls declined sharply during the early sixteenth century, collegiate foundations increasingly dominated the university scene. Not only did they serve as avenues for the introduction of new interests but they also created a closer link between the universities and the government. For one thing, they possessed through their endowments an independence which the halls could not rival; by means of their internal teaching posts (often exercised publicly), their libraries, and their control of student entry they could directly influence the character of the university. The formal arrival of the new learning was signalled at Cambridge by the foundation of St John's (1511) by John Fisher, Bishop of Rochester, as the executor of Lady Margaret Beaufort. Within a few years its alumni would include Sir Thomas Wyatt, Sir John Cheke, Roger Ascham and William Cecil, later Lord Burghley: all figures that point to a new intimacy between the University and the court. At Oxford, Bishop Foxe's foundation of Corpus Christi (1517) was designed to subvert the established order. Scholars and Fellows were required to be sufficiently competent in Latin to compose extempore verses or letters. With an eye to the University at large, Foxe set up three readerships in Humanity (Latin eloquence), Greek and in the 'positive' theology already pioneered by Colet and Erasmus. It seems, incidentally, to have been Foxe who was responsible for the inclusion of quotations from Erasmus' New Testament in the windows of King's College Chapel, Cambridge. Foxe's establishment of a humanist bridgehead at Oxford coincides with Thomas More's public letter to the University, written from the court at Abingdon in March 1518, in which he rebukes the self-styled 'Trojans' who opposed Greek studies and gives a forceful manifesto for the new studies. Later in the same year Wolsey instituted lectures on Humanity and Greek for the University at large.

It seems reasonable to detect in these moves by Foxe, More and Wolsey a three-pronged attack on Oxford, designed to force the pace of adjustment to change. The question is, why should a highly placed group at court take such an interest in these academic issues? There are two answers. In the first place, as far back as Bishop Wayneflete's foundation of Magdalen, a need had been felt for administrators and government servants whose education would enable them to perform their duties with flexibility and style. From its origins in England, humanism was connected with the higher civil service. And this leads us to the second answer, which is that changing conditions in royal service provided a strong incentive to the laity and even the aristocracy to undertake university education. That explains the importance of the steady growth in numbers of undergraduate commoners within the colleges. The provision of places for the sons of the nobility or of wealthy persons became a standard feature of sixteenth-century college statutes. Of course it gave the college useful connections, but it also provided a system whereby members of the governing class who might wish to complete their education in the humanities might attend the universities without necessarily proceeding to a degree or following a profession. Such was the course followed by Sir Thomas Wyatt at St John's, Cambridge, as it was later in the century by Sir Philip Sidney at Oxford. Both cases go to show that the cultural ideal of the courtier as defined for the age by Castiglione was in essence that of a knight who had studied the classics; so the governing classes discovered education and took a firm hold on its institutions.

This was reinforced by other features of the collegiate trend in the universities: the need for the government to control the universities was heightened by the profound religious changes of the century. The rather chaotic, democratic system of university government was gradually overshadowed by the control exercised by heads of colleges, who were closer to the realities of power. The importance of the heads lay not only in the independence of their institutions, but also in the way that the government found them a more reliable means of controlling the universities than the relatively youthful regent masters of arts who formed the largest single group of teachers. When, during Henry VIII's divorce crisis, Oxford hesitated over its declaration of support for the justness of Henry's cause, the University was brusquely instructed to pay heed to the opinion of 'vertuous, wise, sad and profound learned men'. By the last quarter of the century it was such wise and sad men, in the shape of the vice-chancellor and heads of houses, who made important decisions. Moreover, the status of a college headship made it an attractive post, a significant step towards a bishopric or office of state. It was a corollary of the broadened appeal of university education that Oxford and Cambridge were increasingly assimilated into the establishment, and the collegiate system was an essential part of this process, one peculiar to the English universities. Throughout the century and beyond, court patronage was to be active in shaping higher education.

The most ambitious scheme for promoting the new learning was undoubtedly Wolsey's project for Cardinal's College at Oxford. Although his plans gave lavish support to humanistic studies they retained the traditional structure of schools, providing chairs in theology, and law, canon law and medicine as well as philosophy and humanity. But it was, characteristically, the scale that was unprecedented. There was to be a dean, and sixty senior or graduate canons studying in the higher faculties of theology or law, with forty petty canons drawn from a network of grammar schools that Wolsey

planned to endow through the country. Of these only the grammar school in
his home town of Ipswich came into existence. The foundation also included
thirteen chaplains, twelve lay clerks, sixteen choristers, a music master and
other college servants, as well as the six professors. Books were imported
from Rome and Venice and the prized manuscript collections of Cardinals
Bessarion and Domenico Grimani were specially copied for the library.
Although the whole grandiose scheme tottered as Wolsey fell from favour
(that it survived at all owed much to the efforts of Wolsey's faithful factotum
Thomas Cromwell), it must be mentioned as one of the most far-sighted
cultural endeavours of the century. The sheer scale of the college and its
network of schools would have had a major influence on the life of England
and not least on the quality of the clergy. When, at the close of the reign,
Henry VIII endowed Christ Church out of the residue of Wolsey's scheme
and matched it with the foundation of Trinity at Cambridge, these relatively
lavish colleges were designed to further royal domination of the universities.
In 1564 Trinity housed 305 students out of a University total of 1,267 and
had influence accordingly.

Clearly changes in education had a profound effect on the cultural climate
in Tudor England, but the direct beneficiaries of educational change were a
small part of the population. To get some sense of the relation of elite culture
to the country at large we have to grapple with the shadowy concept of
literacy. Here the evidence is scanty and the most authoritative research
largely concerned with the seventeenth century; so any account must be
highly subjective.

As an initial caution it is worth bearing in mind that the modern
assumption that reading and writing are reverse faces of a single skill can be
misleading when applied to the past. Medieval practice distinguished between
the technical skill of writing, an activity for a scribe, and dictation which
presupposed the literary ability to formulate ideas. The growth of literacy in
the later Middle Ages, reflected in the production of smaller books for private
reading, did not necessarily imply the ability to write, at least among the
laity. When we turn to the depressing accounts of 'literacy' in the sixteenth
and seventeenth centuries, then, it is worth bearing in mind that signing
one's name with a mark did not necessarily exclude some ability to read. This
is at least a straw to grasp when we are informed, on the basis of the most
thorough study of literacy in the seventeenth century, that at the outbreak of
civil war in 1643 two-thirds of all males and nine-tenths of all females could
not write their names.

Of course, horror stories in this area are legion. Bishop Hooper of
Gloucester, examining 311 of his clergy in 1552, found that 171 could not
repeat the ten commandments (not such a heinous lapse, conceivably, to
modern eyes but clearly unprofessional), twenty did not know where to find
the Lord's Prayer, twenty-seven could not name its author and ten could not
recite it. Such attainments were not dependent on literacy, but it is unlikely
that these clerical defaulters were strong reading men. It is only fair to
observe that Hooper, a severe and inflexible reformer, was unlikely to have
made the best of his unreformed clergy; within two years they had returned
to the Mass and he died, with great constancy, at the stake. This episode

does point to the difficulty of unravelling the evidence on such a sensitive issue.

Out of the ninety-two men of Little Waldingfield in Suffolk who declared their support of the Act of Succession in 1534, only twelve signed. Of the remainder, thirty-four made their mark and forty-six were simply recorded; of this later group some might conceivably have been *literati* prevented from signing by sickness or absence. But if the twelve who did sign were the only ones in the parish, that gives an eighty-nine per cent illiteracy rate which fits with the general pattern for the time. Class and district were decisive factors: to be gentle born and southern increased the chances; the literacy rate for northern gentlemen matched that of yeomen in the south, and in Elizabethan County Durham one-third of the gentry used marks. Trade and Protestantism were promoters of literacy and in the towns they often went together. Allowing for such local factors, a general estimate can be made that at the start of the century ninety per cent of men and ninety-nine per cent of women were illiterate while at Elizabeth's accession in 1558 the figures were nearer eighty and ninety-five per cent respectively.

This may suggest a steady progression, but that would be misleading. For the bulk of the population conditions did not improve dramatically until the late seventeenth century. What changed most of all during the Tudor period was the nature and availability of secondary education. In other words, while tradesmen and craftsmen show some advance up to the 1550s – when economic decline sapped momentum – it is among the governing and clerical classes that the most striking development is to be found. An increased demand for lay literacy in public affairs, the adaptation of the universities to new social aims, and the new prestige of classical learning all served to prompt a higher esteem of education among the gentle classes.

And here some mention must be made of the effects of printing which made texts available to rural gentry or clergy (and thus to schoolmasters) on a scale inconceivable to earlier generations. The prestige of the classics would have remained very theoretical without pocket editions of Virgil, Horace or Homer which gave the grammar pupil or the travelling diplomat immediate access to their works. The audience crowding into a Shakespeare play, which might number up to 3,000 (at a time when only Norwich, Bristol and Newcastle outside London could muster more than 10,000 inhabitants), would include many who had benefited from the educational expansion and could respond to the figurative intricacy of the language with skills – lost to the modern theatregoer – that had been sharpened in classroom analyses of Terence or Seneca.

It is during the first two decades of Elizabeth's reign (1558–1603) that the full impact of earlier changes became evident, a process that led directly to the literary achievements of the 1580s and 1590s. To some extent this can be credited to the surprising, and unexpected, stability of her government and her cautious, moderate religious settlement. However, the religious turmoil of the previous reigns had left a negative effect. The Dissolution of the Monasteries meant the closure of religious houses in the universities; the abolition of the study of canon law in 1535 closed one traditional career; and theology seemed closer to a minefield than a route to preferment. Thus, although the gentry and the nobility might value education as never before, the medieval figure of the poor scholar climbing to preferment through the church is displaced. Indeed, with the end of clerical celibacy the clergy tend to become a self-perpetuating social group, the children of the manse.

An unusual example of this new kind of dynasty is the family of Edwin Sandys (1516?–88), Archbishop of York. Sandys had studied at St John's College, Cambridge, where he was an associate of John Cheke, the most influential English classicist of the century. He had the misfortune to be Vice-Chancellor in 1553 at the time of Edward VI's death and his rash support of the plot to install Lady Jane Grey as queen led to a period of exile in Strasburg. When, in 1558, Elizabeth succeeded to the throne Sandys was part of the Cambridge connection used by Cecil and Archbishop Parker to provide the new and precarious government with a pool of reliable civil servants and ecclesiastics. From that time his rise was steady: the see of Worcester in 1559, of London in 1570, and of York in 1576. He was a translator for the Bishop's Bible, that moderate version devised by Parker to serve his moderate reformed church, which was published in 1568 complete with portraits of such important patrons of the new order as the Queen and her rival councillors Cecil, later to be Lord Burghley, and Robert Dudley, Earl of Leicester. Sandys' career was not a peaceful one and he must surely have reflected on the irony which bought him, one of the early supporters of Protestant reform, to spend his later years in efforts to control the increasingly radical tendencies of those who found the Elizabethan Church too close to Rome for spiritual comfort.

Sandys was twice married and had seven sons and two daughters by the second marriage. Three of these sons became Members of Parliament, Sir Samuel (1560–1629), Sir Edwin (1561–1629), and Sir Miles (1563–1644), who as 'Milo Sandes' and a Fellow of Queens' contributed to the Cambridge memorial volume for Sir Philip Sidney. Sir Edwin was sent to Corpus Christi, Oxford, where his tutor was Richard Hooker (1553?–1600), and when the latter published his *Of the Laws of Ecclesiastical Policy* in 1593 his pupil acted as consultant and defrayed the publishing costs. Hooker's massive work, the greatest monument of Tudor discursive prose, did not win royal favour because of its constitutional account of the role of the monarch 'in parliament', and a similar resistance to assertions of royal prerogative marked Edwin's often stormy career in the Commons. Between 1593 and 1599 he appears to have made an extended grand tour in France, Germany and Venice, the same route pioneered by Sidney in 1572–5. One result of his experiences was the remarkable *A Relation of the State of Religion* (1605), which in its dispassionate appraisal of the warring churches anticipates something of Locke's rational empiricism.

The youngest son, George (1578–1644), won distinction as a traveller and a poet. His *Relation of a Journey* (1615) records his travels in the eastern Mediterranean where he reached the Holy Land and Egypt. Later he resided for some years in Virginia, and there he completed his verse translation of Ovid's *Metamophoses*, a work of genuine distinction which had a lasting effect on couplet style. Such a family was not possible before the Elizabethan

Church Settlement; not only did the married clergy have a profound effect on cultural life, it also clearly aligned the mainstream of the Anglican clergy with the Tudor political establishment.

Courts and courtiers

It is difficult, when talking about the arts in Renaissance Europe, to avoid some reference to courts and courtiers. We have already noted the increasing presence of undergraduate commoners in the universities, students who were of higher social origin than members of the foundation and who might stay in residence for between one and three years and would probably not proceed to a degree. There are signs that, as in many modern universities, the presence of fee-paying students could be a valuable source of income. But the new interest of the upper classes had its negative side. As Ascham complained to Archbishop Cranmer, too many of the students were the sons of rich men,

and such as never intended to pursue their studies to that degree as to arrive at an eminent proficiency and perfection of learning, but only the better to qualify themselves for some places in the state by a slighter and more superficial knowledge.

Behind the allusion to 'places in the state' lies that concern with counsel which so dominated humanist political discussions. The active, public pursuit of political goals which is assumed in Ciceronian rhetoric and given practical expression in the republicanism of early Italian humanists like Bruni or Salutati had to be modified in the setting of a feudal court. There it became the provision of counsel. Castiglione, whose *The Book of the Courtier* (1528) sketched an entire style of life, made it clear that the ultimate purpose of courtly attainments

is to purchase him . . . in such wise the good will and favour of the Prince he is in service withal, that he may break his mind to him, and always inform him frankly of the truth of every matter meete for him to understand, either without fear or peril to displease him.

This purpose deserve emphasis since *The Book of the Courtier* is often read as though it were simply a handbook of manners, with no higher aim than the cultivation of an acceptable social image. Such a reading confuses Castiglione with Lord Chesterfield, whose letters to his son might be said to mark the last flicker of courtly style.

In reality Castiglione builds on Cicero's familiar orator as defined in the *De Oratore* to meet the needs of his own age; even the fictional dialogue which is used to elaborate his ideal has its source in Cicero's book. And the political goal of wise counsel is what moulds the diverse qualities of the courtier into a coherent whole. In other words, *The Courtier* has to be seen against a background of humanist writing on the public good, and in it the republican ideal of persuasive eloquence is modified to fit the intimacy of life at court. In that intensely semiotic world the whole conduct of life becomes a form of rhetoric,

And therefore in mine opinion, as music, sports, pastimes, and other pleasant fashions, are (as a man would say) the flower of Courtliness, even so is the training and helping forward of the Prince to goodness, and the fearing him from evil, the fruit of it.

Castiglione is thinking here on the very issues that Thomas More reviews in Book 1 of *Utopia*, and though More's scepticism about courts and courtiers may appear closer to modern attitudes, no doubt he too saw his role as servant to Henry VIII in precisely these terms. 'Helping forward' the prince was the justification of the courtier and also, to a quite surprising degree, that of the arts.

The emergence of a courtier style in northern Europe was strongly marked by the rituals of chivalry and the mentality of courtly literature. While there were fluctuations in their comparative importance, the fact remains that there were two traditions which served as sources of value and status during the Tudor period: antiquity and chivalry. The Renaissance obviously gave a new impetus to the adoption of motifs and themes from classical mythology and history, but medieval traditions remained surprisingly active and the long reign of Elizabeth encouraged a revival of knightly service. It was, after all, one way in which her courtiers could relate to a female sovereign. Thus the court ambience provided a meeting point for the classicising aspirations of humanism and the established forms of a military aristocracy.

The central role of courts in the development of Renaissance culture is an inevitable consequence of their control over patronage. The late Middle Ages saw a fall in land values which encouraged the nobility to seek offices, grants and other financial benefits which could be dispensed by the prince in return for service, civil or military. It was this function as a clearing house for political patronage which made the court so important for development in the arts. In time there emerged a 'court humanism' which, in contrast to More's radical analysis, tried to develop a working compromise between new fashions and existing images of power.

Something like this compromise was already present in the court of the Dukes of Burgundy, and this was seen as a model for the English court from the 1460s until the Eltham ordinances of 1526 adopted the new style of the French royal household. On one hand the Burgundian court made use of lavish ceremonial, centred on the Order of the Golden Fleece, which gave an almost liturgical dignity to the public acts of the ruler and drew heavily on the literary conventions of chivalry. As John Paston remarked in 1464, with unconscious irony, 'as for the Duke's court, . . . I heard never of none like it, save King Arthur's court'. On the other hand the Burgundian ideal was a *miles literatus*, a knight who could at least read and give counsel and was thus on the way to being a courtier in Castiglione's sense.

Precisely because Burgundian chivalry was so elaborately devised as a system of display, its outer signs survived even when social reality had changed. Chivalry, originally a way of life designed to promote efficiency in mounted warfare, became increasingly literary in character during the later Middle Ages; in effect it provided a repertory of heroic or courtly roles evoking an imaginary world of knight errantry which bore little relation to real warfare. The costly pageants and tournaments which so impressed John

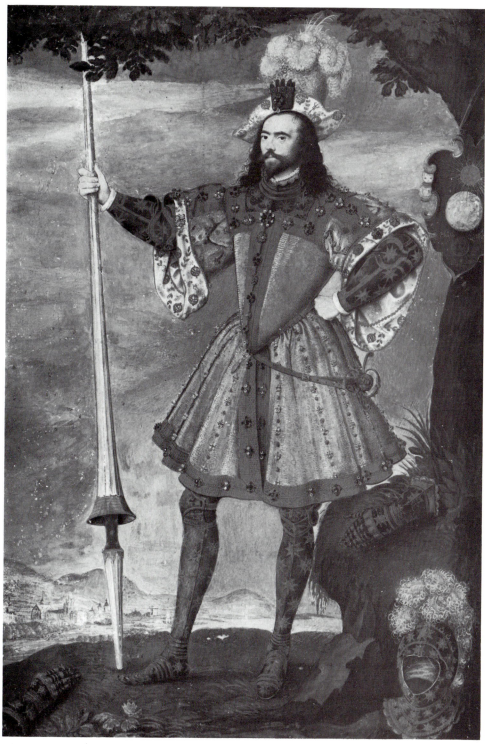

Nicholas Hilliard, portrait of the 3rd Earl of Cumberland as Queen's Champion (c.1590).

Paston were carefully duplicated at Henry VIII's court and even enjoyed a
revival in the Accession Day tilts of Elizabeth I. The ceremonial character of
these events was typical of courtly culture and it bore a degree of similarity
to certain religious practices of late medieval Catholicism: the performance of
a prescribed action was held to indicate the possession of certain qualities.
Thus success in jousting or the completion of a pilgrimage might be taken as
signs of heroism or of holiness. It is certainly the case that Henry VIII's
enthusiasm for jousting was linked in his mind, and in those of his subjects,
with his role as war-leader of the nation.

This habit of externalising qualities and making them visible was
important to the court society (and to the Church) since it suggested a direct
link between social status and the value systems to which society aspired. So
it is not surprising to find that the arts make such a play of ideal figures,
types and roles, to be put on rather like suits of armour. Raleigh's praise of
Sidney as the 'Scipio, Cicero and Petrarch of our time' is wholly conventional
in its projection of idealised persons as qualities. It is the choice of names
that is innovatory.

Nevertheless, the Burgundian spirit was clearly evident in the earlier years
of Henry VIII, and no doubt it was as welcome to the nobility as his swift
execution of his father's 'new men' Empson and Dudley. At his accession the
Upper House included forty-two temporal peers, as well as the bishops and
mitred abbots. By his death in 1547 the abbots had gone and the temporal
peers numbered fifty-one, of whom twenty-eight were his own creation. It is
particularly striking that when Henry invaded France in 1513 at the head of
a well equipped army of 25,000 he was attended by thirty-three peers, whose
retainers made up 13,000 of the troops. The military character of the elite
was convincingly demonstrated. So it is ironical that the close of the reign
saw the triumph of the 'new men', prominent among them John Dudley,
Viscount Lisle, son of the executed minister and now executor of Henry's
will. Although Dudley, as Duke of Northumberland, overreached himself in
1553 in the attempt to place the succession on his own daughter-in-law, Lady
Jane Grey, his third son regained the Earldom of Warwick under Elizabeth
and his fifth son, Robert, won the Earldom of Leicester and became the
greatest faction leader of her reign. Also through his daughter Mary he was
the grandfather of Sir Philip Sidney. It was a remarkable dynastic
performance, made possible by the mobility of Tudor politics.

Slightly less dramatic but still suggestive is the career of Lord Rich
(1497–1567), who won notoriety for his alleged perjury at the trial of Sir
Thomas More. From a mercantile family Rich followed the classic route of
the common law into public life and his career like that of many other men
took off in the general scramble after Wolsey's fall. A protégé of Cromwell, he
went on to give evidence against him at his trial, and later disengaged himself
unscathed from a series of factional involvements. As another executor of
Henry's will he used the occasion to win himself a peerage (the whole affair
produced one duke, a marquess, two earls and four barons) and, under
Edward VI, he rose to Lord Chancellor. When he died of natural causes in
1567 his estates embraced fifty-nine manors (thirty-two formerly monastic
properties), thirty-one rectories and twenty-eight vicarages. In spite of his

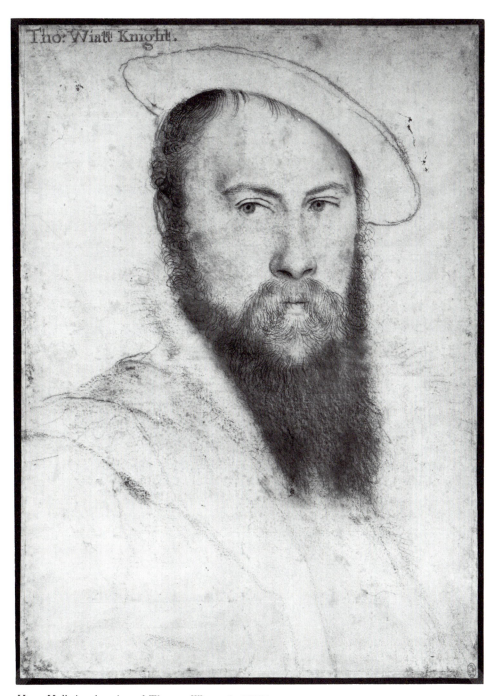

Tho: Wiatt Knight.

Hans Holbein, drawing of Thomas Wyatt (c.1535).
Reproduced by Gracious Permission of Her Majesty The Queen.

reported clash with Archbishop Cranmer over the folly of educating labourers' children, Rich founded Felsted School, presumably for the gentler sort.

For it was, in the last analysis, the gentry who most benefited from the Tudor regime. In the course of the sixteenth century the more substantial figures within that rather blurred category – those rated as esquires – rose from something like 1,000 to 16,000. With the increased centralisation of government, not to mention the drastic changes of public policy which had to be enforced, it was necessary to look beyond the court to those who might promote the royal will locally. It was for such magistrates that Sir Thomas Elyot prepared his *Book named the governor* (1531), the fullest expression of that court humanism which hoped to put new wine in old skins: to install the insights of humanist training within the established political system and thus avoid that radical reappraisal which More's *Utopia* seemed to imply.

The tension between the two orders can be sensed in the career of Sir Thomas Wyatt (1503–42) who, as we have already seen, was one of the early pensioners at St John's College, Cambridge. Born the son of a courtier, he was first presented at court in 1516 before going up to the humanist foundation of St John's, and this double role as a *miles literatus* or scholar-knight contributes directly to his subtlety as a poet. Within the courtly setting the function of the arts was to support social ritual, to promote an ambience in which specific roles might be performed. This applies to the military combat of the tournament as much as to the sexual combat of courtly love: both were the expression of social codes. It is the impersonality of the roles held out in much courtly poetry which may trouble the modern reader looking for an identifiable voice: yet in an age when literature was highly thematic and revolved round a limited number of situations it was the ability to generalise that was admired. Johan Huizinga, the great historian of Burgundian culture, once claimed that 'the whole mental attitude of the Renaissance was one of play'; an attempt, that is, to render an admired model available through the rules of the game. The conventions that one becomes aware of in the arts of the period are part of this effort to invest the individual artifact with the significance of a wider code.

Patronage and the arts

Nevertheless, behind the apparent continuity the qualifications for a political career were changing. Not only was the governing class alerted to education as a way to the benefits of office but the new managerial class of lawyers entered on their inheritance. Families like the Dudleys, the Russells and the Cecils are typical of those who rose to prominence in an age of remarkable social mobility, and who found in the arts opportunities to assert their status and demonstrate their patronage. This is one reason why the visual arts follow such an idiosyncratic course in Tudor England and show themselves indifferent to the kind of creative independence that Titian might expect, since they were so directly controlled by a patron's intentions. Patronage in literature and music was, by the nature of things, less immediately prescriptive. Even when, in the seventeenth century, the growth of foreign travel promoted a broader interest in Renaissance painting, Lord Arundel, friend of Rubens and guiding spirit behind Charles I's great collection, especially valued the works of Holbein because of their historical association with his Howard ancestors. Artists, like builders, were expected to realise the schemes devised by their patrons, and some of the pleasure derived from a portrait would reflect its declaration of status and achievement. Not many Elizabethans appear to have imitated the Dutch lords of Batenberg who scattered stones around their castle inscribed with improbable dates such as 127 BC to impress visitors, but they would have understood the motive.

The patronage system as it operated in Tudor England is inseparable from the faction-principle which controlled politics. Until the Reformation first introduced what can be termed ideological motives into the political scene its driving force was the quest for office and advancement, a quest that was pursued in factions or parties of mutual interests, extending from some notable figure or grouping at court to the lower levels of the pyramid where minor clients scuffled for a place in the sun. Such factions cut across the horizontal strata of modern class consciousness to establish a flexible – and fluid – alliance which could lend support and promote interests at a variety of social levels. While something like the faction-principle might be seen at work in the great households of feudal magnates, it was the process of centralisation of power under the Tudors which gave the system its particular character and its brutality. Since many practitioners of the arts were also connected with factional groups we are faced yet again with the recognition that however much they might appeal, in Sidney's phrase, to the golden world of art they remained firmly in contact with the brazen facts of political survival.

Tudor patterns of patronage were firmly established by Henry VII, despite his unjust reputation for austerity. Perhaps awareness of his insecure position played some part in the support that he expended on the arts; certainly he used them to promote pageantry and dynastic prestige. The most striking feature of Henry's policy is its dependence on Burgundian scholars and artists: the scholar Bernard André was appointed court chronicler and tutor to Prince Arthur, while Gerard Herenbolt, the miniaturist responsible for the Grimani Breviary and the Sforza Hours was lured over with a higher salary than Holbein would receive. Inevitably this Burgundian influence is most significant in the visual arts and in design from tapestry to glazing, but one notable feature of Henry's court was the establishment of a group of 'King's Players'. This small group which seems to have numbered about four members combined duties within the royal household with responsibility for the aspects of royal display or entertainment. Two of its members, for example, constructed the funeral effigy of Elizabeth of York. It was not a troupe of players, therefore, but rather a coordinating office, working together with the resources of the Chapel Royal; as such it bears witness to the emphasis laid on display. The ambitious series of allegorical pageants devised to receive Catherine of Aragon in 1501 were the most sophisticated yet attempted in England.

The tendency to subsume individual experience within an established type or code is particularly evident in court entertainments such as those from the reign of Henry VIII (1509–47) described by the chronicler Edward Hall. These include such alfresco excursions as that on May Day 1516 when Henry and Catherine rode to Shooters' Hill where they were met by Robin Hood and two hundred bowmen and served wine and venison in an arbour of boughs decked with flowers and herbs. More typical, though, are the chivalric displays of jousting or courtly masquerade where the impersonation of allegorical roles was a major feature (colour plate 8). The Shrove Tuesday banquet given by Wolsey to the imperial ambassadors in 1522 was followed by an assault on a mock castle which had three towers hung with banners displaying rent or tormented hearts. In the castle were eight ladies of the court, among them Anne Boleyn, while the entry was guarded by eight Indian ladies who were really choirboys of the Chapel Royal. Eight lords then entered, 'in cloth of gold caps and all, and great mantle cloaks of blue satin', among them Henry in disguise. Led by the figure of Ardent Desire, in crimson satin embroidered with flames of gold, the lords assaulted the castle with dates and oranges, while the ladies threw down rose water and sweets and the choirboys fought with 'bows and balls'. At length the Indian 'ladies' were driven off and the lords danced with the real ladies.

The staging of such an assault was a fairly common diversion, and in this case it is interesting to note the names given to the participants. The ladies are listed as *Beauty, Honour, Perseverance, Kindness, Constancy, Bounty, Mercy* and *Pity*; the lords are *Amorous, Nobleness, Youth, Attendance, Loyalty, Pleasure, Gentleness* and *Liberty*; the troublesome choirboys reveal their function in the names of *Danger, Disdain, Jealousy, Unkindness, Scorn, Malbouche* (Evil Tongue) and *Strangeness*. The names derive from the greatest love allegory of the Middle Ages, the *Roman de la Rose*, and they personify the psychological forces in the conquest of love – here dramatised in the assault. The names in these entertainments were embroidered on the costumes so that the individual courtiers could be identified in their roles.

There is a contemporary tapestry now in the Hermitage Museum at Leningrad which shows a comparable scene: young ladies armed with branches of roses defend the ramparts of a mock castle. Their names are *Franchise, Cortoisie, Plaisance, Largesse* and *Espoir*; with their roses they beat off brutal soldiers – *Faux Semblant, Dangier, Vilonye, Faulte Deseus* and *Traison* – who in spite of ladders fall back. Again the names are carefully embroidered on each figure. In a purely verbal realisation the siege of love is presented in a poem by one of Wyatt's contemporaries Thomas, Lord Vaux (1510–56), later printed in the influential *Tottel's Miscellany* (1551). The cast list is familiar enough,

> There might you hear the cannons roar
> Each piece discharged a lovers look:
> Which had the power to rend, and tore
> In any place whereas they took.

Desire scales the walls, Fancy breaches them, Beauty enters and the lover surrenders. In all three examples – masquerade, tapestry and poem – the names render the *psychomachia*, the inner struggle of love, in conventional terms that make it a social performance. The same thing happens in the joust as well: in 1511 when Henry celebrated the birth of a short-lived son he fought in the lists as *Coeur loial*, and his companions were *Bon voloir*, *Bon espoir* and *Joyous Penser*. Such ritualised conduct was an essential part of the court scene.

Evidently, then, within the domain of courtly display the influence of Burgundy remained strong, though classical motifs make an occasional appearance. Moreover the game of love provided a convenient repertory of roles which could be put to a practical use. It is clear that Anne Boleyn, no less than her daughter, recognised the advantage of using courtly gestures and vocabulary as a model for the dispensing of patronage. The charges of adultery and incest which led to Anne's execution in 1536 were probably based on nothing more substantial than the perverse refusal of her enemies, led by her former ally Thomas Cromwell, to distinguish between public and private codes. As queen and thus as an important source of patronage Anne assumed the role of the courtly lady, granting favours in return for 'service' from clients, be they poets, place-hunters or translators of the Scriptures. Her own indiscretions enabled her political enemies to misrepresent some relationships as adulterous, and to an already alienated husband that was persuasive enough.

Wyatt was, of course, entirely at home in the courtly world and many of his poems articulate its conventions. But he had also reflected on the classics: he translated Plutarch's *Quiet of Mind* from the Latin version of Guillaume Budé and he advised his son to read Epictetus and Seneca. The last figure in particular is an important presence in the poems he wrote against court life. What his humanist education had supplied was a sense of those private moral values which the courtly tradition and its embroidered names deliberately evaded. It is the conflict between these two worlds which gives his writing its individuality and force.

The shock of his imprisonment over the Anne Boleyn affair appears to lie behind Wyatt's adoption of Senecan moralising, notably in a poem from the Blage manuscript, 'Who list his wealth and ease Retain'. Each stanza concludes with the Latin phrase *circa Regna tonat*, 'the thunder rumbles round the throne', a quotation which helps to identify the poem as a free translation of a chorus in Seneca's tragedy *Phaedra*. It is a very characteristic moment in the Tudor Renaissance: the disappointed courtly lover turns to Seneca for a stoic meditation on the dangers of high place and – having invoked classical moral rhetoric – he adapts it to provide a viewpoint on his present anguish, in this case the execution of his friends,

> The bell tower showed me such a sight
> That in my head sticks day and night;
>   There did I learn out of a grate,   [*barred window*]
> For all favour, glory or might,
>   That yet *Circa Regna tonat*.

In a wider context, what is important about this habit of free adaptation is the way in which it stretches and expands the scope of the vernacular as a medium for complex emotion.

Wyatt's humanism, the very education that enabled him to serve his king as ambassador in France and Spain, also provided him with an alternative and anti-courtly perspective. So in his three satires, the finest verse satires in the language before Donne in the 1590s, Wyatt takes over the town–country dichotomy of Horace to expose the brutal opportunism of the court. In the third and most extreme of these, which may be intended as an ironic inversion of Castiglione, Wyatt addresses his fellow courtier and diplomat Sir Francis Bryan. So it is interesting to find Bryan himself translating Antonio de Guevara's *A Dispraise of the Life of the Courtier*, a direct counterpoise to *The Book of the Courtier*:

If a man know himself to be ambitious, impatient, and covetous, let him go hardly [*speedily*] to the court; and contrary, if the courtier feel his nature to be content, peacable, and desiring rest and quietness, let him be dwelling in the village.

Bryan was not inspired by nostalgia for rural England; like Wyatt he drew on the stoic theme of retirement or 'quiet of mind' to formulate a complex attitude. In these aristocratic writers of the 1530s such a pastoral stance can express disillusion or frustration, just as later in Edmund Spenser and his Jacobean imitators it is the medium for direct political criticism. In the end dispraise of the court does not mean total rejection of it; the juxtaposition of the two conventions helps to provide a sharper definition of experience. Courtiers and shepherds need each other, as Shakespeare recognised in *The Winter's Tale*.

Thomas Cromwell and reform

The factional warfare of the 1530s is one symptom of the profound changes that England experienced in what is arguably the most important decade of the century. Securely at the heart of that decade is the figure of Thomas Cromwell (1485–1540). His radical restructuring of Church and State in the years 1532 to 1540 made him the obvious patron of such reform-minded scholars as Thomas Starkey (*c*. 1499–1538). Starkey's application for employment, probably submitted to Cromwell in 1535 when he returned from Italy, is the nearest thing to a manifesto for civic humanism that can be found in English. In it Starkey summarises the years spent in study at Oxford and abroad: philosophy, the two tongues 'both Latin and Greek', and 'the contemplation of natural knowledge'. But his long term motive has been a social one, 'judging all other secret [*private*] knowledge not applied to some use and profit of others to be as a vanity'. What is especially striking is Starkey's sense that 'the politic order and customs used among us here in our country' need to be seen in wider context provided by study of the Roman law, and it is clear that he had looked closely at the Venetian constitution during his travels. This was just the kind of critical detachment and commitment to reform which Cromwell's policies encouraged. No one has gone so far as to label Cromwell as a humanist, but it is clear that he found the kind of orientation which humanistic studies could provide both sympathetic and useful. In such a political realist the latter quality counted for most and there are signs that by the time he fell victim to a new round of factional warfare in 1540 he was no longer so interested in the Erasmian moderation of men like Starkey.

Cromwell was the epitome of the new man, a common lawyer of humble origins who rose through his managerial skills. The evidence suggests that he could command affection, in spite of his ruthless reputation, and he had style: he had visited Italy and the elegance of his house in Austin Friars was noted by the Venetian ambassador; he supported a group of players (who may well have given a performance of Bale's *King John*), and he valued books. In 1530 Edmund Bonner, the future Bishop of London, wrote to ask him for the loan of Italian books, Petrarch's *Triumphs* and the recently published *Courtier* of Castiglione. Obviously Cromwell's political instincts included an appreciation of ideas and the ability to snatch at those which mattered. The policies by which he permanently changed the fabric of English society were carried through because he was able to identify the widespread impatience for reform – particularly strong in the wake of Wolsey's fall – and give it political expression. In the process he became an important patron of English prose.

Although not so directly concerned with policy as Starkey would be, Sir Thomas Elyot (*c*. 1490–1546) was closely associated with Cromwell and it is likely that *The Book of the Governor* was completed with his encouragement. Elyot was directly influenced by Castiglione, as his title may suggest, and he drew on a number of other Italian humanist texts. But he is more than a compiler. Book I, the most original section of *The Governor*, includes a series of proposals for reforming legal education on humanistic lines which may have been formed to catch the eye of More, elevated to the Chancellorship in 1529. The general purpose of the work is to suggest a suitable education for the new style of 'inferior governor', for whom Elyot coins the title 'magistrate'. This is the segment of the gentry on which the government will depend for the implementation of reform and social control.

Elyot follows the familiar pattern of humanist educators in stressing that education is more than professional training; it involves the whole personality and should develop a variety of skills. Among these the playing of musical instruments 'without wanton countenance and dissolute gesture' may be included, together with painting and carving in wood or stone. Elyot is anxious to stress that these skills are for private pleasure only, though sketching may have a military value. But exercise in the arts will help to develop critical judgement 'in discerning the excellency of them which either in music or in statuary or painters' craft professeth any cunning'. The concept of the virtuoso has arrived.

Another aspect of *The Governor* which is often overlooked is that it can lay some claim to being the first critical treatise in English. Elyot's plan, to combine the study of a purified common law snuffed of scholastic barbarisms with the rhetorical training outlined by Cicero, centres on the idea of persuasive speech. It may not be accidental that this ambition to turn a common lawyer into 'a right orator' ties in so closely with the unveiling of Cromwell's plans for reform – reform by parliamentary management and the printing press. Probably at no time before had English political conditions been so open to the persuasive use of language. And it is within the same bracket of persuasive language that Elyot places poetry. This is a consequence of his anxiety to distinguish between a mere versifier and the authentic poet who goes beyond verbal dexterity, just as the orator goes beyond the mere rhetorician by the addition of 'a keep of all manner of learning . . . which is in one word of Greek *Encyclopedia*'.

Elyot's insistence on the elevated status of the poet, as well as his rather coy allusion to inspiration or 'celestial instinction', marks a significant rise in the estimate of fiction as a social force. In several respects his 'right orator' sets the stage for Sidney's 'right poet' fifty years later, and it places the writer, with his training in the liberal arts, on a higher level than the professional painter or musician.

To return to Thomas Starkey, his most ambitious work, the so-called *Dialogue of Pole and Lupset*, remained in manuscript until the nineteenth century. In essence it appears to be a policy paper which he drew up for submission to Cromwell between 1534, when he was still in Padua, and late 1535, by which time he had become a royal chaplain. The *Dialogue* sets out to describe the social problems of the day and to suggest possible remedies. The stark description he gives of the England of the 1530s corroborates the complaints made by Thomas More twenty years earlier: one third of the population live in idleness 'like unto drone bees in a hive', while too many are engaged in luxury trades which fail to cater for the true dignity of man. English ploughmen are the most negligent in Europe and the countryside is haunted by the greatest mob of beggars in Christendom.

Starkey links economic decline to underpopulation, evidence that the Black Death still left its mark on English society. In contrast to the towns of Italy or the Low Countries 'so well builded and so clean kept', English towns display decline and neglect. In the light of Starkey's complaints it is worth noting that from a total population of 3.7 million in 1348 the figure had slumped to 2.1 million in 1400, and in 1524 was still under 2.4 million. It is not surprising, then, that Starkey urges the precedent set by the Roman state in promoting and supporting marriage. His sharp observation of contemporary problems and his common-sense (he notes that dissolving the monasteries will increase the birth-rate) are founded on the characteristic belief that the end of political activity should be

to bring the whole country to quietness and civility, that everyman, and so the whole, may at the last attain to such perfection as by nature is to the dignity of man due.

The dignity of man may not be the most obvious preoccupation of Tudor politics, and it is easy to regard Starkey as naive, but his alertness to the role of economic forces in social development reveals one of the more original aspects of contemporary reform proposals. The roots of such thinking no doubt reached to *Utopia* and to the schemes of the Spanish scholar Juan Vives, briefly tutor to the Princess Mary, whose plans for poor relief had been tested in Ypres and Lyons and were known to Cromwell's policy projectors. It was this kind of practical reform that Cromwell encouraged, and it surfaces again among the 'commonweal' group around Sir Thomas Smith under Edward VI.

Cromwell's plan for a state-controlled Church, the political nation at prayer, developed naturally out of the policies devised by such clients as Starkey and William Marshall. The latter prepared an English version of *The Defender of Peace* by the fourteenth-century anti-papal theorist Marsilius of

Padua, which was published in 1535 to reinforce the claims of royal supremacy. Behind these men one can detect the largely solvent influence of Erasmus: the kind of reformation they envisage parallels the humanist 'philological' model, like a text stripped of later accretions and misreadings, rather than the Lutheran conception of a spiritual community. But the model they produced was to prove a remarkably versatile container for religious change, and the essence of Hooker's defence of the Elizabethan *via media* against radical Protestantism in the 1590s is already anticipated in Starkey's Erastian Catholicism.

The common feature is the appeal to a mean which will preserve 'civil concord' and 'spiritual unity'. In the *Exhortation to Unity and Obedience*, which was printed in 1536 as a justification of government policy, Starkey formulates the central theory of *adiaphora*: the key distinction between fundamental and unchanging truths, and matters indifferent which relate to church organisation and discipline and may be subject to political control. It was precisely this distinction, he argues, which the Germans have failed to observe in their destructive zeal:

they did not discern with right judgement, betwixt things of themselves good and necessary, and other which are only for the time convenient to a certain policy.

This argument was to prove an essential element in the emergence of Anglican thought. It would be anachronistic to overlook the element of political concern which lies behind Starkey's argument: he concludes that princes may enforce the *adiaphora*, and that their subjects must obey them. None the less, the appeal to discernment presupposes the thoughtful response of his readers.

The most immediate physical consequence of these policies was the Dissolution of the Monasteries, and here Cromwell's genuine intentions may well have been distorted by the pressure of events. Starkey, for one, hoped to see the resources liberated by this massive programme of secularisation directed to social ends: educating the governing classes for one thing, no doubt along the lines suggested by Elyot, and various forms of social relief. But the scramble for plunder could not be contained. A suitable emblem for the episode might be the roof timbers of Madingley Hall, outside Cambridge, which to this day carry the tell-tale signs of their original use in the roof of nearby Angelsey Abbey.

On the positive side, Cromwell's propaganda campaign, with its recognition of a new reading public that could be reached through the printing press, was to have important implications for vernacular writing. Apart from the pamphlets designed to lead opinion there was a steady stream of translations, many from the works of Erasmus, and this activity found its most impressive expression in the *Great Bible*, the first English translation to be officially approved which became available in 1539 at a cost of ten shillings, unbound. Revised and reissued in 1540 under Cranmer's super-vision, the new preface referred to the example of Anglo-Saxon translations. In the general course of the Reformation, historical precedent became an invaluable weapon for both sides, and we can see here the first stirring of those antiquarian studies which would develop in Elizabeth's reign under the patronage of Archbishop Parker and find full realisation in the work of William Camden.

Cranmer's preface to the revised *Great Bible* was worked out of Erasmus' *Paracelsis*, the preface that he had prepared for the 1516 New Testament. This had gone behind the whole tradition of the Latin Vulgate to draw on the Greek original. So Cranmer's choice was apt: the provision of a vernacular bible was the next logical step, and Erasmus would have agreed. But since the days of Wycliffe the provision of an English Bible had been a controversial matter. One fifteenth-century writer complained that

Wycliffe translated the Gospel that Christ gave to the clergy and doctors of the Church . . . so that by his means it has become vulgar and more open to laymen and women who can read it than it usually is to quite learned clergy of good intelligence.

The crucial issue of the 1530s was really, who constituted the Church? Was it just the clergy, or did it include princes and their peoples? Lollard was a threat to clerical control since it disregarded the tradition of exegesis and relied on private interpretation; and clerical opposition was not wholly self-centred: it was, after all, the responsibility of the clergy to mediate the perspective of tradition. Thomas More favoured an English version but he was infuriated by Tyndale's tendentious rendering which aimed to subvert accepted doctrine. Erasmus asserts in the *Paracelsis*, with the unfettered optimism that so vexed traditionalists, that anyone who teaches the Gospels in the spirit of Christ is a theologian, even if he is a weaver or labourer. Under that definition even a woman might qualify, and Anne Boleyn was a generous supporter of those who worked to make the scriptures available in English. She must indeed have been aware of French evangelical developments during her long stay as a girl at the French court. The advance of the vernacular Bible was closely linked to the advance of that lay spirit which Cromwell harnessed so effectively in the Reformation Parliament.

Reformation and the arts

Debate about the availability of the Bible led naturally to the impact of the Reformation in the arts. In almost all respects this tended to promote private responsibility for interpretation in place of canonically approved forms. The initial attack by Luther on the doctrine of indulgences was a bitter protest against the institutionalisation of the individual's relationship with God. In the place of a personal encounter with the divine, the system of indulgences provided the believer with precisely-stated rewards for specified acts measured, Erasmus ironically commented, as if by a water clock. Inevitably in many cases such a system encouraged an arid formalism, devoid of inner conviction.

The intensity and, on occasion, violence of the Reformers came from their wish to liberate religious life from such restrictions and to assert the transcendence of God. Where Catholic teaching permitted images as aids to devotion, and specified vestments and ceremonies as outward signs of spiritual worship, the more rigorous Reformers saw only the material distractions which had corrupted the Christian inheritance. Other motives entered the struggle as well; the wholesale confiscation of vestments, plate and other ornaments after the dissolution of the chantries under Edward VI was not prompted by spiritual zeal alone. But the gradual ascendancy of Protestant ideas in worship served to displace a range of arts and skills, from glazing and embroidery to music and the visual arts. In the view of many, a sermon was more beneficial than a sacrament, and this gave priority to the didactic potential of the verbal arts. John Foxe, whose *Book of Martyrs* (1563) was to prove one of the great ideological works of English culture, argued that 'players, printers, preachers . . . be set up of God, as a triple bulwark against the triple crown of the pope'.

The complaints made about images range from charges that they could provoke impure thoughts to the more platonic view that 'material shadows' are a distraction from intellectual truth. Impure thoughts might result from the degree of naturalistic realism provided in paintings or painted statuary, a practice originally developed to assist imaginative intimacy with a devotional episode or a particular saint. Erasmus tells the story of a simple man at Louvain who would say the 'Our Father' at every altar in the church so as to avoid jealousy among the saints. Here the problem lay in the empathetic quality of late medieval art forms. The miniature, however, was hardly likely to stimulate this kind of response, and in the severe formalism of later Tudor portraiture, influenced as it is by miniature techniques, we may see a secular effect of this anxiety. Some rigorists, like the Calvinist William Perkins, might regard even mental images used as mnemonic aids with suspicion; but the general view among reformed opinion seemed to be that images were acceptable if they appealed to the mind and did not stop at the level of sensuous apprehension.

In other words, the image must be internalised in order to provide an occasion for spiritual or intellectual reflection. This requires a formalised sense stimulus in order to activate the viewer's associations and provoke an intellectual response; it results in a view of art as a system of signs or symbols not wholly dissimilar to the concept of the icon. The painted image must be passed through in order to encounter the idea behind the work. Other developments such as the emblem or the *impresa*, which embody an idea or motto through conventional signs, appear to have answered expectations aroused by just such a view of the visual arts, as do the studied violations of realism in the late Hilliardesque 'mask of youth' portraits of Elizabeth. In works of this kind attention is deliberately drawn to the artificiality of the work so that the viewer – in contrast to the misguided worshipper of statues – can recognise the intellectual theme or 'soul' behind it. Protestantism tended to make the book the underlying model for the arts, a text to be read; and the visual tradition of medieval or Catholic art forms was increasingly verbalised. The most important artistic contribution of suppressed Catholicism was, practically enough, in the abstract medium of music.

The Bible was the bedrock of the Reformers, and it had to be interpreted and applied to the peculiar conditions of the individual reader. John Donne (1572–1631), in a characteristically vivid analogy, described the true approach to the scriptures in a Christmas sermon at St Paul's in 1621; the Christian must search the scriptures 'not as thou wouldst make a *concordance* but an *application*; as thou wouldst search a *wardrobe*, not to make an *Inventory* of it, but to find in it something fit for thy wearing'. This clothing image is certainly suggestive; the new familiarity with the translated scriptures meant that such applications became an habitual response, with implication for secular reading habits as well. The medieval romance names adopted in the entertainments of Henry's court are a secular kind of 'application' or role-playing.

Interpretation is such an essential part of the arts in Tudor England because it enables the 'text' – which may also be a painting, a musical setting or a tomb – to work on the reader and to go beyond the merely physical or aesthetic response. An example is the 'Ermine' portrait of Elizabeth executed by the herald Sir William Segar and now at Hatfield House (p. 2). The picture, which probably dates from 1585, shows the Queen dressed in black velvet, richly set with jewels. The exaggerated slimness of the waist and the pale, unshadowed features of the queen (who was fifty at the time) take us out of the sphere of naturalism altogether; the heraldic formality is confirmed by the small white ermine, collared with a jewelled crown, which is poised against her left arm. Not only is the ermine proverbially associated with chastity but, more specifically, it is found in the iconographic tradition which derives from Petrarch's *Triumphs*, the most influential of his poetical writings in Elizabethan England. In the 'Triumph of Chastity' Laura, in the role of Chastity or *Pudicitia*, carries a banner that is embroidered with an ermine. She is shown with this ermine motif in the Flemish tapestries purchased by Wolsey for Hampton Court, and in the identical set now in the Victoria and Albert Museum. As a variant of the theme, the knight Clitophon in Sidney's *Arcadia* has as his device an ermine with the motto 'Rather dead than spotted'.

In Segar's portrait, as well as the ermine there is a sprig of laurel in the queen's right hand, which declares her impersonation of Laura, Petrarch's embodiment of chastity; yet the sword of justice which lies beside her on the table appears to imply the idea of private chastity dedicated to the public service. This association with Petrarch is not an isolated instance: in the 'Sieve Portrait' at Siena, Elizabeth is associated with the vestal virgin Tuccia, who carried water in a sieve to prove her chastity and who is introduced as an exemplary figure in the 'Triumph of Chastity'. In such portraits the material representation is the starting point for a series of associative steps which go beyond the physical likeness of the sitter to indicate ideal qualities. Often political ideas may be insinuated, as in George Gower's 'Armada' portrait now at Woburn, which shows the Queen in French costume in front of the storm-ravaged Spanish fleet.

Such paintings, like the devices in emblem books or collections of *impresa*, demand interpretation; as in the case of a scriptural text the reader is required to play an active part in the process of relating individual persons or events to archetypal concepts. One common charge made by the Reformers against the Catholic Mass was that it confused a sign with the thing signified. To Cranmer the sacrament was a commemoration, a calling to mind of

Christ's unique sacrifice; and the Catholic doctrine of transubstantiation, with its claim that the bread and wine was changed *in substance* into the body and blood of Christ, was idolatrous because it confused the sign with the reality, even as a simple mind might confuse the statue with the saint. So Catholic devotional practice appeared to venerate material things as if they contained a spiritual presence, and this could easily slip into magic. In Spenser's Protestant epic *The Faerie Queene* (1590 and 1596), the evil wizard Archimago is identified with Catholicism for this reason. Protestant reaction against Catholic practice takes the form of a reaching out for the figurative or 'spiritual' sense which lies beyond material signs.

One of the most important statements about the value of the image-making arts of painting and poetry is Sir Philip Sidney's *A Defence of Poetry*, which he probably completed in 1580 although it was not published until 1595. Sidney's aim was to justify the value of the fictional imagination or 'figuring forth', against those who see its products as at best irrelevant and at worst lies. *A Defence* draws on the time-honoured arguments used by humanists since Boccaccio, but it gives them a distinct post-Reformation slant. The key term in Sidney's argument is *moving*: the capacity to convert knowledge into action by moving the affections. This is, of course, the traditional argument, used on behalf of rhetoric; what stands out in Sidney's scheme is the emphasis it lays on the creation of images that can be 'planted' in the mind. The imagination, which Sidney tends to describe in spatial terms, is like a gallery or theatre, stored with memorable figures and episodes which have more force in teaching than scholastic abstractions. The poet 'giveth so sweet a prospect into the way, as will entice any man to enter into it'.

Sidney's distinction between the golden world of the poet and the brazen world of nature has a neo-Platonic basis, but it also reflects his Protestant sense of the gulf between an ideal world, lost by sin and now only accessible to the imagination, and the flawed world of human history. In his own words, 'our erected wit maketh us know what perfection is, and yet our infected will keepeth us from reaching unto it'. The function of the speaking picture of poetry or the frozen poem of painting is to bridge this gulf between wit and will with compelling images that remain active in the memory and provide moral insight and infectious example. Sidney's most original twist to a traditional argument is to assert that 'the skill of each artificer standeth in the *idea* or fore-conceit of the work, and not in the work itself'. In other words the physical medium, whether pigment or print, exists primarily to convey an image from artist to audience. This concern to penetrate beyond the sign to a mental reality, which is so characteristic of Protestant habits of worship and interpretation, finds an outlet in allegorical modes, both in painting and in literature. In Spenser's *Faerie Queene* it finds its fullest expression.

Protestant humanism

The religious upheavals which mark the middle decades of the century have been seen as checks on the spread of Renaissance culture in England. The evidence does not support this. At the universities, humanist studies flourished, and there was a growing traffic between them and the court. The generation of Sir John Cheke (1514–57) and Sir Thomas Smith (1513–77), both of whom matriculated at Cambridge in 1526, marks the ripening of a native classicism linked to government service and committed to Protestantism. Cheke was a brilliant teacher and many of his pupils at St John's went on to occupy positions of importance under Elizabeth. Chief among them was William Cecil (1520–98; colour pl. 4) who drew heavily on the 'Cambridge connection' in 1558 to fill offices in Church and state. The manoeuvring behind Henry VIII's will ensured the triumph of the Reform party under Edward Seymour, Duke of Somerset, and Edward VI's Council included an unprecedented number of highly literate laymen. The steady growth of an educated governing class is reflected in the Commons where, in 1563, out of 420 members some 139 had been to university or the Inns of Court, and this included 36 who had been to both. By 1593 the total had risen to 252 and 106 had been to both. Despite the political instability of Edward's reign the reforms initiated by Cromwell continued to affect cultural life.

Sir Thomas Smith can be taken as representative of this mid-century humanism, combining academic talent with the social concerns of the so-called 'Commonwealth men'. He first won notice at court in 1538, probably through the offices of the royal physician William Butts who had helped to finance his studies. Appointed to the new Regius chair of Civil Law at Cambridge in 1543, he was Vice-Chancellor by the age of thirty. Under Edward VI he was promoted to royal secretary, and the remainder of his career passed in political and diplomatic service. *A Discourse of the Common Weal* (1549), which is now confidently attributed to Smith, takes up many of the issues earlier discussed by Thomas Starkey. Set as a dialogue between members of the various estates, from land-owner to labourer, it sketches the steps necessary to halt economic decline. Smith's policies are managerial rather than radical but they reveal a strong sense of the inter-dependence of the estates, and like John Hales and Hugh Latimer he sees the ruthless enclosure of arable land as a major threat to social justice.

The literature of social protest is a feature of the reign, often voicing bitterness at the wasted opportunities of the monastic dissolution. To Protestant eyes Wycliffe and his Lollard followers were forerunners of the Reformation; Chaucer's criticism of the lax religious drew him into this category, together with Langland. The revival of interest in fourteenth-century texts, which led to Thynne's edition of Chaucer (1532) and Robert Crowley's *The Vision of Pierce Plowman* (1550), is linked to the development of a radical Protestant tradition of popular writing. Spenser's debt to Edwardian medievalism is evident in *The Shepheardes Calender* (1579) and *Mother Hubberds Tale* (1591), as well as Book I of *The Faerie Queene*, and it provides an important caveat against his reputation as an exclusively court poet.

The vigorous literary activity of Edward's reign (1547–53), a result of the tolerant policies introduced by the Protector, Edward Seymour, Duke of Somerset, was largely concerned with the diffusion of Protestant attitudes and beliefs. Nevertheless, the stimulus that it gave to vernacular literary forms, notably to the drama, had an important bearing on the resources available to a later generation of writers. Thanks to the personal tastes and ambitions of Somerset and his successor Northumberland, the reign also saw interesting developments in design and architecture. An interesting figure here is another courtier, Sir William Sharrington, who had been a member of Henry VIII's Privy Chamber and sat for Holbein. He used his monastic prize of Lacock Abbey as the showpiece of a new and coherent classical style which probably owed something to French precedents. Sir Thomas Smith too, whose diplomatic travels had acquainted him with French models, showed a comparable taste in his seat at Hill Hall in Essex which was built in the late 1560s. Closely bound up with these tentative exercises in Renaissance design lay the classical humanism which had its most distinguished representative in John Cheke.

The emergence of an educated, and even erudite, governing class was a necessary factor for the reason that such innovations depended on the initiative of the amateur patron rather than the builder. Until the advent of the trained professional in the person of Inigo Jones, the use of classical design was dependent on an antiquarian taste, guided by the printed works of architects like Alberti, Serlio and in due course Palladio. The association of humanist scholarship with the Protestant interest meant that, in place of the radicalism of Thomas More, it was increasingly bound up with the governing elite. It is intriguing to find how many initiatives in the reign of Elizabeth can be traced back to the circle of Cheke's students.

Cheke died as a broken man in 1557, shortly after public recantation of his Protestant faith. Yet just over a year later his brother-in-law William Cecil, as chief secretary, was at work placing Cheke's pupils and associates in the new administration of Elizabeth, while Cambridge men played a key role too in the moderate Protestant settlement which Elizabeth imposed with Cecil's aid. Yet from the beginning of the new reign there appears to have been rivalry between Cecil as the Queen's closest political counsellor and Robert Dudley, the Earl of Leicester (1532–88) as royal favourite and, in the early years at least, a potential consort. Inevitably this is reflected in their different roles as patrons. Of the two, Cecil was the better educated, having started out in the charmed circle of Cheke, and his wife was one of the formidable daughters of King Edward's other tutor Sir Anthony Cooke, who were said to outshine Thomas More's daughters in their learning. In contrast Dudley, who became Earl of Leicester in 1564, was adequately educated but could not match Cecil's classical training. In 1559 Cecil became Chancellor of Cambridge, following in the steps of Cromwell, Somerset, Northumberland and Reginald Pole.

There was a certain inevitability about Leicester's election as Chancellor of Oxford five years later, and it was in part this rivalry with Cecil which prompted him to become leader of the more radical Anglicans. Certainly his power base was closely associated with that advanced evangelical opinion which looked for an international Protestant league against Spain. Because of his prominence as a court favourite, with a consequent ability to promote the interests of his clients, Leicester played a central role in patronage of the arts and education, as well as in the distribution of political and church offices. In all these areas of activity, advancement was still dependent on the favour of the powerful or influential. It has been calculated that under Elizabeth the Crown could dispose of some 1,200 major offices or places and some 1,200 minor ones. But offices might carry their own petty patronage, and officials would have their private secretaries and assistants. What is clear is that a career could be made at court.

As Chancellor of Oxford, Leicester intervened regularly in University affairs and thus extended his patronage. From 1567 for all practical purposes he nominated the Vice-Chancellor and his influence over appointments within the University and even over policy was considerable. In addition he could advance University men at court and in the Church. It was through his intervention that a special licence was issued in 1584 to permit the establishment of a University printing press – the printer in question was the Joseph Barnes who produced Oxford's tribute to Sidney three years later.

To the modern reader much of the interest of the Sidney commemorative volumes published by Oxford and Cambridge lies in the web of Leicester patronage they reveal, as well as the intimate link still taken for granted between Latin writing and English. The editor of the Oxford elegies, the *Exequiae*, was William Gager of Christ Church, a prolific Latin author whose plays had been performed before Leicester and Sidney in the university. Gager became involved in a heated controversy with the austere John Rainolds of St John's over the lawfulness of stage plays, and received warm support in his efforts from another of Leicester's nominees, the Italian professor of Civil Law, Albericus Gentilis. Among the Oxford Contributors was Leicester's chief agent within the University, Laurence Humphrey, President of Magdalen, whose radical Protestantism dated from his Marian years of exile in Zurich and whose treatise *The Nobles* (1563) provided a thoeretical basis for the kind of aristocratic interference Leicester practised.

The editor of the Cambridge elegies, *Lachrymae Cantabrigiensis*, was Alexander Neville, a pioneer of Anglo-Saxon studies, who had served as secretary to three Archibishops of Canterbury and sat in the Commons, presumably through Leicester's influence. He is a typical mid-century populariser who translated Livy and Seneca (his version of *Oedipus* was included in Thomas Newton's influential *Seneca his Ten Tragedies* of 1581), as well as collaborating with vernacular writers like George Gascoigne (*c*.1525–77), whom Leicester engaged to co-ordinate his spectacular Kenilworth entertainment for Elizabeth in 1575.

The fact that Sidney's death prompted these volumes of academic verse underlines the new alliance between the worlds of learning and power, but they also reveal a further motive: the use of Sidney's death to press the government into open war with Spain. Leicester was the figurehead for the interests of the new Protestant ascendancy, and this meant a Calvinist inclination in religion, bitter hostility to Spain, an interventionist policy in the Netherlands, and with all this a revived cult of chivalry. The most distinguished beneficiary of Leicester's literary patronage was Edmund Spenser, whose *Shepheardes Calender* is a poetic manifesto, but also a declaration of the anxiety of the Dudley faction at the prospect of Elizabeth's marriage with the Catholic Duke of Alençon.

The image of Elizabeth

Elizabeth's government was in no position to impose policies by force and the patronage system was a means of winning the consensus of the political classes. Another means was use of a revived and Protestant chivalry at the service of a queen who was the focus for knightly service. In an age dominated by masculine values, the anomaly of a female ruler could be eased by the fiction of a relationship in which traditions of the love-game were sharpened and sophisticated by the influence of Petrarch and the love sonnet. Such a convention lies behind Hilliard's portrait of Leicester's political heir Robert Devereux, Earl of Essex, which shows him in jousting armour with the queen's glove tied to his right arm. The portrait, with a background of tents, may allude to his 1591 campaign in France in support of Henry of Navarre against the Catholic league; it was during the siege of Rouen that Essex challenged the enemy commander to single combat, a gesture in keeping with the rather anachronistic spirit the English had already shown in the Netherlands.

In the dismantling of Catholic devotion under Elizabeth, St George had remained an exception largely on account of his association with the Order of the Garter; and the annual festival of the Order, together with the Accession Day Tilts, were the chief ceremonial manifestations of Protestant chivalry, in part romantic play and in part serious politics. Sir William Segar, the herald-painter of the 'Ermine' portrait, was also Garter King-of-arms. Spenser's evocation of the Garter in the *Faerie Queene* links those who serve 'that sovereigne Dame, /That glorie does to them for Guerdon [*recompense*] grant' with the recognition that the regenerate Red Cross Knight is 'Saint George of merry England'. Again it is important to recognise the political overtones: behind Spenser's knights gathered to serve the Faerie Queene in Cleopolis lies the memory of Leicester and the dream of a Protestant league against Spain. Further, it is not by chance that Red Cross has been brought up by a ploughman; in this clear allusion to Langland's *Piers Plowman* the chivalric cult of Elizabeth's reign asserts its inheritance of a Lollard past.

The point for the modern reader is not so much to spot the intricacies of contemporary allusion as to see that the romance world conjured up by Spenser or by Sidney is not far removed from the actual conduct and display of the court, and that display in its turn aimed to convey declarations and counsels of a political nature. The patronage exercised by favourites like Leicester or Essex had an enormous influence on the development of the arts and on the introduction of continental models. The splendid Kenilworth entertainments given by Leicester in 1575 as a last effort to urge the queen towards a suitable marriage are far more classical in their conception than earlier festivities, and they show a clear debt to the comparable entertainments given by Catherine de' Medici at Bayonne ten years earlier to promote a Franco-Spanish marriage alliance.

Yet while the use of mythology and classical motifs increased during the reign, there was continuity with earlier tradition; Sir Henry Lee, the Queen's Champion who presided over the Accession Day Tilts and did more than anyone to formulate her symbolic image, had served as a page in the house of his uncle Sir Thomas Wyatt. One of the last uses of the siege motif, which we have already seen at Henry's court, was *The Four Foster Children of Desire*, presented before Elizabeth and the French ambassadors in 1581 and in which Sidney had a hand. The thrust of the argument is that the Foster Children will not win the Fortress of Perfect Beauty: a polite hint that hopes for a marriage alliance are vain. Instead 'they acknowledge this Fortress to be preserved for the eye of the whole world, far lifted up from the compass of their destiny'. As Elizabeth put it on another occasion, 'I am already bound unto an Husband, which is the Kingdom of England.'

Perhaps because of this mystical marriage to her kingdom, Elizabeth showed a marked distaste for marriage among her courtiers. Her own public performances were those of a talented actress, whether in her encounters with foreign diplomats, with Parliament, or her impromptu participation in the pageants that welcomed her on progresses around the country. She knew what people expected and she provided it. This aspect of her personal style supported the erotic vocabulary of Petrarchan politics. The conduct of a courtly lover, even to the extent of writing verse, was a necessary prelude to political favours. Another favourite, Sir Christopher Hatton (1540–91), whose enemies attributed his rise to his skilful dancing, wrote to Sir Thomas Heneage that he intended to leave 'my other shrine', his great house at Holdenby, 'still unseen until that holy Saint may sit in it, to whom it is dedicated'. The queen's negligible personal spending on the arts was a result of this Petrarchan reliance on the devotion of her courtiers. Such a highly artificial mode of relationship was, in effect, a literary code for politics, and it could be recognised as such by its participants: during Raleigh's imprisonment after his secret marriage in 1592, Sir Arthur Gorges alluded to Ariosto's love-crazed epic hero in a cryptic letter to Robert Cecil, 'I fear Sir W. Rawly will shortly grow to be Orlando Furioso, if the bright Angelica persevere against him a little longer.' But it was from prison that Raleigh (*c.* 1552–1618) wrote his finest poetical achievement *The Oceans Love to Cynthia*, a work addressed to the idea of a Virgin Queen whose image had come to displace that of the Virgin Mother.

The native Renaissance

The second half of Elizabeth's reign witnessed an unparalleled flowering of vernacular writing which marks the full assimilation of Renaissance perspectives to the native tradition. But the process of assimilation had been far from smooth. Indeed, for much of the time the two currents – native and classical – were content to run parallel, and one creative outcome of the Reformation was to force the two together in order to propogate the Gospel and win the ear of the common man. The consequences of this interaction can be found in fields quite outside the immediate concern of religion such as the drama, though here the importance of 'players' in the propaganda war was well recognised.

At the start of the century performances of the religious cycles or of morality plays were mounted by guilds or itinerant groups of players and these continued with growing infrequency until the 1570s. Great houses, and above all the court, drew on the resources of their chapels to arrange interludes and entertainments. Whether or not the plays which the young Thomas More joined in at Cardinal Morton's household were Latin comedies, one of the Cardinal's chaplains was Henry Medwall whose *Fulgens and Lucrece* (*c*. 1497) is the earliest wholly secular play in the vernacular to survive. William Cornish (1468?–1523) was the first of a line of Masters of the Children of the Chapel Royal who exploited the theatrical potential of their charges. Richard Edwards (1524–66), another composer–poet, ran the boys as a company of actors – they performed at Lincoln's Inn in 1565 – while Richard Farrant, Master in 1576–81, took out a lease on the old Blackfriars monastery and used the refectory to put on a public series of plays on themes from ancient history. The boys' companies were clearly popular: Sebastian Westcott, a Catholic, held the post of Master of the St Paul's choirboys from 1547 to 1582 thanks to protection of the Queen, and in that period his pupils performed at court no fewer than twenty-eight times. Between the extremes of the traditional and the academic drama the boys' companies trod the middle ground.

While Elizabeth attended Latin plays during her few visits to Oxford and Cambridge, performances at court were in the vernacular, and the importance of the court in the emergence of a mature native drama cannot be overstressed. Growing opposition to plays and to playgoing led to the demise of traditional performances in many parts of the country. At Chelmsford the redundant Catholic vestments in the church were transformed into theatrical costumes and hired out to groups of players, but the last loan was to the Earl of Sussex's Men in 1572 and four years later the wardrobe was sold for £6/13/3. The 1570s marked the peak of religious opposition to plays, but the Queen demanded her 'solace' and the support of the court was decisive in checking the hostility of the City of London. In 1576 James Burbage was able to build The Theatre, the first purpose-built playhouse in London. When the City closed this and the other playhouse, The Curtain, in 1584, the players appealed successfully to Elizabeth's Council. The Earl of Leicester was in this as in so many things a major patron; his own company enjoyed many privileges and he may have given support to Burbage's initiative. The Queen's sympathy is evident in the establishment of her own company, the Queen's Men, who were given the status of grooms of the Chamber in her household. All this meant that the companies, provided with a London base and engaged in frequent tours in the country, had access to a uniquely comprehensive audience.

In addition to the stability and the technical resources which the playhouses offered, the drama profited from the striking advances in verse style. The achievements of Christopher Marlowe and Shakespeare were made possible by all these factors. Dramatic verse and poetry in general sought for a native medium able to match the complex expression of classical or Italian texts. Blank verse, fittingly enough, was first used by the Earl of Surrey during the 1530s for his translation of the *Aeneid* and he revealed the potential of the form for solemn dramatic utterance. This it provided in the important early tragedy *Gorbuduc* by Sackville and Norton, performed by the gentlemen of the Inner Temple as part of their Christmas revels in 1561–2. It clearly went down well since it was repeated at court a few days later. The play stands out for its pioneering use of blank verse, and this enables it to achieve a tragic quality beyond the reach of the cumbersome 'fourteeners' or seven-stress lines favoured by other dramatists.

It is some measure of the Elizabethan achievement in metrical virtuosity that within fifty years of *Gorbuduc* Shakespeare could handle the iambic pentameter with such freedom as makes possible the expression of intense inner conflict, as in Leontes' jealous fit in *The Winter's Tale* (1611),

> Is whispering nothing?
> Is leaning cheek to cheek? Is meeting noses?
> Kissing with inside lip? stopping the career
> Of laughter with a sigh? – a note infallible
> Of breaking honesty? – horsing foot on foot?
> Skulking in corners? wishing clocks more swift?
> Hours, minutes? noon, midnight? and all eyes
> Blind with the pin and web but theirs, theirs only,
> That would unseen be wicked? is this nothing?
> Why, then the world and all that's in't is nothing;
> The covering sky is nothing; Bohemia nothing;
> My wife is nothing; nor nothing have these nothings,
> If this be nothing.   (I, i, 284–96)

Even such apparent dead-ends as the attempt to adopt classical quantitative metres in English verse advanced the technical skills of poets like Sidney and Spenser, and it was from them that Shakespeare learnt his craft. It was this mastery of cadence as much as growing confidence in the expressive resources of the English language that set the scene for the profusion of lyric and dramatic verse, as well as song, which marked the high point of the English Renaissance.

With the benefit of hindsight the defeat of the Armada in 1588 can be seen as a point of transition: the sobering threat of Spanish attack was no longer so imminent. But the removal of pressure only encouraged an increase in internal friction over the character of the Anglican Church. Hooker's *Laws*, although written ostensibly against Catholic opponents of the Elizabethan settlement, was in reality directed at those subversive elements who, in Hooker's ironic terms, 'measure religion by mislike of the church of Rome'. But the dominant issue in the final decade of the reign was the succession, since Elizabeth refused to commit herself to a public acknowledgement of her heir, in spite of encouraging gestures to James VI of Scotland. No doubt it was his anxiety to win the support of the Leicester faction that led James to make a poetical contribution to the Cambridge *Lachrymae* for Sidney.

In any case there are hints of an aristocratic political theory, which would make the nobility guardians of the commonwealth rather as the Huguenot nobles had aspired to be in France, among the members of Leicester's circle and in Sidney's *Arcadia*. The botched rebellion of Essex in 1601 carries overtones of such an intervention. Not only was Essex Leicester's stepson but he had been dubbed banneret at Zutphen and, in a symbolic gesture, Sidney had left him his sword. All this gives added significance to the scheme of his supporters to stage a performance of *Richard II* (1597), a dramatic enactment of deposition. Shakespeare's play was one among many which had covert reference to the succession issue, but none displayed more tellingly the gulf between the public image of the monarch and the private person that it clothed. Such is the disparity between the allegorical projections of late images of the Queen – the Ditchley or Rainbow portraits say – and the faded looks of an ageing woman.

The 1590s were marked by the disengagement of public and private; the popularity of satire and the vogue for Montaigne's *Essays* are symptomatic of the taste for a less idealised delineation of experience. The younger Marcus Gheeraerts' portrait of Essex, presented by the Earl to Trinity College, Cambridge, shows a concern for the private mood of the sitter, a facial mobility which is far removed from the surviving portraits of his stepfather Leicester. At the same period Shakespeare's probing of the metaphors of kingship displays a new introspection about the official signs of authority, 'Tradition, form and ceremonious duty'. It was in the 1590s that the verb 'to monarchise' first appeared, not without ironical overtones.

One aspect of the Elizabethan achievement had been to hold together the two aspects or 'bodies' of royal status: the 'politic' or ceremonial, and the private or 'natural'. No doubt the queen's enactment of her personal myth helped the process, but even during her reign the constitutional tensions that were to overwhelm the Stuarts were evident to the careful observer. When the Parliamentary forces in the Civil War took up arms they were, in their own words, 'fighting the king to defend the King'. It was the heritage of the 1530s, the concept of King-in-Parliament, the assimilation of humanist education and Protestant beliefs, and above all the creation of a new governing class, which made the crisis of the 1640s all but inevitable.

Wales and the preservation of the language

It is ironical that the triumph of the Tudors brought little benefit to Wales. A firm policy of centralisation ruled out any recognition of a separate cultural identity and there was no gesture to compare with Owen Glendower's bold attempt to create a university at Machynlleth. For the most part Welsh affairs were provincial English affairs. However, the memory of Celtic tradition and bardic poetry was preserved by men whose taste for antiquities had been formed by classical humanism. Sir John Prys of Brecon (1502–55), a typical 'governor', married into Cromwell's family and was an active supporter of his policies; but he also wrote a *Defence* of Geoffrey of Monmouth's *History* against the scepticism of Polydore Vergil and he was responsible for the first printing of a book in Welsh (1546). The imposition of religious reform led to Welsh versions of the Bible and the service books, but it also drove out recusants like Gruffyd Robert who, as chaplain to St Carlo Borromeo, drew up a Welsh grammar in the improbable setting of the archiepiscopal palace in Milan. Even in its most distinguished figure John Owen (1564–1628), whose European reputation as a Latin epigrammatist was founded on studies at Winchester and New College, Oxford, Welsh response to the Renaissance was almost wholly dependent on English institutions and presses. It was antiquarian concern for the mythical origins of Wales, and the preservation of the language, which would provide the basis for a later recovery of national identity.

Scotland and the Renaissance

In Scotland political independence encouraged close ties with the continent, above all with France. Although the kingdom supported three universities, a high proportion of graduates continued their studies abroad at least until the 1560s. There were strong trading links with the Low Countries and no doubt it was through such contacts that Hugo van der Goes was commissioned to paint the altarpiece for Holy Trinity at Edinburgh in 1478.

The embassy sent to establish peace with Richard III in 1484 was led by Archibald Whitelaw, an eloquent Latinist and secretary to James III, who had been a regent at St Andrews and at Cologne. He was accompanied by the Bishop of Ross, William Elphinstone (1431–1514), a graduate of Glasgow and Paris and the most masterful patron of the early Renaissance in Scotland. Elphinstone became Bishop of Aberdeen in 1488 and his hand may be seen in the 1496 Education Act which required 'baronnis and frehaldaris' [*freeholders*] to send their heirs to school and to university. It was as part of this effort to improve standards of public administration that he founded King's College at Aberdeen where Erasmus' friend Hector Boece, author of the *Historia Scotorum*, was first Principal. The teaching posts included that of Humanist, held by the grammarian John Vaus, and a professor of Civil Law, the first in Britain, while there is evidence that Greek was taught. Elphinstone was also a supporter of the first Scottish press set up by Chapman and Myllar at Edinburgh in 1508.

Royal patronage of the new learning extended to the engagement of Erasmus as tutor to James IV's natural son, Alexander Stewart, who had been installed as Archbishop of St Andrews at the age of eleven. But, as Erasmus bitterly recorded in the 1515 *Adagia*, Alexander died with his father at the battle of Flodden in 1514, and the aged Elphinstone did not long survive the catastrophe. Among the fallen was Lord Sinclair to whom Gavin Douglas (1475?–1522) had dedicated his Scots translation of the *Aeneid*, the first and one of the greatest native renderings of a major classical poem.

Flodden might be said to end the first, nascent phase of the Scottish response to the Renaissance. In its aftermath two factors distinguished the course of affairs in Scotland from that in England. One was the absence of a settled court life, on account of minority or absence or simple turmoil, with all that meant for patronage of the arts. And closely linked, after the first stirrings of Lutheran influence in the late 1520s, was the issue of religious reform. In contrast to the carefully poised Erastian compromise sketched out by Cromwell, which gave control of the English church to secular power, Protestantism in Scotland grew largely in opposition to the government and its victory in 1559 gave it an ascendancy over the secular arm which Anglicanism could not match.

The foremost literary figure of the second half of the century was the neo-

Latinist George Buchanan (1506–82). Buchanan spent almost forty years abroad, mainly in France where Montaigne seems to have been his pupil, before returning to Scotland around 1562. His Latin poetry and classical-style dramas were admired throughout Europe; as tutor to the youthful James VI he guided him towards Calvinism and literary tastes. James, indeed, showed remarkable cultural ambitions: with the aid of the poet Alexander Montgomerie he established a court coterie to develop 'Scottish Poesie', and kept up contact with the intellectual circle around Sir Philip Sidney. The cultural stimulus provided by the court ended, however, as James moved south in 1603 to claim his new kingdom, and the tradition of courtly poetry faded. Perhaps the most lasting contribution of the Renaissance to Scotland was the broad access to higher education that would later bear fruit in the Scottish Enlightenment.

Part II
Studies in the Individual Arts

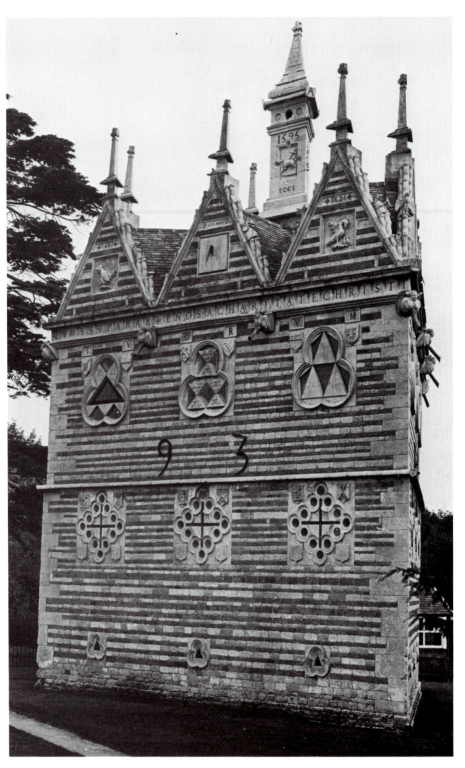

The Triangular Lodge, Rushton, Northamptonshire (1594–7).

1 Architecture

MALCOLM AIRS

Introduction

Over much of England and Wales the sixteenth century was a period of exceptional architectural activity. The appearance of both town and countryside was radically transformed in a building boom which was totally without precedent and which has had few parallels since. By the end of the period the housing conditions and domestic comfort of a substantial part of the population had been improved beyond recognition, the fabric of most towns and many villages had been largely rebuilt, the universities and the Inns of Court had been expanded and the foundations of an enduring school system had been laid. As William Harrison observed in 1577:

Every man almost is a builder and he that hath bought any small parcel of ground, be it never so little, will be quiet till he had pulled down the old house (if any were there standing) and set up a new after his own devise.

The sheer quantity of sixteenth-century architecture is visible in abundance by the large number of surviving examples throughout the country but its particular qualities have been largely underestimated by later commentators who have sought to impose a European perspective on what is essentially an independent and insular development. During a period when most of Europe absorbed the tenets of a classical architectural philosophy rediscovered in Italy in the fifteenth century, England and Scotland pursued a different course which, properly considered, is imbued with great aesthetic excitement and invention and represents a genuinely original contribution to western culture.

The reasons for this notable independence and its spectacular achievements are firmly based on the economic and political circumstances of the time. The great increase in building was a consequence of a period of rapid financial expansion and increasing opportunities for accumulating the capital necessary to invest in construction. Trade and industry were flourishing and a six-fold increase in food prices over the course of the century enabled the primary producers in all spheres of agriculture to prosper. The establishment of the

Tudor peace after the end of the Wars of the Roses and its gradual consolidation under Henry VII and Henry VIII provided a sound foundation for economic growth which was buttressed by a system of strong centralised government and a network of local government administered by the Crown. The important new posts created by this growing bureaucracy were often deliberately filled by new men untainted by the political and dynastic rivalries of the old-established families. They were lawyers and men of proven administrative talents who owed their positions of eminence to the patronage of the state and in consequence had a vested interest in maintaining its supremacy. Such men were handsomely rewarded for their allegiance and they wished to be suitably housed in accordance with the proper status that their new wealth and power required. Families like the Bacons and the Cecils were the mainstay of the system and the stages in their rise to power were marked by the construction of successive new houses, each one notable for an increase in size and splendour.

The Dissolution of the Monasteries, which began in the late 1530s, coincided with the full implementation of the administrative reforms in government and provided the Crown with a timely opportunity to satisfy the housing demands of its new servants and to tie them more closely to the policies of the state. Over the next generation or so large numbers of new country houses rose on the ruins of former monastic houses and the sudden creation of a volatile market in land itself acted as a powerful stimulus to build as the new owners sought to provide a symbol of permanence and family identity on their recently-acquired estates. The form of their houses reflected the growing prospects of lasting domestic peace which was the major achievement of the absolute state that they were helping to create. No longer was it necessary or even advisable to build a fortified house and the removal of this major aesthetic consideration was celebrated by an increasing emphasis on larger areas of ostentatious fenestration. Nor was it essential to accommodate a permanent household of liveried retainers whose major function was to symbolise your power and to demonstrate this by fighting on your behalf. Consequently, apart from those at the very centre of court life in the reign of Elizabeth, there was a growing trend towards a compactness of plan which was encouraged by the abandonment of the requirement to provide ranges of lodgings to demonstrate your rank.

Status was increasingly announced by novelty of design and sophistication of personal comfort rather than any blatant display of mere size or crude military might. The main effect of these developments during the sixteenth century was to render obsolete and visibly out of date the traditional houses and castles which previously had satisfied the needs of many generations of established families. It was a civilising process which was clearly prepared to take advantage of the changed circumstances to exploit to the full the new standards of greater comfort and privacy and advances in heating, lighting and sanitation.

Freedom from rigid cultural restraints and an enthusiastic pursuit of personal and intellectual pleasure shine through as abiding aspects of late sixteenth-century society and contributed significantly to the architectural attitudes current in the reign of Elizabeth when the full effects of the building

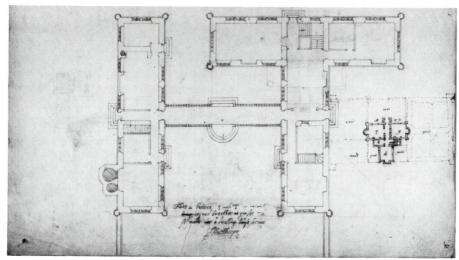

John Thorpe's plan for a house, based on his own initials.

boom were being felt. However, in the early years of the century it seemed probable that the course of both English and Scottish design would follow closely the pattern in the rest of Europe, with the classical style eventually being accepted as the universal aesthetic by all those with any pretension to taste. The recruitment of Italian craftsmen by Henry VIII in England and French craftsmen by James V in Scotland appeared to be an inevitable prelude to European conformity, but the political isolation which followed Henry's break with Rome and the general lawlessness and economic poverty north of the border were powerful factors which inhibited the wholesale absorption of French and Italian culture. The increasing megalomania of Henry VIII was given an architectural expression based on late-medieval Gothic forms as a symbol of the enduring qualities of Kingship and, lacking consistent patronage at the very highest level, the nascent Renaissance of English architecture never proceeded beyond a cautious experimentation with decorative motifs.

The importance of patronage in the introduction of a philosophy of design based on the rigid application of a repertoire of disciplined rules was made manifest during the minority of Edward VI, when the intellectual circle associated with Protector Somerset failed to impose their determined architectural vision on the nation at large solely because their hold on power was of too brief a duration to influence more than a handful of sophisticated disciples. By the time that political stability had returned with the accession of Elizabeth in 1558 the opportunity had been missed and the mood at court had become very different. The result was a burst of creativity which was more exciting and dynamic than in any other period of British architecture. Throughout most levels of society other than the very poor and in both England and Scotland new house designs were evolved which were totally independent of developments elsewhere in Europe and they have an intrinsic interest which derives from the fertility of native traditions rather than the grammar of an alien classical culture.

In Scotland the imaginative transformation of the defensive tower-house form was realised in increasing numbers from about 1560, while in England the full effects of the building boom became apparent at approximately the same time. The growing sense of national identity which was fostered by the apparent vulnerability of a virgin queen dependent on her gallant knights for the protection of her beleagured honour against the forces of darkness, received a great boost of confidence after the successful defeat of the Armada, and was given a direct cultural expression in the chivalric revival which became an important part of court life.

In architecture this led to a re-examination of Gothic forms in a mood of enthusiastic fantasy rather than that of scholarly revival. In an atmosphere of frenzied building, country houses in particular were perceived as status symbols and objects of intense social rivalry which publicly demonstrated the prosperity, wit and modernity of their builders. Architectural symbolism was applauded far more vigorously than any adherence to a discipline based on modular proportion, by men whose favourite word of praise was 'delight'. There can be little doubt that architecture was meant to be enjoyed as fun in just the same way that the cultured contemporary mind delighted at unravelling the real meanings hidden by allegories and 'devices'. The latter were defined in a popular book by Geoffrey Whitney published in 1586 as 'something obscure to be perceived at the first, whereby when with further consideration it is understood, it may the greater delight the beholder', and this is a definition which perfectly captures the intention behind much of the more spirited architecture of the latter part of the century.

Sometimes these architectural 'devices' were serious in intent, such as the lodges built by the Catholic convert Sir Thomas Tresham on his Northamptonshire estate to announce his faith publicly and to symbolise the Holy Trinity and the Passion. At other times they were unashamedly bizarre, as with the design based on his own initials which John Thorpe endorsed with the doggerel verse: 'These 2 letters I and T /[being] joined together as you see /Is meet for a dwelling house for me.' More frequently, however, they took the form of simple geometrical exercises based on the manipulation of squares, rectangles, circles and other plans which can be seen in several examples in both the Thorpe and the Smythson collections of contemporary drawings and which produced such dramatic standing elevations as at Hardwick Hall or Longford Castle (Wiltshire).

The underlying assumption behind all these barely concealed displays of ingenuity was that your friends and peers would be as passionately interested in the novelty of your buildings as you yourself were and it is abundantly clear from contemporary literature and correspondence that in the upper ranks of society, architecture was a subject of great curiosity and enthusiasm to an extent which is difficult to imagine today. Yet in a period when 'every man almost is a builder' such an interest is more comprehensible and its creative vitality less surprising.

Just how much of the architectural achievement of the late sixteenth century was due to the enthusiastic patrons who commissioned the buildings and how much depended on the genius of the master craftsmen who executed them remains a difficult question to answer. There were no architects in the

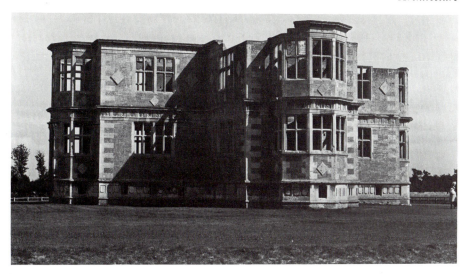

Lyveden New Build, Northamptonshire (c.1604–5).

sense that Inigo Jones was to introduce the concept in the following century, and the finished appearance of many buildings was no doubt the result of a loose partnership between patron and craftsman which varied in the degree of responsibility according to the personalities involved. Men such as William Cecil and John Thynne can be assumed to be the driving force behind both the overall conception and the detailed decoration of their own buildings. But it is equally probable that craftsmen of the known calibre of Robert Smythson, 'Architector and Surveyor unto the most worthy house of Wollaton with divers others of great account', and William Arnold, '. . . so wonderfully sought being indeed the absolutest and honestest workman in England', were given a measure of freedom and independence in designing for less exacting clients and the truly satisfying masterpieces of Elizabethan architecture are as much a tribute to their vision and flair as they are to the economic circumstances and cultural vigour which made them possible.

Royal works

The uneven course of royal patronage in the sixteenth century accounts for much that is of particular interest in the development of architectural taste in the period. Prior to the death of Henry VIII in 1547 it was the Crown which was the main inspiration and the ultimate arbiter of all that was fashionable in domestic building. During the next fifty years the architectural initiative passed almost exclusively to the aristocracy and not one royal building of any significance was constructed or even contemplated. More than any other single factor, this lack of patronage and cultural direction at the very apex of the social pyramid was responsible for the marked resistance to classical architectural doctrine which sets England apart from the pattern followed by the rest of Europe in the second half of the sixteenth century.

The two most important surviving royal buildings of the century are Henry VII's chapel at Westminster Abbey and Henry VIII's country palace at Hampton Court and it is therefore convenient as well as appropriate that they should represent the different personalities and aspirations of the only royal builders of any consequence in the period. Throughout his reign a succession of pretenders and a number of unsuccessful insurrections made Henry VII continually aware of his precarious hold on a crown seized in battle. The successful establishment of the Tudor dynasty demanded radical administrative reform and a careful marshalling of his financial resources which allowed little opportunity for ostentatious building. Nevertheless from the middle of the 1490s onwards Henry felt secure enough to ensure that he was housed in a style fitting his regal status, at least in the area around London to which his travels, for pleasure, were largely confined. Extensive rebuilding works were carried out at the royal houses of Woodstock, Langley, Woking and Hanworth in the period between 1494 and 1507; and his new riverside palaces at Richmond and Greenwich were to have a considerable influence on the form of the palatial house for several decades to come. However, it is principally as a builder of works of piety that Henry is now remembered and it is his increasingly melancholic concern with the salvation of his soul that labels him as a lingering survivor from the medieval world. The untimely death of his Queen and his own growing ill-health produced an air of gloom and introspection at court in the last decade of his reign which influenced the character of his architectural preoccupations.

In about 1500 he founded an almshouse at Westminster Abbey and in the following year he established a friary within the grounds of Richmond Palace. He also made provision in 1508 for the foundation of an ambitious hostel to provide overnight accommodation for 100 poor men and women close by Charing Cross, in a cruciform building known as the Savoy Hospital. These, no doubt, were all acts of sincere devotion, but there was just a suspicion of political propaganda in his determination to secure the completion of the partly-roofed chapel at King's College, Cambridge. This great work had been instigated by his 'uncle of blessed memory', King Henry VI, and the Tudors' claim to the throne partly rested on their ties of blood to the Lancastrian king. The posthumous popularity of his name was assiduously cultivated by Henry VII as a means of consolidating his own position, even to the extent of opening negotiations with the Pope in a vain bid to gain official recognition for his sanctity. Work was re-commenced at King's College in 1508 and continued well into the reign of Henry VIII.

This, however, was merely a late incident in the cult of Henry VI. As early as the 1490s, works had been undertaken for the enshrinement of his bones in a newly constructed chapel at Windsor. This project was abandoned when it was established that the late King himself had selected Westminster Abbey as his chosen burial place. Accordingly Henry VII announced that he would build a new chapel at the Abbey to house the precious remains and that he himself would be buried nearby. Work formally began on 24 January 1503 with the laying of a stone inscribed with a legend recording the generosity of the most illustrious Henry VII. Full provision for the chapel was made in Henry's will of 1509 and the work was finally completed in 1512.

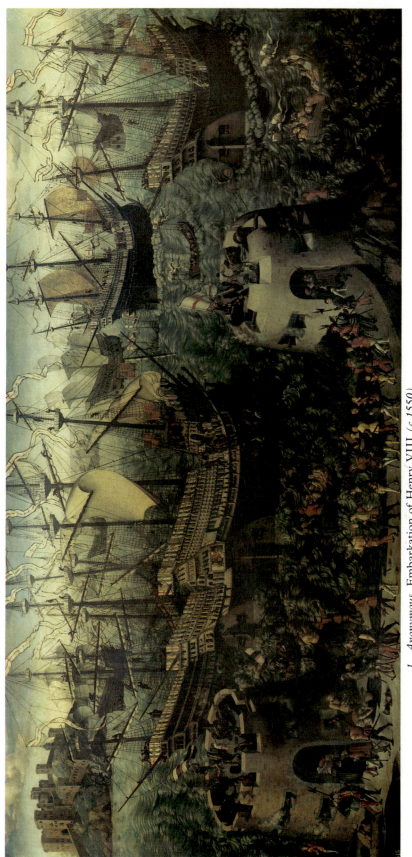

1. *Anonymous, Embarkation of Henry VIII (c.1550).*
Reproduced by Gracious Permission of Her Majesty The Queen. (See p. 226)

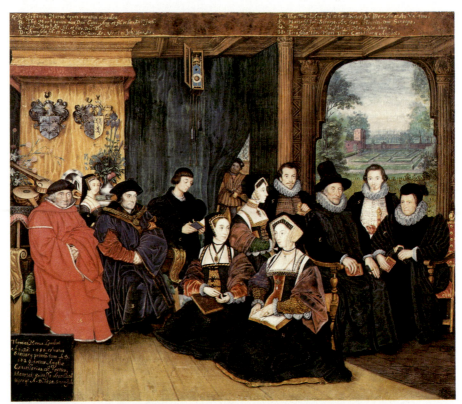

2. *Rowland Lockey, after Holbein,* Sir Thomas More and his family *(1593).*
(See p. 228)

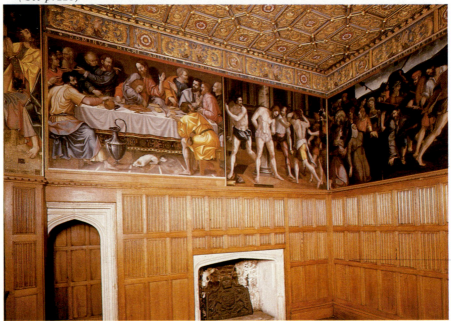

3. *Wolsey's Closet, Hampton Court Palace (1520s). (See pp. 58–60)*

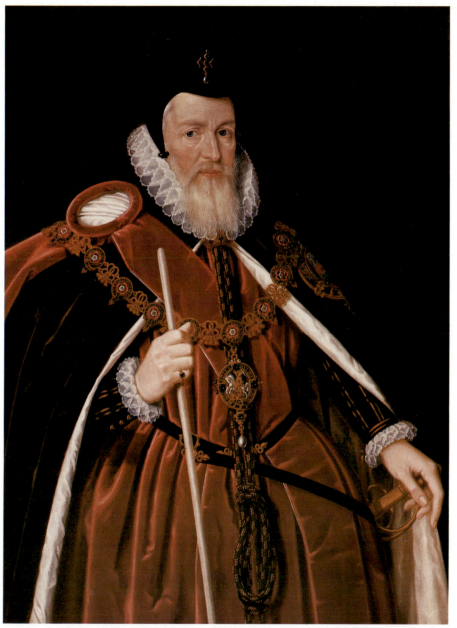

4. *Attrib. Marcus Gheeraerts, portrait of William Cecil, Lord Burghley (c.1585).*
(See p.34)

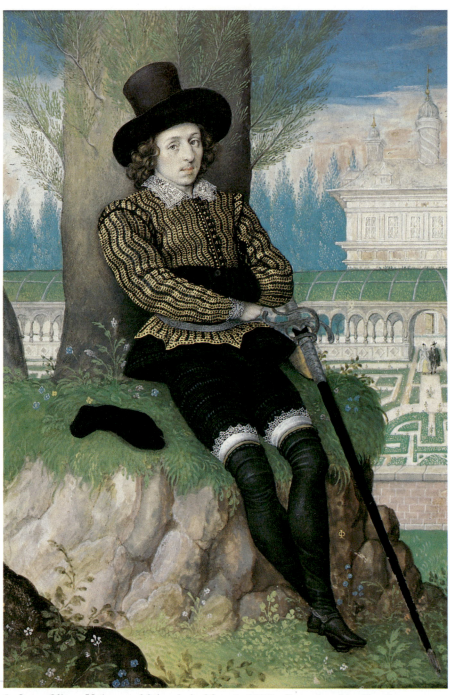

5. *Isaac Oliver*, Unknown Melancholy Man *(c.1590). Reproduced by Gracious Permission of Her Majesty The Queen. (See p.212)*

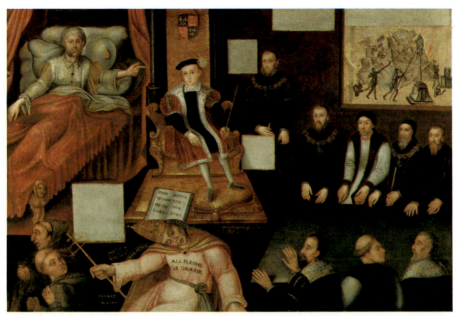

6. *Anonymous*, Edward VI and the Papacy *(c.1548–9)*. *(See p. 226)*

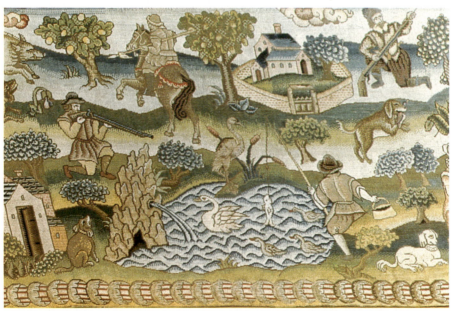

7. *The Bradford Table Carpet, embroidered on canvas in coloured silks (late sixteenth century). (See Chapter 5, also p. 292)*

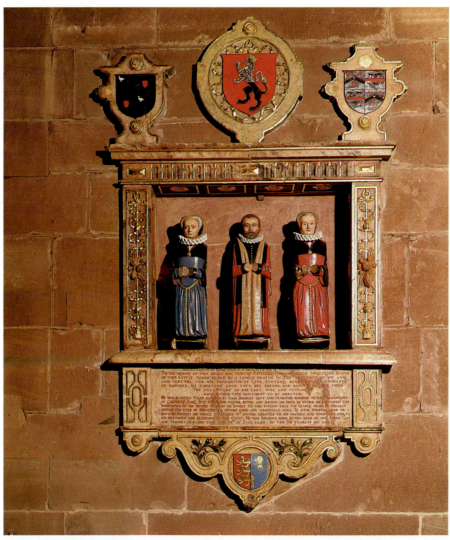

8. *Monument to Thomas Greene (d.1602), Chester Cathedral. (See p.244)*

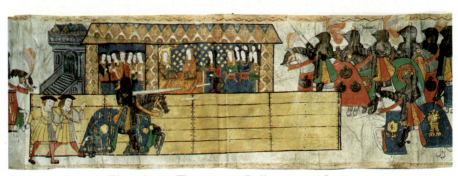

9. *Section from the* Westminster Tournament Roll *(1511). (See pp. 24, 280)*

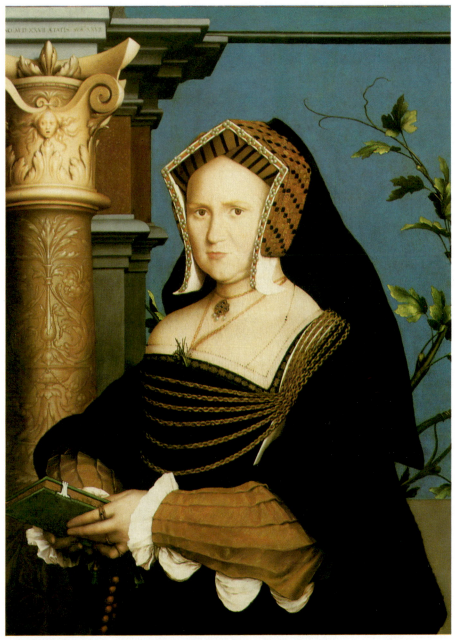

10. *Hans Holbein, portrait of Lady Guildeford (1527). (See p. 228)*

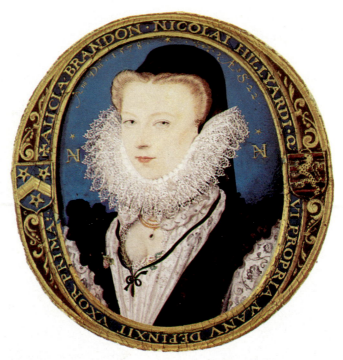

11. *Nicholas Hilliard, miniature of Alice Hilliard, née Brandon, wife of the artist (1578). (See p. 234)*

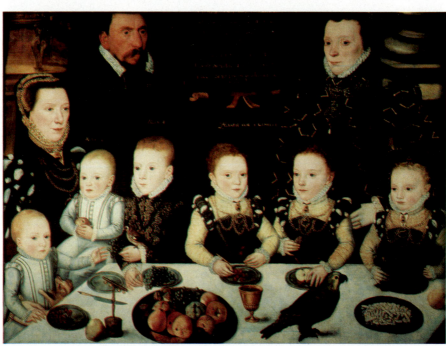

12. *Anonymous*, Lord Cobham and his family *(1567; attributed to the Master of the Countess of Warwick). (See Chapter 6)*

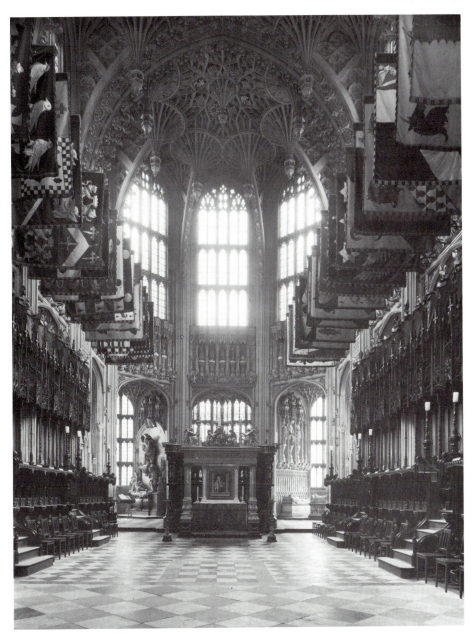

Henry VII's Chapel, Westminster Abbey (1503–12).

The building, which is in fact a Tudor mausoleum, is a breathtaking masterpiece of ostentatious decoration with affinities to French and Spanish Gothic, as well as being the culmination of the English Perpendicular style – unfortunately we know nothing about the individual craftsmen who were involved. Like the Abbey itself, the chapel is composed of a nave and flanking aisles with five radiating chapels at its eastern end. The clerestory of the nave rises high above the aisles and chapels and is connected by sinuously curved flying buttresses to a sequence of slim octagonal towers which form the only areas of solid walling on the external elevations. Yet even so, the surface of each tower is covered with blank panelling in deliberate imitation of the mullioned and transomed pattern of the flanking windows, so that the distinction between solid and void is totally subsumed in a mesh of tracery. The lower windows set up a richly modelled counterpoint to the octagonal towers, those to the aisles being semi-circular bows flanked by half-bows whilst the wider chapel windows are canted bays with a sharply pointed central projection. The prototype for the peculiar form of the chapel windows can be found on the tower which Henry had recently built in the Upper Ward at Windsor Castle and it reappeared on a number of purely residential buildings during the course of the century. The octagonal towers continue above the roof of the aisles with canopied niches which are capped by crocketted cupolas (or small domes ornamented with leaves). The niches originally contained forty-eight brightly-coloured statues of apostles, prophets, evangelists and Old Testament Kings and each cupola was crowned by a metal weather-vane.

If the building now has a somewhat sombre appearance this is due entirely to the darkening effects of age and it must be imagined as a delightful sequence of mobile surfaces all of which were gleaming, colourful and profusely decorated. What Sir Christopher Wren called 'nice embroidered work'.

Something of this quality still remains on the inside of the chapel where the stonework has been protected from the weather and only the bright colours of the statuary and the stained glass destroyed by the Puritans are absent from the original concept. The massive windows flood the interior with light and illuminate the mass of sculptural detail which covers every surface and which is without parallel in any other English church interior. More than a hundred statues of apostles, saints and prophets originally lined the walls and most of them still survive. The roof is a luscious and over-crowded confection of fans and pendants and cusping floating ethereally overhead. The daring manipulation of the architectural forms and the iconography of the religious imagery represents the absolute culmination of the English Gothic tradition and provides a fitting climax to medieval kingship. But instead of the conventional canopied tomb of Henry VI which was originally intended to be the focal point of the chapel and for which the architectural setting was created, the space behind the altar is occupied by a tomb to Henry VII and his Queen in a totally different idiom which at once makes the surrounding sculpture, for all its richness, seem old-fashioned and provincial. The body of Henry VI remained at Windsor and in its place Henry VIII in 1512 commissioned the Florentine sculptor Pietro Torrigiano to create a tomb to his parents which was to bring the Italian Renaissance to England in a complete and fully-developed form.

The shift in royal taste between father and son could not have been more strikingly expressed than in the contrast between the life-like modelling and tender dignity of the effigies on the tomb and the conventional stiffness of the Gothic images on the building which houses it.

Henry VIII was not yet eighteen years old when he succeeded to the throne. The new reign opened with a great burst of spectacular entertainments which heralded a radical change in the atmosphere at court. The motivation was not just the youthful pursuit of pleasure but also a strong desire to impress the whole of Europe with the new King's wealth, taste and accomplishments. From the contemporary comments of various foreign observers it is clear that in the early years of his reign this aim was largely achieved. In the eyes of the world it seemed that the introversion of Henry VII's court had been replaced by the promise of a splendid

Torrigiano's tomb to Henry VII and Elizabeth of York, Westminster Abbey (commissioned 1512).

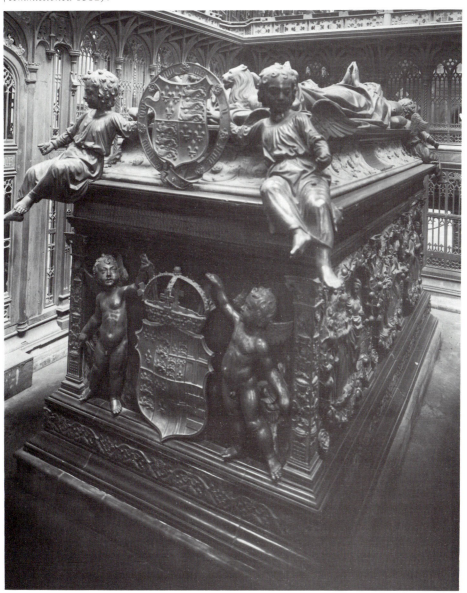

Renaissance under Henry VIII. Henry himself had a particular talent for music which he indulged as a performer, composer and enlightened patron. He was also a committed student of theology and passionately interested in such cultivated pursuits as astronomy and geometry. His personal accomplishments were both intellectual and athletic and were reflected in the able scholars and artists that he attracted to his court from all over Europe. The great humanist Erasmus wrote that

you would say that Henry was a universal genius. He has never neglected his studies, and whenever he has leisure from his political occupations, he reads or disputes – of which he is very fond – with remarkable courtesy and unruffled temper.

And in another letter he claimed that 'There are more men of learning to be found in Henry's court than in any university.' Such men included Sir Thomas More, Thomas Linacre the King's physician, John Colet and Cuthbert Tunstall: all men imbued with the 'new learning'.

It was on the artistic side that the international stature of his court was most manifest. He recruited musicians from Italy, Venice and Flanders, painters from Bruges, Ghent, Florence, Cologne and Naples, engineers from Germany and glaziers from the Netherlands. The commission for Torrigiano to design the tombs in Henry VII's chapel seemed symptomatic of his desire to patronise the best artists in Europe and to introduce the most sophisticated modern taste into his native land. Yet, in the event, with the exception of men such as Holbein, few of the foreigners that he attracted were of the very highest rank, and the brilliant cultural promise of the early years of Henry's court remained largely unfulfilled. By comparison with Francis I of France, Henry's artistic achievements were provincial and disappointing. This is especially true of architecture and its related discipline of sculpture. The cultural values and philosophy of design introduced by Torrigiano were neither understood by his patron nor were they absorbed into the wider field of architecture as happened elsewhere on the continent. They were perceived simply as pretty decorative options totally divorced from the fundamental and universal theory which inspired their actual creators.

Just as the beauty of Henry's well-proportioned body declined into self-indulgent grossness by the end of his reign, so his architectural achievement became little more than a catalogue of ostentatious display rather than a chronicle of refined taste. Without a doubt he was one of the greatest builders in English history, but this was a matter of numbers and sheer expenditure rather than architectural sophistication. At the beginning of his reign he had eight principal residences. By the time of his death in 1547 he owned more than fifty houses, and building works on a greater or lesser scale had been carried out at most of them, often simultaneously. Of all these palaces and hunting lodges, only Nonsuch, begun in 1539 and still incomplete at the time of his death, offered any real indication of architectural innovation. The others all continued the late Gothic forms perfected in the previous century, tricked out with just enough classical ornament to suggest an awareness if not an understanding of what was happening elsewhere in Europe. It was an insular and parochial architecture curiously at odds with Henry's continental ambition in the field of diplomacy.

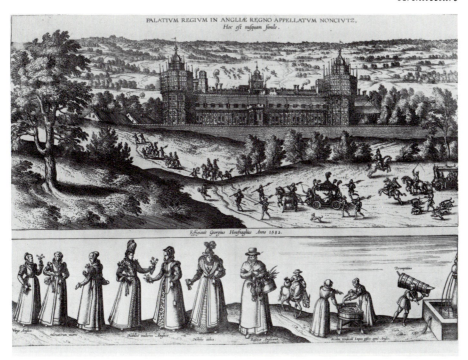

Hoefnagel's view of Nonsuch Palace, Surrey (1568).

Nonsuch was demolished in 1682 and will remain a difficult house to evaluate until the full results of the excavations carried out in 1959 and 1960 are properly published. Despite the studied symmetry of its double courtyard plan, it was the remarkable decoration of the timber-framed inner court which made the building worthy of its name and which showed Henry making a belated attempt to create an architectural monument comparable to Fontainebleau and worthy of the cultural promise of his youth. All the panels of the timber-frame were filled with plasterwork depicting in high relief scenes from classical history, representations of the arts and virtues, and floral and other designs. The major themes included the exploits of Hercules, thirty-one busts of Roman emperors, the cardinal virtues and the seven liberal arts. A seated figure of Henry VIII was placed in the centre of the south elevation with his son Edward by his side. As Edward had been born in the year before the Palace was begun, it is likely that the iconographic programme of the Inner Court was, as *The History of the King's Works* suggests, 'a visual demonstration of the programme of humanist learning which, embodied in the person of the King, the prince would follow'. This immense decorative scheme covered literally hundreds of plaster panels. The timber-framework in between was similarly decorated with carved and gilded sheets of slate.

The whole effect, with the white panels contrasting with the black framework, the deep modelling of the almost-lifesize figures ranked over three storeys and the glistening gold lettering of the mottoes that accompanied them, must have been one of staggering richness. Judging from the accounts of those who saw the building and from the fragments which have been excavated it was also a composition of great quality and classical correctness. However, it is symptomatic of Henry's lack of any consistent interest in the grammar of architecture or patronage of those who were, that when he wanted to build in this idiom he again had to seek his craftsmen from abroad. The actual fabric of the building was erected by native Englishmen but the important sculpture and carving seems to have been conceived and created by foreigners: notably Nicholas Bellin of Modena who had worked for Francis I on the decoration of Fontainebleau, Giles Gering and William Cure.

Nonsuch, had it survived, might have retrieved Henry VIII's reputation as an architectural innovator and patron of classical learning. (Granted by Charles II to his mistress, the Duchess of Cleveland, in 1670, it was no doubt considered unfashionable and out of date. She treated it as an asset which she realised in 1682 by demolition and the sale of the materials.) As it is, we must look to Hampton Court to provide the best surviving example of his taste and here the overall impression is very different, with lavish opulence and sheer size as the main inspiration for what was his principal country palace (colour pl. 3). Originally Hampton Court had been built for Cardinal Wolsey who acquired the manor in 1514. Between 1515 and 1525 he constructed an irregular double courtyard house on a familiar medieval pattern, with an imposing gatehouse leading into a base (or first) court which was surrounded by ranges of lodgings for his immense household. The inner court was entered by another gatehouse and was dominated by the hall which took up the whole of the north side. The layout reflected a common plan adopted by most of the great feudal magnates in the fifteenth century and earlier. By its size and form Wolsey's Hampton Court symbolised great

The Gatehouse, Hampton Court Palace (1515–25).

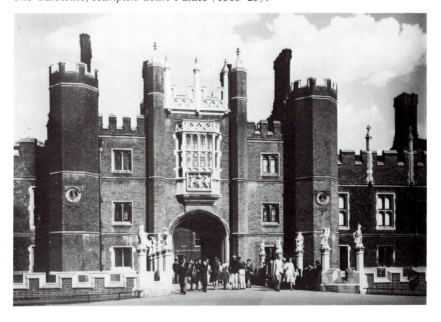

power, and with its 280 rooms permanently prepared to receive guests it was designed to provide the formal hospitality which underpinned that power. However, by the 1520s such an ostentatious display of private strength had become both anachronistic and politically dangerous in the face of Henry's determined pursuit of a centralised government with effective power concentrated in the hands of the king. The achievement of such a system demanded the elimination of all possible rival sources of power, and Wolsey's judicious gift of Hampton Court to his monarch sometime after 1525 did little to alleviate his ultimate disgrace in 1529.

As a power-base, Hampton Court was essentially backward-looking and medieval in its conception. So, too, was its architecture with its emphasis on defensive courtyards guarded by gatehouses and adorned with late Gothic decoration in the form of four-centred arches, flat-headed mullioned and transomed windows, and battlemented walls. Only some of the internal decoration and the remarkable set of terracotta medallions of Roman emperors executed by the Florentine Giovanni da Maiano in 1521 and placed on the octagonal turrets of the gatehouse showed any awareness of Renaissance taste. Henry, after Wolsey's fall, merely embellished and enlarged the themes already established by his predecessor, albeit on a regal scale. He threw out further courts on irregular axes at the east and the north and introduced a form of symmetry to the entrance front by the addition of great projecting wings at either end of the facade. He rebuilt the kitchens and the service courts, redecorated and refitted Wolsey's chapel, provided separate lodgings for the King and the Queen, and built a vast and magnificent new hall to replace the more modest structure which had sufficed for his Cardinal. All of this was done at great speed and considerable expense mainly with English workmen, but with various foreign craftsmen called in to execute some of the classical decoration. Unlike those employed at Nonsuch, the foreigners were men of little reputation. They were hired for their competence in an idiom which formed only a minor embellishment to what was in essence a Gothic palace.

Henry's great hall stands as a token of what he demanded from Hampton Court. It is truly impressive and powerful, towering above the surrounding buildings so that its roof dominates views of the palace from a distance. This architectural emphasis on the hall was an established medieval fashion and the form of the hall with its screens passage, raised dais lit by a tall bay window, and an open hearth in the centre of the room are all thoroughly medieval. So too is the magnificent hammer-beam roof with its Gothic tracery. But the carved pendants and the decorated spandrels of the trusses are incongruously Italianate in design although, because of their height above the ground, this dichotomy is not immediately apparent. They merely add to the richness of the carved and painted decoration overhead and it was this overall opulence which was meant to impress the spectator, not the sophistication of its intricate details. The power which was able to command a structure of such size and to decorate it without regard to the enormous cost was what separated the King from his subjects. The most blatant display of this power seems to have been enough to satisfy Henry's architectural ambitions.

In view of the intellectual and cultural promise of the early years of his reign this is a disappointing achievement. Nevertheless, given the insecurity of the early Tudors' hold on the crown and Henry VIII's continued concern about the succession, it is perhaps understandable that he should adhere to Gothic forms as an appropriate symbol of established monarchy and use the revenue from the dissolved monasteries to reinforce that symbol and to emphasise his supremacy by the number and magnificence of his palaces.

The great house

With the death of Henry VIII in 1547 the supremacy of the Crown as an architectural force effectively came to an end and was not to be revived until the accession of King James in 1603. Henceforward it was to be the courtiers and statesmen who were to influence the course that architecture was to take for the remainder of the century. There was no obvious or immediate break with the past but the different requirements and ambitions of the new patrons inevitably evolved new house types as well as adapting the traditional forms to take account of changing circumstances.

Throughout the century the courtyard house remained the supreme symbol of wealth and power and continued to be the usual solution to the need to accommodate the periodic demands of lavish hospitality without which such power could neither be achieved nor sustained. By the end of the century other alternatives were being considered and preferred, but in the opening decades a great man was only suitably housed behind the enclosing walls of a courtyard. Thus when Sir William Compton came to build in the years before 1520 at Compton Wynyates in Warwickshire, as a close companion of Henry VIII and a principal member of his household, no other type of house would have befitted his station.

Compton Wynyates, Warwickshire (before 1520).

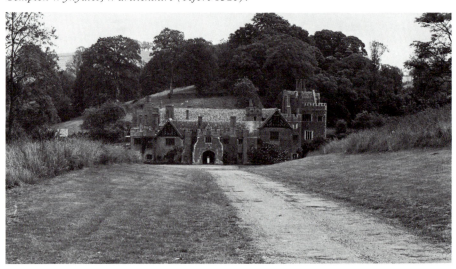

In many ways Compton Wynyates is the epitome of an early-Tudor courtier's house. It is no longer seriously defensible, but the surrounding moat, the battlemented walls and the residential tower on the south front are sufficient to indicate that Bosworth Field was barely a generation past and the times still held the potential for further trouble. Beautifully sited in a hollow surrounded by low hills, the external elevations are totally irregular and sparsely fenestrated with a logic that is entirely determined by the use of the rooms within. Entrance is gained through a buttressed gatehouse asymmetrically placed so that it leads directly across the courtyard to the screens passage at the low end of the traditional hall in the opposite range. The hall occupies the full height of the range and the high table at the upper end is illuminated by a tall projecting bay window which forms the principal architectural feature of the courtyard. The kitchen and service rooms are situated off the screens passage and the parlour is entered through a door placed by the high table. The south range contains a chapel to minister to the spiritual devotions of the household, whose spacious lodgings take up most of the accommodation in the north and east ranges. Similar facilities laid out in a similar fashion were characteristic of most of the major houses of the late medieval period and continued with little change through the first two decades of the sixteenth century.

Although comparatively compact, when it was built it would have been the largest house by far in the neighbourhood and the power and influence of its builder would have been clearly advertised by its form and accommodation. The potency of the house as a symbol of power is unequivocally illustrated in the Bill of Attainder that preceded the execution of the Duke of Buckingham in 1521, where his construction of Thornbury Castle was cited as evidence of his overweening political ambition. Despite its fortified gatehouse range bristling with four towers and two ogee-capped turrets, this was no castle in any understandable sense. In reality it was a triple courtyard palace with ostentatious windows to the privy garden, and was of a lavishness and luxury to rival anything possessed by the king at that date. Such a display was both ill-advised and suspect, as Wolsey was to discover with his great houses at Hampton and York Place a few years later.

The bay windows at Thornbury with their canted and semi-circular projections are unmistakably derived from the windows at Henry VII's chapel at Westminster Abbey and show the way that fashionable innovations were quickly absorbed by the court. Sutton Place in Surrey built in the 1520s is an even more important example of the new influences which were shaping the appearance of the courtyard house. Sir Richard Weston, the builder, was a prominent courtier who later became Under-Treasurer of England. In 1520 he had been amongst the vast retinue which had accompanied the king to his meeting with Francis I at the Field of Cloth of Gold, where he would have had the opportunity to see many of the new developments which were revolutionising French court architecture.

He began to build his own house shortly after his return and he pursued a perfect symmetry for all the internal elevations which was totally unprecedented in English architecture at this date and which can only be explained by his continental experience. The demolished entrance range had a tall

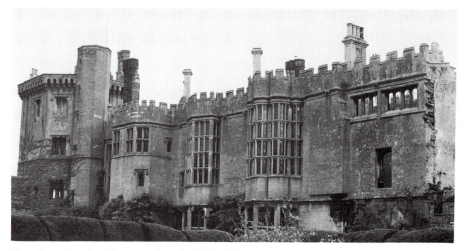

Thornbury Castle, Gloucestershire (c.1511–21).

central gate tower flanked by matching chimneystacks and stepped gables. On the courtyard side the ranges of lodgings to east and west exactly balance each other in the disposition and form of their windows and in the alignment of the single canted bay which punctuates both sides. But it is the symmetry of the hall range facing the gatehouse which is truly remarkable. A battlemented and turretted frontispiece echoes the gatehouse and frames the central entrance which leads directly into the middle of the hall. The projecting bay window at the high end of the hall is replicated by a similar projection at the other end of the elevation, whose large windows merely light insignificant service rooms behind. The emphatic frontispiece, the central entrance into the hall which dispensed with the traditional convenience of the screens passage at the low end, and the deliberate contrivance of a featured projection to balance the bay window were all dictated by the relentless logic imposed by a disciplined symmetry. This was something entirely new in English taste. By the end of the century most of these features had been incorporated into the mainstream of English architecture, but in the reign of Henry VIII there were few builders who were prepared to compromise their immediate comfort for the sake of such a stern aesthetic.

An approximate balance of parts across the entrance elevation rather than rigid symmetry was about as far as most men were prepared to go, as Sir Thomas Kytson ingeniously demonstrated on the south front of Hengrave Hall, Suffolk between 1524 and 1540. Here the gatehouse is offset in relation to the courtyard behind to allow a direct access to the low end of the hall in the conventional manner, but an impression of symmetry is imparted to the principal external elevation by the elongation of the entrance front into a wing projecting to the east. In addition to its flanking towers, extra emphasis is given to the gatehouse by an oriel window with semi-circular bows in the Thornbury manner. However, in contrast to the late Gothic character of the fenestration and other decoration in the remainder of the house, the base mouldings and the supporting *putti* (naked cherubs) in the lower part of the window are thoroughly Italianate in design and intention.

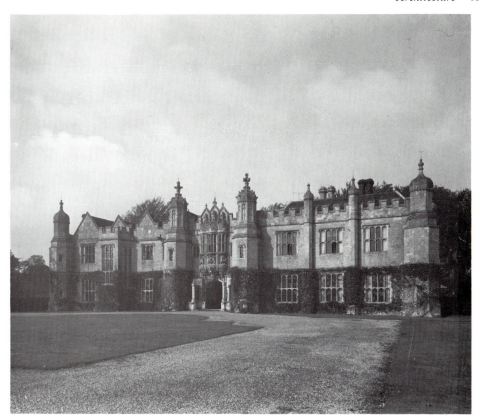

Hengrave Hall, Suffolk (1524–1540).

This application of Renaissance decoration to a prominent location on what is in all other respects a perpendicular building is indicative of the cautious response that fashionable men were beginning to make to the new ideas which were already well established in Italy and France. Wolsey had made a similar gesture with the roundels on the gatehouses at Hampton Court in 1521 and Henry VIII had made a more full-blooded attempt at Nonsuch. Sir Richard Weston, too, as one might expect, had experimented with Renaissance decoration on the symmetrical walls of Sutton Place, placing terracotta panels of naked *putti* and other Italian devices over the hall frontispiece, around various doorways and on the courtyard face of the destroyed gate tower. The use of terracotta as a medium for the new fashion was a growing practice in the 1520s and 1530s and was adopted in a lavish way by Lord Marney for the soaring gatehouse which was all that was completed of his mansion at Layer Marney, Essex, when he died in 1524.

The sporadic use of French and Italian ornament to decorate the houses of the leading courtiers suggests that the time was ripe for the reception of a more comprehensive approach to the ideals of Renaissance architecture. All that was lacking was the consistent patronage that could only come from the very centre of the court, but Henry was disinclined to give this. When he died, his son Edward VI was only nine years old and the country was

effectively ruled by his uncle Edward Seymour, Duke of Somerset, whose
appetite for ostentatious palace building was no less than that of the late
monarch. In his short period as Protector, Somerset built himself substantial
courtyard mansions on the Strand in London, at Syon just outside the
capital, at Great Bedwyn in Wiltshire and at Berry Pomeroy in Devon, in
addition to lesser works on his other houses at Banbury, Odiham and
Reading. As the leading light in a circle of Protestant humanists he seems to
have been instrumental in providing the necessary patronage which had
hitherto been lacking for a group of men imbued with a similar spirit of
learning. It must be emphasised that it was merely an interlude of little more
than five years duration, but it was a period so pregnant with unfulfilled
promise that it demands close attention.

Little now survives of Somerset's own buildings. Syon House has been
completely recased and obscured. Great Bedwyn was never completed. Berry
Pomeroy is a ruin with only the base of a classical loggia to hint at what it
might once have been. Somerset House has been demolished, although John
Thorpe's drawing of its entrance elevation has led Sir John Summerson to
describe it as 'probably the first deliberate attempt to build in England a
front composed altogether in the classical taste'. However, enough is known
of the work and deeds of his disciples and associates to assess the potential of
those short years. The Duke of Northumberland, who succeeded Somerset as
Protector after his execution, sent John Shute, a member of his household, to
Italy in 1550 specifically 'to confer with the doings of the skilfull masters in
architecture and also to view such ancient monuments hereof as are yet
extant'. Sir William Sharington, who acted as steward for the buildings at
Sudeley Castle for Thomas Lord Seymour, brother of Somerset, and

John Thorpe's drawing of Somerset House, the Strand, London.

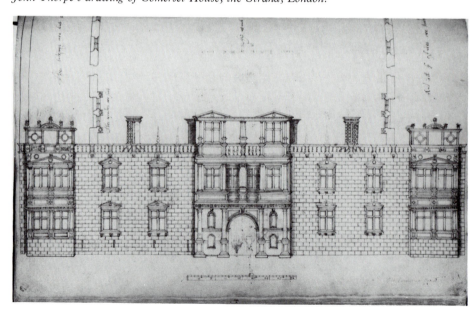

supervised the work at Dudley Castle for Northumberland, used his own unfinished house at Lacock almost as a workshop and exhibition centre of examples demonstrating the correct use of classical design. The plain ashlar-faced muniment tower with its refined balustraded top and richly carved stone tables and vaulting in the French style, the distinctive windows facing onto the cloister court, the Doric fireplace with its correctly moulded entablature in the gallery, the attached Ionic column and the doorcase surrounds in the Stable Court do not add up to a coherent whole but they are all individual salvoes fired in a belligerent commitment to the new style.

Sharington died suddenly in 1553 but by that date the force of the architectural movement to which he subscribed had already been spent. Thomas Seymour had been executed in 1549, Somerset in 1552 and Northumberland in 1553. The radical Protestant cause, of which they had all been advocates, died with them, to be succeeded by a Catholic reaction under Mary which was fundamentally inimical to the humanist learning which had inspired their architectural philosophy. Political expediency demanded that the adherents of that philosophy should temporarily suppress their enthusiasm, but the strength of their intellectual commitment ensured that over the next two decades the fruits of the mid-century Renaissance were revealed in buildings in various parts of the country.

The three gateways symbolising the student's progress from humility through virtue to honour, that Dr Caius incorporated into his refounded college of Gonville and Caius at Cambridge between 1567 and 1575, were given full classical expression by a man who was prominent in the humanist circles at Edward VI's court and was personal physician to the King. Sir Thomas Smith, who had been in the service of Somerset between 1547 and 1549 and after the accession of Elizabeth returned to public life as ambassador to France, used superimposed Doric and Ionic orders on the courtyard elevations and giant engaged Doric columns on the external east elevation on successive remodellings of his house at Hill Hall, Essex, in 1568–9 and in the 1570s.

It was Smith's lifelong friend, Sir John Thynne, however, who was responsible for the most complete expression of the architectural ideas current in this select circle at the middle of the century. Thynne had been Somerset's steward with overall responsibility for the supervision of all his building work. With the fall of his patron he retired to his Wiltshire estate at Longleat and spent the remaining thirty years of his life restlessly perfecting his architectural masterpiece. After three earlier versions had been discarded, Longleat finally emerged in its completed form between 1572 and 1580. Its previous manifestations are preserved in the courtyards which are now buried within the house and in the irregularities of the roofline behind the unifying balustrade. But all four external elevations are perfectly regular and symmetrical, with a command of classical detail and discipline that was a fitting testament to Thynne's relentless pursuit of architectural perfection. His obsession with the house was cruelly mocked in an unpublished satire by his neighbour William Darrell of Littlecote and there can be little doubt that much though we might admire it now, such learned scholarship was very much out of tune with the more robust excitement of the Elizabethan age. Sir

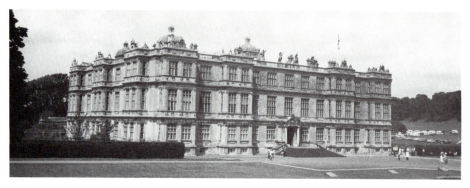

Longleat House, Wiltshire (1572–80).

Hall chimneypiece at Longleat House.

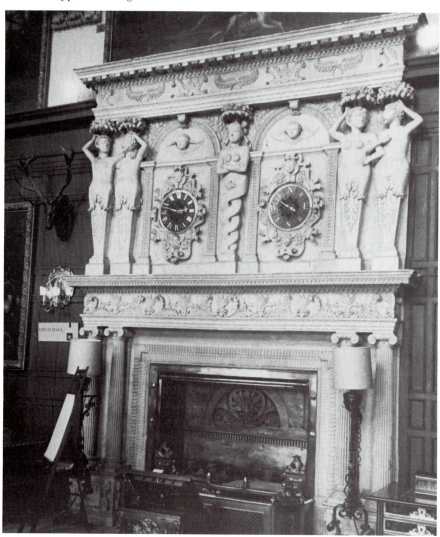

Nikolaus Pevsner has called Longleat 'a milestone in English sixteenth century architecture', but if so, it was a milestone placed on a road which had been effectively bypassed in 1553 and which was to remain a cul-de-sac until the following century.

William Cecil, later Lord Burghley, provides the essential link between what Sir John Summerson has called 'the momentary High Renaissance of Tudor architecture' and the exciting developments of the Elizabethan court. He was another disciple of the new learning who had achieved high public office under both Somerset and Northumberland. Having diplomatically survived the difficult years of Mary's reign, he emerged under Elizabeth as Secretary of State and remained the single most influential man in the land until almost the end of her reign. In matters of architecture no less than in politics or diplomacy he exercised a power and indulged a sincerely held pleasure which dominated the remainder of the century.

During his years of exile from the court, Cecil had started to build a house at Burghley, near Stamford, in a similar learned style to the houses of the other members of the Somerset circle. From its classical beginnings Burghley House was to grow in size as its builder grew in political influence, and its changing appearance from discreet reticence to flamboyant exuberance came to express perfectly the developing architectural preferences of the time. Burghley was a large house, but Theobalds, just north of London, where Cecil started building in 1564, was enormous. By the date of its completion in 1585, it extended across five courtyards with massive three-storeyed towers capped by ogee-roofed turrets breaking the skyline. Its size was far in excess of anything that a courtier, no matter how powerful, could require. However, by the time of its final enlargement it was no longer simply the residence of a private citizen. It was a royal palace designed for the occupation of the monarch whenever she should choose.

Queen Elizabeth built no palaces of her own. Instead she encouraged her noble subjects to build on a scale which in the past would have been seen as a dynastic threat but which now harnessed the ostentatious builder more firmly to the throne. Each summer Elizabeth went on Progress to a different part of the country, showing herself to her subjects and enjoying the hospitality of the principal houses in the locality. She travelled with the court and her own household and they all had to be accommodated, fed and entertained. Her comments at different occasions on the inadequacy of the accommodation provided for her by Lord Bacon at Gorhambury and even Cecil at Theobalds were not lost on her hosts, who both extended their houses to rectify this slight, nor on the other ambitious men who surrounded her. If they wished to receive the rewards of office and patronage which she ultimately bestowed they had to be prepared to build in a manner and on a scale appropriate to the proper entertainment of their sovereign. Without those rewards they might not be able to build at all. Their dependence on the monarch and the financial demands it entailed were succinctly expressed in 1579 in a letter from Cecil to Sir Christopher Hatton, the builder of Holdenby, one of the largest prodigy houses, when he wrote about their respective houses: 'God send us both long to enjoy her for whom we both meant to exceed our purses in these.'

The style that the most powerful courtiers adopted for these 'prodigy'
houses harked back to the great palaces of Henry VII and Henry VIII at
Richmond and Hampton Court with imposing gatehouses, sprawling
courtyards and a skyline punctuated by a mass of ogee turrets, elaborate
chimneystacks, pinnacles and spires. This was partly because there were no
other exemplars of houses on this scale which they could follow with the
demise of royal building after 1547, but it was also a conscious court revival
of the trappings of England's medieval past. The romantic veneration of
Elizabeth as the virgin queen defended by the knights of her court against a
hostile world was a political concept that was deliberately fostered to support
her hold on the Crown and which was bolstered by the growing nationalism
that followed the defeat of Spain. The remarkable explosion of national
confidence and cultural richness which marked the last decades of the century
centred on the person of the queen as both the glorious source and the sole
recipient worthy of all this wealth and achievement. The court became almost
a make-believe world of revived chivalry and fancy-dress tournaments with
the Queen's Champion defeating the forces of darkness to preserve her
honour.

This cultivation of England's historic past was partly light-hearted, but
also of an underlying seriousness which effectively prevented any serious
threat to the position of an unmarried woman with no direct heirs in a
thoroughly masculine and dynastic society. It received its artistic expression
in the clothes and the fanciful posture adopted in the portraits of the time,
the poetry of Spenser and the history plays of Shakespeare. And it received
its architectural expression in the revival of Gothic features that can be seen,
for example, in a building that developed over a long period of time like
Burghley House, where the magnificent hammer-beamed hall, the spire of the
clock-tower, the massed towers of the west front and the projecting bow-
windowed frontispiece on the north front are all later additions of the 1570s
and 1580s.

The most complete example of a building conceived in this Gothic spirit is
Sir Francis Willoughby's Wollaton Hall in Nottinghamshire, built between
1580 and 1588. Here the plan, basically a rectangle with four, almost
detached, corner towers, is directly cribbed from a classical design published
by the Frenchman du Cerceau in 1559. Classical decoration is correctly used
in the orders which climb up all four elevations. But the overall form and
massing, and the overwhelming effect of the detail is that of a glittering fairy-
tale castle set on a hilltop site from which it dominates the surrounding
countryside. It has nothing of the reticence and solidity of a genuine fortress.
Instead, all is light and playful and confident show, from the massed ranks of
windows which cover its outer walls, through the soaring prospect chamber
with its fanciful corner tourelles and tall traceried windows which rise out of
the centre of the house, to the sinuously curved chimneystacks which form
little openwork pavilions on the four corner towers. It is a magical building
which echoes the make-believe atmosphere of the court.

Wollaton is not a courtyard house reserving its full architectural display for
those privileged enough to penetrate its outer walls. It is, rather, an outward-
looking house with its decoration boldly worn on its external elevations. The

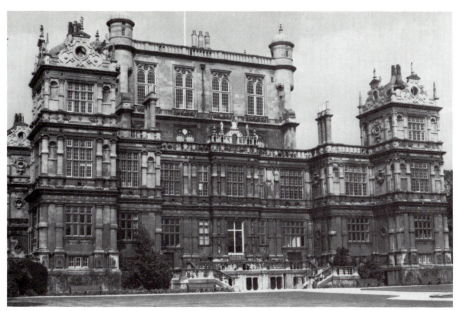

Wollaton Hall, Nottinghamshire (1580–88).

proud public advertisement of the builder's architectural taste was another aspect of late sixteenth-century architecture which reflected the extrovert attitudes at court and the intense rivalry which such confidence and the boom in building had generated. Longleat was another, slightly earlier, manifestation, but it is seen to its best advantage in the E-planned courtier houses which predominated in the latter part of Elizabeth's reign and in the early decades of the seventeenth century. These were basically single courtyard houses with the gatehouse range removed or replaced by an open forecourt with low walls and small pavilions, so that all the architecture of the principal elevations was open to view. The emphasis of the gatehouse was transferred to the entry to the house itself, usually centrally positioned in the main range, and the projecting wings to either side were used to frame the symmetry which was all that remained of that earlier predeliction for the Renaissance (see also p. 228).

An excessive use of applied decoration which threatens to overwhelm the wall surfaces of flamboyant houses such as Wollaton was largely eschewed. Instead the carving was generally confined to the central frontispiece and the ends of the wings, leaving the plain walls and the regularity of the large windows to point up the contrast and to provide their own architectural effect. The essence of these houses was a clear delight in the dramatic effects of massing and the manipulation of the planes of the walls so that they presented a changing progression of projection and recession across a balanced facade, rather than in any ostentatious display of decoration. It would be wrong to deny that the coarse excesses of Flemish decoration were greatly enjoyed, but they were largely confined to the plasterwork and the carved woodwork of the interiors and did not encroach on the more refined appearance of the external walls.

There is a powerful simplicity about these houses which is often overlooked in attempting to analyse them, mainly because of their lively and dramatic rooflines crowded with banks of tall chimneystacks and turrets and adorned with cresting and balustrades and the heraldic achievements of the owner. But this again was all part of a deliberate effect designed to draw the eye upwards from the plainer surfaces below in order to emphasise the height of the building and the hierarchy of the rooms within, as is demonstrated so powerfully in the ascending height of the magnificent windows at Hardwick Hall. The roof, too, was often an integral part of the social space of the building, being used for after-dinner banquets and as a viewing gallery from which to enjoy the surrounding countryside when the weather allowed. What looked like crowded spiky decoration from the ground was also meant to be seen at close quarters as a series of architectural vignettes to amuse and entertain.

The importance of the Cecils in informing court taste can be seen in this aspect of architecture as with all the others in the second half of the century. Wimbledon House, completed in 1588 for Lord Burghley's elder son, Sir Thomas Cecil, has long been demolished but it is known to have been greatly admired in its day. It embraced most of the attributes to be found in the other 'open' houses which followed it. Firstly, careful symmetry about the emphasised entrance into the hall, then plain wall surfaces punctuated by regular rows of large windows, a studied arrangement of the projecting bay at

Henry Winstanley's etching of Wimbledon House (1588; demolished).

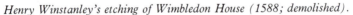

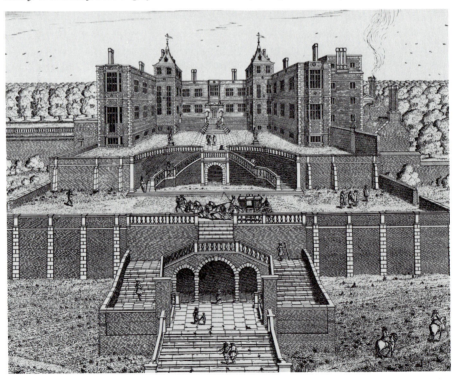

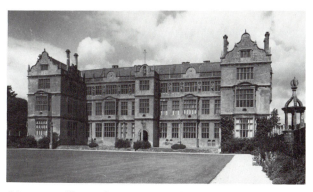

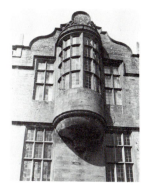

Montacute House, Somerset (completed 1601).

The Gallery Oriel at Montacute House.

the ends of the wings, the balancing staircase towers in the re-entrant angles and the central frontispiece to enliven the walls without diminishing the dramatic effect of their simplicity; and finally a fanciful roofline with two shaped caps to the towers, decorated gables to the principal face of the building, and ordered banks of grouped chimneystacks.

Overall it had the lively discipline and barely restrained dignity which is characteristic of the best houses of the period, with just enough decoration to excite curiosity and delight. Just the sort of qualities that are found at Montacute House in Somerset, begun at the very end of the century and completed in 1601 for Sir Edward Phelips, later to become Speaker of the Houses of Parliament and Master of the Rolls. This is a house which summarises in a very tangible way the architectural achievements of the Elizabethan court. It is both extrovert in its glittering array of showy windows and projecting bays, and yet disciplined in its symmetry about all four fronts. It is suitably learned in its classical references to entablatures and pediments and columned chimneystacks on the entrance front, yet light-heartedly romantic in its castellated pavilions guarding the forecourt and the statues of the Nine Worthies (including such heroes of chivalry as Charlemagne and King Arthur) which separate the almost continuous grid of windows lighting the long gallery along the whole of the second storey. The house stands tall and self-confident, proudly showing off its qualities to the world around. It is also a unified creation which owes very little to the broad sweep of European culture. It is uniquely a product of the country in which it stands and that, in architectural terms, is no mean achievement.

The smaller country house

The particular circumstances which created the great courtier houses could be largely ignored by the builders of the smaller country houses. Men whose power and ambitions did not extend beyond their own locality, and whose wealth derived from farming the demesne or the profits of trade, industry or the law rather than the fruits of office, had no need to flaunt their influence by a display of military might and the provision of surplus accommodation to satisfy the hospitality that was expected of their immediate masters. In consequence, their houses were smaller and less ostentatious and they were able to avoid the excesses of the court whilst acknowledging, should they choose, its more fashionable achievements.

Just how small and how ostentatious depended very much on where they lived, for this governed both the finance at their disposal and the materials that they were able to use. Unlike the courtier houses which could be constructed wherever the builders chose to live, the houses of the gentry present a regional distribution which reflects local conditions of economic prosperity and political calm. The cloth trade and the Tudor price rise which benefited the primary producers of food created marked concentrations of country houses in areas of southern and eastern England and along the limestone belt of the Cotswolds whilst, conversely, there are very few houses of this period built by the gentry in large parts of western Wales and northern England.

All of these houses, too, were built of the materials that were available close at hand, for their builders were not in a position to transport heavy and expensive materials over a long distances just to achieve a desired effect in the way that Lord Burghley, for example, was able to do. The stones of the south-west and the north were less conducive to showy decorative effects than the softer stones of the Cotswolds, the carved and moulded bricks of eastern England and the flamboyant patterns of timber-framing in the north-west. Nevertheless, despite these strong regional variations, it is still possible to make acceptable generalisations about the development of the smaller country houses over the course of the century.

They were comparatively few in number before the reign of Elizabeth, but in the latter part of the century there was a great increase in building which was accompanied by rapid and inventive changes in form and appearance. A courtyard defined and enclosed by ranges of buildings was never a sensible option for the unambitious gentry builder. The medieval prototype might have provided a domestic block protected by a detached gatehouse and surrounded by a moat, but there was rarely any need for the ranges of lodgings necessary in the larger households. In the first half of the sixteenth century the medieval form of the domestic accommodation continued to satisfy the new builder but the concessions to defence were rapidly forgotten. Inevitably some gatehouses continued to be built, partly out of tradition or for reasons of local prestige, but more commonly they were transformed into ornamental gateways which could bear the family's heraldry or the date and initials of the builder and provide a suitable introduction to the architecture beyond.

The grand proportions of the hall continued to dominate the house itself to an extent which had already become old-fashioned at court and this dominance exercised a powerful visual influence over the appearance of the architecture. In most early examples there is no mistaking the position of the hall from an external inspection, because the traditional position of the entry into a screens passage at the low end was invariably matched by the provision of a larger window to light the high end of the hall at a suitable distance further along the elevation. This relationship is clearly expressed in the small manor house built by the Fleming family *c.* 1530 and now called Flemingston Court in the fertile plain of Glamorgan. The entrance passage, marked by doorways with arched heads and moulded jambs, extends from front to rear of the house with doorways off to small service rooms on one side and the hall on the other. The hall was heated by a massive chimneystack in the side of one wall and there was a heated parlour in the room beyond. A Great Chamber was reached in the space above the hall by a projecting staircase turret. There is very little in the way of architectural decoration but the function and hierarchy of the rooms within is clearly advertised by the differing sizes and the irregular disposition of the windows without.

Most English houses of a similar period were slightly larger, with a more varied outline in the form of one or two projecting wings flanking the hall and roofed at right angles to it. But the elements of the house were essentially the same and there was a similar lack of surface decoration. Blackmoor Farm, near Cannington in Somerset, built in the first decade of the century for Sir Thomas Tremaill, gives emphasis to the entry by a two-storeyed projecting porch; but the hall is still entered off the screens passage and the rest of the accommodation is similar to Flemingston Court, with the exception of an integral chapel located in the projecting north wing and adorned with a traceried east window. The difference between these houses and their medieval predecessors is that the hall is only a single storey in height with a room above and is heated by an integral chimneystack, but the asymmetrical elevations dictated by the importance of the hall and its entrance at one end remain.

However, that the balance of parts which was inherent in the hall house with flanking wings was susceptible to symmetrical manipulation was

Blackmoor Farm, Cannington, Somerset (early sixteenth century).

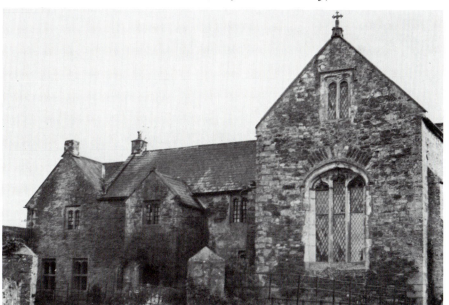

apparent to the gentry builder as soon as such conceits became fashionable. Barrington Court in Somerset, built between 1552 and 1564 for William Clifton, a merchant of Norwich and London investing his wealth in land, shows how easily this could be achieved to great architectural effect. Unlike Sutton Place, the hall is still entered from the screens passage and its importance is still marked by the larger size of its windows, but everything else on the principal elevation is fitted into a scheme of conscious symmetry. The service area to the other side of the screens passage was increased in length to give it equal weight to the hall and to enable the entrance to be positioned centrally. The projecting bay window at the upper end of the hall is carried through the full height of the building to form a tower-like feature in the re-entrant angle with the parlour wing beyond and it is almost matched by a slightly larger staircase projection in the corresponding re-entrant angle with the kitchen wing.

This basic E plan, completed by the projecting porch, was the precursor of countless other examples built during the years of Elizabeth's reign, to whom it has come to be seen as an architectural tribute. In an age of the 'curious device' the connection was probably very quickly made by men of wit and a romantic turn of mind, but it is equally clear that the form was a logical development from the medieval house and was evolved by aesthetic experiment rather than solely as an obsequious gesture.

Barrington was built at the very beginning of the boom in country house building that marks the remainder of the century. The symmetry of its

Barrington Court, Somerset (1552–64).

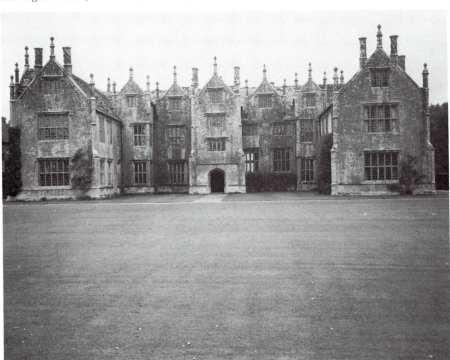

entrance elevation is not quite perfect and that of its other, less public, elevations is non-existent. But it has other qualities which were to become equally characteristic as the century proceeded. The bold emphasis on its central porch, the use of gabled dormers to give a broken skyline and an added impression of height, the interplay of angled buttresses to strengthen the projections of the wings and porch and by their absence to introduce a minor theme with the projecting staircase and bay window towers, and the concentration of decoration on the roofline with its multitude of finials and twisted chimneystacks, all recur again and again in the houses of the Elizabethan period. Their combination with a deliberate symmetry in whatever form was the means by which the Elizabethan gentleman chose to show his architectural sophistication. And in this he was the equal and perhaps on occasion even the mentor of his more public neighbour at court.

There was one aspect of court architecture which particularly commended itself to the gentry builder and which was eventually to become the predominant theme in the development of the smaller country house in the late sixteenth century. This was a marked trend towards compactness of plan whereby all the main rooms were concentrated in a single rectangular block, the projecting wings were eliminated and the appropriate accommodation was provided in added upper storeys rather than dispersed in narrow flanking ranges. It was, in effect, the 'double-pile' plan (two-room deep) which Sir Roger Pratt, writing in 1660, was to commend for its qualities of economy and convenience. It derived not so much from the principal residences of the great courtiers, although the tendency was already there in houses like Wollaton and Hardwick Hall, but rather from their lodges.

These lodges were much smaller buildings which often fulfilled a dual function as grandstands from which to watch the hunt and private retreats to which the owner could escape from the formality of public life in the great house and spend some time in a relaxed atmosphere with a few chosen friends and a greatly reduced staff. For the courtier they offered an opportunity for architectural experiment and fun at a minimal cost and several of them were designed as sham castles in the spirit of romantic chivalry. Notable examples include Sir Walter Raleigh's rectangular lodge with hexagonal corner towers of 1594 in the grounds of Sherborne Castle, Dorset, Lord Howard's Lulworth Castle, also in Dorset, and the gloriously evocative Bolsover Castle, Derbyshire, of the early seventeenth century. Most of them exhibited a common theme of compact rectangular plans two rooms deep coupled with a height of at least three storeys. This of course, was essential if they were to be used to watch the chase but it was also useful as a means of providing sufficient accommodation without cluttering up the outline with subsidiary wings.

These characteristics of compact plans and great height were enthusi-astically adopted by less powerful men for their own wholly residential country houses and had become well-established at this level well before the end of the century. Sir John Games, High Sheriff of Breconshire, built himself a double-pile house at Newton, Llanfaes, in 1582, which a later commentator (Hugh Thomas in 1698) likened to a castle. It is a curiously hybrid building with little attempt at more than token symmetry and the

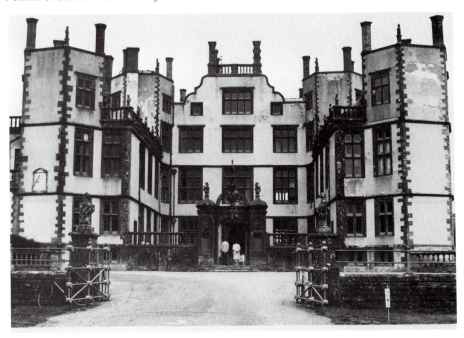

Sherborne Castle, Dorset (central block 1594?; wings c.1600)

traditional importance of the hall still emphasised by its size and the fact that it occupies two full storeys in height. What sets it apart from earlier houses, however, is its four-square, double-pile plan two rooms deep, its towering height rising to four storeys on the elevation away from the hall, the generous proportions of the Great Chamber on the second floor, and the provision of a spacious staircase compartment to create an appropriate entry to the public use of the upper floors.

Similar elements were used with greater sophistication on the other side of Offa's Dyke. Richard Prince, a wealthy lawyer, built what is probably the earliest double-pile house of this status in England just outside Shrewsbury between 1578 and 1582. Whitehall has a simple square plan which allowed for an easy symmetry. The hall, although still traditionally conceived, is no larger than the other principal public rooms and is only a single storey in height. The subtle diminution of window heights draws the eye upwards across the plain surface of the walls to the decorated roofline with its disciplined ranks of gables capped by little finials, tall star-shaped chimneys and a glittering lantern.

It is possible that the lantern at Whitehall is a later addition, but Barlborough Hall in Derbyshire, built at about the same time for Francis Rodes, another lawyer, definitely had a roof-top lantern as an original feature illuminating a central light well. Barlborough is another tall square-planned compact house. It has a similar emphasis on the roof with prospect chambers inset from the four corners complementing the octagonal lantern. It is an altogether more showy design than the reticent Whitehall. The plane of the walls is regularly interrupted by projecting canted bay windows and an

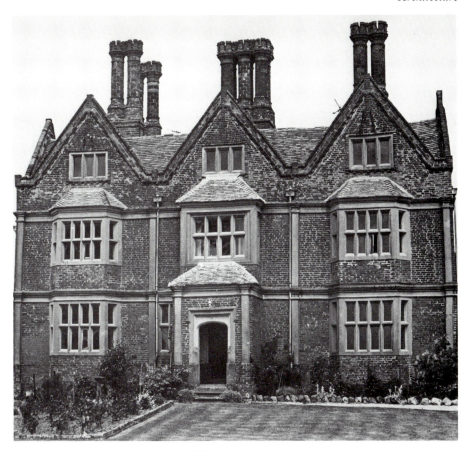

Toseland Hall, Cambridgeshire (c.1600).

emphasised frontispiece: the classical learning of the builder is proudly announced by the coupled columns flanking the entrance and the portrait medallions which decorate the bays; and there is even a reference to the court style of Henry VII in the complex plan of the central bay window projecting on the north front.

Such an ostentatious display of applied decoration, although not uncommon, was becoming less pronounced by the end of the century. Gentry builders, such as the owner of Toseland Hall, Cambridgeshire, of *c.*1600, were more interested in the architectural potential of massing and the appearance of height, rather than costly carving and decorative flourishes which they confined to the symmetrical gables and towering chimneystacks crowning their dignified designs.

The Witney wool merchant, Walter Jones, shows this preoccupation off to perfection in his house at Chastleton in Oxfordshire built just as Elizabeth's reign was ending. Designed on a square plan around a small central court-yard, it is enlivened by tall projections on all four elevations. It provided him with all the amenities of gracious living in a remarkably compact fashion. He had an imposing hall no longer given architectural prominence

at the expense of external symmetry, a first-floor Great Chamber, a long
gallery on the top floor and two very spacious staircases. All this was
achieved at a reasonable cost by making the building both deep and tall, and
placing the staircases in flanking projecting towers. The regular horizontal
rhythm set up by the projection and recession of the wall surfaces harmonises
with the discipline of the fenestration and is triumphantly rescued from
repetitive monotony by the exciting variety of the jagged roofline. There is a
unity of design about the whole composition which is characteristic of the
best gentry houses of the period and which makes them such a satisfying
conclusion to a century of great architectural change and development.

The farmhouse

The most profound architectural changes in the sixteenth century took place
at a lower level in society than the grand houses of the sophisticated courtiers
and the literate country gentlemen. Here the revolution in housing standards
which marked a total and abrupt break with the Middle Ages can be seen
most clearly and they were to have the most lasting effects. The details of
these changes varied both in the form that they took and the time that they
occurred in different parts of the country as a result of regional prosperity
and geology. Nevertheless, beginning in the prosperous south-east about the
middle of the century and continuing in more remote areas of the north and
west until after the Civil War, a significant number of people of middling
social status over a large area of England and parts of Wales either built
themselves new houses in a way that broke completely with their medieval
predecessors or built in permanent materials for the very first time.

The revolutionary context of this development is only manifest when it is
realised that the domestic arrangements from which they escaped were laid
down at the time of the Norman Conquest or even earlier and the new
comforts which they embraced were to endure down into the twentieth
century. In the early part of the sixteenth century, the houses of most people
below the level of the gentry, especially in the rural areas, were dominated by
a single room open to the roof and heated by an open fire placed in the
middle of the floor. By the middle of the seventeenth century this was no
longer true and the majority of the population had begun to go upstairs to
bed for the first time in houses that were divided into a number of different
living rooms heated by enclosed fireplaces and lit by proper glazed windows.
All these fundamental influences on social and domestic life which have been
taken for granted for so long became available to the common people at the
same time as the cultural achievements of the elite which are charted
elsewhere in this book were taking place, the Armada was being defeated, the
foundations of modern trade and industry and religion were being established
and the New World was being colonised by the old. These radical changes
sprang from the same economic base but they had a far greater influence on
the daily lives of the population than the plays of Shakespeare or the exploits
of Raleigh and any account of the architecture of the period would be
incomplete without considering the means by which this was achieved.

In the early years of the sixteenth century, even in the prosperous south-east, open-hall houses continued to be built on the plan that had been established for several hundred years. In its most developed form it comprised a hall extending for the full height of the building, entered by a screens-passage at one end and flanked on either side by storeyed bays with specialised service and storage functions. The hall with its open hearth in the centre of the floor was the only heated room and there was no intercommunication between the upper storey chambers at either end. The grandest examples are indistinguishable from the houses of the lesser gentry and had their storeyed wings separately roofed at right angles to the hall range, which provided sufficient height for the upper storey chambers to be put to regular domestic use. This arrangement can be illustrated by the timber-framed Manor Farm at Chalgrove, Oxfordshire, which probably dates from the latter part of the fifteenth century and only acquired its completed form over two separate building campaigns.

Chalgrove is a large house of relatively high status. Slightly lower down the social scale the same elements of hall and storeyed wings were contrived beneath a single all-enveloping roof as at East End Farm Cottage, Pinner, in

Manor Farm, Chalgrove, Oxfordshire (late fifteenth century).

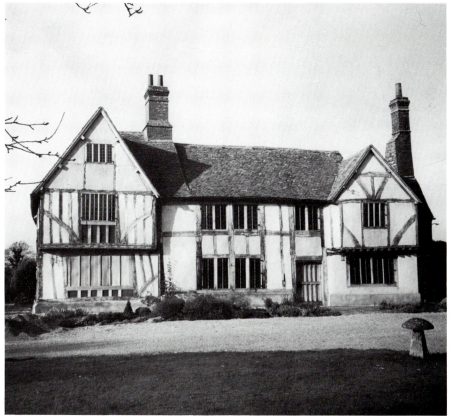

the former county of Middlesex. Here the upper rooms were probably of inadequate size and too difficult of access to have been used for other than seasonal storage. The smallest surviving hall houses of the sixteenth century were simple structures of only two bays, one of which might have incorporated a loft. Although offering only rudimentary accommodation they were by no means the houses of the peasantry, who lived in ephemeral structures rebuilt every generation or so and which are only known from archaeological excavation.

The builders of the surviving hall houses were freeholders or copyholders on fixed rents primarily engaged on agriculture. The staggering rise in food prices which took place through the sixteenth century enabled them to accumulate reserves of capital, which they were able to invest in building, and to contemplate improved standards of comfort and privacy. The way they achieved this goal was by eliminating the open hearth. Initially the hearth was not entirely dispensed with and was merely confined to a single bay of the hall; this enabled the other bay to be floored over with a linking gallery partitioned off from the open smoke-bay, as happened sometime around the middle of the century at East End Farm Cottage. But this was a very short-lived stage in the remodelling of the medieval house and it was not very long before the advantages of housing the fire in an enclosed chimney-stack were fully realised. The growing availability of bricks which made the insertion of a chimneystack into an existing building a comparatively simple matter undoubtedly hastened this trend, so that by 1577 William Harrison could write of his own village in Essex how men marvelled at 'the multitude of chimneys lately erected whereas in their young days there were not above two or three, if so many'.

Once the open hearth had been replaced by a proper fireplace, it was no longer necessary to leave a large part of the house open to the roof simply in order for the smoke to find its own way out. As at Chalgrove, the hall could be horizonatally sub-divided with an upper floor which not only provided an extra room, but also allowed access between the flanking upper storey chambers. The liberation of the upper storey from smoke encouraged the construction of proper staircases to provide easy access and began the trend towards sleeping above the living rooms, which is now entrenched in our domestic lives. Other rooms could be provided with their own fireplaces either from the hall chimneystack or in separate chimneystacks and thus could be brought into comfortable domestic use the whole year round. The glazing of windows, another development available at this social level for the first time, enabled draught-free lighting of the principal rooms. With more light and no smoke from an open hearth it was possible to decorate the interior of these houses with painted cloths, patterned walls and wooden panelling, which in a modified form brought the visual arts developed by the elite into the living rooms of their social inferiors.

The hall house was easily adapted to provide a suitable setting for these momentous changes, and this is why they have survived in such numbers down to the present day. But of more lasting significance were the new house types which were evolved to take advantage from the beginning of all the new possibilities of smaller rooms, better heating and a more extensively used

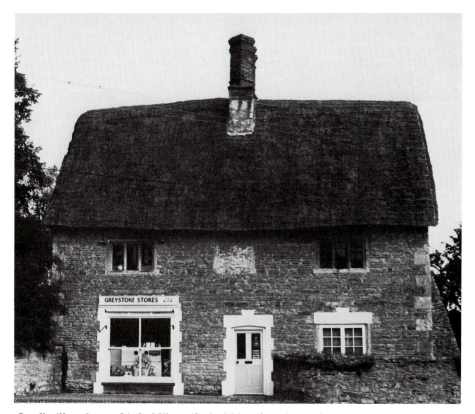

Small village house, Little Milton, Oxfordshire (late sixteenth century).

upper storey that the enclosed chimneystack allowed. Throughout much of lowland England and parts of mid-Wales the lobby-entry plan was adopted whereby the chimneystack was placed in the centre of the house, defining a small entrance lobby at the front and providing space for a staircase at the rear. The single stack could accommodate sufficient fireplaces to heat the rooms to either side on both floors and offered the opportunity for a dominant decorative central feature where it broke through the ridge of the roof. It was an attractively economical plan with a minimum of radiant heat loss and all the essential service elements of chimneystack, draught-free lobby and staircase confined to a narrow bay, leaving the remainder of the building free for unobstructed domestic life.

The courtier Sir John Hussey built himself a lobby-entry house as a hunting lodge at Kneesall in Nottinghamshire sometime between 1522 and 1536, but its true genesis is at a far humbler level amongst the prosperous yeomanry in south-eastern England in the second half of the century. Rook Hall, Cressing, Essex, dated 1575 by deduction from the inscription carved on the framework, is amongst the earliest datable examples. The staircase is housed in a medieval wing at the rear retained from an earlier house on the site, but otherwise it is typical of the lobby-entry house in its fully developed form. Despite a superficial face-lift in the eighteenth century, its front elevation with a central door and tall decorated brick chimneystacks still exhibits the symmetry which commended this plan to its discerning builder. Its symmetry, however, was merely an incidental feature; those who required more accommodation did not hesitate to provide it by building asymmetrical lobby-entry houses with an additional bay incorporated from the beginning at one end of the standard plan, as is graphically shown in the drawing attached to a building contract of 1577 now in the Suffolk Record Office. This document makes it very clear that there was nothing unusual about this type of house in East Anglia by that date. Indeed by the seventeenth century it had become the most common house in southern England and had been exported to the eastern seaboard of America along with the Pilgrim Fathers.

The post-medieval house in the upland areas of the country took a less radical form, almost as though their builders were reluctant to break with the traditional tripartite division of the hall house. The dominant characteristic of their houses was the retention of the through passage running from front to rear of the building and separating the service end from the living quarters. The fireplace was generally placed at one end of the largest ground-floor room backing onto the passage and there was usually a further unheated room beyond. The central room in this plan was initially the only heated room and it therefore retained a dominant position in the domestic arrangements of the house, similar to that previously held by the medieval hall even though reduced to a single storey. It also commanded access to the staircase leading to the upper storey which was usually positioned close to the fireplace. The principal advantage of the through-passage house seems to have been that it provided direct access to the service rooms from both the street and the yard at the rear without interfering with the other rooms of the

Plan of timber-framed lobby-entrance house, to be erected at Holbrook, Suffolk (from a building contract of 1577).

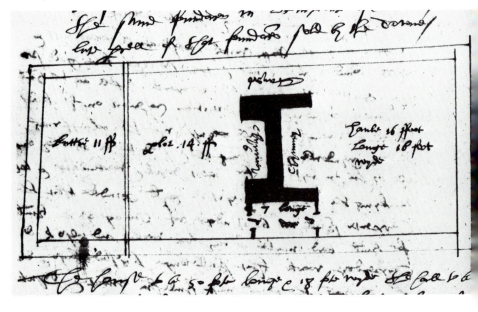

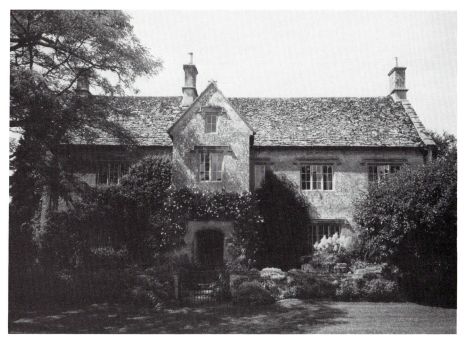

Through-passage plan, Lower Farm, Taynton, Oxfordshire.

house. But it also suggests a more cautious and conservative approach to the domestic changes which gathered momentum in the second half of the sixteenth century, indicative of different cultural preferences in the upland areas where it predominated.

Whatever plan was adopted, all these houses with their new fireplaces and stairs, their smaller rooms with specialised functions arranged on two floors, and their glazed windows, were fully equipped to provide comfortable living conditions for the next 250 years. It is a mark of the enduring strength of the Elizabethan housing revolution that as house types they only became truly redundant with the introduction of central heating and the elimination of the chimney in the twentieth century.

Public building

From the perspective of the end of the century there can be no doubt that the most innovative and exciting developments in architecture were domestic. It is the houses of the great courtiers, the country gentry, the merchants, lawyers and prosperous yeomen that we think of when we consider the accomplishments of that glorious century, and in terms of quantity and architectural quality that is surely correct. Nevertheless there was a great surge of what can loosely be termed public building during the same period which is equally deserving of consideration and respect.

The most public building in any community was the church and as the sixteenth century opened the late flowering of the mature Perpendicular style was in full bloom. Any analysis of the development and achievements of this uniquely English style properly belongs to the fifteenth century, but some of its greatest monuments such as Henry VII's chapel and King's College Chapel, Cambridge, were only completed in the sixteenth century. The emphasis on soaring height and large areas of light fenestration were to find a conscious reprise in the houses of the Elizabethan Court. But the true glory of the style was in the parish church and many of the most splendid examples in the West Country and East Anglia date from this period.

It was a sign of the times, however, that for all their delicate fan vaulting and rich tracery, many of them seem to have been conceived as much as a monument to the wealth and secular achievements of their benefactors as to the greater glory of God. The donors were determined that this celebration of their own names and their conspicuous generosity would not be forgotten long after they themselves were dead. Thus at Lavenham, where a great building campaign was in operation in the 1520s, the church is covered with inscriptions and heraldic devices to the Spring family of wealthy clothiers and the Earl of Oxford, the lord of the manor, who together provided most of

Church of St Peter and St Paul, Lavenham, Suffolk (1520).

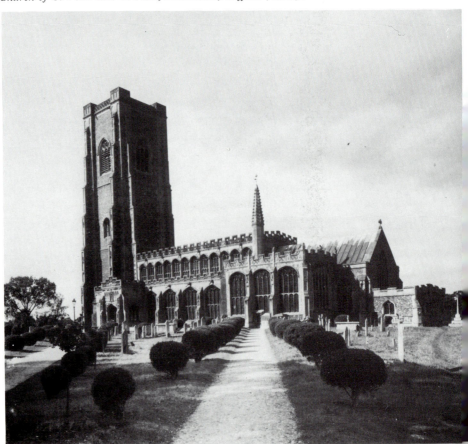

the money to complete the building in such a spectacular form. And at St Peter's, Tiverton in Devon, where the south porch and the sumptuously decorated south chapel were paid for in 1517 by the merchant John Greenway, his donation is proudly announced in a frieze running around the interior, and the exterior is embellished with his initials, his merchant's mark and sculptured ships as tokens of the vessels which carried his wealth.

Such self-glorification was intended to demonstrate the standing of the benefactor here on earth and to improve his chances in the life hereafter. There seems to have been a similar concern with public recognition and, indeed, a weakness for worldly comfort amongst some of the monastic orders and a surprising amount of opulent building was taking place in the monasteries in the years leading up to the Dissolution. Much of it was for the secular benefit of the heads of the houses rather than for the spiritual benefit of the community over which they presided. Such was the Prior's Lodge at Much Wenlock, Shropshire, with its two-storeyed gallery over a hundred feet long, its private hall and even a traceried ceiling in the garderobe. Sir Nikolaus Pevsner's comment on the magnificent lodging that the Prioress built for herself at Carrow Abbey, Norwich, early in the century, that 'in its sumptuousness and worldliness [it] almost seems to justify the Dissolution' could be extended to a number of other examples and evokes sympathy rather than surprise.

All this conspicuous expenditure on building came to an abrupt end with the Dissolution of the Monasteries in the late 1530s, but there was another, more learned, strain in ecclesiastical building which was stifled by the Reformation and died out with the Marian reaction that came in its train. Beginning in the 1520s there seems to have been a greater enthusiasm amongst churchmen for the decoration of the Early Renaissance than can be found in the houses of their lay brethren. It was manifested in the fittings of the church rather than its architectural framework but, nevertheless, it adds up to an impressive testament to the refined taste of those who commissioned the various objects. Some of the carved bench ends and doors in a number of Devon churches are undeniably crude, but the screens at both King's College, Cambridge, and Carlisle Cathedral, the stone pulpit at Wells Cathedral and the exquisite west porch at Sunningwell in modern-day Oxfordshire are as good as anything else in northern Europe at this date.

There was no halt to church building and extension after the Reformation, but the architecture lacks the bravura of the early sixteenth century. The bewildering turns in ecclesiastical doctrine inhibited invention and dictated a watered-down Gothic with none of the flourishes which had characterised the Perpendicular. Such quiet self-effacement must have been an important ingredient in the unmolested survival of many parishioners as they wrestled with their consciences. A lavish display and pride in their accomplishments and lineage was reserved for their colourful monuments which increasingly fill the interiors of their churches, but these properly belong to the story of sculpture rather than architecture (see pages 236–47).

A similar architectural conservatism can be discerned in the fabric of the new educational institutions which were such a noteworthy feature of the age. The need for literate administrators to service the machinery of the Tudor

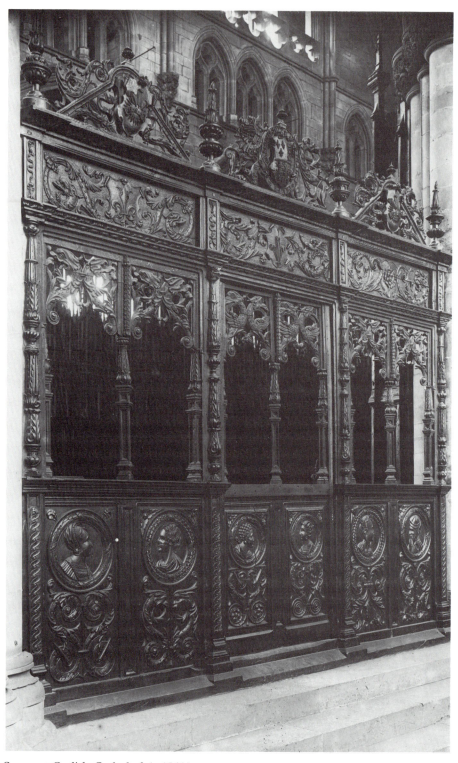

Screen at Carlisle Cathedral (c.1541).

state and the rewards which accrued to families like the Bacons and the Cecils who rose to prominence through this avenue were powerful stimuli to education. The lessons were learnt not only by the ambitious gentry, but also by the hereditary nobility who wished to maintain their position in an increasingly competitive society. As it became clear that the most important public positions were going to those men with trained minds who were capable of clear analysis and who could write official papers and memoranda, rather than to those with the traditional virtues of military expertise or a long-established family name, there was a veritable explosion in education. Men whose wealth might once have been used to extend the parish church now sought immortality through the foundation of an educational institution.

New schools were the basis of the system, and the universities and the Inns of Court were where the process was brought to fruition. Many of the schools were domestic in their scale and in the treatment of their architecture, like the Grammar School founded by Lord Williams at Thame, Oxfordshire, in 1559 with its single great schoolroom and dormitory above and the residential accommodation for the Master and Usher divided by a library housed on the street range. But the individual Oxford and Cambridge colleges founded in great numbers in the second half of the century were medieval both in form and in detail. This was not in any spirit of romantic Gothic revival but rather a reflection that the functional requirements of the colleges had changed very little since William of Wykeham had devised their most practical architectural expression at New College, Oxford, in the late fourteenth century.

The introspective courtyard plan guarded by the Warden's lodge and with its own hall, chapel, library and sets of lodgings was perfectly designed to

Grammar School, Thame, Oxfordshire (founded 1559).

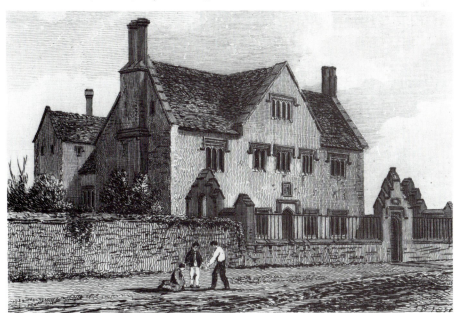

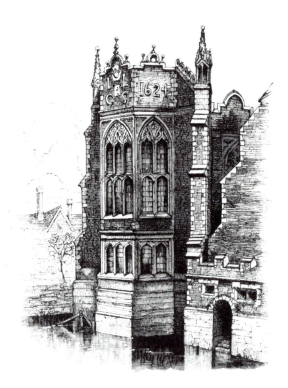

West oriel of the library, St John's College, Cambridge (1624).

meet the needs of the expanded universities of the sixteenth century. It was a
static form with little need to change the details of its architectural dress.
There was a continuity of tradition about the institution which counselled
against any radical tampering with its outside appearance. As the Fellows of
St John's College, Cambridge, explained to the donor of their new library in
1624, 'men of judgement liked the best the old fashion of church windows,
holding it the most meet for such a building'. A like spirit of fitness for
purpose pervaded the buildings of the Inns of Court in London, which acted
as a kind of finishing school in the education of many of the nobility as well
as providing a professional training for the gentry.

Another aspect of the Tudor state was an increasing reliance on local
government as a means of bringing justice and good rule to the provinces and
tying the office-holders firmly to the established order. In combination with
the expanding size of many market towns, caused by a growth in trade and
industry and a massive increase in population, this created a demand for a
suitable building to house the civic authority. Considerable effort was
expended to ensure that the physical symbol of good government was a
dominant feature of the town. It was usually sited in isolation at the head of
the wide market place where it complemented the parish church as the
symbol of spiritual power. Where records survive, it is clear that only the
most respected craftsmen in the locality were entrusted with its construction;
men such as Walter Hancock at Shrewsbury, John Abel on the Welsh

borders, and Lawrence Shipway at Stafford. The conventional form provided for an open arcaded ground floor which offered shelter for some of the stalls on market day and a large chamber which acted as a meeting room for the regulation of the market and for the government of the affairs of the town. Most of them are of a quiet dignity as befitted their civic role, even though they might exhibit advanced architectural taste as in the long-demolished classical building at Stafford begun in 1588.

The most lively of all the sixteenth century market halls is that at Rothwell in Northamptonshire, built ten years earlier, which captures perfectly the brash self-advertisement which so often accompanied acts of public generosity in the Elizabethan period. Although offering the usual facilities of open market hall below and council chamber above, it is much more architecturally ambitious and expensively decorated than most market halls in comparable towns elsewhere in the country. It is in fact little more than a blatant and perpetual billboard to the man who was the prime instigator in the construction of the building. A lengthy inscription running round the walls informs the world that 'This was the work of Thomas Tresham, Knight . . .' It is decorated with shields which were to carry the arms of Tresham's friends and neighbours and the pilasters which rise through both storeys are covered with patterns of trefoils which were his own device.

Rothwell Market House, Northamptonshire (c.1578).

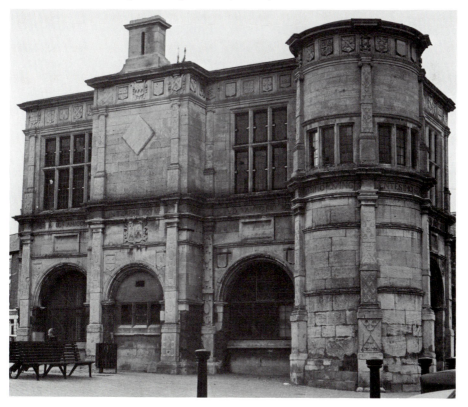

Although undoubtedly a genuine contribution to the civic government of the town, the opportunity has been taken by Tresham to show how architecturally sophisticated he was, and how powerful and well-connected his family was in the county. And he has ensured that whatever else happens, his name will be remembered in Rothwell as long as the building remains standing.

The project for Rothwell Market House was begun in 1578, some three years after Tresham had been knighted but before his conversion to Catholicism. His subsequent symbolically religious buildings demonstrate that he was attracted to architectural showmanship to an extreme degree. Nevertheless, the mixture of learning and self-advertisement apparent in the building, together with its direct bid for immortality, is not uncharacteristic of many of the other arts in late-Elizabethan England and can perhaps be seen as part of a more general spirit of the times.

Scotland

The political, economic and social circumstances in Scotland during the sixteenth century were totally different from those in England and Wales. Scotland was an independent nation and at a time when the Tudors were introducing a system of strong centralised government and reaping the benefits of increasing prosperity south of Hadrian's Wall, it was economically straitened and politically unstable. Consequently, its architectural achievements were separate both in kind and in form. Nevertheless, the century was marked by two distinct periods when developments of great ingenuity and invention were taking place.

Interest in the first period is centred on the activities of James V whose rule effectively began at the age of eleven and who died at the age of thirty in 1542. In 1537 James was at the French Court seeking to revive the Franco-Scottish alliance by marriage to Magdalene, the daughter of Francis I. When she died shortly after her arrival in Scotland, James returned to France to secure the hand of Mary of Lorraine, another, adopted, daughter of the French King. Not only did these visits bring James into direct contact with the distinctive architectural culture of the French Court, but he was also able to recruit French craftsmen into responsible positions in the Scottish Royal Works, with immediate results which were far in advance of anything else in Britain at the time.

Between 1537 and 1541 Falkland Palace was extensively remodelled to receive his French bride. The courtyard elevations applied as thin façades to the existing medieval buildings were of an exceptionally advanced classical character. In view of the absence of any previous departure from native building traditions, it can be confidently assumed that this sudden 'display of early Renaissance architecture without parallel in the British Isles', as Mark Girouard has described it, was due entirely to the impressionable young monarch's exposure to the cultural influences of the French Court and to the talents of the French masons who executed much of the work. The attached columns on high pedestals crowned by inverted consoles and the pairs of

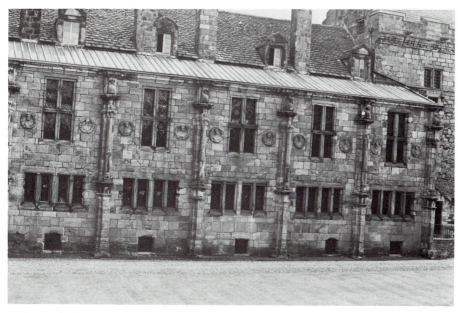

Falkland Palace, Fife, south range (1537–41).

portrait medallions flanking the upper storey windows in each bay are
distinctive motifs of the contemporary Loire school. Although medallions had
been used as a decorative feature at Hampton Court as early as 1521, the
whole ensemble must be considered the earliest surviving example of a
unified classical facade in Britain.

Falkland was part of an intensive campaign of royal palace building under
James which had included earlier work at Linlithgow and Holyrood in a
traditional style. Between 1540 and his death in 1542 he embarked on an
ambitious courtyard palace at Stirling in a more eclectic vein than Falkland
but with a similar French classical spirit. Here it is the external elevations
which are profusely carved with recessed panels decorated by cusped
segmental arches, statues on twisted columns and waisted baluster shafts, and
heavily barred windows under semi-circular sculptured heads. Further figures
stand on pedestals above an enriched cornice and each elevation is crowned
by a crenellated parapet. By European standards the execution is rough and
the design is over-crowded with too many motifs demanding attention.
Nevertheless it is a spirited and exuberant composition which compensates
delightfully for the fortress-like surroundings and the sombre grey stone with
which it is built.

The royal apartments were on the first floor with the King's rooms
occupying the northern range and a complementary set for the Queen in the
southern range. Most of the fittings for the internal decorations were
dispersed in the seventeenth century when the palace ceased to be occupied
as a royal residence, but something of their flavour can be discerned from the
surviving fragments of the wooden ceiling in the King's Presence Chamber.
This was divided into sixty compartments of which fifty-six originally

contained medallion heads of a type similar to those on the courtyard elevations at Falkland. Wooden medallions as part of an internal decorative scheme were frequently incorporated into furniture or panelling, as in the panelled room from Waltham Abbey now in the Victoria and Albert Museum, but the only comparable parallel for the Stirling ceiling is at the royal palace of Wawel in Cracow, where a ceiling executed for Sigismund I in 1531–5 contained nearly 200 carved wooden heads. There is no need to seek any direct link between Scotland and Poland. The details of the heads were no doubt copied from a common source in published wood-cuts and engravings of German origin and the overall design inspired by Italian and French stone ceilings. However, the necessity to consider such influences is a sure indication of the cosmopolitan nature of Scottish palatial architecture in the later years of James V.

The premature death of James in 1542 brought this brief sophisticated interlude to a close. There was very little royal building over the next fifty years apart from various defensive works which allowed little opportunity for architectural learning or display. The Chapel Royal, erected in the Upper Square at Stirling Castle by James VI for the baptism of his eldest son in 1594, is a simple classical building which again demonstrates the cultured taste of the Stuarts but, like the buildings of his father, it had no general influence on the architectural preferences of the majority of his subjects. Instead, they created a national architecture of their own which owed very little to foreign inspiration and almost everything to a dynamic transformation of their native building traditions. As John Dunbar happily described it, in the second half of the sixteenth century 'Scottish architecture remained obstinately Scottish'.

From about 1480 until after the Scottish Reformation of 1560, very few domestic houses of any consequence had been built. The disastrous defeat at Flodden Field in 1513 had decimated the flower of Scottish manhood and the later English invasions in the 1540s had inhibited the next generation. Political uncertainty and financial poverty ensured that the medieval tower-house tradition was effectively interrupted for a period of eighty years or more.

However, by 1561, when Mary Queen of Scots returned from France to rule a Protestant Scotland, an astonishing surge of aristocratic building swept through the land with an impetus which was sustained well into the seventeenth century. No doubt the Dissolution of the Monasteries and the redistribution of church lands and property helped provide some of the funds for this architectural explosion, but it was also the product of a renewed native confidence stemming from the end of the Barons' wars and the new religious settlement. The manifestation was the tower-house, of which a remarkable number of late sixteenth-century examples were built throughout the whole of Scotland. Cumulatively they constitute a unique and highly individual contribution to European architectural history.

The tower-house was one of the most basic and simple kinds of fortified residence. In its medieval form it was usually rectangular and it provided all the standard ingredients of the normal hall house disposed in a vertical rather than an horizontal fashion, with the service rooms on the ground floor

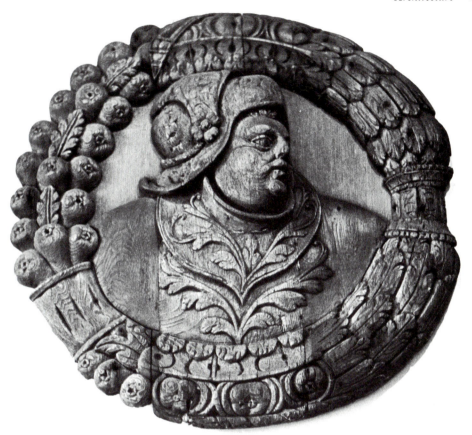

Ceiling detail from Stirling Castle, Stirling (c.1540).

connected by a narrow turnpike stair to a hall above and the private
apartments placed in the upper storeys over the hall. Its defensive qualities
were entirely passive and relied on the minimum of ground area, a heavily
fortified entrance, easily defended internal staircases and a capability for
retaliation from projecting upper works at the very top of the building. Their
height and solidity marked them out as buildings of status but there was very
little architectural distinction between the towers of the grandest barons and
those of the smaller lairds. The balance that they offered between the claims
of domestic comfort and the necessity for defence made them suitable for a
wide section of Scottish society at a time when it had still not achieved the
political stability of the counties south of the border.

The great flowering of the tower-house in the second half of the sixteenth
century modified this traditional form to provide more flexible accommodation and to respond to developments in firearm defence. Extra residential
rooms were contrived in attached wings which were linked with the main
apartments of hall and chamber in the body of the tower. This arrangement
afforded greater domestic comfort and enabled the defenders to capitalise on
the growing availability of hand guns. The defensive emphasis of the tower
moved from the wall-head to the lower storeys where gun-loops offered

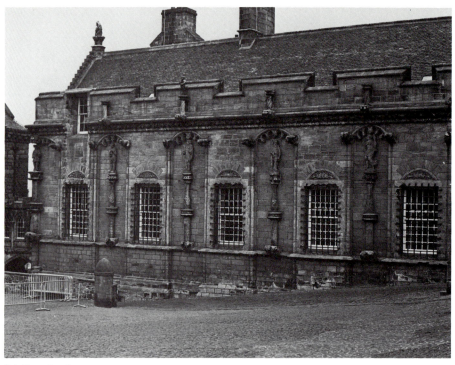

Stirling Castle (1540–2).

greater protection and where the projecting wings could be utilised to provide covering fire along the exposed faces of the main tower, particularly in the vicinity of the vulnerable entrance.

In its simplest form this resulted in an L-plan with a single projecting wing and the entrance sheltering in the re-entrant angle, as at Crathes Castle, Grampian, begun by Alexander Burnett, 9th Laird of Leys, in about 1553 and completed only at the very end of the century. Here the wing is exceedingly truncated and the main tower remains the dominant element in the composition. Built of rough granite, the thick walls are given a smooth appearance by a coat of harling (rough cast) and an air of invincibility by their rounded corners, sparsely fenestrated lower storeys, and distinctive inward-sloping walls. All the original architectural decoration is reserved for the top storey where gabled and conical cap-houses corbelled out from the face of the walls sprout in irregular profusion across the roof-line, and the shift in defensive significance is humorously commemorated by a crenallated string-course and rainwater spouts in the form of mock cannon.

Despite its belligerent swagger, Crathes is unmistakably the domestic residence of a great lord. Claypotts Castle in Tayside is altogether more uncompromisingly defensive in intent. Built for John Strachan between 1569 and 1588, the additional domestic accommodation is arranged in two circular wings which are positioned at diagonally opposite corners of the main tower to provide an unobstructed field of fire around all four sides of the building.

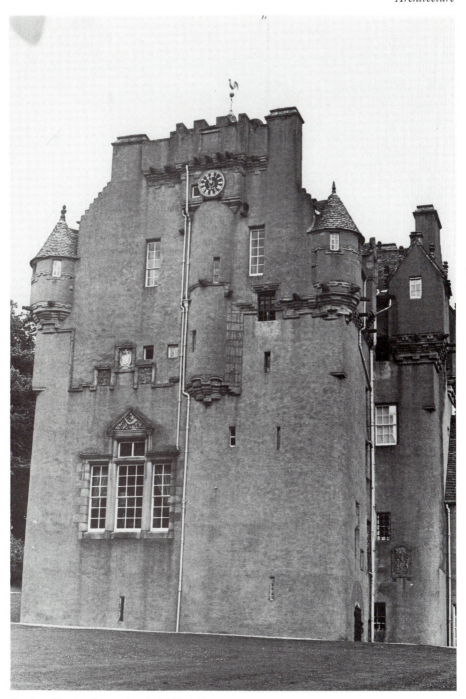

Crathes Castle, Grampian (c.1553–95).

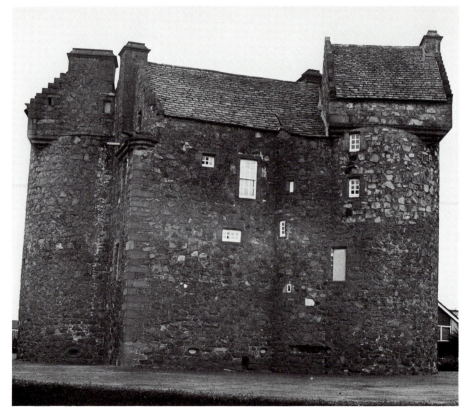

Claypotts Castle, Tayside (1569–88).

This is the classic Z-plan which was one of the most popular forms adopted by Scottish tower-house builders in the late sixteenth century. Even though it is now surrounded by a modern housing estate it is immensely evocative of the troubled times in which it was built, with its towering walls of rough-hewn stones perforated by narrow undecorated windows and threatening gun loops and its fanciful skyline of projecting cap-houses decorated with dormer windows and crow-stepped gables. The exterior is solid and unfriendly for most of its height and it is only at the comparatively secure level of the roof that any semblance of domestic gaiety is permitted to emerge.

The understated entrance is protected by two oval gun-loops. It led into a service area on the ground floor with stone-vaulted cellars and a kitchen located in one of the towers. Two staircases contained in turrets in the re-entrant angles led up to the first-floor hall and there were private chambers on the floors above. Along part of the south and north faces of the main tower there are two open wall-head walks from which the occupants could fire down onto any attackers laying siege to the building.

Such precautions would have been totally incomprehensible to an English builder by this date, but it was the necessity to make prudent arrangements for defence, indicative of the continuing survival of feudal attitudes and the weakness of central government, which dictated the form of Scottish sixteenth-century domestic building and inspired its distinctive architectural qualities. These qualities transcend the merely utilitarian and form an evocative legacy which owes very little to foreign influences and nearly everything to native ingenuity. Although radically different from the country houses of England and Wales, they exhibit the same vigorous spirit of confidence and creative independence which made the architecture of the period such a flourishing and exciting art form.

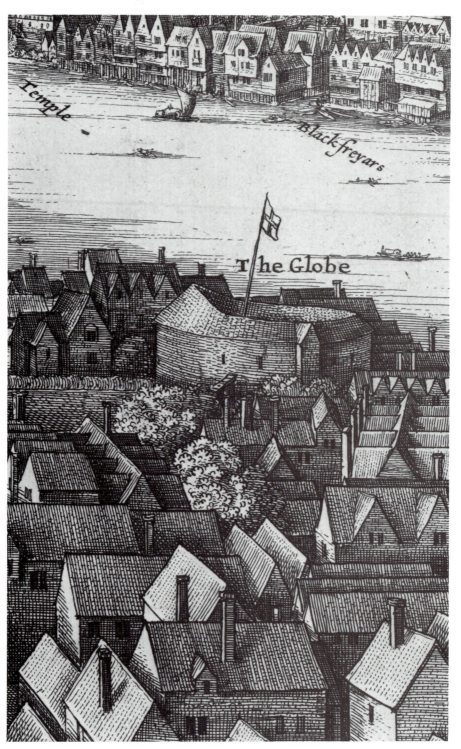

Section of Wenceslaus Hollar's Long View of London, *showing the Globe Theatre (1647).*

2 Literature and Drama

DEREK TRAVERSI

Introduction

Like other outstanding creative achievements, the English literature of the sixteenth century was the outcome of fruitful tensions held in constantly shifting balance. Elements, both intellectual and popular, stemming from the Middle Ages survived side by side with the powerful new forces generated by political and religious transformation; and they were furthered by the various currents we bring together under the general name of the Renaissance.

At the beginning of the period the country was barely beginning to feel its way out of the consequences of the final demise of the feudal order during the preceding hundred years. The collapse of the traditional foundations of society was reflected, in the field of literature, by the unsettled state of the language. Poetry, more particularly, was affected by deep-seated uncertainty concerning such matters as the fall of accents, the value of rhyming words, and the state of the final 'e', a survival from the earlier inflected language which continued to be written but was becoming obsolete in pronunciation. These changes, together with important shifts in the meaning attached to words, meant that the great achievement of Chaucer was no longer readily available to later writers. In Scotland, indeed, a continuing tradition, exemplified in the *Moral Fables* and *Testament of Cresseid* of Robert Henryson (*c.* 1425–1500) and the poems of William Dunbar (*c.* 1460–*c.* 1520) as well as in the notable translation of Virgil's *Aeneid* by Gavin Douglas (*c.* 1475–1522), produced some of the best writing of the early part of the century; but this work, like the vigorous satires and lyrics of the English poet–priest John Skelton (*c.* 1460–1529), may perhaps be best considered in relation to the end of the preceding period.

With the establishment of the Tudor monarchy after Henry VII's victory in 1485 new developments began to assert themselves. The King no doubt thought of his rule in traditional terms, but the needs of government and the virtual elimination of the old aristocracy favoured the creation of a class of administrators, merchants, and professional men upon whom the ability of the kingdom to respond to the challenge of a changing world increasingly depended. These changes were backed by developments which led to the transformation of life in the course of the period. The invention of printing, introduced into England by William Caxton in 1473, came at a time when the religious controversy generated by the Reformation led to an unprecedented expansion of the appetite for argument and confutation. Above all, by making more generally available the work of reformers like Wycliffe and Tyndale in translating the Scriptures, the new processes made possible the publication in 1611 of the Authorized Version of the Bible, perhaps the most influential single book in the entire history of the language.

Side by side with the growing power of the printed word, and furthered by it, was the penetration into educated English circles of the 'humanist' ideas arriving from Europe. The recovery of the texts of Latin and Greek antiquity, and their study and dissemination by scholarly-inclined men at the universities, coincided with the creation of the class of administrators and educators which the political order required. The transformation of literature was furthered by reference to classical ideas of rhetoric and by the early development of what later came to be seen as literary criticism.

The career of Thomas More (1478–1535), who combined dedication to the new scholarship with a public vocation that led him to become, in 1527, the first layman to rise to the office of Chancellor under Henry VIII, is a living example of the tensions which arose when the aspirations of the humanists were confronted by the currents of religious and political violence unleashed by the Reformation. His early years were those of correspondence with Erasmus, who lectured at Cambridge between 1509 and 1511, and with a generation of scholars and educationalists inspired by the new ideals and hopeful of participating in the creation of a better world. The literary expression of this side of More's activities was the *Utopia* (1515), written in Latin and purporting to describe a traveller's account of an ideal commonwealth, the details of which are influenced by Plato's *Republic* and by the ideas of such Italian humanists as Marsilio Ficino (1433–99) and Giovanni Pico della Mirandola. Against highly critical description, in the first part, of the often sad realities of contemporary European politics, More sets a vision, itself slightly ironic beneath the surface, of an ideal state of affairs, of what 'ought to be'. The presence of irony points, however disarmingly, to the pressure of other and more disturbing realities. Side by side with the More who was at home in the world of international humanism is the More whose political responsibilities eventually faced him with intolerable choices. Unwillingly involved in the matter of the King's divorce and forced to take a decision he would have preferred to avoid, More stood by the truth as he conceived it, and died for it. His *Dialogue of Comfort in Tribulation* (1535), written in English whilst facing execution for treason, shows him returning under stress to traditional sources of spiritual comfort and reflects powerfully the changes operated in him by circumstance since the time of the *Utopia*.

After the death of Henry VIII in 1547, and the double swing to contrasted religious extremes under Edward VI and Mary, the way was open for a compromise which was able to take into account, and use, the powerful new forces of Protestantism and nationalism whilst maintaining the link with older traditions. The religious settlement promoted by Elizabeth from 1558 bore fruit, through the *Book of Common Prayer*, in a liturgy which penetrated the national consciousness at every level and exercised an incalculable influence on the later development of literature in English. It also produced, at the end of the period, an impressive monument in Richard Hooker's *Laws of Ecclesiastical Polity* (1593–7): a work seeking to define the Anglican position against what it regarded as the contrary excesses of Counter-Reformation Catholicism and extreme Protestantism and which in the process of restating traditional theology rose to an eloquent assertion of the majesty of universal law.

At the same time as these developments in the religious order, the period was marked by the flowering of a conception of courtliness which married the ideals of humanism to traditional conceptions of chivalry and placed both at the service of a patriotism which found expression in fervent, at times almost idolatrous exaltation of the figure of the Queen. Effective power had largely passed into the hands of the class of royal servants who advised the monarch and guaranteed the continuity of policies. But literature, music, and the courtly arts, celebrated in Baldassere Castiglione's immensely influential treatise of 1528 on the courtly life, flourished in the following of an ideal of gracious courtliness at once intensely pursued and remote from the realities of a world in which intrigue, ambition, and conscious artifice were pervasive. This uneasy balance between ideal and reality marks some of the outstanding literary achievements of the time. Building on the early pioneering work of such poets as Henry Howard, Earl of Surrey (1518–47) and Sir Thomas Wyatt (1503–42) and associated with the idealised figure of Sir Philip Sidney (1554–86), this line finally came to fruition in Edmund Spenser's great unfinished poem, *The Faerie Queene* (1590–6).

Parallel to this flowering of courtly literature, another line of development released powerful forces into the rise of a new secular drama. This, whilst open to humanist influences and building in part on the examples provided by the Latin plays of Seneca in tragedy and of Terence and Plautus in comedy, also preserved and developed older, popular sources of life handed down from previous generations. The unity of intellectual and popular elements established in the theatre was, while it lasted, supremely fruitful. Associated at first with the so-called 'University wits', the first generation of professional secular playwrights, it produced the powerful genius of Christopher Marlowe (1564–93) and led finally to the supreme expression of its possibilities in the work of Shakespeare (1564–1616).

By 1603, as the Queen's long reign came to an end, there were signs that this fruitful combination of aristocratic and popular elements was tending to be replaced by the rise of new issues marking the birth of a new age. The adventurous discoveries of the Elizabethan period were leading to the formulation of the 'new philosophy' which the poet John Donne (1572–1631) saw, in a much-quoted phrase, as placing 'all in doubt'. The prose writing of Francis Bacon (1561–1626), in Latin and in English, marks the transition from a period which had found its prevailing expression in poetry. It might be said that Bacon's *Advancement of Learning* (1605), with its emphasis on the study of effective causes and on the investigation of empirical fact as the only trustworthy source of truth, tended to replace Hooker's traditional celebration of law as the sign of a change in outlook. In social terms the affirmation – already foreseen in the earlier period – of assertive mercantile and financial forces was accompanied by a stress on individual enterprise which became an increasing source of concern for reflective and morally inclined minds. The dramatic work of Ben Jonson (1572–1637), with its exposures of acquisitive greed and the ruthless abuse of material advantage, combines traditional attitudes with the depiction of contemporary evils, giving powerful expression to the moral concerns of a changing time.

Many of these developments can be seen now as reflecting the birth pangs of a new social and economic order; but they did not present themselves under that light to many of those involved in the process of transformation and much of what was written in the first decades of the new century reflects a sense of disorientation and rejection which contrasts strikingly with what had gone before. In more general terms, the fusion of courtly and popular elements which had inspired much of what was best in the literature of the Elizabethan period showed signs of giving way to a separation. Literature in its dramatic and poetic forms became more distinctively, and in some sense more limitedly 'courtly', and the elements of religious and social conflict which were eventually to emerge in the form of civil war made themselves felt as harbingers of a new age.

The literature of humanism and the court; Spenser

The middle years of the sixteenth century were not, generally speaking, favourable to the creation of literature. From the first raising of the question of his divorce from Catherine of Aragon, Henry's court became an increasingly insecure place, where the fortunes and in many cases the lives of those who might have been expected to bring the new literature into being were at stake. The decade that followed his death, marked by violent swings between religious extremes, was also unpropitious. Not until the accession of the new Queen in 1558 and the laying of the foundations, political and religious, of the Elizabethan settlement was it possible for the conditions that produced the great writing of the age – the flowering of elements both courtly and popular in a context of confident and assertive nationalism – to come into being.

The interim period, however, deeply troubled as it was, did produce work that was not only impressive in its own right but indicative of the creative resurgence that was to follow. In 1557 the printer Richard Tottell published a miscellany of poems by courtly writers under the title of *Songs and Sonnettes, written by the right honorable Lorde Henry Howard late Earle of Surrey, and other*: the first and most important of a number of collections of poems and songs that followed in the course of Elizabeth's reign. Tottell's anthology is in fact composed of poems written somewhat earlier. Much of it is conventional and limited in appeal, but the most significant part is devoted to two poets – Henry Howard, Earl of Surrey, and Sir Thomas Wyatt – whose work confirms that the foundations, linguistic and formal, upon which the new courtly poetry was to build, had been well and truly laid.

Surrey's short and brilliant life, which ended in his execution on a trumped up charge of treason, reflects the troubled nature of his times. A number of his poems, including an elegy for Wyatt and the sensitive evocation of a more happy past in the poem beginning 'So cruel prison' written during a period of imprisonment at Windsor, show Surrey at his most appealing. To the historian of literature he is best remembered as a formal innovator, the poet who introduced into England the sonnet form perfected by the fourteenth-century Italian poet Petrarch and who almost accidentally discovered blank verse in his attempt to find an English equivalent for the metre used by Virgil in his version of the *Aeneid*.

Surrey, however, though a finished performer in the best of his sonnets and not without merit in his translation of Virgil, is a less interesting poet than Wyatt. Wyatt too, as a member of Henry VIII's court in its increasingly dangerous later years, led a precarious life in which official posts and diplomatic missions to France, Italy, and the court of the Emperor Charles V alternated with involvement in courtly intrigues and two periods of imprisonment at the time of the downfall of Anne Boleyn and of the arrest and execution of Thomas Cromwell, who had been his patron. This troubled career inspired in Wyatt a disillusionment which is movingly expressed in a series of verse epistles and satires. It led finally to a retirement from public life motivated by the pessimism of a sensitive and concerned man reacting with deep feeling against the brutal and treacherous insecurity of his environment.

The understanding of Wyatt's poetry has been affected, for later ages, by a continuing uncertainty about the nature of the language in which he wrote. Accustomed by the example of later poets to look for metrical regularity in the verse forms used by Wyatt, we are often left in doubt as to where accents were intended to fall or how what we think of as a regular line may be produced from what we read. The difficulty evidently reflects to some degree the uncertain state of a language which was only beginning to emerge from a period of deep and often chaotic change. That these uncertainties were felt in his own time is indicated by the fact that Tottell felt bound on occasions to impose his own sense of metrical regularity on what he evidently saw as Wyatt's irregular lines. We should not, however, be too hasty in imposing our own notions of what is regular. Some at least of Wyatt's apparent irregularities turn out to be inseparable from the meaning of his poems. They appear to derive from the survival of the medieval alliterative line, with its emphasis on spoken stress as opposed to syllabic regularity, shown in the work of such poets as Langland and the author of the *Gawain* poem. To read many of Wyatt's best lines as failures to achieve the regularity which a later and different conception of scansion would enjoin is often to remain blind to some of his most powerful effects.

These difficulties are least apparent in Wyatt's 'songs', where the tendency to 'irregularity' is likely to have been controlled by the need to allow for musical accompaniment. The best of these lyrics, developed in admirably controlled stanzas that lead to a skilfully modulated final refrain, represent poetry of a high order. Typical is the song entitled 'Steadfastness':

Forget not yet the tried intent
Of such a truth as I have meant:
My great travail so gladly spent
   Forget not yet!

. . .

Forget not yet the great assays,
The cruel wrong, the scornful ways,
The painful patience in delays,
   Forget not yet!

Forget not yet, forget not this,
How long ago hath been, and is,
The mind that never meant amiss
   Forget not yet!

Forget not then thine own approved,
The which so long hath thee so loved,
Whose steadfast faith yet never moved;
   Forget not this!

The sense of regularity, occasioned here by Wyatt's deference to the metrical form, does not exclude a carefully controlled cumulative effect. Each stanza is crafted to read as an intensification of the mood conveyed in its predecessor. In the first, the effect is gained by an intensifying use of rhyme ('intent': 'meant': 'spent'), with the emphasis finally resting on the painful contrast between 'great travail' and '*gladly* spent'. In the second stanza printed above, the rhythm is varied, after 'great assays', by the double stress of 'The cruel wrong, the scornful ways', which in turn finds a painful release in the unbroken line which follows. The gathering stress is carried to a further level of intensity in the next stanza, with its urgent repetition – 'Forget not *yet*, forget not *this*' – leading with the calculated shift of the rhythmical break in the line which follows – 'How long ago hath been, *and is*' – into a plea for understanding, acceptance of sorely tried sincerity, in 'The mind that never meant amiss'. As the poem moves to its close, the statement of 'steadfast faith' leads to a modification of the refrain – 'Forget not *this*!' – just emphatic enough to avoid the danger, which the form entails, of mechanical development.

This, evidently, is poetry which is concerned with more than the conventional 'complaints' of the courtly lover. 'Truth' and 'steadfastness' are words which evidently mean a great deal to Wyatt; they represent the central human values which he sees everywhere betrayed around him. A handful of his longer poems show him using a more extended line to remarkable effect. Outstanding among these is the poem entitled 'Remembrance', with its poignant evocation of a bitter and dangerous relationship:

They flee from me, that sometime did me seek
   With naked foot, stalking in my chamber.
I have seen them gentle, tame, and meek,
   That now are wild, and do not remember
That sometime they put themselves in danger
   To take bread at my hand; and now they range
   Busily seeking with a continual change.

Thanked be fortune it hath been otherwise,
   Twenty times better; but once, in special,
In thin array, after a pleasant guise,
   When her loose gown from her shoulders did fall,
And she caught me in her arms long and small,
   Therewith all sweetly did me kiss
   And softly said, 'Dear heart, how like you this?'

It was no dream: I lay broad waking:
   But all is turned, thorough my gentleness,
Into a strange fashion of forsaking;
   And I have leave to go of her goodness,
And she also to use newfangleness.
   But since that I so kindly am served,
   I would fain know what she hath deserved.

The familiar iambic line, with its ten syllables and its alternation of stressed
and unstressed units, serves here as the foundation for shifts of sense and
feeling which play across it to powerful effect, especially in the use of the
metrical break at the half-line, or between lines, to underline situations of
particular urgency: 'With naked foot, | *stalking* . . .': 'it hath been otherwise,
| *Twenty times better*': 'It was no dream; *I lay broad waking*'. Repeatedly, the
accented syllables stand out from the expected pattern; and always the effect
is not one of incoherence or imperfect mastery of the form, but one which
is used deliberately to present an emotional situation raised to very personal
heights of tension. In contrast to these lines, with their stress on remembered
peril – 'stalking', 'wild', 'danger' – others find issue in a present sense of
disillusionment and betrayal: 'But all is turned, | thorough my gentleness, ||
Into a strange fashion of forsaking'. The rhythm carries us with it, forces us
to respond to the contrast between the break which modifies the regular flow
in the first of these lines and the continuity which, in the second, carries the
speaking voice forward in a natural surrender to the rhythmic flow. The
effect is appropriate to a poem dominated by that sense of betrayal, of the
contrast between remembered hopes and present disillusionment, which
marks the reaction of a humane and sensitive man to his stimulating and
dangerous times.

Surrey and Wyatt wrote at a time when the dangers of the courtier's life
were more apparent than its attractions, and both suffered the consequences
of serving a ruthless and incalculable master. It was not until the accession to
the throne of Elizabeth that the conditions were laid for a more stable
development. Effective power, indeed, was increasingly exercised less by
courtiers than by a new breed of effective administrators, the Burghleys and
Walsinghams who directed the control of policy. The life of the courtier came
to be seen as an elaborately formal game, dedicated to the royal fountain-
head of favour and expressive of a highly artificial ideal. The aspiring
courtier was encouraged to see himself as the complete man, trained in the
arts of war which he cultivated in highly formalised tournaments, skilled in
the practice of poetry and music, the exemplar of the ideal advanced by such
writers as Castiglione which so often stood in ironic contrast to the realities
of servility, intrigue, and insecurity which lay not far beneath the brilliant

image presented to the world. If Castiglione expressed the most attractive side of this largely fictitious world, a great part of its reality is to be found in another and notably less idealising treatise: Machiavelli's *Prince* (1527), the text of which became available in English (and then in a form considerably distorted by the passions generated by religious controversy) only in 1577.

The virtues which inspired the new conception of courtliness were felt by his contemporaries to be embodied in the person of Philip Sidney, who was born in 1554 and died thirty-two years later after being fatally wounded on a field of battle in Holland. Acclaimed as poet, scholar, diplomat, soldier and courtier: nephew of the Queen's favourite, the Earl of Leicester, and brother of the Countess of Pembroke, Sidney seems to have been uneasily aware of the expectations which rested upon him and of the difficulty of living up to them. The result is, beneath the artifice which this situation imposed upon him, a body of work which at once answers to his need to give expression to the ideal embodied in the convention and reflects, in its moments of engaging intimacy, a somewhat rueful sense of the absurdity of some of his more ambitious efforts to give them embodiment.

During his life-time, Sidney's writings, like those of many of his contemporaries, remained unpublished, though they were widely circulated in manuscript form. His most extensive work, the *Arcadia*, passed through various stages of re-writing which corresponded to changes in his way of conceiving his project. The earliest version seems to have been written in the 1570s and was only published for the first time in 1926. In his later years Sidney engaged in a series of revisions of his work, which notably altered its character but which remained unfinished at his death. The incomplete revision was published in 1590, and in 1592 the Countess of Pembroke, to whom it had been dedicated, brought out a version consisting of the unfinished revision completed with the text as it had stood in the original manuscript.

The original *Arcadia* is a pastoral love story with a political background. Basilius, Duke of Arcadia, renounces his responsibilities to live in rural retirement with his queen Gynecia and two daughters, Pamela and Philoclea. They are followed there by two princes, Pyrocles and Musidorus, who fall in love with the princesses and pursue their suits by assuming disguises, Musidorus as a shepherd and Pyrocles as an Amazon princess. The assumption of disguises leads them into unexpected situations. Pyrocles in his female impersonation rouses the passions both of the Duke and of Gynecia, who is attracted by the male reality beneath the disguise. After a series of misfortunes, in the course of which Basilius inadvertently takes a potion which seems to kill him and in which Gynecia is accused of murder and the princes of sedition, the situation is saved by the intervention of Evarchus, King of Macedonia. The princes are brought to trial and condemned to death in spite of the fact that they are revealed to be the unrecognised son and nephew of Evarchus. Gynecia also accepts her punishment; but before the story ends the supposedly dead Basilius, reviving and recognising his failure to exercise his royal responsibilities, reverses the sentences and is restored to his wife.

The revised *Arcadia* provides a more complicated plot and a more explicit moral intention. It introduces a wicked sister-in-law, Cecropia, who

persecutes Pamela and Philoclea and one of the princes. The two heroines
overcome these trials with the support of the traditional virtues of fidelity and
patience, which they exhibit in a variety of circumstances. In this later form
the original chronological sequence is largely abandoned, many new episodes
are introduced, and emphasis is laid upon elements tending to the expression
of an ideal of noble and chivalrous gentility.

The *Arcadia* develops its complicated narrative in an elaborate prose which
shares some of its qualities with those shown in the work of Sidney's
contemporary John Lyly (*c.* 1554–1606) to which the term 'Euphuistic' has
been attached following the title of his highly popular prose romance
Euphues, of 1578. Although the style is apt to strike a modern reader as
intolerably artificial, and though it was often satirised in its own time, some
of its qualities make their presence felt in more memorable work, including
some of Shakespeare's most successful comedies. Sidney's romance also
weaves into its narrative a number of poems in a variety of verse forms –
including the intricate sestina 'Ye Goatherd Gods', a form taken from
Petrarch and developed to even greater complexity – which appealed to
contemporary readers for their novelty and for the skill exhibited in handling
the rhyming schemes with confidence and grace.

Sidney's most important poems, however, are those included in the
Astrophel and Stella sonnet sequence, which will be considered below, and a
certain number brought together to accompany the published *Arcadia*. A few,
and among them some of the best, stand apart from the normal conventions
of courtly versifying. We know from Sidney's prose *Apology for Poetry* that
he was responsive to the traditional forms of lyric and ballad which survived
side by side with the new sophisticated forms of poetry. Expressive of this
vein is the hauntingly beautiful poem which opens with the line 'Only joy,
now here you are'. Its successive stanzas concern a lover pleading with his
mistress to respond to his secret passion, only to meet with the refrain – 'No,
no, no, no, my dear, let be' – which binds the poem into a tautly conceived
dramatic progression. As the lover points to the security which the cloak of
night favours – 'Fear not, else none can us spy' – his words become possessed
of an increasing urgency:

> That you heard was but a mouse,
> Dumb sleep holdeth all the house;
> Yet asleep, methinks, they say,
> Young folks, take time while you may;
> Take me to thee, and thee to me.
> 'No, no, no, no, my dear, let be.'

As the thought of the suitor turns to the unsuspecting sleepers who share the
darkness with them, a note of deception enters the exchange, urgent in its
effect and simple in its expression:

> Your fair mother is a-bed,
> Candles out and curtains spread;
> She thinks you do letters write;
> Write, but let me first endite.

In the concluding stanzas, as the lover advances his final plea – 'Sweet, alas, why strive you thus? / Concord better fitteth us' – he recognises the superior power which he has failed to move from its rejecting stance – 'Your power in your beauty stands' – and ends with the reproachful anticipation of his own death which poetic convention imposes upon the rejected suitor: 'Soon with my death I will please thee.' The four stressed beats – 'I will please thee' – which round off this final line serve as an admirably effective conclusion to this tensely moving poem.

With Edmund Spenser (1552–99), the courtly line of poetic writing reached the height of its achievement. First stimulated to an interest in letters at Cambridge by the humanist scholar Gabriel Harvey, Spenser entered the service of the Earl of Leicester and came under the influence of Sidney. Choice and circumstance, in other words, inclined him as a young writer to the courtly conception of literature which he developed to the full extent of its possibilities.

Spenser's poetic reputation rested initially on the publication, in 1579, of *The Shepheardes Calender*, a set of poems which seems to have exercised upon his contemporaries an appeal in some ways greater than that of *The Faerie Queene*. The twelve pieces which constitute the series, one for each month of the year, introduce into English poetry a vein of pastoral dialogue which had its origins in the work of the Greek Sicilian poets of the third century BC, Theocritus, Bion, and Moschus, and which Renaissance writers in Italy and France used extensively, following the example set by Virgil in his *Eclogues*. The attraction of the *Calender* for Spenser's age rested largely on the achievement of a polished and varied literary form capable of covering a wide variety of themes: political controversy and religious denunciation (as in Piers' attack on the abuses of religion in the *May* eclogue), the sophisticated use of popular motives (in *August*), a 'lofty' style to declare Spenser's view of the seriousness of his poetic vocation (Piers again in *October*), the elegiac pessimism of *November*, and the cultivated use of natural motives in *December*. This variety of theme and tone, together with the mastery of a wide range of poetic forms, evidently affected contemporary readers with a sense of novelty which seemed to enlarge the possibilities open to poetry. For a later age, however, *The Shepheardes Calender* must remain one of those works which are more memorable for their historical importance than for any continuing appeal which they may exercise.

The *Calender*, of course, was in Spenser's mind a preparation for other and greater works. Its eclogues were written partly to perfect a style and partly to open the way into the inner circles of court society, at least in its literary aspirations. By an ironic turn of Fortune, however – and there is nothing abstract or removed from lived reality in the court poet's preoccupation with the vagaries of that fickle deity – the publication of the series was followed almost immediately by an exclusion from this society that proved, for Spenser, almost final. In 1580 Leicester's fall from favour affected in varying degrees those who had depended on his patronage. For Spenser, exclusion took the form of a kind of semi-exile, for he was sent to Ireland as Secretary to the Lord Deputy who governed in the Queen's name that remote, barbarous, and unhappy island. Although he returned to England from time to time Spenser evidently felt deeply this banishment from what was for him

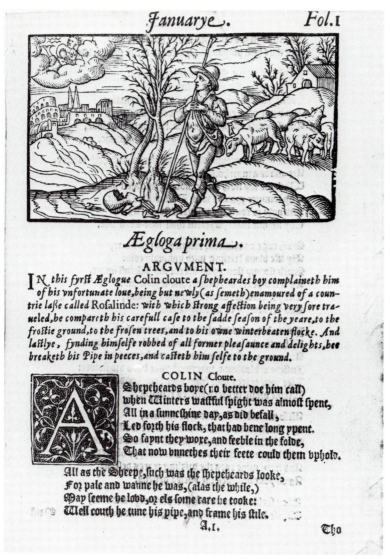

A page from Edmund Spenser's The Shepheardes Calender *(1579).*

the centre of civilised life, and currents of emotion provoked by it play a discernible part in his mature work.

The state of semi-exile did not prevent Spenser from producing a body of poetry which shows at its best a considerable advance from the artificial graces of the *Calender*. The most successful of these poems, perhaps, are *Mother Hubberd's Tale* of 1591, a sharp satire on contemporary affairs in the form of a beast fable in rhyming couplets that makes effective use of a Chaucerian model, and *Colin Clout's Come Home Again* of 1595, which is concerned with a visit to London in the company of Walter Raleigh and with the disillusionment which the spectacle of life at court produced in him and

which led him to return to Ireland. In a more philosophic vein, Spenser
published in 1596 *Four Hymns*, the first two of which, dedicated to Love and
Beauty, were early works, whilst the latter pair, in praise of Heavenly Love
and Heavenly Beauty, belong to his later years. The academic Platonism of
the earlier hymns is largely repudiated in the later poems in favour of
Christian doctrines principally Calvinistic in their formulation. The poems,
important as indications of Spenser's developing thought, hardly add much to
his literary reputation.

This is emphatically not the case with the two marriage poems –
'Epithalamion', of 1594, and 'Prothalamion', of 1596 – which bear
comparison with the highest achievements of his, or indeed of any age.
'Epithalamion', written to celebrate his marriage to Elizabeth Boyle, is
marked by Spenser's superb command of the long and elaborate verse
paragraph, by a splendid musicality, and by the successful weavings of a
variety of elements, ranging from classical myth and Platonising philosophy
to Christian doctrine and English folk-lore, into a controlled progression
which the incantatory refrain at the end of each stanza serves to carry
forward and bind into unity. The poem advances through the events of the
wedding day, culminating in the arrival of the bride, her presence at the
ceremony, and her triumphant return for the consummation of the marriage:

> Now al is done; bring home the bride againe,
> Bring home the triumph of our victory,
> Bring home with you the glory of her gaine,
> With joyance bring her and with jollity.
> Never had man more joyfull day than this,
> Whom heaven would heape with blis,
> Make feast therefore now all this live long day,
> This day for ever to me holy is,
> Poure out the wine without restraint or stay,
> Poure not by cups, but by the belly full,
> Poure out to all that wull,
> And sprinkle all the postes and wals with wine,
> That they may sweat, and drunken be withall.
> Crown ye God Bacchus with a coronall,
> And Hymen also crowne with wreathes of vine,
> And let the Graces daunce unto the rest;
> For they can do it best:
> The whiles the maydens doe theyr carroll sing,
> To which the woods shal answer and theyr eccho ring.

The sheer skill involved in the sustained handling of the intricate pattern of
rhyme and rhythm as the poem moves towards its controlled explosion of
emotion must have struck contemporary readers as unprecedented in English.
Towards the close of the day's long, stately progression, the poet expresses
his longing for the coming of night:

> Ah when will this long weary day have end,
> And lende me leave to come unto my love?
> How slowly do the houres theyr number spend?
> How slowly does sad Time his feathers move?
> Hast thee O fayrest Planet to thy home
> Within the Western fome . . .

As darkness descends, peace and blessing are invoked on the bridal pair, the moon rises, and Juno and Genius, patrons of the marriage bed, are required to bestow the blessing of fruitfulness.

The second marriage poem, 'Prothalamion', written to celebrate the double wedding of Lady Elizabeth and Lady Catherine Somerset, is more formal, less ecstatically personal in tone. A note of heraldry prevails, lending the poem something of a tapestry effect; but Spenser's skill in the deployment of his elaborate stanza emerges in a tone of measured stateliness as it advances to its triumphant conclusion. The invocation to 'sweet Thames' sustained through the entire course of the poem has an important double function. Besides affirming the unity which governs each separate stanza, it serves to relate the development of the whole to the movement of the stream. As the poem reaches its conclusion the onward flow brings the bridal pair – the 'two Swannes of goodly hewe' which come 'softly swimming downe along the lea' – to 'those high Towers', the aristocratic residence from which the 'noble Lord', the presiding genius of this high ceremony, is seen issuing forth, like 'radiant Hesper', in the company of the 'Two gentle knights of lovely face and feature' who are to receive their destined partners 'at th'appointed tyde'.

The most ambitious product of Spenser's years of semi-exile, written in Ireland and brought to England for publication during two brief returns, was *The Faerie Queene*. No English poem of comparable scope and literary stature has appealed, for such widely different reasons, to so many later poets or proved so elusive to critical definition. Milton admired its author as 'our sage and serious Spenser' and as 'a better teacher than Scotus or Aquinas'. Keats, Shelley, and Byron used the Spenserian stanza to varied effect, and Keats in particular was greatly attracted to the sensual qualities of the work. Wordsworth spoke in one of his poems of

> Sweet Spenser, moving through his clouded heaven
> With the moon's beauty and the moon's soft pace.

The variety of these responses, testifying to the continuing fascination exercised by 'the poets' poet', answers to a protean quality in the poem, suggesting the difficulty which faces any attempt to define the nature of Spenser's achievement by confining it to any limiting critical formula.

The difficulty does not arise from any failure on the poet's part to state his purpose. In a letter to Walter Raleigh, prefixed to the 1590 edition of the first three Books, Spenser declared that 'the general end . . . of all the book is to fashion a gentleman or noble person in virtue and gentle discipline'. He also pointed to the influence of previous writers – Homer, Virgil, Ariosto, and Tasso – 'by example of which excellent poets I labour to portray in Arthur, before he was king, the image of a brave knight, perfected in the twelve private moral virtues'. He goes on to say that these virtues are 'the purpose of these first twelve books, which if I find to be well accepted, I may be perhaps encouraged to frame the other part of politic virtues in his person, after that he came to be king'. Finally, he states that 'In that Faery Queen I mean glory in my general intention, but in my particular I conceive the most excellent and glorious person of our sovereign the Queen, and her kingdom in Fairy Land.'

The application to the poem of this plan, which seems to envisage a work four times as long as the huge fragment actually completed, is fraught with difficulties. Most obviously, we have only six books and what seems to be the fragment of a seventh, published for the first time as 'Two Cantos of Mutability' after the poet's death. Further, it is possible to find a certain completeness in the poem as it actually stands. A plan could be discerned in which Book I, devoted to the adventures of the Knight of the Red Cross representing Holiness in search of the Truth to be found in unity, might be linked to Book VI, in which the adventures of Sir Calidore, embodying the virtue of Courtesy, show holiness in action in the ideal courtly world. Similarly Book II, which presents in Sir Guyon the virtue of Temperance responding to a variety of temptations, might be linked to Book V, where the adventures of Sir Artegall show the same virtue engaged in striving to affirm the values of Justice in a difficult public world. According to this plan Books III and IV, dealing respectively with the stories of Britomart and of Cambel and Telamond, would constitute the turning-point of the whole conception. The two Books are united by the presence in them of one of Spenser's most attractive creations, the female knight Britomart, who represents in the third Book the virtue of Chastity, but who is linked in the fourth with Friendship to stress the fact, centrally important for Spenser's work, that the traditional virtue finds its fulfilment, not in ascetic denial of the flesh or withdrawal from the world, but in the socially central and creative relationship of marriage. If this possible scheme has any validity, the two Cantos on Mutability would constitute less the fragment of a seventh Book than a kind of coda placing the whole project in a philosophic context which turns on the relationship between Time and Eternity, the human world of temporal vicissitude and the timeless order of spiritual reality. This, in the last stanza of the work as it has come to us, is 'that same time when no more Change shall be'; for, though it is true that 'all that moveth, doth in Change delight', the poet asks us, as his final word, to join him in looking beyond this temporal truth to the final state in which

> . . . thence-forth all shall rest eternally
> With Him that is the God of Sabbaoth height,

as he addresses what he sees as the final source of all reality: 'O that great Sabbaoth God, graunt me that Sabbaoth's sight.'

The scheme just outlined of a possible plan for Spenser's poem is, like any other that we might propose, tentative and uncertain. We can use it as an anchor for our own perceptions, but would be unwise to claim any final validity for it. What is certain is that Spenser in writing his poem set out to rival or surpass the practitioners of the Arthurian epic as cultivated in Italy, more particularly by Ariosto in his *Orlando Furioso*. It would be difficult, however, to think of two poems more different in feeling and intention. Ariosto is essentially a narrator, who delights in his ability to keep an endless thread of incident moving and who presents his fantastic world in vividly real terms, projecting upon the whole the light of a pervasive comic irony. The effect of Spenser's poem is at once less consistent and more closely tied to the moral vision which has gone into its making.

These influences, indeed, grow into rich complexity as the poem unfolds. The first two Books are those which correspond most obviously to the declared allegorical pattern. In Book I the Red Cross Knight, representing the Holiness which is the source of all virtue, is accompanied by Una, who is Truth made manifest in unity. The pair proceed through a series of adventures which correspond to the temptations of doctrinal error and the moral ills occasioned by it. Already, however, the development of the allegory is not one of simple correspondence. The Red Cross Knight, besides representing Holiness, is also Everyman in pursuit of that virtue and in need of the help of Grace and the possession of Truth to arrive at his goal. The allegory is many-sided, which is not a sign of weakness or intellectual incoherence, but of the inclusiveness of the poet's vision, his unwillingness to be restricted to any single element of the many he is weaving into his conception. Similarly, in Book II, where traces of the simple pattern of allegory persist, we are to see Sir Guyon both as representing the virtue of Temperance, which is a compound of equanimity, prudence, and self-control, and as a figure once again of Everyman tempted from moral and spiritual health by a variety of ills which he overcomes by arriving at a reasonable relationship between body and soul.

Up to this point the reader of the poem can feel that he is following a pattern of allegorical meanings which correspond to the development of the narrative. Already, however, submission to the poetry elicits a more complex response. This becomes apparent, for example, at the end of Book II, in the long description of the Bower of Bliss and of the witch Acrasia, the personified temptation at its heart:

> Upon a bed of Roses she was layd,
>   As faint through heat, or dight to pleasant sin,
>   And was arayd, or rather disarayd,
>   All in a vale of silke and silver thin,
>   That hid no whit her alabaster skin,
>   But rather shewd more white, if more might bee:
>   More subtile web Arachne cannot spin,
>   Nor the fine nets, which oft we woven see
> Of scorched deaw, do not in th'aire more lightly flee.
>
> Her snowy breast was bare to readie spoyle
>   Of hungry eies, which n'ote therwith be fild,   [*would not*]
>   And yet through languor of her late sweete toyle,
>   Few drops, more cleare than Nectar, forth distild,
>   That like pure Orient perles adowne it trild,
>   And her faire eyes sweet smyling in delight,
>   Moystened their fierie beames, with which she thrild
>   Fraile harts, yet quenched not; like starry light
> Which sparckling on the silent waves, does seeme more bright.
>
> (*F. Q.* II. xii. 77–8)

The poetry requires us both to respond to the real force of the passions called forth by Acrasia and to maintain a firm moral judgement in their regard. Words and phrases which stress the languor and artificiality which underlie the surface attraction are interwoven with others which relate to a more positively human perception. Spenser's aim is not to present a pre-established contrast between virtue and vice, but to embody the conflicting pressures which play upon real human experience. The resolution of the conflict will certainly be moral and life-affirming, but it will not be arrived at by prejudging the issue at stake.

By the time we reach the third and fourth Books any attempt to impose abstract meanings is increasingly out of place. In the allegorical scheme Britomart represents Chastity, but in the poem she emerges with the force of a real, breathing person:

> She having hong upon a bough on high
>   Her bow and painted quiver, had unlaste
>   Her silver buskins from her nimble thigh,
>   And her lancke loynes ungirt, and breasts unbraste,   [*unfastened*]
>   After her heat the breathing cold to taste;
>   Her golden lockes, that late in tresses bright
>   Embreaded were for hindring of her haste,   [*pleated*]
>   Now loose about her shoulders hung undight,
> And were with sweet Ambrosia all besprinckled light.
>
> (*F. Q.* III. vi. 18)

Whatever else it may be, this is evidently not the representation of a personified abstraction. The adventures of Britomart in these two central Books concern an exploration of the meaning of real human love, conveyed through contrast and interaction with a series of other feminine figures – Amoret, Belphoebe, and Florimel – who represent varying facets of this moving force in the lives of men and women. In Book III Britomart affirms triumphantly the traditional virtue of Chastity. In Book IV, ostensibly dedicated to Cambel and Telamond in embodiment of male friendship, the exploration of love, its true sense and meaning, continues as Britomart is first involved in combat with Artegall and finally submits to the natural force of love.

Spenser's presentation of Love in these two Books combines elements drawn from Plato's *Symposium* with traditional notions of courtly love, separating in the latter a true ideal from its barren and enslaving shadow. The ideal of chastity represented is not simply one of virginity defended against the assaults of the world, but rather of its natural fulfilment in the creative relationship of lawful wedded love: this against a background of life-affirming acceptance eloquently declared in the apotheosis of Venus in her temple:

> Great Venus, Queene of beautie and of grace,
>   The joy of Gods and men, that under skie
>   Dost fayrest shine, and most adorne thy place,
>   That with thy smyling looke doest pacifie
>   The raging seas, and makst the stormes to flie;
>   Thee goddesse, thee the winds, the clouds do feare,
>   And when thou spredst thy mantle forth on hie,
>   The waters play and pleasant lands appeare,
> And heavens laugh, and al the world shews joyous cheere
>
>   . . .

So all the world by thee at first was made,
  And dayly yet thou doest the same repayre:
  Ne ought on earth that merry is and glad,
  Ne ought on earth that lovely is and fayre,
  But thou the same for pleasure didst prepayre.
  Thou art the root of all that joyous is,
  Great God of men and women, queene of th'ayre,
  Mother of laughter, and welspring of blisse,
O graunt that of my love at last I may not misse.

(F. Q. IV. x. 44, 47)

Representing in part a development from Chaucer's Boethian celebration of the creative power of love in his *Troilus and Criseyde*, the passage evokes some of the most powerful positive forces which animate Spenser's conception, pointing to the principle of life which brings together the various strands of this great and protean poem.

Book V, dealing with the adventures of Sir Artegall, who represents Justice, comes to most modern readers as a disappointment. The sense in the later Cantos of a ruthlessness which seems to reflect the poet's experiences in Ireland acts as a chilling factor which even understanding of the importance, for a Renaissance mind, of the concept of Justice, its relation to a necessary defence against the threat of chaos, can hardly overcome. Book VI, devoted to Sir Calidore and the courtly ideal of Courtesy, is notably less single-minded and more attractive. The virtue celebrated is a development of the medieval conception of 'gentillesse' in accordance with the Platonising philosophy which inspired such works as Castiglione's *Courtier*. The Book abounds in passages of delicate and sometimes nostalgic beauty, the expression of an ideal of courtly perfection which stands in contrast to the often sad realities of human evil and inadequacy. The shadow of the Blatant Beast, representation of the envy and slander which was so rife in Renaissance courts and which no knightly pursuit of personal glory or the tenuous refinements of courtly love could eliminate or contain, lies across the delicate poetry which is perhaps more present here than anywhere in Spenser's work.

In a single passage, towards the end of the Book, this poetry reaches what may be its highest point of perfection. As Sir Calidore, now imaginatively transformed into 'the Elfin Knight', is led by chance to approach a place 'whose plesaunce did appeare / To passe all others, on the earth which were', he is made aware of the 'merry sound' of a 'shrill pipe' and of 'many feete fast thumping th'hollow ground':

There he a troupe of Ladies dauncing found
  Full merrily, and making gladfull glee,
And in the midst a Shepheard piping he did see.

The magic quality of the spectacle moves the knight to awe, making him fearful of entering 'the open greene, / For dread of them unwares to be descryde', or of 'breaking of their daunce, if he were seene'. Remaining under cover of the wood, 'Beholding all, yet of them unespyde', he surrenders himself in contemplation of the dance:

> All they without were raunged in a ring,
>> And daunced round; but in the midst of them
>> Three other Ladies did both daunce and sing,
>> The whilest the rest them round about did hemme,
>> And like a girlond did in compasse stemme;
>> And in the midst of these same three, was placed
>> Another Damsell, as a precious gemme,
>> Amidst a ring most richly well enchased,
> That with her goodly presence all the rest much graced.

(F.Q. VI. x. 12)

The presence of this 'damsel', who 'seem'd' all the rest in beauty to excell', moves the poet to intervene with a series of classical parallels that raise the entire experience to a new imaginative level:

> Looke how the Crowne, which Ariadne wore
>> Upon her young forehead that same day
>> That Theseus her unto his bridal bore,
>> When the bold Centaur made that bloudy fray,
>> With the fierce Lapithes, which did them dismay;
>> Being now placed in the firmament,
>> Through the bright heaven doth her beame display,
>> And is unto the starres an ornament
> Which round about her moved in order excellent.

(F.Q. VI. x. 13)

The vision granted to Calidore is, we are told, of the Graces, 'daughters of delight' and 'handmaides of Venus'. 'All that Venus in her selfe doth vaunt / Is borrowed of them'; but even this beauty is subsidiary to that of the 'faire one / That in the midst was placed paramount': the figure at the heart of the dance 'to whom that shepheard pypt alone'. This is the culminating point of the vision, leading to the introduction into it of 'poor Colin Clout', the poet himself ('who knowes not Colin Clout?'), the humble and yet proud witness of this transfiguring splendour:

> Pype jolly shepheard, pipe there now apace
> Unto thy love, that made thee low to lout: [*bow*]
> Thy love is present there with thee in place,
> Thy love is ther advaunst to be another Grace.

(F. Q. VI. x. 16)

In the face of poetry of this order the attempt to extract from Spenser's enormous poem simple allegorical correspondences becomes irrelevant. The moral purposes declared in the letter to Raleigh no doubt provided him with the starting-point for a work that was certainly intended to embody and advance deeply-held moral convictions; but as we read, we find our awareness of the ostensible moral framework progressively giving way to a surrender to the poetry: not, as some later romantic admirers affirmed, merely to its sensual qualities or to the lulling fascination of sound, but to the imaginative content involved in its world of fiction. The poem, indeed, proceeds by a progressive liberation from the trammels of moralising allegory. As its end approaches, Spenser seems to unite all the rich strands at his disposal to achieve compelling moments of magic vision which answer to the deep-seated humanity of his purpose. Placing himself, with the true artist's mixture of humility and proper pride, in the figure of his Colin Clout at the periphery of a dance of entranced imaginative quality, he has found an image which expresses superbly the unifying and transforming imagination which finally justifies his poem.

The culture of the sonnet

Of the various forms developed by the courtly humanist poets in their efforts to renew the writing of verse in English the most representative is perhaps the sonnet. By the time it reached England in the sixteenth century the sonnet had a long and distinguished literary history. Originating in twelfth-century Provence, it was taken up in Italy and developed by the fourteenth-century poet Petrarch in a series of poems reflecting on the vicissitudes of his idealised love for Laura. Petrarch's poems adapt to his purposes the tradition of courtly love poetry, in which the lover presents himself as the humble servant of a mistress who is alternately complaisant and cruel, and who swings in his devotion between love and despair. His handling of this material, to which he added reflections on mortality arising from Laura's death, is marked by a keen interest in fluctuating states of feeling and by a consistent sense of style which raises the poems to a high level of literary art.

The nature of the sonnet form was such as to make it attractive to poets whose aim it was to refine and extend the possibilities of the language. The convention of courtly love, with its alternatives of precarious exaltation and answering despair, appealed to writers engaged in the elaborate game of aristocratic pretence and in the opportunity for introspective self-projection which it offered. A considerable proportion of Elizabethan sonnets are literary exercises, in which it would be wrong to seek to find any reflection of real relationships or deep emotional commitment. More importantly, the sonnet form presented to aspiring poets a challenge which answered to their literary ambitions. The strictness of its formal limits – the restriction to fourteen lines and the need to conform to a fixed and elaborate rhyming scheme – imposed upon language a distinctive economy and intensity. If many of the poems were conventional in content and expression, making largely mechanical use of 'conceits' which in Petrarch had conveyed real alternations of feeling, their value as literary exercises should not be underestimated; and the best of them allowed the poet to set a precise sense of actuality against a conventional basis which offered enormous possibilities for varying the poetic mood. The relation of personal feeling, where it existed, to an established set of conventions could be used either to intensify the emotional effect or to indicate the presence of irony. Convention, indeed, in the best cases imposed a degree of formal control which only needed to be informed by valid emotion to produce the intensity which marks the outstanding examples of the form.

By the sixteenth century Petrarch's sonnets had become the subject of imitation by poets in Italy, in France, and finally in England. Surrey and Wyatt both attempted the form, often translating directly from Petrarch.

Surrey's efforts in this kind are the more polished and the more faithful to their Italian source. Wyatt's sonnets show more signs of the apparent irregularities which in his best poems often achieve effects of remarkable power and originality. Apart from the poem known from its opening line as 'Whose list to hunt', which appears to spring from a powerful and dangerous personal situation and which hardly falls within the scope of the convention, Wyatt's exercises in this form scarcely reflect the most important aspects of his genius.

The popularity of the sonnet in the final decade of the century owed much to the example of Sidney, whose *Astrophel and Stella*, a sequence of sonnets interspersed with songs, circulated in manuscript form during his life-time and was published after his death in 1591. The sequence, whilst it includes poems which are little more than literary exercises, does seem to reflect upon a personal situation, following the stages of Sidney's unsuccessful courtship of Penelope Devereux, the sister of the Earl of Essex, who rejected his advances in favour of an arranged marriage with the wealthy Lord Rich, who was followed by three other husbands. It would be unwise, however, to lay too much stress upon this possible autobiographical element. The poems offer an anatomy of love presented through an exploration of the lover's mind as it swings between hope and disappointment in the various stages of a continuing psychological action. Sidney's attitude to the conventions on which he largely relies is by no means one of simple acceptance. He is capable of expressing himself somewhat dismissively concerning 'poor Petrarch's long deceased woes' and of refusing to participate in the games of artifice in which, as aspiring poet, he found himself uneasily engaged. When, at the end of the first poem in the sequence, he writes '"Fool", said my Muse to me, "look in thy heart and write"', we are not to attribute to him attitudes to poetic inspiration which belong to a later, more romantic age. He is, however, musing on the insufficiency of his attempts to achieve poetry by following the established literary models –

> Oft turning others' leaves, to see if thence would flow
> Some fresh and fruitful showers upon my sunburned brain –

only to find that 'words came halting forth' and that 'Invention, Nature's child, fled stepdame Study's blows'. Ruefully 'biting' the 'truant pen' which refuses to produce verse which his poetic sense can accept as valid, 'beating [himself] for spite' in frustrated lack of inspiration, he ends by determining to reject empty conceits and by advancing a claim for truth to genuine feeling as the only source of valid poetry.

Some of Sidney's best sonnets turn upon a contrast between the first eight lines (the 'octave') and the concluding 'sextet', a contrast often used to express a conflict between different attitudes to the emotional situations explored. Sometimes a serious presentation in the 'octave' of love in accordance with the accepted conventions is undercut by a 'sextet' which either plays ironically upon it or sets it against a more realistic, a less 'literary' attitude. In the best of these poems artifice and self-centred posturing tend to give way to a recognition of true (though not necessarily directly personal) feeling, and the conventionality which so persistently dogs the sonnet form in the hands of its lesser practitioners is repudiated in favour of a more direct and more honest understanding.

The best of Sidney's sonnets rise beyond these uncertainties to achieve an eloquence that can stand comparison with the highest achievements of this kind. Two poems, from the sequence published posthumously with the *Arcadia* in 1598, may serve as examples. In the first, reflecting on the uneasy compulsions of desire, the poet presents his protagonist as engaged in a struggle to disengage himself from this source of unending disappointment –

> Desire, desire! I have too dearly bought,
> With price of mangled mind, thy worthless ware –

and seeking within himself 'my only hire, / Desiring nought but how to kill desire'. The second sonnet builds on this repudiation to rise to new levels of eloquence:

> Leave me, O Love, which reachest but to dust;
> And thou, my mind, aspire to higher things;
> Grow rich in that which never taketh rust;
> Whatever fades but fading pleasure brings.
> Draw in thy beams, and humble all thy might
> To that sweet yoke where lasting freedoms be;
> Which breaks the clouds and opens forth the light,
> That doth both shine and give the sight to see.
> O take hold fast; let that light be thy guide
> In this small course which birth draws out to death,
> And think how evil becometh him to chide,
> Who seeketh heaven, and comes of heavenly breath.
>   Then farewell, world; thy uttermost I see;
>   Eternal love, maintain thy life in me.

Returning to the great commonplaces in a spirit which might be called that of a Christian Platonism, Sidney's verse rises here beyond its habitual conflicts and uncertainties to achieve a new consistency and rhetorical weight of authority.

Spenser's series of sonnets under the title of *Amoretti* (1595) shows him following Sidney's example in tracing the vicissitudes of a love relationship. The poems are marked by the high level of craftsmanship to be expected from him, but hardly bear comparison with his achievement in such longer poems as 'Epithalamion'. Not until we reach Shakespeare's sequence do we find anything to take us beyond the level of Sidney's best sonnets. Shakespeare's poems were published for the first time as a sequence late in his career, in 1609. It seems certain, however, that most of them were written well before the end of the century and before the fashion for sonneteering had been largely replaced by other literary models.

Much of the power which distinguishes Shakespeare's sonnets from other sequences resides in the dramatic quality which pervades them. This can be exemplified by considering one of the most familiar poems in the series in its full development:

> They that have power to hurt and will do none,
> That do not do the thing they most do show,

> Who, moving others, are themselves as stone,
> Unmoved, cold, and to temptation slow;
> They rightly do inherit heaven's graces
> And husband nature's riches from expense;
> They are the lords and owners of their faces,
> Others but stewards of their excellence.
> The summer's flower is to the summer sweet,
> Though to itself it only live and die;
> But if that flower with base infection meet,
> The basest weed outbraves his dignity:
> > For sweetest things turn sourest by their deeds;
> > Lilies that fester smell far worse than weeds.   (*94*)

To read this sonnet is to respond to a process which works itself out in the course of its development. The opening line seems to offer a simple and approving picture of virtue, though there are indications in 'power' and 'hurt' of an uneasiness which seems, however, to be countered by the assertion that those who possess these powers will 'do none'. The second line, by making a distinction between what is 'shown' and what is *not* 'done', introduces a moral ambivalence which the following lines, with their stress on 'stone' and 'cold' and on the quality of remaining passively 'unmoved', confirm. To be 'to temptation slow' is no doubt a sign of the virtuous man; but 'slow' allies itself uneasily to 'cold' and 'stone' to cast a doubtful light on the initial assumption of rectitude.

Indeed, if what is being celebrated here can still be thought of as 'virtue', it is 'virtue' achieved at a price. It seems that those who 'rightly' inherit – or claim to inherit – nothing less than the 'graces' of 'heaven' are those who 'husband', avariciously hoard, the abundant 'riches' of nature, ostensibly to protect them from the risk and the living justification of 'expense'. The final lines, corresponding to the sextet, endow familiar, almost proverbial commonplaces with a strange and sinister complexity. They contrast the temporary, but real and poignant 'sweetness' of the summer flower which 'only' lives and dies in the course of nature to the state of the same flower as 'infected' and reduced to the base condition of a 'weed'. This merges in turn into the final contrast between the conventional purity of the 'lily' – with its beauty balanced by its connection with funeral rites and with death – and the 'festering' of corrupted virtue. The poem, holding contrary moral judgements – virtue and vice, self-control and self-affirmation – in a constantly shifting state of suspense, proceeds by a method which is characteristic of Shakespeare's great dramatic soliloquies, including very notably those of Hamlet. Like the sonnet, these project into dramatic utterance not the finished statements which critics have sometimes sought to find in them, but developing states of thought and feeling as they move towards clarification. The effect of the language is dynamic rather than stationery in a way that corresponds to an essential feature of Shakespeare's dramatic expression.

A similar tendency to the dramatic can be discerned, indeed, in the grouping of the poems, which are likely to have been written separately over a considerable period, into what emerges roughly as a narrative sequence notably more complex and varied than anything attempted by Sidney or Spenser. After an opening set of poems (*1–18*) addressed to an aristocratic patron and urging him to marry, the long central part of the sequence (*19–118*) seems to be concerned with the poet's relationship with a young man (the patron or another) who rejects his offered friendship and who, at one stage, betrays him with a second poet. The final segment (*119–54*) deals mainly with the poet's hopeless love for a woman who fails to respond to his advances. It would indeed be rash and profitless to attempt to relate these poems to any supposed process of self-confession. All we can safely say is that the entire sequence, thus loosely constructed in accordance with a narrative plan that points to something other than the relatively conventional vicissitudes expressed in other sonnet collections, has produced poems in which we can sense the hand of a dramatist exploring themes which he will use effectively in some of his greatest plays.

Some of the themes which engage the poet in these sonnets emerge in what may seem, at first sight, unpromising contexts. The opening sequence, in which the patron–friend is urged to marry and promised immortality in verse, is likely to strike a modern reader as bizarre; but, by urging the person addressed to accept the necessity of commitment, of the creative risking of self as a condition of being truly alive –

> Profitless usurer, why doest thou use
> So great a sum of sums, yet canst not live?
> For having traffic with thyself alone,
> Thou of thyself thy sweet self dost deceive. (*4*)

and by relating this imperative to the poet's desire to find fulfilment in his own creative action, Shakespeare is addressing concerns which will occupy a central position in some of his greatest comedies.

All the poems, conventional or otherwise, show signs of the way in which the sonnet form imposes upon language a distinctive economy and intensity. The most striking sonnets in the long central sequence develop these qualities in relation to themes that, once again, Shakespeare will develop in his plays. Prominent among them is a sense of the hostile action of time as a destructive reality in human experience:

> Time doth transfix the flourish set on youth
> And delves the parallels in beauty's brow. (*60*)

> Ruin hath taught me thus to ruminate,
> That Time will come and take my love away. (*64*)

> O fearful meditation! where, alack,
> Shall Time's best jewel from Time's chest lie hid? (*65*)

The apparent solidity and permanence of natural objects – 'brass', 'stone', and 'gates of steel': 'earth', 'boundless sea', and 'rocks impregnable' – appear destined to decay in a process against which the best human endeavours, associated with the effort to achieve a precarious 'permanence' through the creation of verse, can only set a fragile aspiration to 'value'. The theme, developing and transforming a commonplace of the day associated with the Platonising philosophy which contrasted the ideal perfection of eternity with the corruptible realities of earthly existence, is one which found powerful expression in Spenser's *Cantos of Mutability* at the end of *The Faerie Queene*.

This concern with the action of time produces attitudes towards love and friendship which are various and even contradictory. Love is seen not only as valuable in its own right, but as a source of the creativity by which a poet may hope to assert, or at least to extend, his own sense of value. It is also, and at the same time, seen as subject to a process of temporal decay which threatens to make these aspirations vain. At times, the poems express a conviction of the permanence and unique validity of emotions expressed in time-defying verse; and then the attitude is that proposed in one of the most familiar of the sonnets:

> Love's not Time's fool, though rosy lips and cheeks
> Within his bending sickle's compass come.   *(116)*

Splendidly as this conviction is expressed, however, there is about the poem, particularly in its closing couplet, a suggestion of the rhetorical, of a self-conscious determination to carry conviction by unsupported weight of affirmation:

> If this be error, and upon me prov'd,
> I never writ, nor no man ever lov'd.

The couplet reads with an odd sense of weakness after the powerful development which has led up to it. The poet seems to say that the experience which he has sought to project into verse *must* have a time-defying validity, because to accept the contrary would be to leave it tragically meaningless. The value of the affirmation is found to be inseparable from the desolate reality which it seeks to evade.

Given such pressures, it is not surprising that in other moods a contrary attitude prevails. Such is the case in the equally famous sonnet 129 from the final segment of the sequence:

> Th'expense of spirit in a waste of shame
> Is lust in action.

'Love' has become 'lust', changing from the most potentially affirmative of human relationships to one which involves an expenditure which is indeed of 'spirit', because it involves some of the deepest human aspirations, but which seems destined to lose itself in a sterile 'waste of shame'. Both these sonnets can be seen as contrasted reflections upon the reality implied in human subjection to the temporal. Love, and the friendship of which it constitutes the most intense expression, presents itself as a reaction against the process of temporal decay; but what is rooted in time, and requires time as a condition of its being, time inexorably destroys. What is involved is not – I must repeat – any exclusively personal drama connected with possible facts of an autobiographical nature. All great art is indeed involved in some kind of personal experience; but what concerns us here is the more universal human urge to seek fulfilment in creativity, to become in some sense the creator of its own 'reality'. The urge is one which rises from, and is threatened by, the circumstance against which it seeks to react. The very value perceived in the most intensely pursued of human emotions, failing to maintain itself by unsupported force of affirmation, only makes them by an extreme paradox more potent to corrupt. 'Lilies that fester' indeed 'smell far worse then weeds'.

Players and playwrights

Side by side with the flowering of a sophisticated literature born of a fusion of humanistic and courtly elements, the age saw the spectacular birth of a purely secular theatre. Elements derived from the past, going back to the religious and folk origins of drama, preserved in festivals of a seasonal nature, in ritual mimings and the performances of wandering mummers, survived to play their part in the new developments. So too did the memory of the miracle plays and the moralities of the medieval period, though these had come to be seen as old-fashioned and had encountered the disapproval of the religious reformers of the Reformation. The essential precondition of the new flowering of dramatic art was a secularisation of what survived of the traditional forms. The earliest extant purely secular dramatic entertainment in English is Henry Medwall's *Fulgens and Lucrece* (*c.* 1515?): the story of the wooing of Lucretia, daughter of a Roman senator, by a rich and worldly aristocrat and a poor but virtuous rival. It is worth noting that Medwall was chaplain to Cardinal Morton who was in turn connected with More; More served as a page in the Cardinal's household and is known to have been interested in dramatic performances.

Medwall's play is the first of a number of so-called 'interludes', the most important of which were those by John Heywood (*c.* 1497–1580), who was also connected with More by marriage with his niece. Entertainments by Heywood, such as *A Merry Play between Johan the husband, Tyb his wife, and Sir Johan the Priest* (1533) and *The Four Ps* (1545?), are rudimentary farces, the interest of which lies in offering a transition between the traditional representations and the new secular drama. The first, modelled on a French original, presents the typical fabliau triangle of jealous husband, amorous wife, and priestly lover, the second a debate between a Palmer (or Pilgrim), a Pardoner, an Apothecary, and a Pedlar as to who can tell the most convincing lie.

The full development of these early efforts had to await the consolidation of the Elizabethan Settlement. The earliest dramatists to explore fruitfully the possibilities of an openly secular drama derived their inspiration largely from the humanist outlook encouraged by education in the new grammar schools and the reformed universities. The translations of Seneca's Latin tragedies, brought together as late as 1581 in the form of *Ten Tragedies*, proved influential in providing the model for a neo-Classical form of tragedy in English. The first play to develop this vein, Sackville and Norton's *Gorboduc*, was presented in 1561 for an audience of lawyers in the Inner Temple. It was followed by a small number of academic tragedies by other authors. These plays existed side by side with comedies of more directly popular inspiration, such as Nicholas Udall's school play *Ralph Roister Doister* (*c.* 1553), which combined the Roman theme of the *miles gloriosus*, the vainglorious soldier, with strong elements of popular song and rural farce, including memories of such folk entertainments as the May dances and the traditional representations of Misrule.

For these beginnings to expand to the full range of their possibilities it was necessary for the idea of a playhouse, and of the professional actors who performed in it, to become a reality. The traditional dramatic entertainments were originally performed in the open air, by occasional 'actors' to fluctuating audiences. By the 1570s the strolling players were beginning to form themselves into regular companies attached for patronage and protection to prominent noblemen: such a company, known as the Queen's men, was formed by Elizabeth's Master of the Revels in 1583. Already, James Burbage had established one of the conditions of the new drama when, as leader of the Earl of Leicester's men, he built in 1576 The Theatre, the earliest construction of its kind in England, on an open field near Shoreditch. In spite of the opposition of the authorities of the City of London, fearful of possible disorder and moved by Puritan prejudice against dramatic performances, other permanent theatres rapidly followed: the Curtain, also in Shoreditch, in 1577, the Rose, on the South bank of the Thames, about 1588, the Swan in Southwark, around 1595, and the Globe Theatre, to become associated with Shakespeare, in 1598.

The formation of permanent companies led naturally to a new conception of the profession of actor. The first performer to achieve national status was Richard Tarleton (d. 1578), a clown who wrote ballads and extempore verses, and even apparently a lost play, for performance and who seems to have enjoyed favour with the Queen. By the end of the century such names as those of Richard Burbage (*c.* 1567–1619), for whom Shakespeare wrote many of his greatest parts, and his chief rival, Edward Alleyn (1566–1626), who became prosperous enough to finance the building of the Fortune Theatre and eventually, after retiring from the stage, to endow the charitable foundation of the College of God's Gift at Dulwich, testify to the revolution in status which the new developments made possible.

The provision of permanent public playhouses, depending on the patronage of spectators who paid fixed sums for entry, was a necessary condition for the rise of the new theatre. A parallel development – of less lasting importance, but the cause at times of considerable rivalry – was the rise of private theatres, offering dramatic performances in structures which – unlike the public playhouses – were roofed. These were used in the early years by child actors, drawn from the choirs of St Paul's Cathedral and the Chapel Royal. The first private theatre, the Blackfriars, opened in 1576 for the children of the Chapel Royal, who offered plays generally more scholarly and sophisticated than those performed on the public stages and with settings rather more elaborate than those in use elsewhere. When, towards the end of his career, Shakespeare's company felt the need to respond to changing fashions, they used the Blackfriars Theatre as an alternative to the Globe.

The open stage, of which the Globe was an example, can be seen as a successor of the platforms set up at strategic places in medieval towns, or moving on wheels from one point to another for the performance of the 'miracle' cycles. The platform, however, in the process of evolving into a

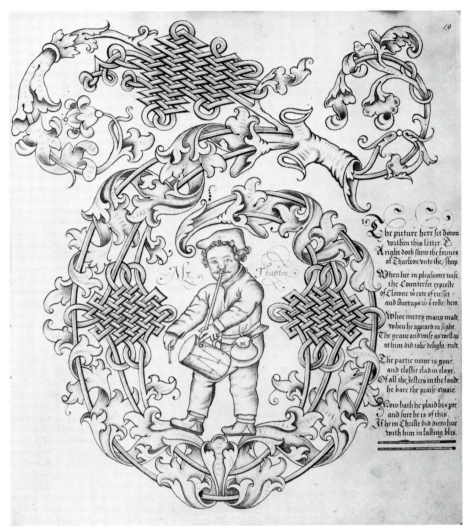

Portrait of Richard Tarlton by John Scottowe (1588).

stage, had grown considerably in complexity. The exact nature of the
arrangements in question, for which our knowledge depends on imprecise
contemporary accounts and on such illustrations as Joannes de Witt's sketch
of the Swan Theatre (*c.* 1596), is often uncertain in matters of detail; but the
main features are sufficiently clear. To a main stage, projected forward
sufficiently to allow an actor to detach himself from the general action
and address the audience more directly (a matter of importance for
understanding, for example, the soliloquies in many Elizabethan plays), there
was added at the back an inner space which could be curtained off but was
capable of being used when required. This inner stage had a balcony above
it. Entries and exits to and from the 'tiring' (attiring) space were provided on
either side of the principal platform and there seem to have been windows at

the upper levels which were available for use, as well as a musicians' gallery on the highest level of all. A trapdoor afforded access to a space beneath the stage which could be used for representations of Hell, or other demonic interventions, and at the Globe the stage seems to have been covered by a canopy representing the Heavens in their reflection of the majestic divine order which traditionally governed the universe in which man, on his earthly 'stage', acted out his temporal drama by exercising his distinctive privilege of responsible choice to ends alternately of eternal salvation or damnation.

Much in these arrangements may strike a modern playgoer as makeshift and primitive. It is possible, however, to hold that they offered the dramatist certain advantages. This was, in the first place, an intimate theatre in which the contact between actor and public was close and direct. The spectators, who practically surrounded the stage platform on three of its sides, were intimately present, participating in the unfolding of the action. The stage arrangements offered, moreover, a superior degree of flexibility. The divisions of the platform stage, complex but not rigid, together with the absence of the isolating drop-curtain, enabled a continuous and uninterrupted action to be developed and so ensured the maintenance of a tension necessary to the theatrical illusion.

These advantages were in certain important respects enhanced, rather than hindered, by the fact that there was practically no provision for lighting in the open theatre and by the almost total absence of scenery and stage properties as we understand them. Once again we should not be over-hasty in imposing any narrowly realistic point of view. A play – and especially an Elizabethan play – is not in any primary sense an imitation of 'real' life. It is rather a spoken and visual action, unrealistic and conventional in its nature, which calls for public participation. If, as we may believe, the art of the theatre is essentially poetic in nature and if realism, as narrowly conceived, tends to destroy it, we shall find this view amply confirmed by three centuries of Shakespearean theatrical production.

The poetic nature of the Elizabethan dramatic illusion was supported by a language which maintained the rhythms of common English speech as yet unmodified by the abstracting influence of the printed word. The sources of linguistic vitality in English, as conditioned by social, economic, and intellectual developments in medieval England, were to a considerable degree local, closely connected with the largely self-contained society of the village and the country town. It was this reality that enabled dramatists to introduce colloquial expressions in situations where a continental writer, more accustomed to think in terms of a literary, cultivated idiom, would have found them incongruous.

This continuity of popular linguistic tradition, however, represents only part of the situation. During the course of the sixteenth century, the new forces of the Renaissance combined with the natural mental agility of the Elizabethans to bring into circulation a great new body of words and concepts. This development was not without its dangers for lesser writers. Words, followed for their own sake, often lacked the necessary minimum of logical connection and overreached the limits imposed by the structure of the sentence. Some of Shakespeare's writing, especially in his youth, has

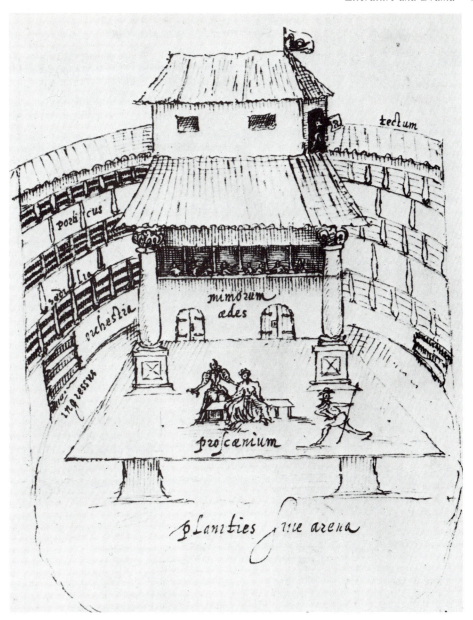

Joannes de Witt's sketch of the Swan Playhouse (c.1596) as copied by Arend van Buchel.

connections with this type of excess which, however, he came to satirise in such plays as *Love's Labour's Lost* and eventually converted from a danger into an opportunity. The speeches of his greatest characters derive their effect from a vast vocabulary and sometimes seem to twist sense to extravagant ends; but the words they use are charged with meaning, rarely empty or merely rhetorical. Language and emotion, which may derive equally from the most direct and popular speech or from the most intellectual sources, are fused by the action of the poet's creative power. To believe that so perfect an instrument for the recording of states of thought and feeling can be described adequately in terms of baroque fantasy or rhetorical excess is to misinterpret the writer who developed further than any other the possibilities of English speech as an instrument of dramatic expression.

The full potentialities of the new theatre only began to take shape with the rise of the so-called 'University wits': a group of writers who chose to make their living by writing for the stage after attending one of the traditional centres of learning, where they had access to the new currents of humanistic speculation and gained, in several cases, a reputation as literary bohemians. Such men as John Lyly (*c.* 1554–1606), Robert Greene (*c.* 1558–92), and George Peele (*c.* 1558–96) were among the first to set up as professional playwrights and to introduce new concepts of dramatic form. Lyly, who turned to drama after his success with prose romance, wrote most of his plays for the children of St Paul's and for performance at court before the Queen. The themes are often mythological or pastoral. The medium is the intricate stylised prose which he had developed for his novel and which, although scarcely adapted in his use of it for dramatic dialogue, contributed to the graceful wit of Shakespeare's prose in such plays as *Much Ado about Nothing* and *As You Like It*.

The work of Robert Greene, an early rival of Shakespeare, reflects a very different temperament. Some of his plays, such as *A Looking-Glass for London* (*c.* 1590), are exposures of social evils which reveal their connection with the medieval 'morality' plays and seem in some cases to be intended as responses to the alleged atheism of his contemporary Christopher Marlowe. Other works by Greene, such as *Friar Bacon and Friar Bungay* (1589?) and *James IV* (1591?), make use of contrasted plots in ways which anticipate, however imperfectly, the effects obtained by Shakespeare in works of greater complexity and wider human content. The weaving together of plots reflecting different levels of life in town and country, court and tavern, came to have a function exceeding that of comic relief. That function certainly exists in these early plays, as it continued to do in the work of the later dramatists; but the more essential purpose of this device, as it came to be developed, was to explore a dramatic situation, enabling it to be seen from contrasted points of view and grasped in its full range of complexity.

Peele, unlike Greene, was himself an actor and, as such, closely connected with the new theatre. Some of his plays, like the early *Arraignment of Paris* (*c.* 1584), are courtly entertainments, combining in this case the praise of Elizabeth with the retelling of the classical story of the Apple of Discord and interweaving songs in Latin and Italian with elements of folk tradition. Such plays, bringing together elements of popular sport and public pageantry, were intended to find their unifying principle in the celebration of the universal harmony of Nature, symbolised in the human order by the unity of peasant and courtier in their common devotion to the Virgin Queen. In *The Old Wives' Tale* (*c.*1595?), perhaps the most attractive of his plays, Peele returns to pure folk-tale, thus giving testimony to the continuing strength of the element of popular tradition at this relatively late date in the development of the drama.

Other plays of this period – such as *Arden of Feversham* (1592), a play by an unknown author which deals, powerfully at times, with a sordid tale of nearly contemporary murder in a 'bourgeois' setting, show more sombre imaginations at work. The most interesting figure in this kind was that of Thomas Kyd (1558–94), who specialised in the writing of plays on the theme of revenge. A play of his on the story of *Hamlet* seems to have been in existence by 1589 and to have provided Shakespeare with some of the material for his tragedy. Kyd's most popular play which has come down to us, *The Spanish Tragedy* (*c*. 1589), was immensely popular and exercised great influence upon later playwrights. The theme of revenge, the madness both real and feigned of the main protagonist, the device of a play within the play which turns from acting to deadly earnest, and the Machiavellian villain who combines murderous violence with malicious plotting: all these offered themes and devices which were taken up and developed by generations of later dramatists, including some of the greatest.

What the new theatre needed was a figure of outstanding genius capable of firing the imagination of audiences in the process of creating fresh dramatic worlds. Such a need was met in the short and meteoric career of Christopher Marlowe (1564–93) whose first plays, the two parts of *Tamburlaine the Great* (1587), introduced a new order of imaginative power to the stage. The prologue to the First Part has the effect of a declaration of intent:

> From jigging veins of rhyming mother wits,
> And such conceits as clownage keeps in pay,
> We'll lead you to the stately tent of war,

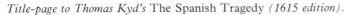

Title-page to Thomas Kyd's The Spanish Tragedy *(1615 edition).*

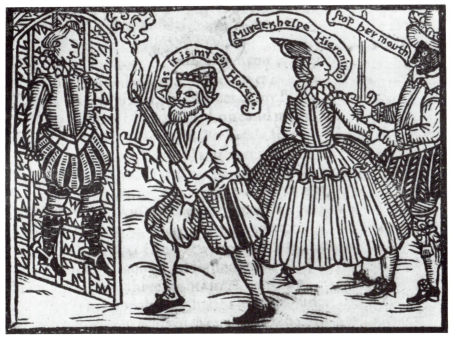

> Where you shall hear the Scythian Tamburlaine
> Threatening the world with high astounding terms
> And scourging kingdoms with his conquering sword.

In his scornful dismissal of 'rhyming mother wits' and 'clownage' Marlowe is rejecting the theatre as he found it and declaring his determination to follow paths of his own making. This purpose found its most immediate expression in the creation of a new kind of dramatic verse. The Marlovian 'mighty line' opened to dramatists possibilities hitherto unimagined, and echoes of it continued to permeate the work of writers for many years.

Part of the fascination was connected with a sense of the overweening and the precarious that was characteristic of Marlowe's sense of life. Something of this is implied in Tamburlaine's claim near the opening of his first play:

> I hold the Fates fast bound in iron chains,
> And with my hand turn Fortune's wheel about,
> And sooner shall the sun fall from his sphere
> Than Tamburlaine be slain or overcome.

There is much in Tamburlaine's aspiration to which Marlowe's audiences must have thrilled, but such audiences were still close enough to traditional medieval notions of Fate and Fortune – the philosophy of the turning wheel – to perceive the danger implied in seeking to maintain human life on this level. Marlowe certainly recognised this danger. In Part Two the reality of death interposes, bringing with it a descending curve to set against the hero's vaulting aspirations. Tamburlaine's desire to immortalise his love for the 'divine Zenocrate' is powerless to prevent her death, and his conquests are contrasted at the end with the reality of his mortal situation: 'For Tamburlaine the scourge of God must die.' It is typical of Marlowe's genius that this conclusion, which might have been the occasion in a lesser writer for a moralising lesson, is presented with detachment, as a simple fact which no rhetorical assertion can overcome or disguise.

Marlowe's *The Jew of Malta* (1589?) presents a central figure who achieves the wealth and power which he covets, only to fall a victim to the forces which he aspired to manipulate. Barabas, beside being a Jew, is a Machiavellian, in the Elizabethan sense of the term: one who conceives of the world in terms of effective power and who, being excluded by his race and religion from a supposedly Christian society, sees wealth as the instrument through which that power may be exercised. In this he does not differ from the world around him: the Christians who reject him and profess to live by superior standards are no better than himself. No edifying moral emerges from a story that combines theatrical melodrama with what T. S. Eliot called a note of 'savage comic humour'.

Doctor Faustus (1588? or 1592?), the greatest of Marlowe's plays, may have been written either before or after *The Jew of Malta*. The theme as he found it in his source, the English version of a German legend, has strong medieval overtones which Marlowe may have viewed with detachment, but which he had no interest in evading. Faustus' aspirations are those of Tamburlaine translated from the world of conquest to that of intellectual achievement and sensual gratification. They are expressed in a tone which is not dissimilar in its craving for 'infinity':

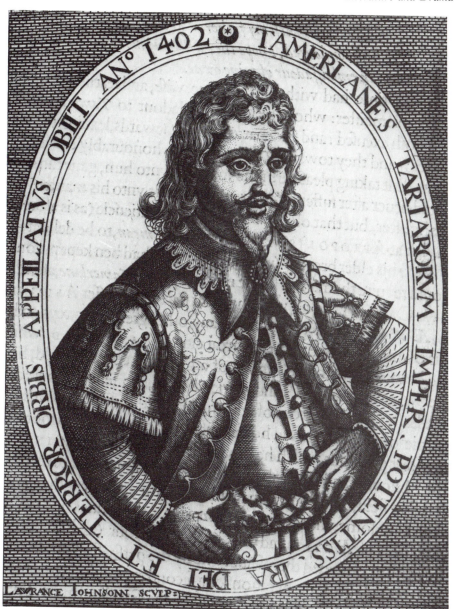

Edward Alleyne as Tamburlaine, from Richard Knolle's A Generall Historie of
the Turkes *(1603)*.

> O, what a world of profit and delight,
> Of power, of honour, of omnipotence,
> Is promis'd to the studious artisan!
> All things that move between the quiet poles
> Shall be at my command: emperors and kings
> Are but obey'd in their several provinces,
> Nor can they raise the winds, or rend the clouds;
> But his dominion that exceeds in this,

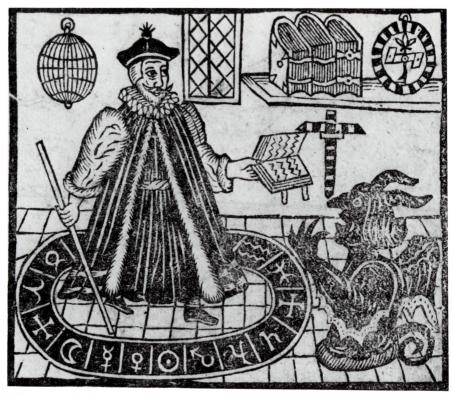

Title-page to Dr. Faustus *(1624 edition)*.

Stretcheth as far as doth the mind of man:
A sound magician is a mighty god,
Here, Faustus, tire thy brains to gain a deity.

Marlowe's contemporary reputation as an atheist should not prevent us from seeing that, whatever his own beliefs may have been, he is attuned to the moral spirit of his source. Like Tamburlaine, Faustus overreaches himself. He sells his soul to Mephistopheles in the desire to obtain 'profit' and to exercise 'power', to make for himself a caricature of 'omnipotence'. To obtain these ends, which amount to an 'infinite' extension of what is of its nature passing, he deceives and dramatises himself until he is left with nothing but despair: that absence of the saving gift of 'hope' which is, in the strictest sense, 'damnation'.

Faustus, who began by expressing confidence in his power to manipulate time, ends by desiring to hold up its inexorable course: 'Stand still, you ever-moving spheres of heaven / That time may cease and midnight never come.' The desire is, of course, vain: and Faustus, having sought his 'immortality' in an impossible extension of the trivial and the temporal, is left at the last with the wish to see annihilated that same soul in the unending extension of which he originally conceived his 'bliss':

> O soul, be changed into little water drops,
> And fall into the ocean, ne'er be found;
> My God, my God, look not so fierce on me!

To believe that Marlowe wishes us to identify with his hero is to ignore the contrary evidence which the play provides. This is not to say that he necessarily wrote in an avowed Christian spirit or meant his audience to understand it so. The prevailing tone, as in his other plays, is one of notable detachment, and what the play seems to put forward is not any moral doctrine, or any assertion about the providential nature of the real, but simply the price of following illusion in an attempt to raise trivial and self-deceiving aspirations to the level of governing obsessions in the conduct of human life.

The scope and fusion of Shakespeare's art

Shakespeare, 'of all modern, and perhaps ancient poets, had the largest and most comprehensive soul'. Dryden's tribute, the more generous as coming from an age that prided itself on a superior standard of polite sophistication, sums up what students of Shakespeare have at all times sought to express. No writer of comparable greatness is more elusive to final definition. None has exercised a more diverse appeal or shown a greater capacity to inspire continual and fruitful renewal in the minds of succeeding generations. (Given the impossibility of discussing all of Shakespeare's plays in the space available, I have focused on as many representative plays of different kinds as possible. This has inevitably meant excluding a number of plays – *Othello* and *Measure for Measure*, for instance – which are in no way inferior to those included.)

The history plays

This protean genius came only gradually to full expression. The earliest plays by Shakespeare, respectively historical dramas and comedies, show him concerned to advance the mastery of his craft. The three early plays on the reign of *Henry VI* (1591–2) can be seen as attempts to discover what a 'history play', built upon dramatically viable ideas as distinct from an episodic pageant, might be. The three plays show, by the end if not at the beginning, a remarkable continuity of purpose in weaving together two contrasted ideas. The first is the notion, derived from a great body of medieval thought, that sin is eventually repaid in the form of retribution upon the sinner; the second, more modern in its implications, relates the existence of disorder in the body politic to elements of weakness in the ruler. Both elements are developed consistently and side by side. The first finds expression in the unhappy fate of nearly all the principal contenders as they become involved in the consequences of their blood-thirsty appetite for power; and the unhappy figure of Henry VI serves to join the two, in so far as he is at once a good man against whom sin is almost continually committed, and a feeble ruler who is at times disposed to admit that his claim to the throne is uncertain.

By the end of the series, in *Richard III* (1593), Shakespeare presents in the person of the villainous royal hunchback whose presence dominates the action (it is, after Hamlet, the most extended role in Shakespeare's work) a character without precedent in English drama. His opening definition of his own nature is marked by a notable extension of the possibilities of blank verse of a kind that differs decisively from Marlowe's achievement:

> I, that am not shaped for sportive tricks,
> Nor made to court an amorous looking-glass –
> I – that am rudely stamp'd, and want love's majesty
> To strut before a wanton ambling nymph –
> I, that am curtail'd of this fair proportion,
> Cheated of feature by dissembling nature,
> Deform'd, unfinish'd, sent before my time
> Into this breathing world, scarce half made up,
> And that so lamely and unfashionable
> That dogs bark at me as I halt by them –
> Why, I, in this weak piping time of peace,
> Have no delight to pass away the time,
> Unless to spy my shadow in the sun
> And descant on mine own deformity.
> And therefore, since I cannot prove a lover
> To entertain these fair well-spoken days,
> I am determined to prove a villain
> And hate the idle pleasures of these days.   (I. i)

Feeling himself excluded from the forms and fictions of polite society and indeed from the sources of love, Richard makes the pursuit of power his obsessive aim. In following it he shows a combination of intense commitment and ironic clear-sightedness which causes him to stand out in the world of shallow, time-serving politicians and helpless moralists in which he moves; but in the act of achieving the Crown the cost of success is revealed as he reflects, before his final overthrow, upon the inevitability of his isolated doom: 'Richard loves Richard: that is, I am I.' The result of a life-long dedication to the egoist's drive for power is seen to be the impossibility of self-evasion, escape from the limits of the isolated self. The realisation will be taken up, in various and more complex forms, in the great tragedies to come.

These early experiments bore fruit a few years later in a second series of historical dramas, running from *Richard II* (1595–6?) to the two parts of *Henry IV* (1596–8?) and *Henry V* (1599). The broad conception which provided a point of departure for these plays answered to the current political notions, intensely nationalistic and monarchical, of the age. All four plays were conceived as successive stages of a study in kingship. The power of the monarch was assumed to be conferred upon him by God as a guarantee of order and of that hierarchical structure of society which cannot be rejected, according to this line of thought, without plunging it into anarchy and chaos.

The interest of the plays, however, lies less in these traditional conceptions than in their consequences in terms of human behaviour. In *Richard II*, where the pattern of feudal loyalty is broken by the murder of a king, the play turns upon a contrast between Richard, a monarch lawfully enthroned but personally irresponsible, and a born politician, the Lancastrian Bolingbroke, who achieves his ends through what is, in the traditional terms to which his victim appeals, an act of sacrilegious rebellion. In the two *Henry IV* plays, the new King calls his subjects to unite in a Crusade which is intended to provide a focus for national unity, only to find that his original crime fatally engenders the strife which he aims at ending. The political success which eludes him is finally achieved in *Henry V* by his son. In describing the achievement, and in the process of giving it full value, Shakespeare develops a conviction, finally tragic in some of its implications, that political capacity and human sensibility tend inevitably to diverge. When Henry, weighed down by his responsibilities on the eve of Agincourt, moves in disguise among his soldiers, he is moved to reflect that the King 'is but a man as I am'; and just because he shares this common humanity there is something precarious in the iron self-control which his necessary vocation imposes upon him and in the absolute claim which he is required to make on the allegiance of his subjects.

It is as a reaction against this precariousness that Falstaff, Shakespeare's greatest comic creation, appears in these plays as both the embodiment of 'riot and misrule' and as a reminder of the human loss which his necessary repudiation implies. In Part I of *Henry IV*, where the comic spirit prevails, he is a connecting link between the tavern world of broad if at times corrupt humanity in which he is at home and that of political rhetoric and power intrigue to which he also has access. Thus situated between two worlds, and not entirely limited to either, he is able to throw a detached light on the heroic sentiments to which the more responsible characters are given and to comment, bitingly if irresponsibly, on the 'honour' which they invoke on the battlefield, often to urge others to die in their cause. 'Why, thou owest God a death' is Prince Hal's parting remark to Falstaff on the field of battle, leaving his tavern associate to comment ruefully ''Tis not due yet: I would be loath to pay him before his day' and to add his deflating comment on the concept of honour itself: 'What is honour? A word. What is that word honour? air – a trim reckoning. Who hath it? He that died a Wednesday.'

The Falstaff of Part II is a different character in a different kind of play. Age has replaced youth in the main action and success is sought without illusion in a world where the action of time seems to carry all the human actors helplessly before it. Falstaff himself, who in the previous play was engaged in an exuberant attempt to ignore the reality of time – as the Prince tells him on his first appearance 'What a devil hast thou to do with the time of the day?', is subdued to the changed spirit. Finding his companions among ageing dotards, and himself haunted by disease and the premonitory thought of death, he strips them of their pitiful pretensions:

I do see the bottom of Justice Shallow. Lord, Lord, how subject we old men are to this vice of lying! This same starved justice hath done nothing but prate to me of the wildness of his youth and the feats he hath done about Turnbull Street, and every third word a lie . . . I do remember him at Clement's Inn like a man made after supper of a cheese-paring. When a' was naked, he was, for all the world, like a forked radish, with a head fantastically carved upon it with a knife.

(III. ii)

The repudiation of verbal honour in the preceding play is reinforced by a more sombre evaluation of the human condition, in relation to which the comment just quoted can be linked to Falstaff's attitude to the Lord Chief Justice – himself an old man on another level of authority – with whom Prince Hal is required to come to terms in the pursuit of his vocation. Whereas in Part I Falstaff's attitude on the battlefield had implied an affirmation of life beyond the selfish calculation of politicians, in Part II he is content to live on the bribes offered by those who have the means to buy release from service and to accept the resignation of the helpless to their fate: for such, and no other, is the nature of things. The 'young dace is a bait for the old pike', and a blind 'necessity' justifies all.

The growing conviction that the claims of the human and the political order can barely be reconciled finds expression at the end of *Henry IV* Part II when Prince Henry, newly crowned, rejects the dissolute companion of his younger days. 'I know thee not, old man. Fall to thy prayers'. Here, as so often in Shakespeare, we must not simplify the issues. Henry, with the responsibilities he has just shouldered, *must* abandon Falstaff; but the public declaration of his resolve strikes us as an imposition, rigidly and almost violently asserted, upon his normal humanity. It is significant that in *Henry V* Falstaff is only remembered in the Hostess's account of his death. No doubt the dramatist drew his Henry V with a sense of necessary public vocation in mind. One aim need not, in Shakespeare, exclude another, and the human necessity of choice is always governed by a balancing sense of the cost, in terms of other possibilities excluded, which choice of its very nature implies. As we follow the various stages in the uncompromising study of achieved success which rounds off the trilogy, a certain coldness takes possession of our feelings as it took possession, step by step, of the limbs of the dying Falstaff. We too find ourselves, like him, in our own way disposed to 'babble of green fields'.

The comedies

Side by side with his early experiments in the chronicle play, Shakespeare was engaged in the early 1590s in exploring the possibilities of the comic convention, shaping it by a process which initially resembled trial and error into an instrument for expressing the finished statements – more especially about love and the human need to live imaginatively – which he was already, beneath the desire to entertain, concerned to make. Whereas the history plays tend to tragedy in as much as they concentrate on a central figure, the king, whose vocation imposes upon him a degree of responsibility and isolation that borders on the inhuman, the comedies are concerned with release and reconciliation: release from the constraints which accompany the human need to live in society, and reconciliation through the creative and life-giving relationship of marriage.

The early stages of Shakespeare's exploration of the comic form, from *The Comedy of Errors* (*c.* 1592) to *Love's Labour's Lost* (*c.* 1594), led eventually to *A Midsummer Night's Dream* (1595), which can be thought of as a comic counterpoise to the romantic tragedy of *Romeo and Juliet*, which equally engaged his attention at this time. Within the framework of a rational and social attitude to marriage, expressed in the opening scene through the preparations for the union of Theseus and Hippolyta and confirmed at the end of the play by the actual marriage ceremony, the action transports two pairs of young lovers – Lysander and Hermia, Demetrius and Helena, who feel they cannot achieve their largely wilful aspirations in the daylight world – from civilised life in Athens to nocturnal wandering in the mysterious woods. There the irrational but potent impulses which love normally covers are released and the capacity of the young lovers to master them tested. The woods become the scene of jealous rivalry between Oberon and Titania, respectively king and queen of the fairies. The spell which Oberon, acting through his elusive servant Puck, casts upon Titania, obliging her to 'dote' on the 'translated' figure of Bottom the weaver with his ass's head, is evidently a central symbol of the irrationality and absurdity which form part of the reality of love.

With Titania alienated from her reasonable self, the love of the human pairs is turned into misapprehension and hatred until, having followed their fanciful purposes to a sorry end, they are ready to confess themselves thoroughly chastened. Their delivery depends on that of Titania, whom Oberon is at length willing to release from 'the hateful imperfection' of her eyes. He declares that everything that has happened in the woods shall be remembered as 'the fierce vexation of a dream' once the dreamers have been restored to their true selves, awakened from the following of desire in the night of error to the light of day and the truth of reason.

On the heels of this declaration Titania awakes and Theseus and Hippolyta re-enter the action as the sound of hunting horns greets the morning. The stress is now on daylight and harmony, the bringing together of 'discord' into music, the uniting of the sounds of nature to those of human sociability in 'one mutual cry'. Lysander and Demetrius confess that their behaviour during the night has reflected an unreasonable fury, and even Bottom, in the act of standing confirmed as an object of ridicule, asserts after his own incongruous fashion the power of the vision which he too has been afforded:

I have had a most rare vision. I have had a dream, past the wit of man to say what dream it was. Man is but an ass if he go about to expound this dream. Methought I was – there is no man can tell me what. Methought I was, and methought I had – But man is a patched fool if he will offer to say what methought I had. The eye of man hath not heard, the ear of man hath not seen, man's hand is not able to taste, his tongue to conceive, nor his heart to report what my dream was.   (IV. i)

The substance of Bottom's dream turns out to be nothing less than an echo, comically confused but compacted of reality, of St Paul's celebration of love as a transforming power. From his attempt to describe what he has experienced we may gather that Bottom too has his contribution to make to the play's variations upon its central theme. Love, as it is here conceived, is seen to be at once a folly and to carry within itself, obscured indeed and subject to absurdity, but none the less real, a glimpse of the divine element in human life.

In the conclusion, as we return to the framing action, the various elements of the play are drawn together in a social and civilising vision of love. The marriage union is presented as life-giving, joining body and soul, reason and feeling, imagination and fancy in an assertion, qualified indeed but none the less humanly potent, of essential 'truth'. It is this 'truth' which Hippolyta, hinting at the limitation of her husband's rational distrust of poetry and the imagination – the domain, as he somewhat sceptically dismisses it, of 'the lunatic, the lover, and the poet' – celebrates in lines which can be read as the definition of a 'comic' action in the theatre:

> . . . all the story of the night told over,
> And all their minds transfigured so together,
> More witnesseth than fancy's images
> And grows to something of great constancy,
> But howsoever, strange and admirable.   (V. i)

Against this assertion of imaginative truth Theseus, as he looks forward to the entry of Bottom and his mechanicals with their Pyramus play, speaks feelingly of 'the anguish of a torturing hour'. In easement of this anguish the lovers, whom we have watched in the woods following their absurd impulses to 'preposterous' conclusions, are to witness an action in which romantic love is exposed to ridicule. Their reactions to what they see – their charity or lack of it – will show what kind of men and women they are. To accept this 'lesson', balancing truth against the ever-present possibility of illusion, is to affirm the faith in life and its ongoing processes which comes readily to the simple-hearted and which the arrogant and the sophisticated ignore at their mortal peril.

Some six years after *A Midsummer Night's Dream* came *Twelfth Night* (*c.* 1602), replacing the 'framework' structure of the earlier work by one which turns upon the interplay and contrast between two connected levels of plot. The play seems to have been intended to mark the festivity – the end of the Christmas season – which the title recalls. It adds to many of the qualities of an aristocratic entertainment those of a children's merry-making, an occasion for dressing-up to mock the absurdities committed in all seriousness by their elders. In so doing it gives recognition to that sense of the incongruous, and to the need for providing it with an outlet in the interests of continued social and personal harmony, that is one of the most persistent aspects of the comic impulse. Very roughly, one could say that the element of masque prevails in the poetic part of the action, and that the sentiments and situations developed in this are given a comic reflection in the prose underplot which is interwoven with it.

The serious part of *Twelfth Night* deals principally with conventions of romantic love derived from the literary taste, aristocratic and sophisticated, of the day. Orsino's passion for the unresponsive Olivia is a blend of sentiment and artifice, true dedication and elaborate self-centredness. We might say of him that he is to a large degree in love with love, with his awareness of himself as an uncorresponded suitor, just as Olivia is initially confined to her grief for her dead brother. This in no way makes them ridiculous or ignoble characters. Precisely because they are capable of *real* feeling, because the human potentiality revealed in the poetic quality of their utterances exceeds the common measure, they will have to learn to go beyond their initial attitudes, to accept the experiences which life offers, as it always does in these comedies, on terms not exclusively of their own making.

The primary instrument of this transformation is Viola, whose readiness to rely on her own resources and to allow the currents of life to sustain her (much as she had done in the initial shipwreck which brought her into the action) contrasts with the restricting attitudes which prevail at Orsino's court. In her male disguise as 'Cesario', and obliged by circumstances beyond her control to carry to another the message of the man she loves, Viola becomes the agent by which each of the relationships in which she has become so unpredictably involved find their proper object. Both Orsino and Olivia are brought to a recognition that the compulsive force of their passions is such as to draw them out of the various disguises which they have created for themselves and to accept the element of risk, of unforeseen commitment, which a more natural and spontaneous way of living involves.

This conclusion is reinforced by the more avowedly comic underplot. In particular it is conveyed through the exposure of Olivia's steward Malvolio when he finds himself, in a scene (III. iv) which occupies a central position in the play, imprisoned in darkness and visited by Feste the clown in his disguise as a curate. The comedy at this point is not devoid of a disturbing quality. Malvolio, though impenetrably deceived as to his own nature – and therefore plunged in 'darkness' – clings to what he recognises as solid reality against the illusions to which he is subjected: 'I am no more mad than you are.' In so far as it is a matter of distinguishing between external realities, Malvolio's protest answers to the truth. He is no more – and no less – 'mad' than the rest of the characters in the play, or – we might add – than the members of the audience who find their amusement in his predicament. The comedy of his situation lies in the fact that, lucid as he is in his attitude to his physical surroundings, he is yet – like those around him, but to a less curable degree – the 'prisoner' of his own self-estimate.

Malvolio, accordingly, excludes himself from the final resolution much as the finally self-deceiving 'philosopher' Jaques does at the end of *As You Like It*. It is characteristic of Shakespeare's comedies that when the time comes to work out the final dance of married harmonies to which they tend, and which is a faint reflection in the human order of the great dance of cosmic harmonies in which nature itself is involved, some character should be excluded or some situation left unresolved. So it is here with Malvolio, who responds to the Duke's invitation to forgive and be forgiven with a bitter protest against his treatment and a cry – 'I'll be revenged on the whole pack of you' – which constitutes his last word.

It only remains to add that Feste, the most enigmatic, thus far, of Shakespeare's clowns, stands equally somewhat apart from the prevailing mood of reconciliation. The spirit of his comedy responds to constantly shifting attitudes, moods more complex and varied than may at once appear. He answers, perhaps, even better than most to the tendency of Shakespearean comedy to qualify its imaginative harmonies with a sense of relativity, of a final uniqueness and autonomy in human experience. Illyria too, in spite of the beauty of imaginative fantasy which has gone to its creation, is a dream; and it is of the essence of Shakespeare's mature comedy to touch the poignant and to extract from its sense of the passing and the insubstantial some of its deepest effects.

The tragedies

At about the turn of the century, Shakespeare's work, reflecting the changing mood of the time, turned in the direction of tragedy. *Hamlet* (1601?) extends the possibilities of drama in ways foreshadowed in earlier plays but now realised in their full range of complexity. The motives of the central character touch the action at every point, seeking clarification through contact with it and illuminating it in turn by his central presence. Hamlet sees himself alternately as a tragic and as a grotesquely comic figure. Always and uniquely self-conscious, he brings to light, in pursuing the duty imposed upon him to avenge his father's murder, a corruption which embraces the entire field presented to his consciousness; and, as his action penetrates beyond 'seeming' – 'I know not seems, good mother', to expose the ramifications of the infection which pervades Denmark, he reveals progressively the depths of his inner disaffection.

In accordance with this conception, the early part of the play is concentrated on the revelation of the Ghost. This shows that Claudius, the seemingly competent and self-confident ruler of the Danish state, has not only supplanted Hamlet's father in his mother's bed, but has also been his murderer. As a result of this discovery the world, as Hamlet sees it, becomes infected with what proves finally to be the infirmity that preys on his own mind. The extent of this disaffection emerges in his enigmatic exchange with Rosencrantz and Guildenstern, the courtly parasites sent by Hamlet's uncle to probe his condition:

Hamlet:	What have you, my good friends, deserved at the hands of Fortune that she sends you to prison hither?
Guildenstern:	Prison, my lord?
Hamlet:	Denmark's a prison.
Rosencrantz:	Then is the world one.
Hamlet:	A goodly one, in which there are many confines, wards, and dungeons, Denmark being one of the worst.
Rosencrantz:	We think not so, my lord.
Hamlet:	Why, then, 't is none to you, for there is nothing either good or bad but thinking makes it so.
Rosencrantz:	Why, then your ambition makes it one. 'T is too narrow for your mind.
Hamlet:	O God, I could be bounded in a nutshell and count myself a king of infinite space, were it not that I have bad dreams.

(II. ii)

The depreciated value of 'friendship', which has become for Hamlet a sinister mockery, extends itself to ever-increasing areas of his consciousness. His thought, embracing the universe in the process of turning in upon itself, offers him the prospect of seeing himself as 'king' of a space at once 'infinite' and empty. In so doing, it leaves him victim to the 'bad dreams' to which he is led by the contrast between the 'infinity' to which his thought aspires and the reality of the 'prison' – Denmark, the world, his own mind – in which an inner incompatibility condemns him to live.

The intrigue to which Hamlet is exposed by his uncle's efforts to penetrate his motives has a further, more intimate consequence. His love for Ophelia, in which his nostalgia for purity – purity, nobility, and infinity represent the persistent aspirations of his thought throughout the play – might have been confirmed, becomes the occasion for the 'politic' devices by which Polonius offers to discover the truth for his master:

> *Hamlet:*   . . . I did love you once.
> *Ophelia:* Indeed, my lord, you made me believe so.
> *Hamlet:*   You should not have believed me, for virtue cannot so inoculate our old stock but we shall relish of it. I loved you not.
> *Ophelia:* I was the more deceived.
> *Hamlet:*   Get thee to a nunnery. Why wouldst thou be a breeder of sinners? I am myself indifferent honest, but yet I could accuse me of such things that it were better my mother had not borne me. I am very proud, revengeful, ambitious, with more offences at my beck than I have thoughts to put them in, imagination to give them shape, or time to act them in. What should such fellows as I do crawling between earth and heaven?
>
> (III. i)

Hamlet's rejection of Ophelia is only in part explained by his discovery of the deception to which he is being exposed. The reference to 'our old stock' implies nothing less than the universal human inheritance of sin derived from our first parent. Reacting against this fate with an asceticism based finally on resentful denial, Hamlet incorporates his disgust into the 'madness' which is at once a disguise, a refuge, and a manifestation of despair. At once involved in his own action and able – actor-like – to contemplate his involvement in detachment from it, Hamlet swings between the poles of intimate tragedy and bitter farce, becomes in a very real sense his own 'fool', a tragic protagonist acting out a role and engaged in an unending effort to evaluate, and so to distance himself from, his own predicament.

To this exposure of Hamlet's infirmity there corresponds the undermining of Claudius' 'seeming'. The play-scene (III. ii), in which he causes his father's murder to be re-enacted, provides a turning-point for the entire action. It shatters the appearance of regality which his uncle has so far presented to the world – like a painted mask covering the reality beneath – and brings to the surface the division which his awareness of guilt implies. With Claudius' crime confirmed, Hamlet is ready to confront his mother. The reproaches he directs against her combine moral indignation with a cruelty that answers to his own moral state. As he arraigns Gertrude he at once leaves her hopelessly divided against herself – 'O Hamlet, thou hast cleft my heart in twain' – and, under the guise of performing a salutory act of moral surgery, finds a savage release in exposing further the roots of division in his own soul.

The distortion which increasingly affects him through the course of the action ends by affecting Hamlet's attitude towards the task to which his father's Ghost has called him. As he is stirred, in a crucial soliloquy, to enthusiasm by the sight of the Norwegian prince Fortinbras and his marching army, he affirms initially the necessity of action as a sign of the rational and undivided personality:

What is a man
If the chief good and market of his time,
Be but to sleep and feed? a beast, no more.   (IV. iv)

In his own inaction, Hamlet is moved to admire Fortinbras – 'a most delicate
and tender prince' – but with an admiration that turns almost imperceptibly
to criticism. If the soldiers before him seem to be motivated by an 'ambition'
that partakes of the 'divine', he sees them nevertheless as 'puffed' by its
presence in themselves. The word carries a sense of vanity and inflation, so
that we are ready, as Hamlet's meditations move towards their conclusion, to
coincide with him in seeing them absurdly 'making mouths at the invisible
event', grotesquely agitating themselves for an 'egg-shell'.

   The final stages of the tragedy reflect the divisions in Hamlet's nature.
Nothing in Denmark is what it seems to be, every action has an underlying
content which belies its surface appearance. Claudius' final intrigues – the
dispatch of Hamlet to England with secret orders for his execution, the use of
Polonius' death and Ophelia's tragic end to involve her brother Laertes in a
web of plotting – are no more than attempts to cover the infirmity of his
condition, the 'imposthume' or carbuncle which is the symptom of the
'rotten' state of Denmark, by extending the area of the disorder. In the final
scene, something not very different can be said of Hamlet himself. His return
to Elsinore is from the first involved in death – he reappears in a cemetery,
exchanges jests with grave-diggers, and struggles with Laertes in Ophelia's
grave – and the final resolution which fate puts into his hands is surrounded
by obscurity and misunderstanding:

   There's a divinity, that shapes our ends,
   Rough-hew them how we will.   (V. ii)

Claudius, intending to poison him, poisons his own wife. Laertes, hoping to
avenge his father's death, is caught in the trap he has agreed to lay for his
enemy. Hamlet himself only carries out the command imposed upon him
after he has realised that he is involved in the pattern of death that has
woven itself round his person. By the end of the play he has uncovered all
the evils which surround him and has shown them to be variously, if
obscurely, related to the stresses in his own being.

   The setting of *Hamlet* in a remote, barbaric Denmark need not obscure
from us that the world of the play is that of a Renaissance court, dominated
by the ruthless appetite for power and by the intrigue and insecurity that
went with it. Some five years later, Shakespeare chose a story that has
initially some of the marks of a fairy-tale to present what might be called a
dramatic metaphor of the human condition. The central character of *King
Lear* (1605–6) is father and king, head of a family and ruler of a state, and
his tragedy affects us under both these aspects. Age has weakened Lear's
control over his own impulses, making him the prey of anger and resentment
obscurely rooted in the passions. By wilfully banishing his youngest
daughter, Cordelia, he breaks bonds which precede reason and order, but
upon which the unity of the family – and, in the long run, the significance
and coherence of experience itself – depend. The crime against natural
paternity is balanced by his elder daughters' disregard of all natural ties.

A similar division explains the parallel situation of the courtier Gloucester, whose illegitimate son Edmund undoes the bond of nature by dispossessing his true-born half-brother Edgar and bringing his father to blindness and death. Edmund is a personable and intelligent young man, whose actions are governed by a philosophy of Nature which, in his own view, justifies him in brushing aside the traditional restraints which stand between him and the achievement of the power which is his all-absorbing purpose in life:

> Thou, Nature, art my goddess; to thy law
> My services are bound. (I. ii)

In certain respects, Edmund is a logical development from the conception that, more than a decade earlier, had produced Richard III. Witty and disillusioned like his predecessor and, again like him, feeling himself excluded from a world which he sees as resting upon unexamined and finally meaningless assumptions, Edmund, acting in conjunction with Lear's elder daughters and their husbands, finally contributes to bringing about a world which his father uneasily contemplates:

These late eclipses in the sun and moon portend no good to us. Though the wisdom of nature can reason it thus and thus, yet nature finds itself scourged by the sequent effects. Love cools, friendship falls off, brothers divide. In cities, mutinies; in countries, discord; in palaces, treason; and the bond cracked 'twixt son and father.

(I. ii)

Under these pressures family and state in *Lear* are alike disrupted. The process of dissolution culminates, in the central scenes of the tragedy, in the storm in which Lear, shut out by his daughters, and Edgar, supplanted in his rights by Edmund, meet in the depth of human deprivation. Both are accompanied by the Fool, the last and greatest of Shakespeare's creations in this kind, whose wry and disillusioned comments serve to express the bitter truths which his master recognises in spite of himself but which he is unwilling, or simply unable, to accept.

Even before his exposure to the elements, Lear, faced by his daughters' inhumanity, has been moved to ask himself what constitutes true human need. 'O reason not the need!' he cries, in response to Regan and Goneril's ruthless cutting down of his own 'needs', and goes on to say:

> Our basest beggars
> Are in the poorest thing superfluous,
> Allow not nature more than nature needs,
> Man's life is cheap as beast's. Thou art a lady;
> If only to go warm were gorgeous,
> Why, nature needs not what thou gorgeous wear'st,
> Which scarcely keeps thee warm. But, for true need . . . (II. iv)

Now, exposed to the storm and deprived of every natural support, he confronts the unadorned human condition in the person of Edgar disguised as 'poor Tom', the houseless and apparently crazed victim of a cruel world:

Why, thou wert better in a grave than to answer with thy uncovered body this extremity of the skies. Is man no more than this? Consider him well. Thou ow'st the worm no silk, the beast no hide, the sheep no wool, the cat no perfume. Ha! here's

three on's are sophisticated. Thou art the thing itself; unaccommodated man is no
more but such a poor, bare, forked animal as thou art.

(III. iv)

At this point the external action has become a reflection of Lear's own
condition. Conveyed to us on a bare stage through his words and those of his
fellow-sufferers, the tempest becomes an extension of the personal mood.
Man and his environment are seen as organically related; natural
relationships are shattered and the state of 'unaccommodated man' is
conceived in terms of subjection to the beast of prey in his own nature. By
the end of the storm scenes Lear and Edgar are united in their common
frailty, and as the old King's wits collapse into madness the Fool, whose
words have provided a crazed reflection of his master's inner stresses, finally
leaves him.

At this stage the blinding of Gloucester (III, vii) represents the lowest
depth of man's subjection to the beast in his own nature. It is followed, first
by a kind of lull as misery passes into Stoic resignation, and then by a
compensating moral development in Lear's own reactions. Out of his
consideration of the pitiful condition of basic, unadorned humanity, there
springs a recognition of the failings which have brought him to his present
plight. The wounded egoism of the passion-driven animal gives way to a
moral awareness of the terrible wound caused by suffering in human nature.
Not only is Lear's past 'unkindness', his neglect of natural feeling, opposed
to the solicitude and paternal affection to which he is painfully feeling his
way back: but many of his words at this stage suggest the cauterising of a
deep injury, as though his very grief were a necessary prelude to restoration.

In this way we are led to Lear's awakening and recognition of Cordelia
(IV. vii). Bound up to this moment on what he calls a 'wheel of fire', so that
his tears 'scald like molten lead', he reacts to her presence as to the vision of
'a soul in bliss'; and the suggested idea of resurrection ('You do me wrong to
take me out of the grave') contributes to the same effect. His grief has
become such that it can at least contemplate the possibility of beatitude.
Cordelia's prayer for his benediction and his answering plea for forgiveness
imply feeling of a kind that surpasses the possibilities of expression. This is
the central reconciliation, the restoration of the natural relationship between
father and child, which is seen – while it lasts – to figure the resolution of the
ruin originally caused by passion. The vision of an intimate 'bond', broken
by perverse choices and restored through the atoning action of love, is one
which will haunt Shakespeare's later conceptions, up to *The Winter's Tale*
and *The Tempest*.

In *Lear*, it is not allowed to prevail. We are engaged in an exploration of
the human reality under its tragic aspect, not elaborating the supposedly
beneficial effects of suffering in promoting moral understanding. The armies
of Cordelia and her husband, who have returned to restore her father to his
throne, are defeated by the realist Edmund who becomes for a brief moment
the undisputed master of the political action; and though he finally dies at the
hands of the disguised Edgar, neither his death nor his last-minute
repentance can prevent the hanging of Cordelia at his orders. As the play
ends, Lear returns with her dead body in his arms and, in a world dominated

by emotional petrifaction and a sense of returning darkness, the curtain falls. Lear dies, gaining in death the only relief conceivable from 'the rack of this tough world', which has proved so consistently indifferent to the spiritual intuitions which suffering has brought so painfully to birth. His faithful follower, Kent, announces his readiness to follow his dead master and Edgar, joining hands with the surviving Albany, is left with the mission of restoring the wounded state in a spirit in which exhaustion and sincerity, purged of all excessive pretension, meet in a gesture of mutual sustainment.

Macbeth, which must have followed *Lear* very closely in 1606 and which seems to have been conceived with the recent coronation of a king from Scotland in mind, offers an unusually short and concentrated action. A king is murdered, his assassin attempts to maintain a grotesque parody of kingship, and is finally overtaken by the consequences of his perverse choice. The presence of equivocal 'supernatural' forces looming over the decisions of men in a blood-soaked and storm-ridden world to mirror a fundamental reversal of natural order confers a unique 'metaphysical' dimension upon this tragedy of regicide.

Macbeth's fall from grace is determined at a very early stage in the play. On the way home from his latest campaign, the loyal general victorious over domestic traitors and their foreign allies, his encounter with the Witches brings to the surface unconfessed ambitions lurking in the recesses of his soul. 'This supernatural soliciting', he reflects, 'cannot be *ill*, cannot be *'good'*. His words, which seem to echo the elemental confusion already announced by the Witches in their opening chorus – 'Fair is foul, and foul is fair' – mark the entry of equivocation into his thought. They suggest a mind already threatening to collapse, 'against the use of nature', into a purposeless fumbling with ideas, the first obscure intimations of a state where fundamental values are inverted and where, in Macbeth's bemused conclusion, 'nothing is / But what is not'.

The decisive part in resolving the dilemma which exercises him is played by Macbeth's wife, who recognises the lack of consistent purpose in her husband – 'wouldst not play false', she says of him, 'and yet wouldst wrongly win' – and opposes to it her own show of logical determination. The resolution, however, is won at a cost to herself. As her purpose takes shape her first prayer is a rejection of her natural femininity: 'unsex me here': the second is an appeal to the darkness which accompanies the exclusion of reason and pity. By doing violence to her own nature Lady Macbeth succeeds in making her husband act in accordance with his hidden desires; but the success involves a rejection of nature which finds intimate expression in the passionate distortion of her attitude to the bearing of children and which will bring them both to disaster.

From the moment in which he submits to the logic which inspires his perverse determination to force time, wresting its natural course to his purposes, Macbeth's musings – expressed in soliloquies which perhaps penetrate even further than those of Hamlet into the hidden sources of decision – are accompanied by the growth of a hallucinatory quality in his thought. The great speech in which he pauses on the threshold of his victim's bed-chamber to take stock of his situation moves from an unwilling recognition of insufficient motive to a distraught assertion of the play's overriding 'metaphysical' theme:

> If it were done when 'tis done, then 'twere well
> It were done quickly. If th'assassination
> Could trammel up the consequence, and catch
> With his surcease success, that but this blow
> Might be the be-all and the end-all here,
> But here, upon this bank and shoal of time,
> We'd jump the life to come.   (I. vii)

The succession of uneasy suppositions and the breathless compounding of urgent sibilants – 'a*ss*a*ss*ination' followed by 'con*s*equence', '*surcease*' by '*success*' – proceeds from a mind enmeshed in the flow of its ideas and succumbing to the state of incoherent intensity which the speaker will bear with him to the final extinction of feeling.

Nor is this all. Beneath the incoherence, rising to take possession of the murderer's mind, is a tide of submerged natural feeling which testifies to the outraged values he is attempting to set aside:

> Besides, this Duncan
> Hath borne his faculties so meek, hath been
> So clear in his great office, that his virtues
> Will plead like angels, trumpet-tongued against
> The deep damnation of his taking-off;
> And pity, like a naked new-born babe
> Striding the blast, or heaven's cherubin horsed
> Upon the sightless couriers of the air,
> Shall blow the horrid deed in every eye,
> That tears shall drown the wind.   (I. vii)

In spite of himself, Macbeth is moved to contrast the brutality of his projected deed with the 'meekness' of his victim, the guilt it inspires in his divided thought with the 'clarity' he recognises in the king he is about to kill. 'Meekness' and 'clarity', however, when associated with Duncan's sacred office, are not merely innocent and pacific qualities. They embody a power that will impose itself to plead 'trumpet-tongued', with apocalyptic force, against the horror of the deed; and this sense of outrage merges, in the great complex image which converts the 'naked new-born babe', embodiment of vulnerable innocence, into a power 'striding the blast', into the assassin's fear of the 'damnation' that the intrinsic evil of his act will draw upon him.

From the moment of the murder, and after the superb scene (II. ii) in which he issues from the death-chamber as one walking in his sleep with the blood of his victim sticking on his hands, Macbeth's career proceeds on lines of rigid determinism. The man who began by planning the murder of his king to gain 'solely sovereign sway and masterdom' ends as a puppet in the grasp of circumstance. By the middle of the play, after a central scene (III. iv) in which the 'blood-boltered' image of the slaughtered Banquo seems to prevent him from taking his place at the head of his table, he is engaged in an effort to evade the recognition of his failure. Turning for support to the 'supernatural' mentors in whom he has placed his trust, and clinging to the fallacious 'philosophy' which assures him that 'Things bad begun make strong themselves by ill', he wakens from illusion to find himself in the position of one who has stepped into a river of blood only to find that his real desire is to return, to recover his original innocence, but that – being what he has now become – he is no longer free to do so.

The play, then, emerges finally as a tragedy of 'damnation', with Macbeth consigned in his life-time to the 'hell' he has fashioned for himself. It does not, however, end on this note alone. As the armies of Duncan's natural heir approach his last refuge, the once formidable tyrant shrinks to something small, even absurd. After the death which follows the exposure of his last illusions, the coronation is announced of a king who can properly refer to 'the grace of Grace' as sanction for his healing authority: a king to whom the loyalty of free subjects is once more due, and from whom royal bounty may again be expected to flow.

The final plays

As Shakespeare's art approached its final stages, he showed himself to be increasingly unwilling to be bound by the limitations of literary genre. *Antony and Cleopatra* (1607) combines the normal features of tragedy with those of a chronicle play and even, in certain scenes, with a comedy that approaches the farcical. Its Cleopatra is at once the Egyptian queen of history, engaged in a struggle to maintain her freedom of action in what is essentially a Roman order, and a woman approaching her declining years, experienced in the ways of a corrupt and cynical world and conscious of having been, not a few years before, Julius Caesar's discarded mistress. In the opening scenes Antony expresses the scope and aspiration of his passion for her in words which read like a splendidly theatrical, even operatic gesture for an audience:

> *Cleopatra:* If it be love indeed, tell me how much.
> *Antony:* There's beggary in the love that can be reckoned.
> *Cleopatra:* I'll set a bourn how far to be beloved.
> *Antony:* Then must thou needs find out new heaven, new earth.
>
> . . .
>
> Let Rome in Tiber melt and the wide arch
> Of the ranged empire fall! Here is my space.
> Kingdoms are clay: our dungy earth alike
> Feeds beast as man; the nobleness of life
> Is to do thus; when such a mutual pair
> And such a twain can do't, in which I bind,
> On pain of punishment, the world to weet   [*know*]
> We stand up peerless.   (I. i)

Already, however, we have heard the soldiers who follow Antony speak of his infatuation in terms of 'dotage', and Cleopatra's own words, cunningly calculated to stimulate his passion by an assertion of contraries, have stressed the realistic view which limits these flights of imaginative lyricism. This double vision persists throughout the play. Whatever else it may be, Antony's love for Cleopatra is the infatuation of a man past his youth, who has chosen to give up the public responsibilities which rest upon his shoulders to become the dupe of an emotion which he knows to be unworthy. It is a sign of the dramatist's confidence in his powers that he chose this apparently unpromising material for what emerges as the most triumphant and, in some sense, the most positive of all his tragedies.

A detailed study of the play, which would stress the effect of its uniquely rich and subtle poetry, would show the dramatist obtaining this aim in a series of definable steps. The first concerns its presentation of the public, political action. This covers a vast field – vaster, perhaps, than any in Shakespeare – and imagery which stresses the concept of the world or the universe is constantly in the mouths of the principal characters. The three triumvirs, who uneasily divide authority between them until Caesar disposes of his two rivals, are seen as 'pillars of the world' and Antony's unhappy wife Octavia, torn in her loyalties between her brother and her husband, speaks of rivalry between them in typically universal terms:

> War 'twixt you twain would be
> As if the world should cleave, and that slain men
> Should solder up the rift.
>   (III. iv)

This emphasis relates in two ways to Antony's own choices. He is evidently to blame in setting aside responsibilities so great for an irrational and dubious infatuation; but side by side with this realistic judgement, which the play constantly underlines, there is an implication that the measure of his passion may be, at least in his eyes and while the effect maintains itself, correspondingly compelling. Seen from this point of view, the theme of the play becomes the necessity, and the danger, of living by the imagination. Men live, and in some sense *need* to live, imaginatively, by a process of creating their own 'reality' and imposing it upon the world around them; but the following of this human compulsion involves an element of illusion which, in the inevitable recall to what is objectively and inescapably real, assumes the form of tragedy.

At the heart of the action thus conceived lies the contrast between Antony, the political failure, and Octavius, whose success in worldly and practical terms is as impressive as it is necessary. It is easy to dislike Octavius, and many have done so. We can think of him as the last of Shakespeare's great series of public men: those whose acceptance of their vocation conditions them to think of moral issues in Machiavellian terms of effectiveness and practical success. It would be wrong to underestimate Octavius on this account. In the struggle with Antony he prevails and – in the public order of things – we would not have it otherwise. His are the ends of empire, firm rule and universal order: ends necessary and indispensable if civilised and humane living are to be possible in a world that desperately needs them. As he says, at the turning-point of his fortunes,

> The time of universal peace is near:
> Prove this a prosperous day, the three-nooked world
> Shall bear the olive freely.
>   (IV. vi)

'Universal peace' and its classic symbol, the olive: no mean things to depend on one man's conscientious and effective choices. The cause of victorious empire – the vision, so compelling to Renaissance minds, of the *pax Romana*, the universal peace celebrated in Virgil's great poem – wins the day justly in the interests of humanity; but because in human affairs every victory has its cost in terms of other possibilities rejected, the fall of Antony is there to remind us, beneath the squalor, the degradation, and the self-deception, of what has been left out, what might have been. From this point of view, the rejection of Falstaff at the end of *Henry IV* Part II and the death of Antony answer, each in its entirely different way, to a common intuition of life.

For Antony's decline, the inevitable consequence of his choices, lays the imaginative foundation for a certain elevation to tragic stature which is achieved, together with the corresponding exaltation in Cleopatra which follows it, at the end of the play. No play is more ruthlessly realistic in its exposure of failure. Yet, just as the folly of renouncing the responsibilities of empire was felt, at certain moments, to be balanced by a sense of the paltry nature of the pursuit of political success for its own sake, so death, which is the consequence of the hero's prodigality, comes to represent, for certain moments and while the imagination imposes itself upon the real, a liberation from triviality. Bungled and pathetic as it is to the realistic eye, Antony's suicide can become in his mind the noble action of 'a Roman by a Roman / Valiantly vanquished'.

This final attempt at self-affirmation finds its counterpart – but only after his death, which alone has made it possible – in Cleopatra's imaginative transfiguration of her dead lover:

Cleopatra:	I dreamt there was an Emperor Antony,
	O, such another sleep, that I might see
	But such another man.
Dolabella:	If it might please ye –
Cleopatra:	His face was as the heav'ns, and therein stuck
	A sun and moon, which kept their course and lighted
	The little O, th' earth.
Dolabella:	Most sovereign creature –
Cleopatra:	His legs bestrid the ocean: his reared arm
	Crested the world: his voice was propertied
	As to the tuned spheres, and that to friends;
	But when he meant to quail and shake the orb,
	He was as rattling thunder. For his bounty,
	There was no winter in't: an autumn 'twas
	That grew the more by reaping: his delights
	Were dolphin-like, they showed his back above
	The element they lived in: in his livery
	Walked crowns and crownets: realms and islands were
	As plates dropped from his pocket. (V. ii)

This is the reflection of a process by which Cleopatra *creates* an Antony in tune with her emotional mood. The images flow together from the most varied sources to compose a compelling dream sequence. The Colossus whose 'legs bestrid the ocean' becomes one with the heraldic device implied in the 'reared arm [that] crested the world', and both merge into the evocation of a supernatural 'bounty' immune to the action of the seasons (it had 'no winter in't') and into the strange folk- or fairy-tale quality suggested by those two eyes, like a 'sun and moon' adorning the 'heaven' of their owner's face, and confirmed by the effect of the two final lines. That an apostrophe of this scope and splendour can be accepted as natural, unstrained, is a sign that Cleopatra, while she speaks, is living her dream; but that it *is* a dream, that there never was an 'emperor' Antony (that place of eminence is occupied in the real world by his rival), is a sign that warns us to maintain a necessary measure of detachment in its regard. Challenged by Cleopatra to confirm the reality of her vision – 'Think you there was or might be such a man / As this I dreamt of' – her Roman captor's reply – 'Gentle madam, no' – at once sympathetic and gently deflating, warns us against making excessive claims upon it. Cleopatra is living, or seeking to live, in a world that is the projection of her own emotions. That world, as she creates it, is splendidly valid in the effect that it works upon the Roman who feels himself, almost in his own despite, fascinated by it; but the fact remains that in the real world only death can prevent an awakening from it. For that reason, if for no other, Cleopatra is resolved to die.

Accordingly, Antony's final attempt at self-affirmation finds its counterpart – but only after his death, which has made it possible – in the poetry of Cleopatra's end, the deliberately staged conclusion which she so splendidly contrives on her mortal throne –

> Give me my robe, put on my crown, I have
> Immortal longings in me –   (V. ii)

as she takes the asp to her breast, calling upon it to 'untie' the 'knot intrinsicate' of life in the act of dismissing Caesar as 'ass unpolicied'. There is here, of course, an element of imaginative illusion which remains relevant to the last. The serpent at her breast is not the 'baby' which she presents as a symbol of life, but death, its negation. Yet, for so long as the theatrical effect imposes itself, we are led to join her in feeling that the 'dungy earth' of Antony's opening speech, the baser reality of life seen now from the distancing perspective which death imposes, is imaginatively transformed under our eyes into fire, air, and 'immortality'.

Shakespeare seems to have abandoned whole-time dedication to the theatre in or around 1613 to return to his native Stratford. In his last years as a dramatist he turned to the writing of a new kind of play, a development from comedy to which critics have given the name of 'romance'. In this new form, he was following a general taste, observable in other writers of the time, such as John Fletcher (with whom he is likely to have collaborated in *Henry VIII* and, possibly, in *The Two Noble Kinsmen*), for old-fashioned tales embodying elements of magic and reconciliation. Shakespeare's first complete success in this manner, *The Winter's Tale* (1610), shows him adapting a popular form to his own ends. The play, a dramatisation of Robert Greene's *Pandosto: The Triumph of Love* (1588), concerns Leontes and Polixenes, kings respectively of Sicily and Bohemia, whose life-long friendship is broken up, as the play opens, by the jealous conviction of the former that his friend has betrayed him with his wife Hermione.

The nature of this division is made clear in Polixenes' account of the foundations upon which the friendship rested. 'We were', he exclaims,

Two lads that thought there was no more behind
But such a day to-morrow as to-day,
And to be boy eternal.

. . .

. . . What we chang'd
Was innocence for innocence; we knew not
The doctrine of ill-doing, nor dream'd
That any did.   (I. ii)

The bond between the two kings, which dates from childhood, has rested on
the youthful state of innocence, the assumption that it might be possible to
remain 'boy eternal'. The realities of human nature make this impossible.
Boyhood is necessarily a state of transition. Time corrupts those unprepared
to oppose its action with a corresponding moral effort, and youthful
innocence, left to itself, falls under the shadow of 'the doctrine of ill-doing'.
The reality of a 'fallen' condition in man needs to be recognised in the
process by which each individual passes from the state of original 'innocence'
to that of maturing 'experience'.

In particular, and as a potent factor separating the mature man from his
childhood, time brings a capacity for sensual passion which may be good, if it
leads to its natural fulfilment in the creative unity of the family, or evil and
destructive in the form of egoism and its consequences, jealous possessiveness
overcoming all restraint of reason. In Leontes, the evil impulse comes to the
surface. Moved by the spirit of unreason, he condemns his new-born child
first to death, then to abandonment, and his wife to prison, without pausing
to wait for the sentence of the divine oracle. This, when it comes, proves
Hermione to have been innocent; but not before she has died – or so Leontes
believes – of grief, and before his son has perished, his new-born child 'lost'
and his friendship with Polixenes shattered beyond all apparent remedy. The
opening phase of destruction and disintegration is complete with Leontes'
broken reaction to those blows: 'Apollo's angry; and the heavens themselves /
Do strike at my injustice' (III. ii).

At this point a single short scene provides the turning-point which is, in all
these plays, an essential feature of the symbolic structure. It opens in a storm
which at once carries on the idea of the divine displeasure and serves as the
background to a new birth. When the peasant who has witnessed the
hurricane describes the drowning of a ship's crew in the angry seas, his father
replies by showing in his arms a newly found child – the child, as it will turn
out to be, of Leontes, delivered from his cruel exposure to the elements – and
adding, in words of transcending simplicity which are central to the entire
conception: 'Thou mettest with things dying, I with things newborn.' The
significance of the discovery is clear. The child, born of Leontes' flawed
passion, has no part in his sin. Born in tempest and looking forward to future
calm, it will connect the tragic past with the restored harmony of the future
and become the instrument of reconciliation.

Before this can begin to take shape time has to play its necessary part.
Sixteen years pass. Leontes' child reappears as Perdita (the 'lost one') and
meets Florizel, the disguised son of Polixenes, at the rustic sheep-shearing

organised by her supposed father, the shepherd who discovered her as a baby
in the storm. Once again, this great scene (IV. iii) makes highly personal use
of established pastoral conventions. Early in the scene the conflict between
'innocence' and 'experience' emerges when Perdita, as 'queen of the feast',
rejects the flowers – 'carnations' and 'streaked gillyvors' – in the name of
what she sees as 'nature', unsophisticated simplicity. To this rejection the
disguised Polixenes responds with his plea for 'experience', harmonising
growth:

> . . . over the art
> Which you say adds to nature, is an art
> That nature makes. You see, sweet maid, we marry
> A gentler scion to the wildest stock,
> And make conceive a bark of baser kind
> By bud of nobler race. This is an art
> Which does mend nature – change it rather; but
> The art itself is nature.   (IV. iii)

To Perdita's view of 'art' as a deformation of 'nature', Polixenes opposes
another, of 'art' as completing 'nature', based on it indeed but as its crown
and perfection. According to this view, it is the nature of man to be *artful*,
and human nature expresses itself in human art. The conception is capable of
expression in social terms, and Polixenes makes this explicit by discussing the
process of grafting in terms of marriage: the union of the 'wildest stock' (in
other words, what Shakespeare sometimes calls 'blood', unregenerate
sexuality) to a 'scion', the product of civilised urbanity, of 'nature' in its
completely human, fulfilled sense, which is 'grace'. Man, unlike the rest of
the creation, is in a very important sense what he makes of himself, at least as
much as what he was before the making (artful) process began.

  The force of Polixenes' argument is conditioned by the element of a
jealous, old man's possessiveness which will bear fruit in his actions before
the end of the scene. In her reply Perdita speaks from her youth and
simplicity, her right rejection of what in human relationships is corrupt,
cynical, unnatural, and – as we might add – the necessary incompleteness of
her state of innocence. Promise and incompleteness, blended to correspond to
the present state of the action, are both present when, in offering her pastoral
flowers to Florizel, she celebrates the return of life after the long winter of
discontent:

> Now, my fair'st friend,
> I would I had some flowers o' the spring that might
> Become your time of day – and yours, and yours,
> That wear upon your virgin branches yet
> Your maidenheads growing. O Proserpina,
> For the flowers now that, frighted, thou let'st fall
> From Dis's wagon! daffodils,
> That come before the swallow dares, and take
> The winds of March with beauty: violets dim
> But sweeter than the lids of Juno's eyes
> Or Cytherea's breath; pale primroses,
> That die unmarried ere they can behold

Bright Phoebus in his strength – a malady
Most incident to maids; bold oxlips, and
The crown-imperial.   (IV. iii)

Beautiful as the speech is, and for all its conclusiveness as a sign that the
spring of reconciliation has dawned, the love it expresses still lacks the full
maturity which only experience can provide. The emphasis on Spring, on
birth, inexperience, virginity, is balanced by an implicit sense of death, which
the vitality associated with the 'royal' flowers – 'bold oxlips' and the 'crown-
imperial' – only partly counter. Other flowers to which Perdita refers are
'pale' and 'dim': they die 'unmarried', in unfulfilled promise, having failed to
'behold Phoebus in his strength'.

Florizel's reply expresses movingly a similar desire to live outside time and
to hold up the course of mutability:

What you do
Still betters what is done. When you speak, sweet,
I'd have you do it ever. When you sing,
I'd have you buy and sell so, so give alms,
Pray so, and for the ord'ring your affairs,
To sing them too. When you do dance, I wish you
A wave o' the sea, that you might ever do
Nothing but that, move still, still so,
And own no other function. Each your doing,
So singular in each particular,
Crowns what you are doing in the present deeds,
That all your acts are queens.   (IV. iii)

The most striking feature of the speech is its sensation of balance, of a
continual relationship between motion and stillness. Every action of Perdita's
– so Florizel asserts – involves *all* her perfections, is a complete expression of
her natural queenliness: 'All your acts are queens'. This, in turn, connects
her with the central image of the speech – that of the wave, which is always
in movement and yet ever the same. This intuition of the relation between
the mutability of life – for change is its law, and it is made by changing –
and the infinite value of the human experience which is conditioned by
change but finally incommensurate with it, is one which will eventually be
taken up into the complete pattern. Not yet, however, for at this moment of
idyllic celebration Polixenes casts across it the shadow of impotent anger,
taking away his son, threatening Perdita with torture, and falling into
something very like Leontes' sin.

The final resolution requires a return to Sicilia, where Leontes' courtiers
have been urging him to marry again. His response is a blend of apparently
contrary emotions. Bound by a 'saint-like sorrow' which the memory of his
queen keeps alive in him, he none the less shares the universal desire for an
heir as fulfilment, as manifestation of the natural fertility of which his sin has
deprived him. The child he so intensely desires can only be born of
Hermione: can only, therefore, be the daughter whom he condemned to die.

At last, however, Leontes has repented enough. In the presence of all the
chief actors in the fable – including Florizel and Perdita, who have fled
before the displeasure of Polixenes to take refuge at a wiser court – Leontes

is placed before the life-like statue of his 'dead' wife, which gradually comes to life by a process which corresponds to the birth of a new life out of the winter of penance and suffering. The 'statue' tortures Leontes with the poignancy of a sorrow that he desires to hold, to make eternal. Deluded, as he still believes, into thinking that the image has the appearance of life, he exclaims:

> Make me to think so twenty years together!
> No settled senses of the world can match
> The pleasure of that madness. (V. iii)

Finally, as though in answer to his prayer, the 'statue' comes to life. It is not an accident that this slow awakening is conceived in religious terms. Paulina, just before Hermione 'descends', says to Leontes:

> It is required
> You do awake your faith:

'faith', perhaps, not so much in any set of doctrines or beliefs as in the presence of life 'graciously' renewed. Paulina's final call makes it clear that what we are witnessing is a kind of resurrection:

> 'Tis time; descend; be stone no more; approach;
> Strike all that look upon with marvel. Come,
> I'll fill your grave up. Stir; nay, come away,
> Bequeath to death your numbness, for from him
> Dear life redeems you. (V. iii)

'Redeems you': though this is not said, and is not to be understood, in a Christian context, the Christian reverberations of the word are there, powerful as indications of a life renewed, restored to the full measure of its human possibilities. It is not a resurrection, of course, in the sense that it reverses or undoes the past. Hermione, who has never died, is restored to Leontes with the added signs of age and grief upon her. He has passed through an equal period of sterility and death, and there is no reason to suppose that his restored marriage will not be subject to the normal human destiny in time. His son, too, died in the now distant past, and no miracle will bring him back to life. Men and women have to face, to recognise – in time – the cost of their perverse choices, and this Leontes has done. He cannot now escape, but he can build, on the recognition of his fault, a new and humanly fruitful life with his 'redeemed' wife.

The last play in this series of 'romances', *The Tempest* (1611), may be Shakespeare's last fully committed dramatic statement. It also seems to reflect the final state of his reflections, developed through a lifetime dedicated to the stage, on the nature and limitation of the dramatic illusion. Prospero, who controls the action and brings it to the reconciling conclusion we expect from these plays, is less a 'god-like' figure than a very human agent, possessed indeed of powers of 'magic' which reflect the imaginative, creative element in human nature, but only with notable difficulty mastering his own less 'divine' impulses and bringing out the harmonising conclusion for which his set of 'characters' has been brought together on his island 'stage'. The newcomers from the real world beyond the island have been brought there, as Prospero recognises, by a process not initially in his control:

By accident most strange, bountiful Fortune,
Now my dear lady, hath mine enemies
Brought to this shore; and by my prescience
I find my zenith doth depend upon
A most auspicious star, whose influence
If now I court not, but omit, my fortunes
Will ever after droop.   (I. ii)

The relation to the dramatist's art seems clear. The materials of his action,
including the characters whose stage lives he aspires to mould into an
imaginative pattern, are initially given, cast on the shore of his predisposed
awareness. Coming together at an auspicious time, they become the material
for a play: material that he must be ready to grasp and shape to his ends
before it is carried away on the tides of life and escapes his controlling action.

Seen from this point of view, the action of the play concerns the working
out on the island stage of Prospero's projected drama by distinguishing
between the various degrees of responsibility of the characters who were
instrumental in his exile or who, in the case of Caliban, he found on the
island. A corresponding personal drama concerns Prospero's need to separate
justice from his craving for revenge and to accept that 'The rarer action is /
In virtue than in vengeance'. Two plots – one conceived by his unnatural
brother Antonio, the other by Caliban and the drunken sailors Stephano and
Trinculo – are launched against his life. He overcomes them by the
intervention of his servant-spirit Ariel whom, at a turning-point in the action
(III. iii), he sends to his enemies transformed from his usual ethereal self into
an avenging harpy. In the name of a shaping Destiny, Ariel calls the
assembled characters to repentance. Unless their sojourn on this 'most
desolate isle' has disposed them to recognise their own evil, their doom is
certain. For it is in the nature of uncontrolled passion, as the great tragedies
have consistently revealed, to lead its victims to self-destruction: and
Prospero's action, with its insistence upon notions of repentance and
amendment, is conceived as nothing less than a counterpoise to the processes
of ruin.

By the end of the play Prospero's purposes seem to have been achieved. As
in the previous romances, the instruments of reconciliation are the children of
the parents whom passion originally divided. Prospero's daughter Miranda,
awakened to the realities of a world beyond the limits of the island, marries
Ferdinand, the son of his former enemy: the young man whom she first saw
in her innocence as a vision proceeding from the 'brave new world' of her
awakened imagination, but whom she has come to love as a man. The 'brave
new world' becomes an ennobling vision of love in the light of an enriched
experience. In the words of the faithful courtier Gonzalo, the 'gods' –
whatever they may be – are invoked to 'crown' the newborn vision of
restored humanity with a symbol of royalty. The crown that they bestow is a
sign of the 'second', the redeemed and 'reasonable' life which has been given
to the characters through their experience on the island. For a moment it
seems that here, if anywhere, the design pursued by Shakespeare through his
mature work is substantially complete.

To leave the matter there, however, is seriously to underestimate the scope
and subtlety of the conception. We must remember that what we have been

following as *Prospero*'s 'play' is not necessarily the same thing as Shakespeare's. There are indications in *The Tempest* that the two do not necessarily coincide. The point (IV. i) at which Prospero celebrates the successful conclusion of his contrivances by offering a masque – a further play within a play – to mark the betrothal of Ferdinand and Miranda is also the moment in which his presentation is interrupted by a darker reality that forces itself upon his consciousness:

> I had forgot that foul conspiracy
> Of the beast Caliban and his confederates
> Against my life.

The shadow game of 'spirits' has to be ended and a return made to a more problematic reality. The recall moves Prospero to a deep uneasiness which communicates itself to his famous reflections on the 'insubstantial pageant': words which, far from being uttered in Olympic detachment, seem to reflect the anxious mood of an ageing man burdened with his weight of responsibility, conscious of the limitation of his 'magic' in the face of the mysterious and always ungraspable reality that so insistently breaks into, and dissolves, the imaginative harmonies it has brought so painstakingly into being.

In the final Epilogue in which Prospero, stepping forward on the now empty stage to address himself to the spectators, seems to be recognising that the dramatic illusion is the product of a convergence between the author's creative imagination and that of the audience, the implication seems to be that a play – *any* play – has no single meaning, of the kind that can be abstracted and proposed for approval or dissent in terms of any claim to exclusive validity. It may be that Shakespeare finally refused to contemplate the kind of play which such an affirmation might have implied: that he chose to remain true to a vision which has indeed its 'wonders', but 'wonders' of human creation, and sharing in the limitation of all that is human. For, in the words spoken by Theseus at the end of *A Midsummer Night's Dream* in relation to another, and very 'human' entertainment, 'The best in this kind are but shadows; and the worst are no worse, if imagination amend them.'

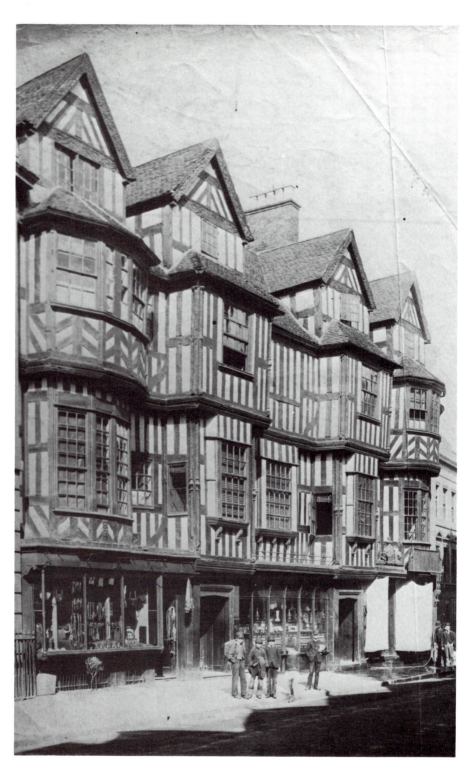

Ireland's Mansion, Shrewsbury (late sixteenth century).

3 The Town of Shrewsbury

ERIC MERCER

In its origins, its commercial and strategic advantages, its social character and its fluctuating fortunes Shrewsbury was a typical medieval and early modern English town.

The Anglo-Saxon 'burgh' of Shrewsbury was in existence by 901 and later gave its name to the Mercian shire of Shropshire. It was the centre of the great semi-independent palatine earldom created by William the Conqueror for Roger de Montgomery and in the late thirteenth century was one of the two main bases for the conquest of north Wales. Although in decline during the late fifteenth century, it was one of the most important towns in the country in the time of Henry VIII, ranking among the first fifteen. Recent calculations, perhaps more reliable than earlier ones, suggest that it then had just under 3,000 inhabitants. A small wealthy group, mostly merchants, contributed half of the total sum paid in the occasional tax levied in 1524–5 on lay fortunes, and owned about forty per cent of the taxable wealth. Below them, probably about one third of the citizen body, were the small masters and independent craftsmen. At the bottom, more than half the population, were journeymen, labourers, apprentices, servants, and the destitute poor. To these last the rich must have seemed rich indeed, but in comparison with many others of the time the town was ill-provided with exceptionally rich men and ranked higher among its rivals in souls than in taxable wealth.

The Tudor town, however, was not a purely bourgeois community. From early times local potentates like the Charltons and the Abbots of Haughmond and Lilleshall had maintained their town houses. In the Middle Ages many aspiring local gentlemen fashioned careers for themselves as officials of great magnates and needed accommodation in the town. The Talbot earls of Shrewsbury were among the greatest of the great in the fifteenth century and maintained Talbot's Inn to lodge their senior officers when they came there on duty. In the next century service to the Crown generally on behalf of the Council in the Marches of Wales was a better road to success for Shropshire men. That body had its headquarters in Ludlow Castle, but it had a seat in Shrewsbury as well and Gibbons' Mansion and Shearer's Mansion were probably built by, or with the wealth bequeathed by, two of its officials.

Many large late-medieval houses such as Vaughan's Mansion and Cole Hall belonged to men who, whatever their origins, had achieved knightly or gentle status, and throughout the sixteenth century local families had their town houses. Further, many Shrewsbury merchants of the period were of gentry descent. Between 1560 and 1620 around fifteen per cent of all the members of the powerful Drapers' Company were sons of gentlemen and, conversely, many leading drapers married into gentry families. The names of such families occur in the lists of bailiffs and provosts all through the century; not all of these were active businessmen and many seem to have aspired to the office for the prestige they considered it to confer. This participation increased as the years went by and at the end of the century the MPs for the borough were almost exclusively local gentlemen. At high social levels the county town was firmly integrated with its shire.

At the accession of Henry VII the town was, in the jargon of the time, 'decayed'. Its population was less than it had been a hundred years before and it had lost much of its former trade to smaller towns sited within easier reach of the Welsh hinterland, such as Welshpool and Oswestry. Its fortunes were reviving by *c.* 1540, but not significantly before the last third of the century. The first sign of its future dominance of the Welsh wool market was the passing in 1566 of an Act to give the Drapers' Company a monopoly of the trade. The Drapers had, in fact, over-reached themselves and the Act was partly repealed a few years later, but mainly through the efforts of other Shrewsbury companies, the Mercers and the Shearmen, unwilling to let their upstart rivals have all the plums. Both the Act and its part-repeal illustrate the political and economic power that the town was acquiring *vis-à-vis* its smaller competitors. It may be supposed, too, that over and above 'get-richer-quicker' schemes by the rich there was a rise in general prosperity, for from the 1580s onwards the rent receipts from the numerous urban properties held by the Drapers' Company rose considerably, and at the same time the population increased at a faster rate than in any nearby town of comparable size.

So much rebuilding has occurred over the last 500 years that one may only guess at what Shrewsbury looked like in 1500. There were then a number of grand houses wholly or mainly of stone and large enough to be built around one or more open or closed courtyards. Scattered throughout the centre of the town they were numerous enough, together with religious houses more on the periphery, to give an unenclosed and spacious air to some parts. This effect was enhanced by their generally low proportions, modelled upon the rural houses of the great, and by the even lower proportions of the houses of many of the ordinary citizens. It was further accentuated by the amount of open space not only at the rear of many tenements, but in the front as well. Some idea of the effect may still be seen in Dogpole, where the Old House and Nos. 14–16 have retained some of the originally much larger open space that lay between their main ranges and the street.

There is a myth, as popular among academics as among laymen, that periods of prosperity and of architectural splendour go hand in hand, and at Shrewsbury the outburst of fine building in the late sixteenth and early seventeenth centuries accompanied a marked rise in the economic fortunes of

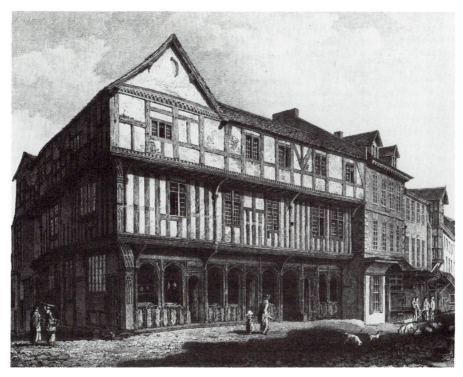

The Abbot's House, Butcher Row, Shrewsbury (c.1500).

the town, or at least of its wealthier citizens. Nevertheless, some of the surviving timber-framed buildings of the depression of a hundred years before were only once surpassed and rarely equalled by those of the later more prosperous age. The dating of timber buildings is something of a guessing game, but probably the best guess is that such grand houses as Mytton's Mansion, the so-called 'Henry Tudor House' on Wyle Cop and 'The Abbot's House' in Butcher Row, were erected in the years around 1500. They differed in many respects from their predecessors. They were of timber and not of stone; of three jettied storeys; their main ranges parallel to and aligned along the street and, apart from a passage to the rear, presenting an unbroken front to the roadway. In function, too, they were wholly different, for the ground floor was occupied by several shops and the upper floors by living accommodation. There was not necessarily any connection, either physical or tenurial, between the shop and the chambers above it, and it is known from documented examples in other towns that every shop and nearly every chamber might be in separate occupation. Very few ground-floor arrangements in houses in the main streets of towns have survived the changes in commercial practice of the last 500 years, but at the 'Abbot's House' and to a less extent at Mytton's Mansion, the original disposition can still be made out. At the former, each shop has its own doorway flanked on one side by two wide windows. Whether the 'Abbot's House', often said to be the town house of the Abbot of Lilleshall, has any connection with the abbey is uncertain, but it may well have been a speculation by that institution

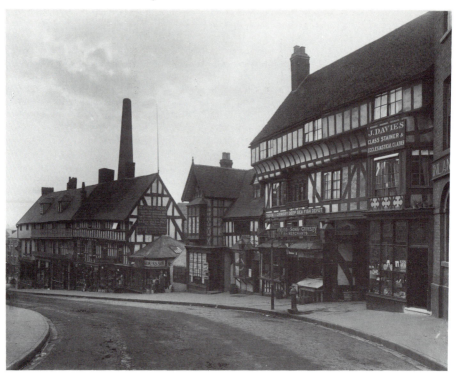

Henry Tudor House and Mytton's Mansion, Shrewsbury (c.1500).

similar in intent to the tenements which Tewkesbury Abbey was erecting in that town at much the same time. In other cases even when the owner himself occupied a shop and chambers there were still some to let out, and so even then the building was as much an investment and a speculation as a dwelling.

Large timber houses were not wholly new in Shrewsbury *c.* 1500 but earlier ones, even those of three storeys like the King's Head in Mardol, had been smaller and lower. Further, the new houses used a new mode of decoration, no longer emphasising but attempting as much as possible to disguise the main structural divisions. Their street-fronts eschewed the old large panels with heavy curved braces, conforming to and delineating the outlines of the timber frame, and instead hid the bay divisions beneath an overall pattern of small panels or of narrowly-set slight uprights in a manner known as 'close-studding'. That these elaborate elements were employed for decorative and not for structural reasons is shown by their absence from those elevations that were not easily seen: at Nos. 51–52 Mardol the contrast between the close-studding of the three-storeyed front and the large braces of the side wall is visible from the road. The applied decoration upon these buildings is, however, still in a late-medieval manner: the bold mouldings, the crenellation and the canopy of Mytton's Mansion; the tracery worked upon the dragon-posts and the knopped colonettes at the 'Abbot's House'; the use of slight cusped braces at 'Henry Tudor House' and, if the restoration may be trusted, the tracery of the window there.

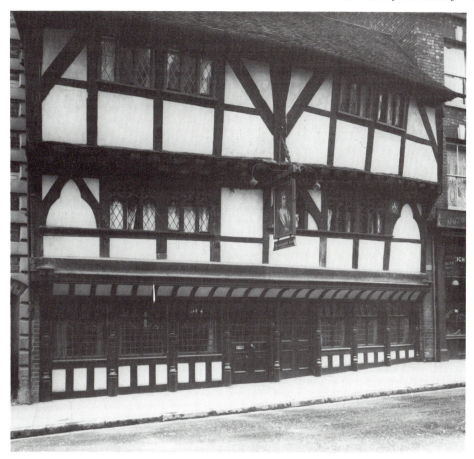

The King's Head, Mardol, Shrewsbury (before 1500).

By the second half of the century such large timber houses were only rarely built; Ireland's Mansion is exceptional, the most splendid timber building in the town, and still intended for more than one occupant. Far more typical of the time were houses of less height, with gables to light an attic storey, and often of only two bays to the front, like Owen's Mansion of 1592 in the High Street and Nos. 27–28 Mardol. Their size makes it likely that they were not speculative ventures for multiple tenancies, but rather were intended as a single dwelling or as a single shop-cum-dwelling. One which survived more or less unaltered until its demolition in 1944 and was then carefully recorded, was Gibbons' Mansion. The single door at the end of the main elevation suggests strongly that it was intended for single occupation, and in view of Gibbons' connection with the Council in the Marches it may well have been a residence only. Most of its contemporaries have had their fronts wholly removed for modern shops and their ground floors gutted, but it may be thought, to judge from the entrance porches of Lloyd's Mansion and of No. 16 High Street that they too were meant for single occupation, probably with a dwelling above a shop. The appearance of the large number of such houses at this time probably reflects the tardy rebuilding by solid but not outstanding citizens of their out-of-date medieval houses.

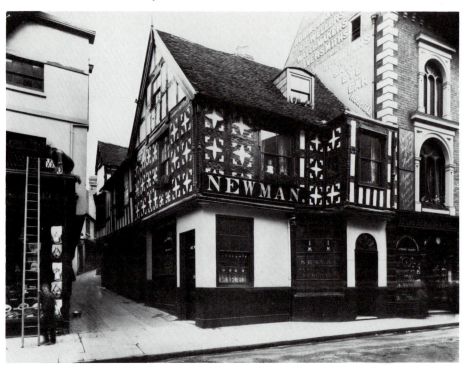

No. 16 High Street, Shrewsbury (16th century).

The earlier and generally somewhat larger houses of this type, like Lloyd's Mansion and 'The String of Horses', both now demolished, were appearing by the 1570s, and with them yet another new mode of ornament. The old mode, and especially a plain version of it which dispensed with cusping, continued for a long time and Fellmongers' Hall in Frankwell may date from as late as *c.* 1580. The new and more flamboyant manner may best be described in contrast with its predecessor. The slight cusped braces of the first, often in association with close-studding, developed an S-curve, generally uncusped; close-studding and plain panels declined before small panels filled with quatrefoils or larger panels enclosing multiple lozenges where space permitted or, where it did not, a single lozenge or a herring-bone pattern. Two small houses in the High Street (Nos. 16 and 17) which face each other across Grope Lane illustrate the small-scale forms, the one with herring-bone patterning the other with quatrefoils. Often the timbers themselves were worked with sunken quatrefoils and the plain colonettes of the 'Abbot's House' turned into twisted 'barley-sugar' columns. The barge-boards and tie-beams of the gables were often decorated with a running vine-leaf pattern.

The amount and nature of the rebuilding much impressed visitors. Thomas Churchyard had been born in Shrewsbury *c.* 1520 and when he returned there in 1587 he commented on its 'buildings gay and gallant finely wrought' and on the changes in the look of the town: 'I walked the streets and marked what came to view. Found old things dead, as world were made anew.' One such change, from the earlier more or less open aspect to the modern unbroken lines of tall buildings has taken many centuries to complete. It had only begun by the accession of Henry Tudor, but by the death of Elizabeth I had gone a long way towards transforming the street-scene.

The new style may justly be termed 'urban' in the sense that in the countryside it had a different emphasis, for there large panels with multiple lozenges were more common than in the town, where small scale ornament was seen to best advantage at close quarters in narrow streets. It has been said that Elizabethan Shrewsbury was curiously medieval in its style of ornament, but it is more accurate to say that it was late in adopting fashionable Anglo-Flemish forms. How late it was appears from the number of Jacobean porches and bays clapped onto not very much older Elizabethan street-fronts, as at No. 29 Castle Street and No. 41 Pride Hill.

No such charge of backwardness can be laid against the interior decorators of the time. In the Old House on Dogpole is a wall-painting incorporating the pomegranate badge of Catherine of Aragon which must be earlier than 1532. It is in full contemporary fashion with well-designed naturalistic foliage. In the same house an overmantel with a date of 1553 has almost certainly been brought from elsewhere, but is certainly the work of a known local craftsmen, Robert Sego. It is as advanced in style and in the attempt at correctly-classical columns as anything else in the country at the time. In the later years of the century plasterwork became common and those ceilings which survive, for example in a wing of Windsor House in Castle Street, are in a wholly up-to-date vein.

Throughout the later Middle Ages, stone had been common in the houses of the great in Shrewsbury, but it was virtually neglected in the sixteenth century, not because it had become unfashionable or impractical but because men of the standing to build great stone houses were few. Only two are known from the whole period. Bellstone House in Barker Street was completed with an open courtyard by Edward Owen. His social ambitions moved him to obtain a grant of arms in 1584 and probably explain the traditional form and material of his house. Whitehall, at the end of Abbey Foregate, was built *c.* 1578 and is of national importance as the first known double-pile country house in England, but its closest relevance to the architecture of the town is that it was built of stones from the nearby abbey.

In contrast, stone buildings erected not by great men but by the citizen body are the architectural manifestation of the town's rise to independence of any local power. In 1567 the old Market Hall was built in timber, but within a generation had been pulled down and replaced by the present structure, erected in 1596. In the same decade the rebuilding of Shrewsbury school was begun with the present north wing. Founded, or refounded, in 1552 and intended for the sons of local gentlemen as well as of townspeople, Shrewsbury was on a par with Eton and Winchester, was claimed to have more pupils than any other school in the country, and numbered Philip Sidney and Fulke Greville among them. Both buildings are in a severe style in white Grinshill stone, the Market Hall with Tuscan columns and responds to the arcades of its open ground floor and the School with the mullioned and transomed windows of the age and with no extraneous ornament at all. Both have a solidity and assurance that outdoes any comparable urban

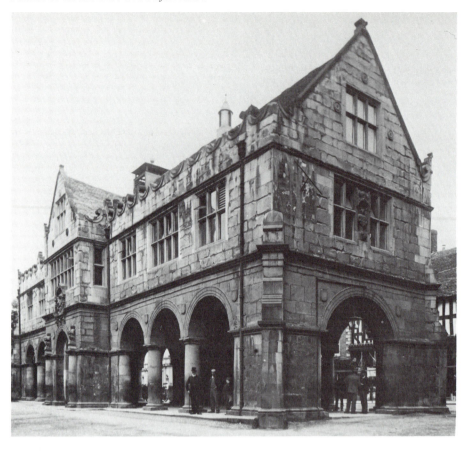

The Market Hall, Shrewsbury (1596).

structure throughout the marches and proclaims the town's commercial and cultural dominance of its wide hinterland.

With the exception of Bellstone House all the stone houses in the town were manifestly old at the death of Elizabeth, and the sparkling novelty of the Market Hall and the School symbolised the change in the distribution of wealth and power which had occurred during the sixteenth century. That age has been seen by some historians as one in which urban oligarchies, encouraged by Tudor monarchs, developed rapidly. The surviving buildings of Shrewsbury, for all their fragmentary character, suggest that the development was not so straightforward; it was less that a late-medieval democracy was subverted as that an urban oligarchy dominated by a few great men both within and without the town threw off that control and, in alliance with men of comparable standing in the countryside, achieved something like homogeneity within its own ranks. With that went an increased sense of common interests and identity and of independence of all but the Crown. These changes were progressively reflected architecturally in the cessation of the building of large stone houses based on rural models, in the building instead of large timber properties as whole or part-speculations, in the appearance later of many smaller houses with appropriate small-scale decoration, and finally in the erection of magnificent municipal structures that no neighbouring town could equal.

(I am grateful for much information and many helpful suggestions and comments to Mr George Baugh, Mr Anthony Carr, and the staff of the Shrewsbury Local Studies Library, Dr David Cox, Mrs Madge Moran and Dr Paul Stamper.)

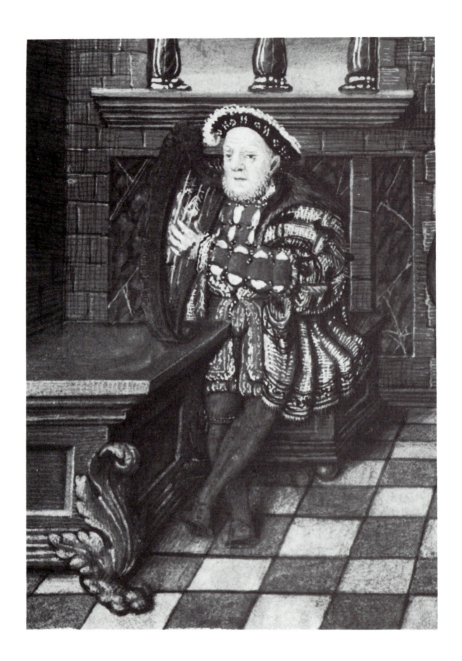

Henry VIII playing the harp.

4 Music

JOHN MILSOM

Introduction

> On Thursday morning, her Majesty was no sooner ready, and at her gallery
> window looking into the garden, when there began three cornetts to play
> certain fantastic dances, at the measure whereof the Fairy Queen came into
> the garden . . . After [a] speech, the Fairy Queen and her maids danced
> about the garden, singing a song of six parts, with the music of an exquisite
> consort; wherein was the lute, bandora, bass viol, cittern, treble viol and
> flute . . . [the bandora and cittern were related to the lute] This spectacle
> and music so delighted her Majesty that she commanded to hear it sung and
> to be danced three times over, and called for divers lords and ladies to
> behold it . . .

So began the fourth and last day of Elizabeth I's visit to Elvetham House,
the Hampshire home of Edward Seymour, Earl of Hertford, in September
1591. From beginning to end the entertainments had been conceived on the
grandest scale. Some were acted out on the great crescent-shaped lake that
had been specially constructed for the occasion, complete with artificial
islands and a fleet of elaborate barges; others took place in the grounds or
within the house itself. Grand orations greeted Elizabeth with all due
reverence; fireworks blazed in her honour; the pageantry was magnificent, the
banquets sumptuous; and the music too had amounted to a veritable feast of
assorted courses. A further extract from the contemporary account of the
festivities gives another glimpse into the brilliance of the musical contrivances
that so absorbed the queen:

Near to her [on a barge] were placed three excellent voices, to sing to one lute, and in
two other boats hard by, other lutes and voices, to answer by manner of echo . . . The
three voices in the pinnace sang a song to the lute, with excellent divisions
[ornamentation], and the end of every verse was replied by lutes and voices in the
other boat somewhat afar off, as if they had been echoes.

That music should have occupied such a central position in these
entertainments is not surprising, for Elizabeth herself is known have been

deeply musical. A few years after Elvetham she recalled to the French ambassador how in her youth she had 'danced very well, composed balletts and music, and played and danced them myself'. This was no idle boast. For the Queen, no less than for many of the courtiers who surrounded her, the ability to dance and to make music served not only as a means of recreation but also as a social grace, one by which good taste and evidence of a good upbringing might be gauged. We know, for example, that Elizabeth was a skilful player of the delicate virginals – the fashionable, harpsichord-like keyboard instrument of the day – and that she maintained a pride in her achievements. It irked her that Mary, Queen of Scots, was thought by some to be a better keyboard player than herself. During a visit to London in 1564, Sir James Melville, one of Mary's courtiers, was trapped into making a comparison between the two queens. To judge by the entry in his memoirs, the encounter must have been stage-managed by Elizabeth herself:

After dinner my lord of Hunsdon [Elizabeth's first cousin] drew me to a quiet gallery, that I might hear some music (but he said he durst not avow it) where I might hear the Queen play upon the virginals. After I had hearkened a while, I took by the tapestry that hung before the door of the chamber, and seeing her back was towards the door, I entered within the chamber, and stood a pretty space hearing her play excellently well. But she left off immediately so soon as she turned her about and saw me. She appeared to be surprised to see me, and came forward, seeming to strike me with her hand; alleging she used not to play before men, but when she was solitary, to shun melancholy . . . She asked whether my queen or she played best. In that I felt obliged to give her the praise.

Elizabeth acquired her love of music in her childhood, and for this she had her father, Henry VIII, to thank. From his youth, Henry himself was fascinated by music, and during the early, relatively carefree years of his first marriage he surrounded himself with the best musicians he could find to employ. For his Chapel Royal he sought the cream of English singers, many of whom were also composers. For his household musicians he looked mainly to foreigners: Italian and Flemish minstrels, trained to standards higher than England could produce, who became his employees. Court records of the time also mention the various visiting musicians who performed before him. Henry himself sang and played a variety of wind, string and keyboard instruments. Even more remarkably, he composed music – pieces of somewhat limited accomplishment that were recorded for posterity, one suspects, more on account of their royal authorship than for their intrinsic merit. Perhaps most important of all, Henry ensured that all three of his heirs – Edward, Mary and Elizabeth – were trained to read and perform music, and he brought them up to value its presence in their daily lives, whether in court or chapel. The sheer musicality of the English royal family, and its patronage of musicians throughout the sixteenth century, accounts at least in part for the extraordinary proliferation of art music during the Tudor era. It is an inescapable fact that their music-making resonated through the upper levels of English society. What the ruling monarch appreciated, the courtier could barely choose to scorn.

The musical expertise of Henry VIII and his children in turn bears witness to a social trend characteristic of the sixteenth century throughout

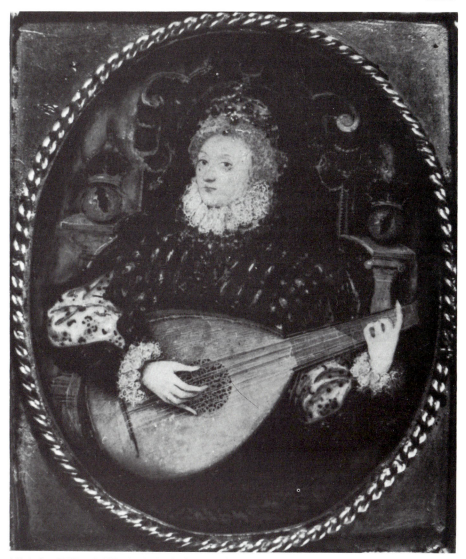

Nicholas Hilliard, Elizabeth I playing the lute.

Renaissance Europe. In an age of increasing literacy, the ability to read music itself became an accomplishment to which the educated readily aspired. Not content merely to pay others to sing and play before them, members of the nobility found pleasure in making music themselves. Baldassare Castiglione's *Il libro del Cortegiano*, translated into English as *The Book of the Courtier* by Sir Thomas Hoby in 1561, actively encouraged amateur musicianship. Other so-called courtesy books added their support. Foreign travel brought the English face-to-face with domestic music abroad. To judge by the following entry from his autobiography, the Elizabethan composer and musician Thomas Whythorne (1528–96) was deeply impressed by the situation he witnessed during his visit to Italy:

Ye shall find in that country, in most men's houses that be of any reputation or account, not only instruments of music, but also all sorts of music in print, having sets of books in their houses for singing and for instruments . . . Because that when there be many in one company together who can sing pricksong [part-music] perfectly, ye shall in those books find songs of diverse trades for them to sing. And for that the printers would have every day new songs to print, they do fee the best musicians that they can retain . . .

One wonders what proportion of the Elizabethan upper and merchant classes joined Philomathes, one of the imaginary interlocutors in Thomas Morley's *A Plain and Easy Introduction to Practical Music* of 1597, in his acute embarrassment at not being suitably equipped to share in social music-making:

Supper being ended and music books (according to the custom) being brought to the table, the mistress of the house presented me with a part earnestly requesting me to sing; but when, after many excuses, I protested unfeignedly that I could not, every one began to wonder; yea, some whispered to others demanding how I was brought up, so that upon shame I go now to seek out my old friend Master Gnorimus, to make myself his scholar.

The spread of musical literacy during the second half of the century, and the amateur's newly acquired ability to sing a part in a song or a madrigal or to turn his hand to the lute, harpsichord or viol, steadily increased the demand for new music. Symptomatic of this change during Elizabeth's reign is the considerable number of surviving music manuscripts that were copied for or by amateurs, and also the first flowering of the music printing industry in England. By the last decade of the sixteenth century the printing of secular music, madrigals, metrical psalms and lute-songs in particular, reflected a demand that would have been inconceivable at the beginning of Henry VIII's reign. Music notation which for reasons of design lent itself less easily to the printing process, such as keyboard scores and tablature (a form of music notation) for the lute, relied instead on manuscript copies for its circulation, though here too the music symbols were often copied on to pages of blank staves that had themselves been mass-produced and sold as 'ruled paper imprinted'. Viewed as a whole, these various books of music, both manu-script and printed, give the impression that the 'golden age' of Elizabethan music was, to a large extent, also the golden age of the amateur performer.

The situation had been significantly different during the first half of the sixteenth century. Without a doubt, one of the chief glories of early Tudor culture had been its church music, the extravagance and sensuousness of which had entirely suited the late-medieval richness of the English Catholic liturgy. Not only the Chapel Royal but also the royal collegiate foundations (such as St Stephen's, Westminster), the private household chapels, the colleges of Oxford and Cambridge, and the principal cathedrals, abbeys and parish churches of the country, all maintained choirs made up of minor canons or staffs of professional lay singers, variously directed by an organist or a choirmaster. Their aim was to embellish the annual cycle of daily religious observances, both during mass and in the offices. From the ranks of these church musicians a succession of distinguished composers emerged –

the task of writing music being at this time an adjunct to playing or singing it rather than a profession in its own right. A simple roll-call of these musicians' names is enough to evoke the wonders of the early Tudor era: Robert Fayrfax, William Cornysh, John Taverner, Nicholas Ludford, Hugh Aston, Christopher Tye, Thomas Tallis, John Sheppard, and other, smaller talents too numerous to mention, epitomise the best in Henrician music, just as the names of William Byrd, Thomas Morley, Thomas Weelkes, Orlando Gibbons and John Dowland symbolise the wonders of Elizabethan and Jacobean musical culture.

For professional church musicians, however, the mid-century was a period of deep uncertainty. Two crushing blows were dealt to the musical establishment, blows that few choral foundations withstood without sustaining severe damage. First came the Dissolution of the Monasteries, an act of wholesale plunder designed by Henry VIII to raise revenue at the Church's expense; and second, on the accession to the throne of Henry's son Edward VI in 1547, England witnessed the reformation of its state religion, imposed by authority and organised largely along lines previously laid down by the Calvinists and other Protestant sects on the continent. The effects on music were compound and sometimes devastating. Whether by closure or impoverishment, the Dissolution effectively decimated the number of institutions that were capable of maintaining choral services, and this in turn reduced the number of places at which a budding musician, whether chorister or adult, could learn his craft. Moreover, the Protestant reformers actively sought to change the function of music in divine worship by playing down its decorative quality, demanding instead a more austere idiom in which words and music were welded together into close, utilitarian union.

The full significance of these changes can most readily, and poignantly, be understood by considering the early career of one of the leading English church musicians of the mid-sixteenth century. Thomas Tallis was born around 1505 and, by the early 1530s, had already begun to stand apart from his contemporaries on account of his considerable promise as a young organist and composer. One of his early appointments, to Waltham Abbey in Essex, came to an abrupt end when, in 1540, the entire choir of twelve singing-men and five choristers was pensioned off, and the abbey itself suffered dissolution. Tallis moved to Canterbury Cathedral, but remained there only as long as it took him to secure election as a Gentleman of the Chapel Royal. Once installed in this latter post, he remained in the comparative protection of royal service for the remaining forty-four years of his life.

Like his colleagues, Tallis provided music of whatever kind the Chapel Royal authorities asked of him. At first the musical fare was relatively traditional, since neither Henry's break with Rome over the issue of the divorce nor the Dissolution affected the Church's demand for rich masses, magnificats, and antiphons addressed to the Virgin Mary. During Edward VI's reign, on the other hand, Tallis was required to cut his cloth according to an entirely new fashion. Where flamboyance and extravagance of melody had reigned supreme, there was now to be sobriety and economy; where textures had been rich and complex, simplicity was to be cultivated; where the words had been lost among details determined by purely musical considerations, they were now to emerge with plain, didactic clarity, and the music was to subordinate itself to their total audibility. In addition, the texts of the new, unfamiliar liturgy were to be in English rather than the traditional Latin. Almost overnight, the very basis of the church composer's craft was called into question, and it was the musician's responsibility to alter his ways.

There was further confusion to come. On Edward's early death, the new queen regnant reinstated the Catholic liturgy complete with all its familiar trappings of rich ceremony. For five years Mary encouraged her Chapel Royal musicians – and, by example, presumably English church musicians at large – to indulge in the luxury of resorting to old fashions. Experienced men such as Tallis simply resumed where they had left off, sometimes with even greater extravagance than before. Younger colleagues such as Robert White and William Mundy tried their hands at the florid style for virtually the first time. And one even younger chorister, William Byrd, almost certainly began his career by singing this music, as well as making his first tentative steps towards writing similar works himself. Even now, however, the number of institutions that could support a choral service was small when compared with the situation thirty years earlier. In Elizabeth's reign, this number can hardly have grown, if indeed it did not shrink even further.

By 1558, the year of Elizabeth's accession, much of the talent in English church music had become focused on the Chapel Royal, a handful of buildings in or around London (the most prominent being Westminster Abbey, St Paul's Cathedral and St George's Chapel, Windsor) and the college chapels of the universities, places where reasonably large-scale anthems and settings of the canticles were still deemed acceptable. It is often forgotten that the period we regard today as being the resplendent culmination of a golden century of English music was in effect a dark age for all but a very few of the institutions that had formerly nurtured musicians in quantity: the church choirs.

There is an additional reason why Elizabethan church music seems to us less significant than the songs, madrigals, consort, lute and keyboard music practised in courtly circles at that time. The music books that once contained this ecclesiastical repertory have, almost without exception, disappeared without trace, largely because their contents gradually fell out of fashion, or the books themselves disintegrated with use and were never replaced. Not a single manuscript copy of anthems or services that formerly belonged to the Chapel Royal or a major cathedral or collegiate chapel survives from the years of Elizabeth's reign, and what we have of the church music of the age is known largely from sources of much later date. Even the prolific William Byrd (1543–1623), whose long association with the Chapel Royal must have resulted in a significant quantity of Anglican music, is today credited with only a handful of English-texted works that can have been suited to the official liturgy of the time. There is little doubt that much Elizabethan church music has simply been lost.

What does survive in considerable quantity, however, is the music Byrd composed for the Roman Catholics: Latin-texted motets for singing privately, and both masses and settings of Roman liturgical texts that served the Catholics in their clandestine services. This music was printed in Byrd's lifetime, partly as propaganda, and copies survive where manuscripts of his English-texted church music have perished. Like several other musicians of his generation, Byrd's personal commitment to the old faith was total, even though he remained professionally associated with the Protestant church for his entire career. Quite simply, he led a double life, with one hand serving the Chapel Royal as organist and composer, and the other composing music that expressed his own faith and met the needs of the Catholic underworld, in particular the network of patrons in whose circle he moved and to whom several of his publications of motets were dedicated. It is due to the vehemence of his personal religious convictions that the masses and motets of William Byrd – the composer who was, in any case, without doubt the most prodigious musical talent of his age – seem today to form the very apogee of the tradition of Tudor sacred music. There is a delicious irony in the fact that this music has, in the cathedrals and collegiate chapels of our own time, been accepted back into the Protestant liturgy that Byrd himself must privately have abhorred.

Although church, collegiate and cathedral employment provided the principal means of support for many professional composers, it is often the case that these same church musicians also wrote secular music for entertainment, recreation and educational purposes. Particularly during the earlier part of the sixteenth century, named composers of songs and instrumental music are almost always the ones familiar from the repertory of the church. This may seem surprising in view of the fact that Henry VIII employed a substantial body of instrumentalists and singers, quite separate from the members of his Chapel Royal, to entertain the court with secular music. What did these household musicians sing and play, and – assuming that they composed music themselves – why does so little of it survive?

The answer partly lies in an understanding of the minstrel's profession, which differed in fundamental ways from that of the church musician. Minstrels were in general artisans of relatively low social status whose craft, often learnt by rote and handed down through families and colleagues, relied little upon the ability to read and write music. Unlike the members of the Chapel Royal, Henry VIII's lutenists, trumpeters and viol players must have committed to memory most of the music they could play. Like jazz and popular musicians in our own century, their performances grew more out of collective improvisation, rehearsal and memorisation than from reliance upon written musical scores. For this reason, more is known about the names, life-histories and even the salaries of these men than about the actual music they played. Church musicians, on the other hand, were by necessity literate; their own songs and instrumental pieces were readily committed to paper, and some have survived, though admittedly in meagre quantity when placed beside the rich store of secular music from Elizabeth's reign. It is almost as easy today to hear the courtly, chivalric songs of Robert Fayfrax or William Cornysh, written for the amusement of Henry VIII and his court, as it is to encounter the masses and antiphons these men composed for the services of the Chapel Royal.

The demand for recreational music created by the rise of the new class of amateur performers in the later sixteenth century made it feasible for musicians to supplement their incomes, or to win patronage and favour, by turning their hands increasingly to the composition of music for domestic consumption. Typical of this trend was the sudden rise in popularity of the madrigal in England, a vogue that began in the late 1580s and waned some thirty years later. The fact that the madrigal as a genre was Italian by origin may in part explain its attraction to a society that was in general keen to absorb the latest in transalpine trends and ideas. For many Elizabethans, however, there was the barrier of language. A London singer, Nicholas Yonge, acknowledged the existence of this problem in his preface to the collection of Italian madrigals he published in London in 1588 under the title of *Musica Transalpina*:

Since I first began to keep house in this city, it hath been no small comfort unto me that a great number of gentlemen and merchants of good accompt (as well of this realm as of foreign nations) have taken in good part such entertainment of pleasure as my poor ability was able to afford them, both by the exercise of music daily used in my house, and by furnishing them with books of that kind yearly sent me out of Italy and other places, which being for the most part Italian songs are for sweetness of air very well liked of all, but most in account with them that understand that language. As for the rest, they do either not sing them at all, or at least with little delight.

The success of Yonge's venture, and others like it published in its wake, was due in no small part to the fact that these selections of Italian madrigals were furnished with English texts, some of them more or less related in subject-matter to those of the Italian originals, others following nothing more than the verse-forms and general style of the poetical models. However hybrid the net results may have been, there is no denying the fact that these early examples of English-texted madrigals caught the imagination both of amateur singers and many English composers. Several of the latter, including Thomas Morley, Thomas Weelkes and Thomas Tomkins, were established professional church musicians who derived profit and – to judge by the gaiety of their settings – pleasure from this side-line. Others such as John Wilbye and John Ward were employed as personal musicians to individual families; Wilbye's patrons, for example, were the music-loving Kytsons of Hengrave Hall in Suffolk, and it was from them – as well, presumably, as from the sale of his music to (or through) his publisher – that he derived his income. A further group of musicians that included William Byrd and Orlando Gibbons participated in the vogue only with some reluctance, shunning in particular the artifice, levity and frequent lack of substance of fashionable madrigal verse, and making only occasional contributions to the genre.

Many Elizabethan madrigal collections were advertised as being 'apt for voices or viols', a flexibility of usage that reflects not only the rise of singing amongst amateurs but also the spread of performing proficiency on instruments. The delicate voice of the viol had first been heard in England during Henry VIII's reign, played by professionals at court, though there are very few surviving consort works by English composers from before the 1560s. As the century progressed, the viol became one of the most popular domestic instruments, largely because the frets of its fingerboard encouraged the untrained hand to fall correctly into place, and many late Tudor composers added fantasias, stylised dances and other consort works to its repertoire. Here again, William Byrd stands out as a leading exponent of the genre. Ensemble songs for solo voice accompanied by viols, often setting serious verse or metrical versions of the psalms, found favour in circles that cared little for the new fashion of the madrigal. The music manuscripts of the Norfolk gentleman Edward Paston, for example, demonstrate his preference for the consort songs of Byrd over the madrigals of Morley, Weelkes and their followers.

The viol, which differs from the violin in its stringing and in being held on or between the knees, was a relatively easy instrument for the amateur to master, as well as being one ideally suited to undemanding social music-making. The more intimate solo instruments, on the other hand – the lute and the virginals – called for greater dexterity on the part of the soloist, and Elizabeth was just one of the many players who found the lure of attaining a degree of virtuosity hard to resist. Records of payments for instruments, for repairs, tuition and the purchase of music to play abound in the household accounts of the late Tudor nobility. Again, the truly great music for these instruments dates from Elizabeth's reign, though in each case the development of the repertoire can be traced back to early Tudor times, even if only tentatively because of the scarcity of sources.

As one might expect, it was the professional organists who furnished the Elizabethans with most of their keyboard music. More surprising, however, is the fact that only a small proportion of their surviving music was composed specifically for performance on the organ or for use in church services. There is possibly a simple explanation for this. No less in Tudor times than in our

Title-page to William Daman's The Psalmes of David in English meter *(1579)*.

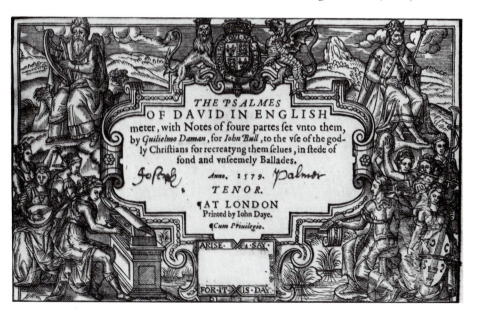

own, the church organist was expected to be able to extemporise. The demand for written copies of organ music suitable for performance before, during and after church services may not have been great for the very reason that most players were competent improvisers, or because they carried much of their solo repertoire in their heads. Music notation, on the other hand, was the only effective means of delivering new works into the hands of amateur performers. Put another way, the fact that so many of the surviving sources of Tudor keyboard music contain exclusively secular pieces yet again illustrates the amateur's quest for good new music during the late sixteenth century. It is largely because of the different conditions of supply and demand that we know so little about the organ music that was heard in the chapels, churches and cathedrals of Elizabethan England, but so much about the pavans and galliards, fancies and variations that were played by (or before) educated men and women in the privacy of their halls or chambers. It was largely for these people that the extant keyboard works of William Byrd and Orlando Gibbons, John Bull and Thomas Tomkins, were composed or ultimately destined.

The lute, together with other related plucked instruments such as the cittern and bandora, called for performance techniques all of their own, and there is little evidence to suggest that many church-based musicians attempted to master them. For this reason, the composers of lute music – and, to a lesser extent, of ayres for solo voice accompanied by the lute – tend not to be names familiar as composers of anthems, motets, and music for viols or keyboard. Virtually no lute music by Byrd is known, for example, and it is almost certainly an instrument that he never chose to explore, though other hands may have arranged his music for playing on the lute. Thomas Morley wrote lute songs, and happily accepted the lute and its relatives into his works scored for mixed consorts of instruments, but again he composed little for solo lute. The solo repertory is instead dominated by men who were themselves skilled players, and above all by the works of the leading court lutenist, John Dowland (who is discussed by Wilfrid Mellers in Volume 4).

Whether scored for voices or instruments, destined for Protestants or Catholics, played before magnates or by merchants, Tudor music is, above all, distinctive by its Englishness of style. Leaving aside the fashion for the Italianate madrigal during the final decades of the sixteenth century, it is on the whole true to say that English composers were inclined to honour forms and techniques inherited from their forefathers and to maintain a strong sense of national identity, whether out of ignorance of the alternatives that existed elsewhere in Europe or in the full knowledge – and pride – that their music preserved an English character. This is not to say that foreign influences were insignificant, but rather that the English tended to absorb ideas from abroad selectively, and they rarely indulged in pastiche. To take a specific example, it is clear that however much William Byrd may have learnt from singing and studying the motets of his foreign counterparts, in particular those of his Italian friend Alfonso Ferrabosco, his own motets ultimately reveal the sheer depth of his respect for the music of his native English heritage.

It is perhaps not surprising to find that the few passages of music criticism that survive from Tudor England invariably view the tradition of English music as one quite distinct from that of the continent, and declare both preference for and pride in the works of English composers. Perhaps most famous of these is a poem in praise of Byrd by John Baldwin, a chapel singer, music copyist and composer. Dated 1591, it prefaces one of his manuscript anthologies of music, and names the composers whose music is included (or was intended to feature) in the collection, including some of the most prominent foreign writers of the age. As Morrison Comegys Boyd says of it in his study of Elizabethan music, the following extract is 'poor poetry, but good criticism'. It also epitomises the sense of national identity that was held by many musical circles throughout Tudor England.

> I will begin with White, Sheppard, Tye and Tallis,
> Parsons, Giles, Mundy (th'old one of the Queen's palace),
> Mundy young, th'old man's son, and like wise others moe;
> Their names would be too long, therefore I let them go.
> Yet must I speak of moe even of strangers also;
> And first I must bring in Alfonso Ferrabosco.
> A stranger born he was in Italy as I hear;
> Italians say of him in skill he had no peer.
> Luca Marenzio with others many moe,
> As Philippe de Monte, the Emperor's man also;
> And Orlando [Lassus] by name and eke Crecquillion;
> Cipriano Rore, and also Andreon [Gabrieli?].
> All famous in their art, there is of that no doubt.
> Their works no less declare in every place about.
> Yet let not strangers brag, nor they these so commend,
> For they may now give place and set themselves behind
> An Englishman, by name William Byrd, for his skill,
> Which I should have set first, for so it was my will;
> Whose greater skill and knowledge doth excel all at this time,
> And far to strange countries abroad his skill doth shine.
> Famous men be abroad, and skilful in their art;
> I do confess the fame, and not from it start.
> But in Europe is none like to our English man,
> Which doth so far exceed, as truly I it scan,
> As ye cannot find out his equal in all things
> Throughout the world so wide . . .

Music and worship in Tudor England

During the first three decades of the twentieth century, a team of British musicologists set about the task of reviving and publishing the religious music of Tudor and Jacobean England. Although a little of this music had enjoyed more or less continuous exposure through the centuries, having never completely fallen out of use within the liturgy of the Anglican church, much of the repertoire that survived attracted little interest except among antiquarians and collectors. (This was particularly true of pre-Reformation works with Latin texts, and of other pieces so overtly Catholic that their usefulness to British worship was severely limited.) Ignoring such issues of practical relevance and emphasising instead the intrinsic quality of this long-ignored music, the editors began the process of sifting through the manuscripts and early printed editions, bringing together the works of the most conspicuous composers, and publishing them in imposing folio volumes under the broad and evocative title of *Tudor Church Music*. Ten such volumes appeared between 1922 and 1929, and many more would have been issued had the project not run out of money and foundered, leaving much of these pioneer editors' work unpublished.

Subsequent generations have helped themselves liberally not only to the contents of these books but also to the vague, generalised concept of 'Tudor church music', a concept epitomised today by the sound of a choir of boys and men singing in the resonant ambience of a large, vaulted church such as Westminster Abbey or the Chapel of King's College, Cambridge. Like all performance arts, however, music lends itself to misrepresentation through the very act of being revived in sound, misrepresentation that may not immediately strike an audience whose contact with the object is made primarily or exclusively through its sound in performance rather than from the more innocent printed page. In this respect, a piece of Tudor music differs fundamentally from a building, a painting or even a poem of the age, all of which can confront us today – albeit as objects from a distant, foreign world – in much the same manner as they confronted men and women of their own time.

A setting of the mass by William Byrd is open to as many different interpretations as is (say) one of Shakespeare's plays. Whether or not it necessarily suffers from being performed in a manner that would have been alien to the composer himself is a difficult issue to resolve, and one that is warmly debated today. Certainly a deep level of appreciation is possible through any encounter with the music itself, however fanciful the performance itself may be and irrespective of the extent to which its original historical context is known to either performer or listener. It is equally true, however, that an understanding of this context often provides clues that are useful, and sometimes vital, to interpretation and valid criticism. It is largely through the investigation of these contexts that the generalised view of 'Tudor church music' has begun to break down into a more sensitive appreciation of the various roles that music played in specific acts of Tudor worship.

The strands that contribute to this appreciation themselves intertwine in a delicate counterpoint. There is the theme of function, of the use for which a piece of music was originally conceived; and this often connects with the issues of patronage and church history. Then there is the theme of nationality and heritage: all Tudor composers recognised the strength and individuality of their native musical tradition, and many of them chose to celebrate this by emphasising their Englishness rather than accepting wholesale the way in which composers in other countries chose to write. Words such as 'emulation', 'homage' and 'nostalgia' are difficult to avoid in any discussion of Tudor religious music.

There is the theme, too, of internal development within the canon of any one individual composer – development in the sense that a man who writes music is alert not only to the various kinds of commission he receives, and to the extent of his allegiance to his heritage, but also to the growth of his own musical personality, to the exploration of techniques that seem pregnant with possibilities and the rejection of others that are better left to rest. The works of a composer, like those of any other artist, can be viewed as statements of self-criticism, revealing evidence in one work of a moment of discovery, in the next of an act of consolidation, and this often helps to explain why a particular work behaves in the way it does.

In practice, of course, these various themes prove to be interdependent rather than independent, just as the lines of Tudor musical counterpoint themselves weave into a web of mutual support. Conservativism and the deliberate cultivation of 'Englishness', for example, were issues that could concern the patron no less than the composer. In an age of political and theological isolation from other nations on the continent of Europe, there are examples of pieces of music that seem to proclaim not just their nationality but equally a defiant spirit of nationalism. Although we lack documents to prove that patrons directly influenced the ways in which Tudor composers wrote, there are good reasons for believing that this particular law of demand and supply sometimes did obtain, even if less so than with the visual arts.

Among the composers who were singled out for publication by the editors of *Tudor Church Music* was John Taverner (*c.* 1490–1545). It is largely because of this early exposure in modern printed form that Taverner's music has acquired a currency among performers today, while the works of his contemporaries such as Robert Fayrfax, William Cornysh, Nicholas Ludford and the Scottish composer Robert Carver (*c.* 1490 – after 1546), none of whom are represented in the pages of *Tudor Church Music*, are still rarely heard. Providing a context for Taverner's music is made difficult by the fact that his biography is sketchy. In addition, many of his works have been lost. For one brief period of his life, however, the documentation is sufficiently full to allow background, biography and surviving music to meld in such a way that detailed interpretation becomes possible; and this helps to shed light not only on the way in which an early Tudor church composer went about his business, but also on the ways in which that business might itself be shaped by the hands of a specific patron, in this case Cardinal Thomas Wolsey.

Between 1526 and 1530, Taverner acted as instructor of the choristers (in effect, musical director) at the chapel of Wolsey's newly founded Cardinal College in Oxford – the college that was later refounded under its present name of Christ Church. Taverner's 'contract' with Wolsey is typical of its time, and relatively easy to summarise. Like all church composers, his duties were primarily administrative, and concerned with the practicalities of day-to-day liturgical requirements: the recruitment and training of a choir of men and boy singers, the numbers of which were controlled by the statutes of the college; collecting and assembling suitable music, and where necessary or desirable, composing new pieces himself; rehearsing this music, and directing performances during the services.

Wolsey's choice of Taverner as his chapelmaster is significant, for he could not have selected a more quintessentially English composer. Nor was

Wolsey's choice made out of ignorance of the alternatives open to him; the alternative, above all, of importing a musician from abroad. That he should have chosen not to do so, at a time when the English were keenly watchful of foreign ideas in general, is important. It is worth recalling that on 23 June 1520 the chapels royal of France and England had sung mass together during the service that formed a highlight of the showy and not entirely sincere peace-seeking encounters between Henry VIII and Francis I at the Field of Cloth of Gold. Wolsey himself had officiated as the English and French organists accompanied one another's choirs, the French singers performing the first introit, the English the second, and so on in alternation. Notwith-standing the sense of rivalry that must have coloured the event, it is clear that during this service – and on several other recorded occasions – Wolsey was confronted with the extreme stylistic differences that distinguished French music from English.

Inspired by humanistic ideals, French composers such as Jean Mouton and Claudin de Sermisy sought a rhetorical style in which declamatory melodic lines, shaped in such a way that they captured and stylised the rhythm and inflexion of speech, were built up into tidy terraces of entries in the various voice-parts. There is a feeling for economy, orderliness and symmetry in their work, bound up with a deep desire to relate music to words in a direct, rational way; and this stood in fundamental opposition to the aims of the composers from Henry VIII's chapel royal, composers such as Fayrfax and Cornysh. The early Tudor aesthetic, by contrast, favoured an abundance of florid melody that maintained relative indifference to the projection of the verbal text, musical lines that often span dozens of notes to just one or two syllables. Frequently they owe little if anything at all to the rhythm, stress-patterns and meaning of the words, and instead they seem to have been contrived so as to stream against one another to form as complex a tissue of sound as possible.

Since both Wolsey and Henry VIII seem to have been discriminating about music, it is significant that neither man appears to have made any attempt whatever to emulate the music-making of the French chapel royal – nor, for that matter, of any other foreign church or chapel choir. In fact, to judge by the lists of musicians who provided music in the various Tudor choral foundations through the sixteenth century, foreign composers and singers never entered their ranks. Chapel singing in England was exclusively a job for Englishmen, and new generations of composers were trained up as choristers under the tutelage of English choirmasters. Equally telling is the fact that early Tudor music books contain virtually no works by foreigners. Although Henry VIII was presented with various finely executed manuscripts of Burgundian, French and Italian church music, there is no evidence to suggest that his choirmen ever sang from them. The fact that their contents did not subsequently disseminate in English manuscripts may well support the view that they were met with indifference. In its turn, English music was virtually unknown abroad.

Considered in this light, Wolsey's choice of John Taverner as *informator choristarum* of his new, richly-endowed Oxford college in 1526 reflects a prevailing sense of nationalism bordering on chauvinism. That a collection of

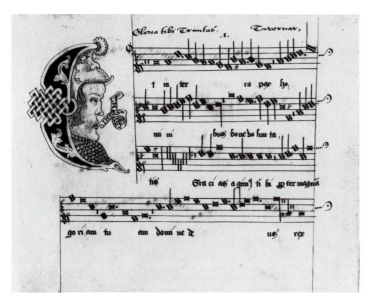

Page from John Taverner's Missa Gloria tibi Trinitas.

mass-settings copied at Cardinal College during Taverner's years there – the so-called 'Forrest-Heather' partbooks – contains no foreign music bolsters this impression. Above all, there is the evidence of Taverner's own music, which is so emphatically florid and extravagant that it must surely indicate Wolsey's aim to fill his chapel with sounds of thoroughbred Englishness.

Nowhere is this quality heard to better advantage than in Taverner's *Missa Gloria tibi Trinitas*, a huge, complex and extremely long setting of the mass that must have been stimulated by Wolsey's desire for splendour and displays of rich ceremony. It offers a classic example of how patron and composer proceeded hand in hand, the one offering facilities in the form of buildings and a virtuosic choir, the other writing music that was capable of testing that virtuosity to its limit, and which exploited the physical space of the church to best advantage. Not surprisingly, it is music that calls for unusual stamina and technical competence on the part of the singers, to the extent that it is among the most difficult works of its time to perform. Typically, Taverner's concern here is less with the clearly audible enunciation of the texts of the mass than with pure melody, melody in which the meaning of specific words or phrases is all but lost among the vast vaulting lines and constantly renewing bursts of energy. Rarely does Taverner try his hand at the modern continental techniques of imitation. According to this principle, a melodic idea that emphasises the speech-pattern of a phrase of text is announced by one voice-part and is then passed to others in turn, resulting in a texture that is shot through by varied repetitions of thematic cells. Imitation gives rise to textural unity; on the whole, Taverner's music is concerned with variety, and his mass uses the technique sparingly.

Deep within the *Missa Gloria tibi Trinitas* is order of another kind, order that Taverner calculated when designing the work but which communicates itself to the modern listener only by its general effect. Like the contemporary architect, the early Tudor church composer traditionally worked with sets of numbers and ideas of ratio and proportion in his head, schemes relating to the duration of movements and sub-sections that ensured overall balance in the finished product and provided an initial grid on which he could then work out detail. The result is music that proceeds as a succession of blocks, sometimes of several minutes' duration, which are contrasted from one another by texture but are internally relatively stable. Taverner's mass opens, for example, with a passage of music for the full six-part choir. After a pause, the number of voice-parts reduces to just three for another substantial section. Thereafter, various long spans of duos, trios and quartets alternate with the *tutti* in a manner that seems – and is – schematic rather than intuitive.

Equally lost on the modern listener is the melody that, in theory at least, serves as the work's foundation and gives it its name. Taverner's method was a well established and time-honoured one: he took a traditional plainchant melody, 'Gloria tibi Trinitas', and stated it in long, slow-moving notes in one of the inner voices, all but inaudible among the profusion of melodies that he then freely composed around it. Rich in symbolism – not least because the mass was composed for Cardinal College, itself dedicated to the Holy Trinity – there is logic to the method, but logic that the eye appreciates more readily than does the ear. It is a memorable moment, then, when at the words 'in nomine Domini' of the Benedictus the plainchant tune suddenly assumes a quicker rhythmic guise and proceeds at a confident, steady pace. During this passage the exposed chant is accompanied by three voices whose melodies are for once made up of shared, imitative material: as one voice announces a snatch of thematic idea, the other voices pounce upon it, evaluating and reinterpreting it in turn.

The genius of this passage provoked an astonishing array of responses (in the form of homage and competition) by Taverner's English colleagues and successors, responses that point to the existence of a close-knit, insular school of composers. The challenge was to take the same plainchant melody and compose new music around it, in emulation of Taverner's original, not for church use but rather to be played on viols or keyboard instruments. Christopher Tye alone wrote more than twenty 'In nomines', William Byrd perhaps as many as seven, and virtually no major composer of the later sixteenth century failed to contribute at least one setting to this curious and exclusively English secular genre.

The enduring impression left by a performance of Taverner's *Missa Gloria tibi Trinitas*, however, is not of the logic of its structural bases but rather of a huge display of vigorous, powerful and long-spanned melodies that mesh together into luscious harmony, a supremely musical experience that reflects in a vague yet powerful way the nobility of the text. Like a great vaulted cathedral, it serves as an ambience in which worship can take place, a spectacular sound-world that impresses by its sheer size, magnificence and, at times, the complexity of its detail. It is also a manifestation of wealth and benefaction – in this case, Wolsey's. Works of its kind, if not always quite on the same scale, are common in early Tudor manuscripts that can be linked with the richest collegiate, cathedral and monastic choral foundations of the time, in particular those with royal connections. This was no music destined for the provincial parish church.

It comes as no surprise to discover that such florid music had its opponents, particularly among those members of the clergy who feared that the trappings of worship could all too easily encourage idolatry, drawing attention away from the more fundamental ideas and beliefs that lay (or, to their minds, ought to have lain) behind them. Left to their own devices, Tudor composers might well have continued to compose with extravagance and abandon. That they did not was, to a large extent, due to the restrictions that were placed upon them by authority. Respect for this florid style does, however, remain a constant theme in later Tudor religious music, particularly music associated with the Catholics. Old works such as Taverner's *Missa Gloria tibi Trinitas* continued to be cherished and recopied even into the early seventeenth century; in many cases, whole pieces would have been lost today had they not been saved by Elizabethan and Jacobean collectors. Even more telling is the way in which the florid style continued to breathe life into English sacred music long after the Reformation.

During the reign of Mary Tudor (1553–8) the style was deliberately resuscitated, presumably by royal demand, in an attempt to evoke stable days long before the divorce, the break with Rome and the spread of Protestantism. It is from the brief span of her rule, for example, that two of the most massive and marvellously ornate Tudor votive antiphons appear to date: Thomas Tallis's *Gaude gloriosa Dei Mater*, in which the text seems deliberately to refer ambiguously both to the Blessed Virgin and the queen herself, and *Vox Patris celestis* by William Mundy. More distant echoes of Taverner and his generation continued to reverberate gently through the religious music of much later composers, not least the motets and masses that William Byrd provided for the Elizabethan recusants.

While composers and Catholics inclined towards tradition, the Protestants demanded change. Unimpressed by music that arguably distracted attention away from the words, and which certainly made no effort to underline the meaning of the texts, the reformers set out to prune music back as hard as they could, or to eliminate it altogether along with statuary, vestments, and all the traditional adornments of worship that they associated with popery and superstition. Even before the end of Taverner's lifetime, the relationship between employer and the employed musician was becoming increasingly affected by the intervention of this third and hitherto apparently indifferent party: the churchman. The extraordinary extent to which English church music was transformed during the reign of Edward VI (1547–53) cannot easily be attributed to changes of heart by composers themselves. On the contrary, it must have been a period of deep uncertainty and lost opportunity for those skilled musicians whose craft was denounced by influential clergymen such as Thomas Becon, chaplain to Cranmer and Somerset:

There have been (would God there were not now!) [men] which have not spared to spend much riches in nourishing many idle singing men to bleat in their chapels, thinking so to do God on high sacrifice . . . A Christian man's melody, after St Paul's mind, consisteth in heart, while we recite psalms, hymns and spiritual songs, and sing to the Lord in our hearts . . . All other outward melody is vain and transitory, and passeth away and cometh to nought . . . So ye perceive that music is not so excellent a thing that a Christian ought earnestly to rejoice in it.

Not all the reformers went so far as this, but even those who accepted that music could legitimately contribute to worship also insisted that it should adopt a new sobriety and serve a more explicitly didactic function.

Music books surviving from the reign of Edward VI show that one of the first confused responses to the new restrictions was compromise. The Latin words of existing compositions, for example, were simply deleted and new English ones added in their place. In this way, two of Taverner's less extended masses were converted into English Communion settings, and the words of Thomas Sternhold's metrical version of Psalm 20, 'In trouble and adversity', were somehow fitted under the music of the celebrated 'In nomine' of the *Missa Gloria tibi Trinitas*. But adaptations such as these were never anything more than makeshift experiments. A few composers set the new English texts of the canticles around long-familiar plainchant melodies, simply because this had always been their practice, but since books of 'popish' plainchant were themselves being outlawed and destroyed in their thousands throughout the land it was hardly a promising solution. Compromise, in short, was impossible. The only effective response was to accept the situation, abandon the principles of past tradition and cut according to the cloth.

Chapel Royal composers such as Thomas Tallis and John Sheppard were among the first to find an answer. They fashioned a new intimacy in their church music by adopting the simpler, declamatory style they used when writing partsongs for the king's chamber. Tallis's anthem 'If ye love me' has little in common with the liturgical works he composed during Henry VIII's reign, nor for that matter with the renewed freedom he was allowed under Mary Tudor; but it is a very close cousin indeed to his secular partsong 'When shall my sorrowful sighing slack', which is probably roughly contemporary with the anthem.

The scrupulous economy of 'If ye love me' is, in its way, no less striking than the spendthrift luxury of the old florid style. In this anthem, forty-one syllables are declaimed in just twenty-six bars of music (compare this with Taverner's 'In nomine', where seven syllables are made to last all of fifty-seven bars), and most of the syllables are set to a single note – certainly never more than three at the most. Form is generated by the syntax of the text rather than any abstract, 'architectural' scheme: each clause or phrase becomes a short musical unit, set off from its neighbours by a pause, cadence or change of texture. Melodies grow directly out of the spoken word: by lengthening notes or leaping upwards to stress accented syllables, for example, Tallis effectively makes music that heightens the pattern of speech:

> If ye *love me*,
> keep my com-*mand*-ments,
> and I will *pray* the *Fa*-ther,
> and he shall *give* you a-*no*-ther *Com*-forter;
> that *he* may bide with you for *e*-ver,
> e'en the *spir't* of *truth*.

Taken only this far, the recipe guarantees good declamation but not necessarily interesting music. What saves Tallis's setting from mere routine efficiency is the fact that, at the Chapel Royal at least, composers were not banned altogether from weaving melodic lines against one another in counterpoint. Tallis's anthem begins with block chords; but the body of the work is made up of short bursts of imitation which allow more opportunity for shaping the text and adding climax and variety. The result brought English music closer into line with the liturgical music of Italy and, in particular, France, though there is little evidence to suggest that in their church music Tallis and his contemporaries actually modelled their works on foreign examples. Outside the Chapel Royal, some English composers were denied the right to use even the simplest forms of imitative counterpoint, the 'reports or repeatings which may' (as the York Minster Injunctions of 1552 put it) 'induce obscureness to the hearers'.

The Reformation forced English church composers to rethink the fundamentals of their work. No longer could considerations of melody and design be regarded as ends in themselves; instead, music was to be arranged so that the notes were in harmony with the text (the phrase is Martin Luther's). It is arguable, however, that in the long run the lesson was worth learning, and that the fusion of the two extremes made possible by the more liberal attitudes towards music of succeeding generations of church reformers ultimately accounts for the success of later Tudor sacred music, music that powerfully exploits the advantages of each.

This marriage between old and new can clearly be heard in Elizabethan motets. The term 'motet' today signifies a musical work with Latin text, and as the majority of such works are of an explicitly religious nature, it has become natural to think of motets as church music. To Elizabethan musicians, however, the word was rather more broad in its meaning, and less commonly used. In Thomas Morley's *A Plain and Easy Introduction to Practical Music*, for example, the motet is defined as music made upon a 'grave ditty', with the cautious amplification that 'a Motet is properly a song made for the church'. Morley's choice of the word 'properly' is telling: in reality, many Elizabethan motets are not and were never intended to be church music at all – or at least, not 'church' in the sense of the official Anglican church of Elizabethan England.

In the title-pages of their publications, Tallis and Byrd described these works as *cantiones sacrae*, or 'sacred songs'. Clearly this too is something of an umbrella term. Some of these pieces almost certainly came from the repertoire of Elizabeth's Chapel Royal, of which both Tallis and Byrd were senior members. Certain 'sacred songs', on the other hand, were anything but suited to Anglican worship, since their texts implied a deep sympathy for the Roman Catholic faith – texts which, had they not been chosen or assembled directly from the Bible, would have been read as unequivocally recusant and sometimes even seditious testimonies. It is now accepted that many Elizabethan motets are in fact Catholic expressions of faith and solidarity, a form of protest song. We must imagine them having been sung not by church or cathedral choirs but by families or gatherings of Roman Catholics in the privacy of their homes.

The power of this music is due in no small part to the fact that the composers who wrote it were themselves Catholics – William Byrd and (almost certainly) Thomas Morley, for example – or older men of unknown persuasion such as Tallis who had lived through decades of doctrinal change. Their motets speak with a true depth of commitment to the texts, using careful, persuasive word-setting. The result is quite different from the free, more purely musical invention of Taverner's art or the didactic utilitarianism of the Edwardian anthems. What comes to mind most immediately, in fact, is the close identity that now exists between English and continental vocal music – an identity, however, that never becomes total, owing to the survival of certain specifically English musical characteristics. It is surely no coincidence that this stage of evolution occurred at the very time when foreign music was beginning to circulate widely in England, largely in the increasingly numerous, cheap and easily accessible printed editions that issued from the presses of Venice and the Low Countries.

Tallis's two settings of verses from the Book of Lamentations offer a vivid view of this world of turmoil. The texts themselves seem delicately balanced in their ambiguity, for these particular Biblical words could be (and almost certainly were) read as a thinly-disguised metaphor for the state of the Catholic church in late Tudor England:

All her gates are desolate, her priests sigh, her virgins are afflicted, and she herself is in bitterness; her adversaries are become the head, her enemies prosper . . . Jerusalem, Jerusalem, return unto the Lord thy God.

In musical terms, these two motets show Tallis balancing old against new. Traditionally English is the rich, ornamental counterpoint, worked out most exquisitely in the luxurious settings of the Hebrew letters that preface each verse of the text: 'Aleph', 'Beth', and so on. Transitional is the bald, sometimes almost unrelieved rhythmic regularity of the declamation – a slight drabness that Tallis, like other composers of his generation, first cultivated during the Reformation, and which Byrd later succeeded in transcending. There is too still a stiffness about some of the imitative writing.

Entirely new for Tallis, however, and indeed new for English music as a whole in the 1560s, is the sheer expressiveness of the overall conception, expressiveness that is achieved largely by sophisticated long-term harmonic planning of a kind that Tallis most likely discovered in the music of foreigners such as Gombert, Clemens non Papa and, above all, Orlande de Lassus. This is particularly evident in the first motet, 'Incipit lamentatio Jeremiae', in which the effect is achieved not so much by local dissonances or the use of affective chromaticism but rather by the sheer instability of the music's point of tonal reference. Tallis unsettles the listener by moving farther and farther away from the key of the opening, emerging at the centre of the motet in a remote region for the words 'Plorans ploravit in nocte' ('She weepeth sore in the night'). When the process is reversed in the remainder of the motet, home itself seems no less strange and unfamiliar a place. The sophistication and confidence of this music is all the more astonishing for the fact that this should be the work of an elderly English composer who had been reared with the sound of Taverner's music in his head.

The religious works of William Byrd fall into three categories, marked off from one another by function and, to an extent, by scope and style. First there are the English-texted anthems and services, works that he composed for Anglican worship initially in his capacity as organist of Lincoln Cathedral and then, for the major portion of his mature career, as a Gentleman of Elizabeth's Chapel Royal. More numerous and ostensibly more personally motivated are his Latin motets, many of which possess an intensity and seriousness of tone that immediately distinguishes them from the English church music. For all the richness of their counterpoint, these are essentially chamber works, and they benefit in performance from the sensitivity and expressiveness of solo voices. The third category, written later in Byrd's life, is again of genuinely liturgical music, but this time written for use in actual Roman Catholic worship: settings of the mass, and mass Proper texts drawn from the church's annual cycle of feasts. Each category commands an individual character; binding them together, however, is the resourcefulness of Byrd's craftsmanship, which outshines that of any other English composer of his generation.

In both quantity and quality, the motets are Byrd's most outstanding achievement, at least within the bounds of vocal music. Given the topicality and political sensitivity of many of the texts, their earnestness comes as no real surprise. In several, the 'Jerusalem' theme of Tallis's 'Lamentations' is further developed, most memorably in the second part of 'Ne irascaris', with its extended and deeply poignant setting of the words 'Sion deserta facta est; Jerusalem desolata est' ('Sion has been deserted, Jerusalem laid waste'). Even more pointed is the setting of the opening four verses of Psalm 78 (according to Vulgate numbering), 'Deus, venerunt gentes', which was composed in the wake of the martyrdom of Edmund Campion and his companions in December 1581. The aptness of the words to the reality of that event is macabre:

God, they have invaded your heritage, and desecrated your holy temple; they have reduced Jerusalem to ruins. They have left the corpses of your servants to the birds of the air for food, and the flesh of your devout to the beasts of the field. They have shed blood like water throughout Jerusalem, and there is no one left to bury them. We are insulted by our neighbours, made the buff and laughing-stock of all those around us.

The success of these motets can be attributed to a wide variety of factors. Even a casual hearing reveals the sheer rhetorical power of Byrd's word-setting, his extraordinary ability to create and combine melodic lines that not only grow out of the rhythm and inflexion of heightened speech but which do indeed seem to be 'framed by the meaning of the words', to use Byrd's own expression. This power is heightened by the manner in which the melodic lines are then combined to create a contrapuntal fabric. In Byrd's hands, imitation acquires a potency quite new among English composers: his technique transcends the level of creating mere textural unity and the quality of dialogue, and instead becomes a means of achieving a sense of genuine growth, of development and climax. Through the use of varied repetitions, of expansions and compressions of the musical ideas, each section of a motet becomes a discrete expressive unit that focuses attention on its clause or phrase of text. In the final passage in 'Ne irascaris', for example, the three words 'Jerusalem desolata est' are dwelt upon for some two minutes' worth of music, during which Byrd brings four quite separate imitative points into play one after another, each of them opening up new possibilities for intensification and, ultimately, cadence. Perhaps even more important than the internal logic of the passage itself is the way that it contributes climactically to the motet as a whole.

Byrd's ability to pace an extended piece of music, to reserve or release tension, is no less impressive than his handling of detail, and few composers of his generation show such an awareness for the need to think through the strategy of an entire work.

Old and new lie side by side with one another in Byrd's sets of *cantiones sacrae*. The collection published in 1591, for example, juxtaposes works composed around a plainchant melody in the pre-Reformation fashion ('Descendit de caelis'), music that owes a debt to the expansive, florid style of Taverner's generation ('Infelix ego'), a paraphrase of Psalm 150 in neo-classical elegiac metre that allows Byrd's rhythmic invention to run riot ('Laudibus in sanctis'), pieces that invade the world of the madrigal, with their extremes of textural contrast and pictorial word-setting ('Haec dies'), and motets of a more intimate, compressed nature that bear first witness to the economy of Byrd's late works ('Domine, salva nos'). To turn the pages of such a collection is to see the world of Tudor sacred music expressed in microcosm.

Byrd's liturgical works for the Catholics are no less wide-ranging than his motets, and they show the same deep concern for celebrating both the past and the present, though in scale the music is generally more compact. In the Mass for Four Voices, for example, the homage to early Tudor music is frequently audible – to the extent that several passages can be shown to have been inspired by Byrd's knowledge of one specific mass-setting by Taverner. The emphasis on concision, intelligent text-declamation and variety of material, however, would have been beyond the means of any earlier English composer. Again, Byrd's ability to judge the intensity, the timing and the duration of events is remarkable. Here, the Credo is no routine catalogue; instead, each article of faith is underlined with a different colour and a varying degree of emphasis. (It comes as no surprise to find that one of the most heightened passages occurs at the words 'Et unam sanctam Catholicam, Catholicam et Apostolicam Ecclesiam'; the repetition, which is Byrd's own, receives further stress by the use of plain block chords rather than the staple of imitative counterpoint.) Here too, Byrd calculates the effect of an individual moment in the light of its contribution to the setting as a whole.

Nowhere is this heard more clearly that in the celebrated 'dona nobis pacem' at the end of the Agnus Dei, one of the most expansive passages in the entire mass-setting. By limiting his material to a single melodic shape, repeated obsessively over long-held droning notes, the passage acts as an anchor that checks the momentum of the preceding music and, little by little, brings it to a close. The effect is also calculated, however, to create a chain of clashing dissonances, the stringency of which have no precedent elsewhere in the work. This paradoxical combination of slackened pace and heightened tension in the final moments of the mass brilliantly serves to remind the listener that, for the Catholics of England, the peace for which the text so urgently supplicates was not so readily forthcoming.

Unlike his masses and motets, which are properly a form of vocal chamber music, Byrd's anthems and service music genuinely do belong to the world of the church choir, and as such they reveal the more public side of his character. From what we know about the immediately preceding Anglican traditions on which he had to build, Byrd's contribution to this repertoire again seems to have been particularly significant for the development of English music. Before him, few composers had written pieces for Protestant worship that could be described as weighty or spectacular – not even Tallis, whose English church music is almost universally modest in scope. With Byrd, both anthems and settings of the canticles (the Magnificat and Nunc Dimittis, for example) acquired a new degree of substance or seriousness and, often, a distinctly ceremonial quality; and this in turn must reflect Elizabeth's liberal acceptance of splendour into her chapel services, shunning the asceticism of the early reformers.

Some of Byrd's English church music may in fact be genuinely occasional. The sheer size of the Great Service, for example – it is his largest single work – implies that it was written for a specific event rather than for everyday use, and there is a strong whiff of festivity about the anthem 'Sing joyfully unto God', with its pealing onomatopoeic cries of 'Blow the trumpet in the new moon'. Anthem-like works by Byrd's younger contemporaries were evidently used in increasing quantity to mark events of state: both Thomas Weelkes and Orlando Gibbons wrote settings of 'Hosanna to the Son of David' that appear to have been used as royal welcome-songs, and a flush of pieces based on the theme of David's lament for Absolom followed the death of Prince Henry in 1613. There was also something of a trend towards solo writing in Elizabethan English church music. In Byrd's hands, the 'verse' service and anthem became fully fledged forms in which a heightened, oratorical style of solo delivery accompanied by organ could effectively be set off from the interjections of the full choir. The expressive and sometimes even dramatic potential of such schematic alternations can be heard worked out to best advantage in verse-anthems such as Morley's 'Out of the deep' and Gibbons's 'This is the record of John'.

Viewed as a whole, the repertoire of Tudor sacred music is astonishing for its sheer variety. In no other nation of the sixteenth century was resistance to the Reformation expressed in such emotive musical terms as in England; nowhere else did the cross-fertilisation between Renaissance humanism and nostalgia for the medieval tradition give rise to such a vigorous musical hybrid. Few foreign institutions promoted festive church music with anything approximating the enthusiasm of the monarchy and prelates of Tudor England. Considered within this European context, the extent of England's musical isolation and insularity is most strikingly evident in those works that are associated with worship, whether official, ceremonial or sectarian, works that proudly proclaim their nationality even after selectively absorbing styles and techniques from abroad. Arguably, it was this very sense of national identity combined with the struggles of reformation and resistance that

contributed most potently to the strength and sheer quality of so much
Tudor religious music.

Songs, fantasias, and madrigals for entertainment

Music readily falls prey to the vicissitudes of fashion. Few things are so
easily destroyed as a sheaf of papers, and such sheaves were the medium
through which most Tudor secular music was circulated for as long as
anyone cared to preserve it. Unlike musical expressions of religious faith,
which were never left without friends in a country deeply divided into
factional denominations, the songbooks of one generation readily became the
litter of the next, unless something externally appealing about the book itself
– its binding or its calligraphy, for example, or its association with royalty –
ensured it a longer shelf-life. Considerations of this kind certainly helped to
save the three large manuscripts of early Tudor song that survive from the
first two decades of the sixteenth century, books whose contents vividly evoke
the thriving court cultures of Henry VII and the young Henry VIII.

What these books sorely lack, however, are successors. Between them and
the madrigal publications of the 1580s onwards, so little Tudor secular music
has come down to us that we might be forgiven for thinking that virtually
none existed. Songs, dances, music for lute, keyboard and consort: all are in
short supply, and even those pieces that can be retrieved may conjure up only
a pale image of the way things really were. It would be misleading to arrive
at the firm conclusion that music for entertainment began the sixteenth
century in a state of high spirits only to decline rapidly during the years of
Reformation and pick up again in the closing years of Elizabeth's reign.
There is certainly some truth in this, but it is not the whole truth.

The early Tudor songbooks offer a wealth of material to enrich our view of
courtly life. Admittedly even these books are far from complete records of the
full extent of court music. They tell us nothing, for example, about dances
(many of which were probably improvised anyway), nor do they contain any
of the virtuoso pieces for solo instruments, plucked and keyboard, that Henry
VIII is known to have prized. In a sense, however, the songs are the most
valuable evidence that we could have wished for, since their words speak so
directly about courtly values, pastimes and obsessions. Even when the music
itself is of slight value, the lyrics have the capacity to fire the modern reader's
imagination.

Early Tudor court culture has been described as carrying the strong scent
of Burgundian influence. To only a limited extent, however, does this apply
to musical style. One of the songbooks includes a small collection of foreign
pieces, most of which have been described as the 'international song-hits' of
their day. A degree of emulation of this foreign repertoire is evident in a few
indigenous songs, but substantially more of them are as English in their
manner as is the church music of the same time. The rich idiom of 'Woefully
arrayed' by William Cornysh, for example, is barely a dilution of the style of
this same composer's sacred antiphons. Tiny snatches of imitation lead into
extended and exuberant passages of florid, textless writing that commands

more of the listener's attention. Technically the work is a carol – which is to say that the stanzas of its text always lead back into an unvarying refrain. Its subject, not unusually for a late medieval lyric, is the story of the Passion related through the voice of Christ himself, expressed in blunt, rhythmical and often alliterative verse:

> Of sharp thorn I have worn a crown on my head,
> So pained, so strained, so rueful, so red;
> Thus bobbed, thus robbed, thus for thy love dead;
> Unfeigned, not deyned, my blood for to shed:
>   My feet and handes sore
>   The sturdy nailes bore;
>   What might I suffer more
> Than I have done, O man, for thee?
> Come when thou list, welcome, to me.
>   Woefully arrayed.

Cornysh's musical setting emphasises the versification of the poem and aptly matches the vigour of the language. What it does not set out to do, however, is to pick up anything more than the lyric's general mood. Never does the music dwell expressively on a particular phrase of text; never is there a direct mimetic response to a word such as 'pained' or 'bobbed' such as a later madrigalist would have written almost without thinking; climax and resolution are achieved largely through successive returns of the refrain. As in Taverner's mass-setting, considerations of melody and of overall architectural design prove to be the generating forces behind this music.

Other pieces from the songbooks reveal the social (as distinct from the devotional) side of courtly life. Here the music is often simpler and slighter in its proportions, and no less vigorous in style. It is the liveliness of the tune, for example, that breathes such fresh air into Cornysh's semi-erotic 'Blow thy horn, hunter', the speed and wit of the musical exchanges between milkmaid and suitor that turn the anonymous 'Hey trolly lolly lo!' into a genuinely funny little scene. Here too, foreign influence seems insignificant when set against the strength of the native elements in the music. By international standards it is not the greatest music of its age, but in its miniature way it does wield a uniquely Anglo-Saxon strength.

During its ensuing dark age, English song seems gradually to have fallen increasingly under the spell of fashions from abroad, specifically those from France and the Low Countries. Anne Boleyn may well have brought a taste for foreign songs back with her from her childhood spent abroad. Both Henry VIII and Cardinal Wolsey had the opportunity to hear chansons in the latest fashion when they were entertained overseas, and this may have encouraged them to promote similar music in England. In addition, the king increasingly peopled his court with foreign musicians, many of whom arrived with their heads and pocket-books full of music that was not indigenous to England. It is revealing that the man who rose to the position of highest prominence and responsibility among Henry VIII's court musicians was not a Briton but the Flemish lutenist and composer, Philip van Wilder. Barely a note of his lute music survives, but several dozen polyphonic chansons by him, scattered among English manuscripts of the later sixteenth century, testify to his activity and, almost certainly, his influence in this field.

The few extant English songs that survive from the mid-sixteenth century, most of which either exist only in wordless keyboard reductions or are in a state too fragmentary to allow for any kind of performance or reconstruction, owe an evident debt to musical trends on the other side of the English Channel. The authors of their lyrics are often unidentifiable, though the presence among them of texts by the Earl of Surrey and Lord Vaux implies that these pieces are linked to courtly circles. There is a new strictness of metrical regularity in this poetry that tends to have an adverse effect upon the composer: even the relatively flexible rhythmic patterns of Surrey's widely admired poem 'O happy dames', for example, are not enough to save John Sheppard's four-voice musical setting of it from becoming stuck in the grooves of its prevailing iambic metre. Though rarely of great intrinsic merit in themselves, songs of this kind illustrate how English composers first attempted fully to come to terms with the techniques of imitation and economical, declamatory word-setting. Even if the first fruits were not always of the highest quality, it was a stage of development that simply had to be lived through, and later generations reaped the benefits, both in recreational and religious music.

It was during these central decades of the sixteenth century that the English began to pay serious attention to writing music for consorts of viols. Here too, the appeal of an imitative texture with its debate-like quality became increasingly difficult for composers to resist. Tallis's two four-part 'In nomines' are symptomatic of the trend. In each, a few pithy melodic shapes are subjected to all manner of extension, abbreviation and other forms of mutation (being turned upside down, for example, or played at twice the original speed), all this wittily taking place against the solemn progress of the 'Gloria tibi Trinitas' plainchant melody, which is played in slow motion on one of the instruments. Being free from any considerations of word-setting, the composer's imagination simply ran riot, juggling familiar shapes into different patterns and throwing in new ideas as he thought fit.

By the end of the century, consort music had acquired a seriousness of intent in the composer's mind that placed it on a level with the motet. To the generation of Byrd and Gibbons, few musical forms offered a greater challenge than did the fantasia (or 'fancy'), an instrumental piece in which, to use Thomas Morley's words,

a musician taketh a point [melodic idea] at his pleasure and wresteth and turneth it as he list, making either much or little of it according as shall seem best in his own conceit. In this may more art be shown than in any other music because the composer is tied to nothing, but that he may add, diminish and alter at his pleasure.

The art that went into Byrd's two six-part G minor consort Fantasias, composed probably in the 1580s, reveals the sheer fertility of his invention when fired by purely musical concerns, free from the external influence of a text. Proceeding first as a series of logical developments of a few key ideas, each piece moves through a passage of rhythmic intensification before launching into wilder abandon as the music moves into faster, dance-like triple measure.

Brought together, the sound of human voices and viols produced one of the most characteristic combinations of Elizabethan chamber music. Any partsong, madrigal, motet or anthem could be performed in this manner, but the medium also attracted a literature of its own, starting apparently with pieces written for court entertainment or for inclusion in choirboy plays, and gradually moving into the domain of the amateur performer. To Byrd in particular, the consort song presented the endlessly fascinating challenge of setting a carefully fashioned declamatory vocal line against a free fantasia played by the viols. In his 'Lullaby, my sweet little baby' – later published in a compromised form, like so many of his consort songs, with words added to the viol lines as well as under the 'first singing part' – the melodic material is shared by all the parts, although it is the accompaniment that contributes most to the ebb and flow of the music. Other composers exploited the possibility of pitting the voice (or voices) in even bolder contrast against the instruments. Gibbons, Weelkes and Richard Dering, for example, all discovered the fun of embedding the calls of street traders within the texture of a rich and thematically independent viol fantasia. Little Tudor music carries quite so much latent humour as does Weelkes's 'Cries of London', with its various voices bawling out 'new great cockles, new' or 'a good sausage, and it be well roasted' against the tongue-in-cheek seriousness of the four viols who busily make decent music underneath.

From the 1580s through to the second decade of the seventeenth century, English society variously revelled in or deeply disparaged the rise of a new

Hans Holbein, Jean de Dinteville and Georges de Selve ('The Ambassadors') *(1533)*.

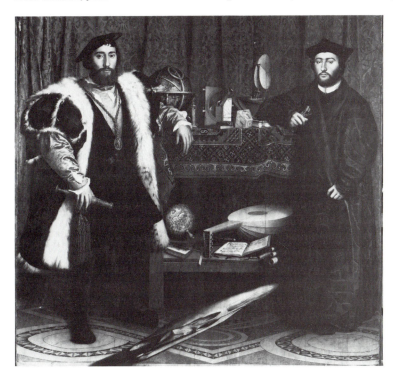

musical fashion: the madrigal. Imported as it was from Italy, both direct and by way of the Low Countries, the madrigal could in no way be described as an indigenous English form, and there were certain English composers, patrons and amateur performers who remained wholly indifferent to the arrival of the genre. Thomas Morley (*c.* 1557–1602) was not among them. Speaking through the character of the Master in his *A Plain and Easy Introduction to Practical Music* of 1597, Morley has this to say in commendation of the madrigal:

. . . it is, next unto the motet, the most artificial and, to men of understanding, delightful [form of vocal music]. If therefore you will compose in this kind, you must possess yourself with an amorous humour, . . . so that you must in your music be wavering like the wind, sometime wanton, sometime drooping, sometime grave and staid, otherwhile effeminate . . . and show the very uttermost of your variety, and the more variety you show the better shall you please . . . for as you scholars say that love is full of hopes and fears, so is the madrigal, or lovers' music, full of diversity of passions and airs.

Morley's definition is telling: by laying stress on the need for artifice and variety rather than on consistency of tone and the need to choose verse of high literary merit, Morley immediately distinguishes his view of the English genre from that held by many Italians – and indeed by some of his English colleagues as well. Morley's own madrigals tend towards the display of highly-polished frippery, good humour and tuneful patter, and they identify closely with the Italian forms of the *canzonetta* ('little song') and the dance-inspired *balletto* – both of which find a place in English terminology as 'canzonet' and 'ballett' (or 'fa la'). Morley's lead was followed by several English contemporaries who, like Morley himself, recognised the commercial implications of the vogue and published a string of collections aimed at the general market. Undoubtedly the most talented of these successors was Thomas Weelkes.

Musicians in private employment, on the other hand, in general looked to more serious Italian models for guidance. George Kirbye, John Wilbye and John Ward inclined towards a more discreet elegance and greater musical breadth, and their settings are often tinged with a passion and melancholy almost unimaginable in the madrigals of Morley or Weelkes. Members of a third group of composers which included Byrd and Gibbons maintained a certain distance from the madrigal, and strictly controlled the level of Italianate influence they were prepared to allow into their music. There is nothing madrigalian, for example, about Gibbons's exquisitely-turned consort song 'The silver swan', nor his sombre setting of Sir Walter Raleigh's searching lyric, 'What is our life?'.

Italianate madrigals began to arrive in England long before English composers themselves tried their hands at writing pieces of a similar nature. As far back as the late 1520s, Henry VIII had been given a fine Florentine manuscript of madrigals and motets. Often printed copies were brought back from European tours; one set of such books that survives appears to have been owned by Sir Thomas Hoby, translator of Castigione's *Il Cortegiano*, and it was probably purchased during his travels abroad in the 1550s. Sir Thomas Chaloner's payment of ten shillings 'to a Flemish musician who teaches my daughter for song books Italian in four parts' was certainly not an isolated transaction. By the 1570s the great library of Henry Fitzalan, 12th Earl of Arundel, included not only books of Italian madrigals by Arcadelt, Gero, Rore and Willaert but also a set of pieces in manuscript by Innocenzo Alberti that is actually dedicated to the Earl and was perhaps commissioned by him during a visit to Padua. Records such as these show how the ground had been prepared for English publishing ventures such as Nicholas Yonge's *Musica Transalpina* of 1588 and Thomas Watson's *Italian Madrigals Englished* of 1590, pioneering anthologies whose contents were made more enjoyable to English audiences by being given English texts.

These early publications to an extent helped to establish the very tone of the English madrigal itself. Prominent in the collections are works that are light, pastoral in nature, tuneful, full of rhythmic vitality, and rich in texture: madrigals, in other words, that might appeal as much for their musical content as for any intimate relationship that existed between verse and music. Many of the pieces were already known and popular in the Low Countries, where Italian was equally still a foreign language to all but the most educated; they simply crossed the Channel to England. Today the madrigal books of Yonge and Watson rarely receive an airing. In their own time, however, their novelty must have created a genuine thrill.

Following hard on the heels of the publication of these various 'Englished' pieces, the entrepreneurial Thomas Morley was among the first native English composers to enter the field and write his own canzonets, balletts and madrigals for home consumption. (Byrd had contributed two madrigals to Watson's 1590 anthology, but thereafter he wrote few works that can correctly be called madrigals.) Between 1593 and 1597 Morley issued five sets, several of them published not only with English words but also in Italian-texted editions, presumably for export, together with a further anthology of foreign madrigals in translation. It was also Morley who commissioned and edited what is perhaps the most famous of all collections of English madrigals, the set of twenty-five pieces 'composed by divers several authors' and dedicated to Elizabeth under the title of *The Triumphs of Oriana* (1601).

Morley's aim was to capture as far as possible the general spirit of his transalpine models, and it comes as no surprise to discover that several of the pieces he published under his own name are in fact reworkings of Italian originals. Even among the pieces that seem genuinely to be his own, there are many that show such deep indebtedness to Italian pieces as to be virtually indistinguishable from them. Placed beside the *balletti* of Giovanni Gastoldi, for example, there is little that one might call English about pieces such as 'Sing we at pleasure' or the well-known 'Fire, fire'. Even Morley's verses are often constructed so as to simulate the lyricism and feminine endings of Italian canzonet poetry:

> Sing we and chant it
> While love doth grant it;
> Fa la la la . . .
> Not long youth lasteth,
> And old age hasteth;

Fa la la la . . .
Now is best leisure
To take our pleasure;
Fa la la la . . .

Morley's world is essentially one of pastoral elegance, peopled by nymphs
and shepherds who, decked in flowers and garlands, live out their lives
troubled only by the cruelty of love or the shadow of old age, and to whom
the only real threat of death is the longed-for 'death' of sexual fulfilment.
Occasionally the Arcadian back-drop becomes more readily identifiable as
England, as morris dancers and May-queens take the places of Daphne,
Cloris and Philomela. To the Elizabethans, this offered pure escapism and
superb light entertainment, expressed in music that was, on the whole,
technically undemanding and readily singable by amateurs. It is hardly
surprising that Morley's successful recipe set the standard for imitation over
the span of some two decades. Lesser writers such as Thomas Bateson, John
Bennett, Thomas East, John Farmer, Robert Jones, Francis Pilkington,
Thomas Vautor and Henry Youll soon followed him into print.

Although Thomas Weelkes (1576?–1623) is in a sense Morley's spiritual
cousin, his madrigals tend to be more individually striking works; larger
jewels, and more intricately cut. Many also possess a sonority and density
that bespeaks their Englishness in a way that Morley's light-hearted
Italianism rarely allows. Like Morley, Weelkes published a batch of four sets
of pieces in close succession, starting in 1597 and culminating in collections
of five- and six-part works of 1600, the two sets that contain many of his best
(and, today, best known) madrigals.

Weelkes's resourcefulness is often astonishing. Given a short, plain poem
such as 'O care, thou wilt despatch me', Morley might have entertained the
listener with quicksilver changes of mood in a compact, transparent setting.
Weelkes, on the other hand, turns the mere eight lines of this ballett into a
sustained work of significant dimensions and true pathos. In each of the four
main sections (setting two lines each), the musical material is genuinely
developed and reworked to climactic effect, most poignantly at the words
'Hence care, thou art too cruel', with its strange and dissonant chromatic
twists. Interleaving these main paragraphs are the typical ballett interludes
set to the nonsense syllables 'fa la' which, far from breaking the tension,
introduce a wistful tone of resignation that has been brilliantly calculated to
blend artifice with melancholy. Perhaps most impressive of all, however, is
the way Weelkes sustains the argument over an extended span of music – an
ability not always evident in his lighter pieces, which tend to dwell more on
the moment than project the totality of the poem.

Equally resourceful, and arguably the most skilful of all his works, sacred
or secular, is the great six-part madrigal 'Thule, the period of cosmography'.
Admittedly any madrigalist would have regarded this text as a gift, with its
references to 'Hecla, whose sulphureous fire doth melt the frozen clime and
thaw the sky' or, in the second half, the Andalusian merchant who 'reports in
Spain how strangely Fogo burns amidst an ocean full of flying fishes'. These
things do indeed 'seem wondrous' in Weelkes's brilliantly scored music,
which explodes into a lava of fast-running scales before itself freezing for a

moment into held chords, slithers strangely and chromatically in sympathy with Fogo or, like the flying fish, skims the surface in a shoal of short energetic bursts. Yet what convinces above all is again the sturdy architectural plan of the entire piece, the continuity that underlies the surface variety.

For all that they belong (in modern parlance, at least) to the same 'school' of composers, Morley and Weelkes have only a few features in common with the most talented member of the English madrigal movement, John Wilbye (1574–1638). Unlike them, Wilbye seems not to have worked at lightning speed to produce sets of pieces in rapid succession. His first book of madrigals appeared in 1598; his second, of 1609, is evidently the accumulation of a decade's work. These pieces apart, virtually no music by Wilbye survives, and there is good reason to believe that he wrote little else for his patrons, the Kytson family of Hengrave Hall in Suffolk. If the music of Morley and Weelkes sometimes has a commercial ring to it, the same is rarely true of Wilbye's madrigals, which appear to grow out of a sense of personal motivation and earnestness.

Symptomatic of Wilbye's character are the texts he chose to set. Though admittedly never great poetry, these verses nevertheless transcend the casual pastoral narrative and strong sexual innuendo of many English madrigal lyrics. Above all, they have a tendency to sustain their mood and imagery in a manner that positively encourages long-term musical planning, and it is not surprising that several of Wilbye's pieces have been described, anachronistically but with some justification, as being 'symphonic' in scope. The mix of local detail, logical connection of parts and projection of an overall message within a text is a recipe that Wilbye found particularly suited to his musical needs. The following lyric (from his Second Set of 1609) is typical:

> All pleasure is of this condition:
> It pricks men forward to fruition;
> But if enjoyed, then like the humming bee
> (The honey being shed) away doth flee –
> But leaves a sting that wounds the inward heart
> With gnawing grief and never ending smart.

In his setting, Wilbye is as responsive to details of word-setting as any of his colleagues: the urgent rhythmic anticipations do indeed 'prick men forward', for example, and the humming of the bee is, as one would expect, nicely simulated in musical terms. Never, though, does Wilbye allow any one of these short term 'madrigalisms' to become purely an object of interest in itself. The passage from line to line is critically paced, with musical sentences left open-ended and the joints cleverly dovetailed. Like the poem, the music presses forward to the final couplet, and it is truly the 'gnawing grief and never-ending smart' of the setting that ultimately lingers in the mind after the work's close.

Wilbye's ability to achieve genuine climax and resolution can be heard to excellent advantage in his two best known pieces. The early 'Adieu, sweet Amaryllis', a miniature so lacking in Italianate features that one hesitates even to call it a madrigal, is justly famous for its final passage, in which the prevailing minor modality suddenly brightens – wistfully and pathetically – into the major, as the lover bids his final parting farewell. Rarely in the madrigal literature does an English composer touch so sensitive a nerve of real human emotion as Wilbye does through this astonishing change of musical mood. 'Draw on, sweet night', from the Second Set, is also a work that trades on antithesis and volatile changes of mood, here projected on a large scale and scored for Wilbye's richest six-part texture. It is also potentially one of his most anguished works, though English institutionalised performances tend to see the brighter side of it. Here the constant vacillation between major and minor combines with techniques of thematic recall to simulate effectively a mind that is not merely troubled but rather completely obsessed. (The cause of the 'painful melancholy', much to the madrigal's advantage, is never made specific.) In one sense it is a work that evolves, for the musical material genuinely undergoes a process of thematic development, just as the lines of the poem successively develop the theme of complaint. In another sense, however, it is Wilbye's most remarkably holistic conception; the meaning of the work as a whole does indeed seem to be more than the sum of its parts. Compared with this, even the despair of Weelkes's 'O care, thou wilt despatch me' appears affected and artificial.

In their different ways, Weelkes and Wilbye represent the apotheosis of the Elizabethan madrigal. Few of their Jacobean successors could match them in quality, though the publications of Gibbons, Tomkins, and above all John Ward's serious collection of 1613 built effectively upon the tradition. Newer Italian fashions, however, undermined the popularity of the genre. By 1620, the English madrigal was all but dead.

Lute ayres, and music for solo instruments and dancing

Longer lived than the madrigal – and, for that matter, than the contrapuntal consort song – was the most intimate and literary form of Elizabethan secular vocal music: solo song accompanied by the lute. The ancestry of this genre, which first properly broke the surface in the 1590s, is not entirely clear. Almost certainly some form of solo song had existed in courtly circles since early Tudor times, most likely as an improvised tradition rather than a written one. Controversy still surrounds the issue of whether the lyrics of Sir Thomas Wyatt (for example), with their frequent allusions to the lute and the singing voice, were once performed musically. The root of the problem lies in the fact that the lutenist's art was a solo rather than an ensemble one, and that until the spread of amateur lute-playing late in the sixteenth century, few court lutenists took the trouble to write down or circulate the pieces they played and, very likely, sang. There is a double poignancy about the anonymous elegy written on the death in 1553 of Philip van Wilder, chief court musician to Henry VIII, in that it stands as an epitaph both to the player himself and to the fragile, lost tradition that he represents:

> Bewail with me, all ye that have professed
> Of music th'art by touch of cord or wind.
> Lay down your lutes and let your gitterns rest.

Philip is dead whose like you cannot find,
Of music much exceeding all the rest.
Muses, therefore, of force now must you wrest
Your pleasant notes into another sound.
The string is broke; the lute is dispossesed;
The hand is cold; the body in the ground.
The low'ring lute lamenteth now therefore
Philip, her friend that can her touch no more.

There is an irony in the fact that some of the earliest surviving lute songs were written down precisely because they were adaptations of ensemble music and not idiomatic lute music at all. Partsongs, consort songs and even madrigals were sometimes performed with their lower voices conflated into chords that could be strummed on a lute. To a composer such as Thomas Morley, the lute-song texture was barely more than an extension of the sound-world of the madrigal. There is little in either the scoring or the nature of its verse to distinguish his solo setting of 'It was a lover and his lass', with its scurrying imitations and nonsense syllables, from an ensemble ballett like 'Now is the month of maying'. Even those song-writers who maintained a greater distance from the madrigal offered performers the choice of either a lute accompaniment or four fully worked-out contrapuntal lines that could be sung like a partsong or played on instruments in the manner of the consort song. Many of their songbooks were published with the various voice-parts displayed on a single opening, facing in different directions so that as many singers and players as desired could gather round it.

Elizabethan lute-songs (or 'ayres') are essentially reflective or at most narrative pieces; the idea of writing more overtly dramatic or declamatory song falls outside the aesthetic and belongs rather to the later generation of Nicholas Lanier and Henry Lawes. The two chief exponents of the Elizabethan ayre themselves epitomise the two main and contrasted approaches. Thomas Campion (*c.* 1567–1620), himself no less a poet than a musician, stands for the 'literary' ayre, in which the principal concern is with the lyric itself. Disdaining songs that are 'long, intricate, bated with fugue [imitation], chained with syncopation, and where the nature of every word is precisely expressed in the note', Campion instead aimed to write musical settings that emphasise the poem's form and its general mood. This may make him the true inheritor of a courtly improvised tradition that laid stress on lyrical melody and simple supporting accompaniment. John Dowland (1563–1626), representing the more 'composed' ayre, inclined instead towards a denser, fully worked-out musical quality in which locally expressive details and a feeling for counterpoint added variety and weight. Placed beside the stark emptiness of Campion's 'The cypress curtain of the night' (published in 1601), Dowland's 'Sorrow, stay' (1600) positively bulges with rhetorical devices: exclamations, emphatic repetitions of certain words, plangent turns of phrase, even mimetic musical contours in the concluding lines ('But down, down, down, down I fall, / And arise I never shall'). In Dowland's song, an interpretation is virtually composed into the music; in Campion's, much more depends upon the singer's ability to communicate through the intonation of the voice, since the music itself is internally less expressive.

It is worth pausing briefly to consider the place of songs on the
Elizabethan and Jacobean stage. Beneath the thick layer of composed music
in Tudor England there existed a seam of semi-popular songs and dances,
and it was this that the dramatists tended to mine. Many of Shakespeare's
stage-songs allude to ballad tunes and other forms of popular melody;
Desdemona's Willow Song, for example, genuinely is 'an old thing' that
surfaces in manuscript as a simple lute arrangement several decades before
Othello was written. References in Shakespeare to polyphonic music are
rarely more than that, and they never call for a straight performance of the
piece as an integral part of the play. Peter's broken rendition of the partsong
'When griping griefs' by the playwright-composer Richard Edwards in Act
IV of *Romeo and Juliet*, for example, is built into the dramatic action, quite
unlike the songs that served as interpolations in contemporary masques and
choirboy plays. Public theatre thrived on music that was known to as wide an
audience as possible, and this inevitably tended to exclude the madrigals,
ayres and consort songs that belonged to courtly society and the circles of
wealthy amateurs.

Popular music also makes its presence felt in fully composed works scored
for solo lute, keyboard and viols. A simple Elizabethan arrangement of
'Greensleeves' may not in itself possess enough artistry to impress us deeply
today, but it is another matter when that same tune emerges triumphantly
out of the dense polyphony of Byrd's first G minor Fantasia for six viols; and
our own delighted responses at such a moment would have been shared by
audiences of the day. There is a potential problem here: modern listeners
usually lack familiarity with the object that ought to give so much pleasure as
it peers out of its new, unexpected and often sophisticated setting.
'Greensleeves' has withstood the test of time, but how many people today are
sufficiently familiar with the popular song 'Sick, Sick and very Sick' to
recognise it as it makes its extraordinary entry into Byrd's five-part Fantasia
in C? Some of Byrd's most complex and alluring works, both for consort and
keyboard, are built around tunes that come literally from the streets of Tudor
England: the 'Browning' for five viols, for example, which comprises a chain
of twenty statements of the song 'The leaves be green, the nuts be brown',
variously clothed in different contrapuntal guises; or the brilliant sets of
keyboard variations on 'Walsingham' and 'John come kiss me now'.

With dance music, a distinction between 'high' and 'low' states of the art is
particularly pronounced. As a general rule, the closer a piece comes to being
suitable for accompanying an actual dance, the less likely it is ever to have
been written down. Collections such as the Dublin Virginal Manuscript and
odd lute-books from the mid-sixteenth century provide occasional glimpses
into the physical reality of Tudor dance, but heard on their own without the
spectacle they were meant to accompany, these anonymous little pieces are
themselves often disappointing. 'Art' dance music, on the other hand,
occupied the minds of the most learned and serious-minded Elizabethan
composers. In *My Ladye Nevell Booke*, a retrospective manuscript anthology
of his keyboard music, William Byrd brought together a cycle of nine pavans
and galliards that collectively stand as one of his most towering achievements.
Arranged partly by chronology, partly by key, and otherwise by various

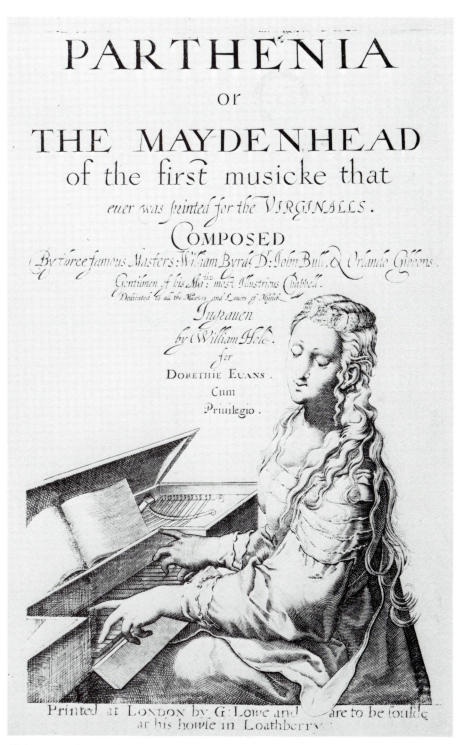

Title-page to Parthenia or the Maydenhead *for the virginal (1612–13).*

considerations of symmetry or diversity, this collection of deeply stylised dances seems no less carefully planned and thought out than a contemporary sonnet cycle. Even the ending has been calculated to act as a true culmination, for the Ninth Pavan and Galliard – the great *Passing Measures* pair – is a work of truly enormous proportions.

Here, as in so much of his Latin sacred music, Byrd pays homage to his past by recalling the intricate figuration of earlier generations of organist–composers: John Redford and William Blitheman, for example. At the same time, the sheer thrust of the music, the logical thematic connections and developments that make every bar seem to generate the next, the gradual intensification from long note-values to slow, from duple metre to triple, all combine to make this a piece as remote from Byrd's predecessors as it is from the world of dancing. It is also a piece of quite formidable technical complexity for the performer; if Queen Elizabeth had been capable of mastering passagework of the difficulty this work presents, her keyboard playing would have been impressive indeed.

Dance music for instrumental consort tends to be of a rather different character. Some was evidently composed for inclusion in processions and masques. For example, the mixed (or 'broken') consort of bowed, plucked and wind instruments shown playing at Sir Henry Unton's wedding banquet in the National Portrait Gallery mural (reproduced on the jacket of this volume) was associated with a particularly stately form of dance music in which certain instruments – the flute and lute in particular – engaged in rapid, often extemporised embellishment, creating a filigree of sound around the more steady progress provided by the other instruments. Unlike Byrd's pavans and galliards for keyboard, the consort dances of Daniel Bacheler (*c.* 1574–*c.* 1610) are at heart simple pieces with low polyphonic content. It is the sonority and complex interplay of the instruments, however, that lends such a thrill to the music.

Many of these dances, like so much instrumental music from around 1600, bear the names of specific courtiers in their titles, suggesting that a close relationship existed between composition, patronage and a network of connoisseurs, at least some of whom must have taken part in performances themselves. It was for men and women like this that Dowland compiled his collection of consort dances for viols, published in 1604 as *Lachrimae, or Seven Teares*. The title refers to Dowland's melancholy ayre, 'Flow my tears', a pavan-song so widely acclaimed that Dowland went on to compose a set of seven 'Lachrimae' pavans in similar vein, using snatches of the song's melody as starting points for their thematic content. Here too, melody and sonority take the place of Byrd's more intellectual invention, qualities that Dowland further emphasised in the remaining music in the collection – pieces such as *Sir Henry Umpton's Funeral* and *The King of Denmark's Galliard*.

With dances of this kind, modern audiences come about as near as is possible to the ceremonial music that surrounded Elizabeth on events such as the 1591 Elvetham entertainment. The specific piece that was performed by the six singing maids and consort of flute, lute, bandora and cittern, treble and bass lutes as Elizabeth came out on to her gallery still exists, though admittedly only in the muted colours of a consort song arrangement for solo voice and viols. The music, by Edward Johnson (*f.* 1572–1601), follows the lilt if not the formal structure of a galliard:

> Eliza is the fairest queen
> That ever trod upon the green.
> Eliza's eyes are blesses stars
> Inducing peace, subduing wars.
> O blessed be each day and hour
> Where sweet Eliza builds her bower!
>
> Eliza's hand is crystal bright,
> Her words are balm, her looks are light.
> Eliza's breast is that fair hill
> Where virtue dwells, and sacred skill.
> O blessed be each day and hour
> Where sweet Eliza builds her bower!

Of the pieces Elizabeth herself composed, not a note survives that can be identified with certainty. The music that once surrounded her, however, still exists in quantity; and there are few more telling musical tributes to her than *The Triumphs of Oriana*, a collection of madrigals published in her honour in 1601, little more than a year before her death. The array of composers represented here is dazzling: John Wilbye and Thomas Weelkes; Thomas Morley (who devised and edited the collection); Thomas Tomkins, John Farmer, the lutenist Robert Jones, Edward Johnson, even John Milton, father of the poet. (By now Byrd had all but withdrawn from court; Dowland, never a madrigalist, was in any case working overseas.) If not all the music, let alone the verse, is of the very highest quality, the collection nevertheless brims over with high spirits, splendid imagery and downright flattery of the Queen. Even if no other piece from the collection had survived, John Wilbye's madrigal 'The Lady Oriana' alone would have served as an eloquent testimony to the sheer heights Tudor secular music attained during Elizabeth's reign and, to a large extent, under her patronage.

> The lady Oriana
> Was dight all in the treasures of Guiana;
> And on her grace a thousand graces tended.
> And thus sang they: 'Fair queen of peace and plenty,
>   The fairest queen of twenty!'
> Then with an olive wreath, for peace renowned,
>   Her virgin head they crowned;
>   Which ceremony ended,
> Unto her grace the thousand graces bended.
> Then sang the shepherds and nymphs of Diana:
>   'Long live fair Oriana!'

Music in Scotland

Time has not dealt kindly with Scottish music of the sixteenth century, and
the few sources that survive give less of an impression of a continuous
tradition than do those from contemporary England. To an extent, however,
this broken chain of evidence may well reflect the reality. Conspicuously
absent are major Scottish composers, men whose music circulated generally
and was imitated by others. Even those names that stand out tend to do so
because their works are recorded in reasonable quantity in a single
manuscript; never does the evidence go on to show that their works won a
wider audience. Without the choirbook that contains his masses and
antiphons, for example, we should not possess a single note of music by
Robert Carver (*c.* 1490–after 1546), nor for that matter more than a couple of
pieces of liturgical music from before 1560, the date of the Reformation in
Scotland. Possibly further symptomatic of the situation are the facts that both
English and French pieces seem to have supplemented the works of local
men, and that Scottish musicians are known to have travelled abroad in order
to gain experience and consolidate their techniques.

Carver's music is immediately distinctive in style, though whether the
accent is in reality a regional rather than personal one it is impossible to tell,
since there is so little to compare with it. His *Missa L'homme armé* has the
distinction of being the only mass by a British composer of the sixteenth
century to belong directly to a Continental tradition, in that it is composed
around the melody of this popular French chanson in the manner of the late
fifteenth-century settings by Dufay, Ockeghem, Obrecht and Josquin. But
this is the full extent of his debt; the melodic lines of Carver's mass have in
fact much more in common with the English style of writing than with those
of the French and the Burgundians. Floridity here combines with insistent,
nervous ornamentation and a strongly modal flavour to create music that is
bluntly unsophisticated and yet, in its general effect at least, startling and
memorable. At its best – as, for example, in the massive *Missa Dum sacrum
mysterium*, whose ten independent voice-parts represent St Michael and the
nine orders of angels – there is something deeply stirring about the wildness
of Carver's musical imaginings. Certainly his masses overshadowed the blunt,
functional metrical psalms and few motets that replaced them in the latter
part of the sixteenth century. Carver may have been Scotland's Taverner, but
no equivalent of a Tallis, Byrd or Gibbons seems to have followed on from
him.

Records of courtly song, at least from the reigns of Mary, Queen of Scots
and her heir, James VI, are a little more complete. Given the country's
political allegiance, it is not surprising to find that the debt to France is
particularly strong and more continuous than in England. Scottish court
poets and composers can be shown to have shaped their indigenous tradition
by accepting French chanson styles as actual models. The hybrid this
produced, in the form of simple, lyrical partsongs and, later, also lute-
accompanied songs, proved strong enough to survive well into the
seventeenth century, untouched by the vogue for the madrigals that raged
south of the border. Being stylistically derivative, largely unattributed in the

sources and undemonstrative in character, Scottish Renaissance songs tend to be passed over rather more readily than their intrinsic quality merits. Placed beside some of the less imaginative music of late Tudor England, anonymous Scottish miniatures such as 'Richt soir opprest am I' and 'Lyk as the dum solsequium' stand up remarkably well, and they deserve a wider audience – as indeed does sixteenth-century Scottish music in general.

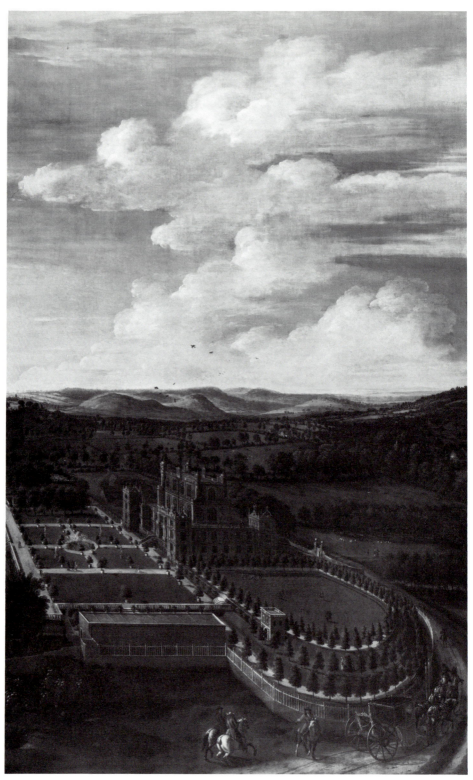

Painting of Wollaton Hall and Park, Nottinghamshire, by Jan Siberechts (1697).

5 Renaissance Gardens and Parks

JOHN STEANE

Renaissance gardens

> God Almighty first planted a garden: and indeed it is the purest of human
> pleasures. It is the greatest refreshment of the spirits of man: without which,
> buildings and palaces are but gross handyworks: and a man shall ever see,
> that when ages grow to civility and elegancy, men come to build stately,
> sooner than to garden finely, as if gardening were the greater perfection.

(Francis Bacon, 'Essay on Gardens')

The Crown, aristocracy, church, gentry, and merchants all created gardens
which served this complex hierarchical society in four main ways. Gardens
were one expression of the belief of order in nature, and the desire for order
appealed to the spirit of the age.

> Why should we, in the compass of a pale
> Keep law and form and due proportion
> Showing, as in a model, our firm estate
> When our sea-walled garden, the whole land
> Is full of weeds, her fairest flowers choked up.

(Shakespeare, *Richard II*, III, iv, 40)

Robert Laneham described the Earl of Leicester's garden at Kenilworth as
'the place in which the mind reassumed its absolute dominion over a world
from which all savagery has been purged'. A more particular and political
function was fulfilled by what Strong called 'heraldic gardens'. These were a
convenient mode for displaying the triumphant success of the Tudor dynasty.
At Hampton Court and Whitehall Palaces there were parterres surrounded by
rails, painted in Tudor white and green, amidst a forest of posts surmounted
by vanes held by heraldic animals. All centred on majestic stone fountains.
Here, in her fifties, the Queen walked, sat on specially made seats, and kept
state among diplomats and her own courtiers. They, in turn, indulged their
passion for display in extravagant building and gardening programmes.
World systems were intermixed with bogus genealogies. At Theobalds, for
instance, Burghley planned the 'conspectus' of the universe, the nations of

England and her governors, considered as a setting for England's queen. He extended the garden into the house, installing his presence chamber with a kind of grotto where water streamed out of rock; the Zodiac with sun and moon were painted on the ceiling, and on the walls were six trees, 'all complete and natural', hung with bird's nests and the heraldic shields of England's nobility. It is said that in the morning when the steward opened the windows overlooking the pleasure gardens birds flew into the hall, perched themselves upon the artificial trees and began to sing. The gardens of these palaces and 'prodigy' houses were settings for courtly entertainments and pageantry including water spectacle of an ephemeral nature. The bowers, knots, and mazes were full of emblems of royal virtues because adulation of the sovereign had a horticultural dimension.

A sterner view of the functions of gardens came from moralising Puritans who connected gardens with the Fall. Adam sinned in a garden, Christ was betrayed in one. They were dangerous places. William Lawson stressed that in a garden 'there will ever be something to doe, weeds are always growing'. The haven is reached only through 'the Straits of painfull toyle'. There are always weeds to be rooted out, trees to be 'reformed' by 'good government', walls to be held rigidly against a world of invaders. The converse was a nostalgic yearning that Paradise might be regained. This idea was embedded in the punning title of *Paradise Retrieved, Paradise Regained, Paradisus in Sole*, by the apothecary, John Parkinson (1567–1650), who was promoted on the strength of it to become Botanicus Regius Primarius by Charles I. The pun derives from the fact that in the later Middle ages the term 'Paradise' had been applied to the pleasure garden of a convent. In Oxford today Paradise Street commemorates the former garden of the Greyfriars. For Renaissance Britain the enclosed garden was a symbol of repose and harmony; walking its alleys and arbours, herbal in hand, the Elizabethan could recognise in flowers and trees emblems of spiritual truths, and gain in this outdoor cloister something of the same spiritual reflection as did a medieval monk.

As in building, so with gardens, the patron sometimes intervened with ideas of his own. Among Burghley's papers are 'plots', measurements and estimates for waterworks in the gardens at Theobalds, all annotated by him. Robert Cecil's garden plans went ahead at Hatfield during the years 1609–11 under the confused direction of three men, Jennings, Chaundler, and Tradescant, with the Earl himself as ultimate authority. Gardening theory was also increasingly available in book and essay form. Bacon's famous 'Essay on Gardens' shows the informed interest in horticultural planning of a distinguished lawyer. Many owners, however, were content to rely on the advice of experts such as Hill, Lawson, and Markham in planning their gardens and orchards.

There was a pronounced tendency to favour regularity, both in architectural and horticultural design. At Wollaton (Nottinghamshire) for instance, the house is centred in a garden grid of nine squares. Hatton at Holdenby (Northamptonshire) sited his palatial residence on the top of a slope stepped symmetrically with double terraces. In these constituent elements the square or rectilinear plan was preferred, being more suitable for

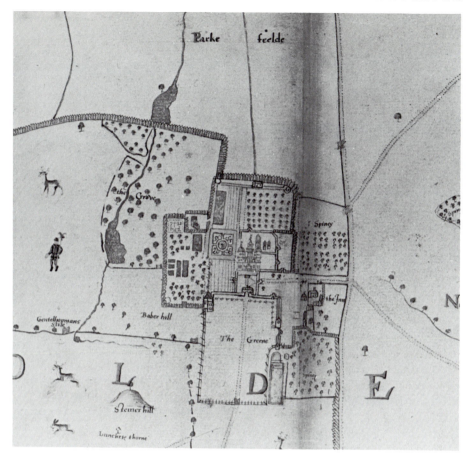

Section of estate plan for Holdenby House gardens, Northamptonshire, laid out in 1580–7.

'straight walkes'. For Markham the 'perfect ground plot' was 'a great large square', sited 'on the south side of your house . . . as wel for the prospect thereof to all your best rooms, as also because your house will bee a defence against the northerne coldness'. Parkinson disliked a vegetable garden near the house 'for the many different sents that arise from the herbes, as cabbages, onions and are scarce well pleasing to perfume the lodgings of any house'. He added the revealing point, reflecting the current obsession with regularity: 'the many overtures and breaches as it were of many of the beds thereof, which must necessarily bee, are also as little pleasant to the sight'.

Once the siting was agreed on, the first task was to enclose the garden. If this was not done, Hill thought, it 'be many wayes endamaged as wel by beastes, as by theeves, breaking into them'. Enclosure could be done rapidly by a quickset hedge, a dead hedge (made of clippings) wattle, or paling surrounded by bank and ditch; dry stone, brick or slate walls were also built. This sense of enclosure might be gained more expensively, or on a sloping site, by digging terraces and stepping banks. Holdenby (Northamptonshire) is a prime example; it vies with Italian Renaissance gardens in its multiple terraces and water works. Another, recently displayed by archaeology, is at Aberdour in Scotland where terraced gardens were probably created by James, 4th Earl of Morton, Earl from 1548–81.

A further mode of defending the garden was to surround it with a moat. Lawson's idealised garden had moats on two sides, 'for fish, fence, and moysture to your trees', and he pictured the owner sitting on his mount angling 'a peckled trout, or weightie eele, or some other fish' or rowing with a boat and fishing with nets. Sir Thomas Tresham's water orchard at Lyveden (Northamptonshire) was such a garden, punctuated with mounts at each corner linked by wet moats, set beside the cruciform New Bield, 'my garden lodge', in 1597. Some garden works were set out in military fashion, with bastions and water defences. Markham's plan was carried out literally in the mini-fortified garden at Tackley (Oxfordshire) attached to the seventeenth-century manor house.

But there was more to it than simply defence and a sense of order. Walled gardens in the Middle Ages had a special Christian symbolism. In Solomon's Song of Songs the virgin bride (seen as foreshadowing the Virgin Mary) is referred to: 'A garden enclosed is my sister, my spouse, a spring shut up, a fountain seated.' That this idea continued into the Elizabethan age seems certain; fountains were built at the centre of the palace gardens at both Hampton Court and Whitehall for the delight of the Virgin Queen. More ambitious gardens involved running water; at princely Hatfield the water was contained in two cisterns at the upper end of the garden and ran into a great container in the centre on which were painted artificial rocks and a statue of Neptune. De Caux's contribution was to add a huge marble basin, more fake geology and a shallow meandering river paved with coloured pebbles and sea shells. Further constructions included a dam, a water pump and an island.

Large scale Renaissance gardens were studded with minor architectural and earthwork features used for open air entertainments and activities. Mounts or small hills were thrown up either in the middle or on one side of the garden. They were vantage points from which the complexities of knots and parterres could be viewed and whereby a prospect could be enjoyed of the country around. Steps spiralled up and on the top were built banqueting houses or arbours. These might be temporary structures run up for a specific occasion or more solid little buildings such as are seen peppering the gardens in Wyngarde's view of Hampton Court. A substantial one built during the last years of Henry VIII's reign was excavated at Nonsuch (Surrey), 400 metres walking distance from the palace. Here desserts, light refreshments of marzipan, sugar, cakes, fruits, marmalade and spices were consumed during entertainments.

Figures exercising under cover, while overlooking gardens, are often seen in embroideries of Elizabethan gardens. Wyngarde again shows us timber-framed galleries erected over the Privy garden at Richmond Palace. A more usual (and cheaper) method of covering walks was by means of pleached limes (colour pl. 12).

> The Prince and Count Claudio, walking in a
> thick – pleached alley in mine orchard were
> thus much overheard by a man of mine.
>
> (*Much Ado about Nothing*, I, ii, 9)

Hill recommended that the alleys be covered with fine sand 'least by raine and showres the earth showde cleave and clag on your fete'.

The alleys led to arbours and here carpenters were much in demand in Renaissance gardens, making the rails which lined paths and alleys and the trellis work over which were intertwined plants, such as 'Vine, Mellon or Cucumber, running and spreading all over, might so shadow and keep both the heat and sun from the walkers and sitters thereunder'. The only unlikely element here is the heat of the sixteenth-century English summer.

The rigid geometry of the 'plotte' or 'forme' of a garden necessitated its subdivision into beds lined with borders and decorated with knots, elaborate patterns planted in low clipped evergreens 'where all kinds of plants and shrubs are mingled in intricate circle as though by the needle of Semiramis' (so said Thomas Platte). The patterns of these knots formed the subject matter for woodcut illustrations in garden books; and are found in the background of portraits; they equally delighted embroiderers who stitched them in behind narrative subjects. To ensure regular planting, John Evelyn,

The King's Knot, Stirling Castle, Scotland; the remains of the garden laid out 1627–8.

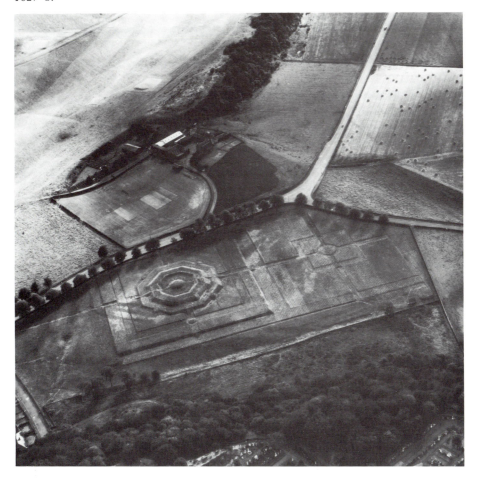

by the middle of the seventeenth century, advised the use of a lattice and even advocated carrying a four poster bed into the garden 'to draw over and preserve the choysest flowers'. Interspersed among knots, 'bankes and seates of Camomile, Peny royale, Daisies and Violets are semmly and comfortable'. All the surrounding borders of thyme, hyssop and savory required constant trimming and Parkinson recommended the use of 'dead' materials with which to line knots such as lead, oaken boards, the shank bones of sheep and tiles.

The use of topiary was widespread. Bacon advised in 'ordering of the ground within the great hedge' that 'it be not too busy or full of work' (ie not too elaborate). For other writers the more fantastic the topiary work the better. Yew and rosemary were preferred. Parkinson considered that yew 'is so apt that no other can be like unto it, to be cut, lead and drawn into what forme one will, either of beasts, birds or men'. The plants were trained up wire or over trellis frameworks, and intertwining of different species is found in painting, as in the portrait of Margaret Laton (*c.* 1610) where roses, honeysuckle and pinks spring from a single coiling stem, and it was a commonplace in Tudor and Stuart embroidery. The most elaborate development of topiary was found in mazes. Hill illustrated a maze as a 'proper adournment' and suggested fruit trees could be grown in the corners of a square (notice how reluctant he was to give up rectilinearity), within which is set a circular maze. These traditions of the gardener carving his images out of box and yew instead of marble carried on into the eighteenth century, where their excesses were ridiculed by Alexander Pope as 'verdant sculpture'.

Frontispiece to Gerard's Herball *(1597).*

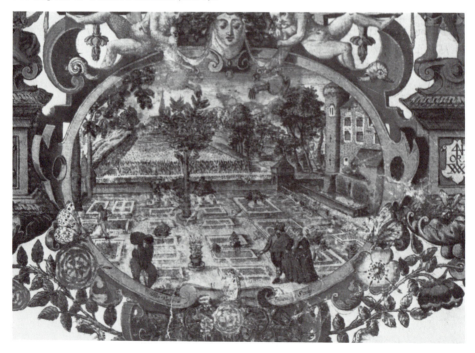

In representations of medieval gardens, plants seem almost to have been an afterthought. They occur sparsely or in pots, regimented behind railings or topping raised beds. The number of species represented was distinctly limited. Flower gardens as such are a Renaissance development. It was the availability of exotics brought in from abroad (what Parkinson called 'outlandish' flowers) which excited British gardeners, for until now English gardens had been limited in their floral displays to spring flowers. Parkinson contrasts the 'English' flowers, primroses, cowslips, rose campions, stock, gilliflowers (carnations) violets, with the newly arrived foreign imports which gave 'the beauty and bravery of their colours so early before many of our owne bred flowers . . . Daffodils, Fritillaries, Jacinths, Safron-flowers, Lillies, Flower deluces, Tulipes, Anemones, French Cowslips or Beares eares'. Gardeners became ever more skilful in propagating by slips and grafting multi-coloured varieties of gilliflowers which they pursued as keenly as their Dutch colleagues hunted the almost black tulip half a century later. Tulips, when they came in, were sought after of every hue; the rich spectrum of early seventeenth-century floral vocabulary distinguished between tones of gredeline (pale grey), quoist (colour of a dove's breast) and gilvus (very pale red). Almost a hundred sorts of daffodil are listed.

Plants were imported from nurserymen in Holland and Paris; merchants were commissioned to bring back exotic specimens from Turkey and Russia. The Tradescants, the gardeners of Hatfield and Oatlands, took great care of their plant introductions. They oversaw the watering of the plants on board ship and their protection from salt spray. They covered plants with straw during the winter, their citrus trees were planted in hooped wooden barrels with lugs for ease of movement by workmen. Experiments were made in building the earliest orange houses, wooden sheds with windows and stoves.

There appears to have been a considerable enrichment of vegetables in the diet of Tudor England. Holinshed (d. 1580), describing England in his day, pointed out that their cultivation had greatly increased . . . 'I mean of melons, pompions [marrows], gourds, cucumbers, radishes, skirets [skirets of Peru were potatoes], parsnips, carrets, cabbages, navares [rape roots], turnips and all kinds of salad herbes', and he reckoned that 'their use is not only resumed among the poor commons' but also 'fed upon as daintie dishes at the tables of delicate merchants, gentlemen and the nobilitie who make their provision yearlie for new seeds out of strange countries'. Harvey has traced the general introduction of root crops back to the fifteenth century and already by the early sixteenth century the 'Fromond' list of 'Herbys' necessary for a garden includes forty-nine sorts of herbs for pottage, and nineteen for salad as well as seven roots.

The interest in herbs, however, continued to be predominantly medieval. Much contemporary medical treatment still relied on the archaic doctrine of signatures whereby the helpful Almighty was thought to have endowed plants with signs by which their curative properties could be recognised. *Aristolochia* or birth wort, for instance, was associated with the womb because of swellings at the base of the flower and considered to be efficaceous 'to bring away the women's after burden'. It is said still to grow at Carrow Abbey in Norwich, a floral relic of a long vanished monastic garden.

Orchards were seen as an essential part of a large garden and as much care was lavished on their layout as on other areas. Renaissance garden writers recognised that different species needed to occupy the various habitats within the orchard; nectarines and peaches, for instance, were trained against south-facing walls. Fruit trees were planted in rows with plenty of room for their roots to spread. Air photography has recognised the regular pattern of tree holes dug for trees in Sir Thomas Tresham's garden at Lyveden (Northamptonshire). Among the 'outlandish' fruits introduced from the Middle East was the apricot which required care in pruning. Henry VIII paid his gardeners at Hampton Court and Richmond for bringing pears and damsons, grapes and 'philberts' to court. The staple fruit remained, however, the apple. Intense interest was shown during the period in grafting and pruning; Shakespeare apparently shared in this:

> O what pity is it
> That he had not so trimm'd and dress'd his land
> As we this garden! We at time of year
> Do wound the bark, the skin of our fruit trees
> Lest, being over-proud in sap and blood
> With too much riches it confound itself.
>
> (*Richard II*, III, iv)

The newly discovered worlds also provided Renaissance Britain with many novel timber trees. Sycamore came in from Central South Europe in the sixteenth century or earlier. The first North American tree to be introduced into Britain was the *Arbor Vitae* in 1597. The early seventeenth century saw the common lime, *Tilia Vulgaris*, a hybrid between our native lime *T. Platyphyllos* and *T. Cordata* imported from continental nurserymen in large numbers for use in avenues.

Gardeners may have produced exciting experiments in plant propagation and grafting but they remained conservatively attached to their habitual tools. In the realm of water supply, however, elaborate pumps were used in the more sophisticated garden causing water to 'flee forthe of the pipe holes . . . in the form of raine'. These were supplemented by ceramic watering pots and butts trundled on wheels. Alleys and gravel walks were levelled using rollers, 'of the hardest marble' such as could be 'procurred from the ruines of many places in *Smyrna* when old *Colomns* of demolished antiquities are being sawd off' (Evelyn). Tools had to be provided by the gardener himself. An illustration in Evelyn's unpublished *Elysium Britannicum* shows two sorts of spade, one with an iron shod wooden blade, two types of rakes, an axe, a hoe, a mattock, a fork and a large spoon-shaped object. Hollow glasses were put over cucumbers to bring them on.

Attempts to control pests were crude and often based on misinformation. Earthworms were wrongly thought to be harmful. 'Toades and frogges are very poysonous and great destroyers of young plants.' Scattering kite dung and the shavings of harts-horn was thought to be helpful. 'Moales' were trapped in pots buried in the soil. Ashes, lyme and scalding water executed 'pismires' (ants).

The Renaissance witnessed a growth in the social status of the artist;

The maner of watring with a pumpe in a tubbe.

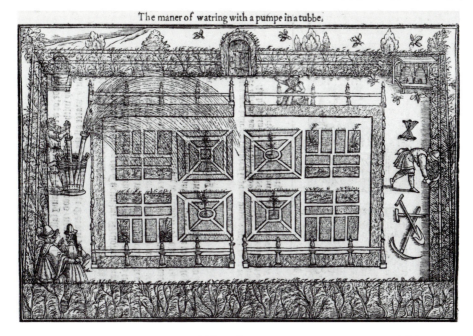

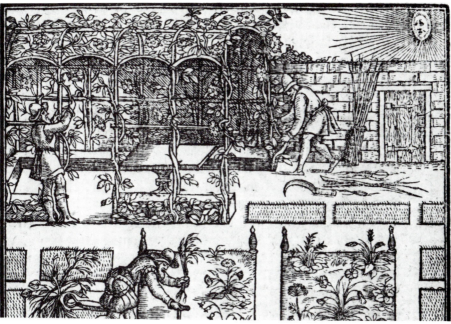

Illustrations from The Gardener's Labyrinth *(1586 edition) by Didymus Mountain. The top picture shows a trellised enclosure, and parterres crisscrossed with gravel paths.*

similarly gardeners made some progress from lowly craftsmen to prized professionals by the beginning of the seventeenth century. Shakespeare certainly endowed the Queen's gardener in *Richard II* with a discourse on political theory, but in general writers on gardening had a low opinion of gardeners. Lawson reckoned that such must be honest and 'painfull' (i.e. laborious) and 'had not need be an idle or lazie lubber, for so your orchard being a matter of such moment, will not prosper'. Parkinson too was suspicious of his fellow professionals, reckoning they were quite likely to steal valuable plants from their patron. Cogan was rather contemptuous of 'husbandman craftsmen' but regarded digging as contributing to their longevity. The search for respectability and recognition led to the foundation of the Company of Gardeners set up in 1606 and incorporated by royal charter. The motive was to put a stop to frauds practised by gardeners in the City who sold dead trees and bad seeds 'to the great deceit and loss of their customers'. The writers of gardening books adopted the same sycophantic and adulatory approach to their patrons as did other writers, but for all that they were the professionals and their employers were the amateurs.

Comito hit the nail on the head when he remarked 'Great princes like Burghley or Elizabeth were required only to contemplate the wealth of 'The plentifull treasury of Nature', not actually to toil in its production.

Renaissance parks

One of the characteristic features of the medieval landscape in England had been the park, an enclosed area of land (either open or wooded) designed to keep in game, to act as reservoirs for timber and underwood, and for use as pasture. Parks belonged in large numbers to the crown, and were permitted under royal licence to ecclesiastics such as bishops and abbots. The nobility and gentry similarly aspired to this territorial badge of status. An Act of 1390 confirmed the alliance of king and landed gentry in protecting their hunting privileges from the lower classes. Hunting in fact was a recreational obsession and occupational hazard of the medieval ruling class.

Already in the fifteenth century there were signs of a reduction in the total number of parks. Many medieval parks had been founded in areas of heath, forest, and waste on the edges of parishes and were seen as standing in the way of agricultural expansion. They began to be converted to other uses. In Cornwall, the bishops of Exeter lost interest in their parks in the fifteenth century, ceased to visit them, and split them up into smaller units, letting them out to tenants as farmland. Robert Ryece (in the *Breviary of Suffolk*, written before 1603, and published in 1618) explained why parks were thought to be wasteful of good land and why so many more were being disparked than newly enclosed. Staffordshire by repute had a hundred parks during the Middle Ages. Christopher Saxton's map (1577) shows a total of only thirty-eight.

Undoubtedly one of the reasons for the dissolution of the late medieval landscape was the break-up of the great ecclesiastical estates following the downfall of the monasteries in the 1530s. The conversion of parks into productive farmland involved extensive agricultural operations such as timber clearance, marling, liming, hedging, ditching, fencing, and provision of buildings. Normally these tasks were carried out by a succession of lessees, each improving and then paying higher rentals than their predecessors.

Conversely there are also signs that in other parts of the country, parks were being enlarged during the Tudor period. It seems that some parks absorbed land which had already been deserted by peasant farmers and on occasions there is evidence that cultivated land was deliberately laid waste to make a park. This could arouse intense opposition from those who thought themselves divested of agrarian rights. In *c.* 1490 the Wilstrop family of Yorkshire 'dydd caste downe the town of Willistrop, destroyed the corne feldes and made pasturs of theym, and hath closed in the commen and made a parke of hytt'. Similarly, Sir Christopher Hatton, Chancellor to Queen Elizabeth, greatly enlarged his park at Holdenby (Northamptonshire) between 1580 and 1587 by absorbing 600 acres of open fields in the southern half of the parish and surrounding them with a five mile circuit of pointed oak pales. In this way he provided a suitable setting for his house, the largest and most magnificent of the prodigy houses built by members of the Elizabethan court circle. Hatfield House, the seat of Robert Cecil, Earl of Salisbury, another essay in conspicuous consumption, was similarly surrounded by a swollen park, the greatest in Hertfordshire.

These examples highlight the different functions now fulfilled by parks in Renaissance society. Parks, like houses, mirrored ways in which the ruling elite saw itself. The internal design of houses tended to emphasise the social separation of the landed family from its servants by physically consigning them to living and working in attics or in basements. A similar sense of social hierarchy was instilled in the distancing of the new courtier house from the village by setting it in the middle of the park. As life for the ruling classes became grander, more bound round with etiquette, so the park was the background against which a rigorous set of social conventions was acted out. Changes in the practice of hunting illustrate this. Instead of, as in the Middle Ages, a wild gallop following the beasts of the chase over wide tracts of rough country, the Tudor hunt was much more formalised. Large numbers of deer were rounded up and driven down rides and through clearings to set places (called standings) where they were shot down. This ritualised slaughter assumed some of the characteristics of grand theatre. Such hunting expeditions to parks were integral to the ponderous progresses of Elizabeth I and James I. They had the effect, deliberate or otherwise, of crippling the economy of their lordly hosts. Parks were now criss-crossed with rides. Lodges were now less places from which to rest after a hard day's hunting than vantage points from which elaborately-dressed members of the nobility (and their hangers-on) witnessed the *battues* performed by their social superiors.

When we consider planning and planting in parks it is possible to detect the same artificiality, the same separation from the worlds of nature and reality. The first deliberate plantations of trees (a century before Evelyn's *Sylva*) were recorded in a remarkable series of inscribed stones in the Spencers' park at Althorp (Northamptonshire), beginning as early as 1567.

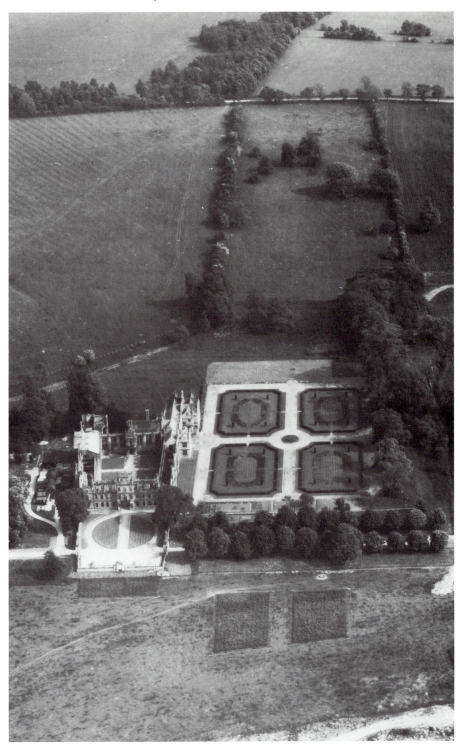

Kirby, Northamptonshire, with long garden, canalised river, gravel walks and terracing (late sixteenth century).

New species like the sycamore were introduced and their rapid growth soon made an impact on the English landscape. Parks were demarcated by mounded boundaries, lined with internal ditches and topped with timber palings. Saxton's county maps, published in 1577, show parks as little oval and circular enclosures ringed round with fences. The sites of Tudor parks can still be recognised in the English landscape. The lodges survive as moated earthworks or adapted as ancient farmhouses. Clues are provided by place and field names. The most vivid evidence is botanic – the presence of aged, freestanding or hedgerow trees growing on enclosed lands. Ancient pollard oaks dotted over Woodstock Park (Oxfordshire), Windsor Great Park (Berkshire) and Parham Park (Sussex) are among the oldest surviving things. In Cornwall (at Boconnock for instance) ancient parks abound in lichens and in the invertebrate fauna of dead wood.

Towards the end of our period, the park began to be recognised as something contrived and set apart. The Civil War witnessed the wholesale destruction of parks and the diminution of forests. From the Restoration of the monarchy the gentry began to introduce formal elements of planning in the French manner. Also, canalised water systems, bridges, rigidly straight avenues opening up vistas were inspired by the authoritarian regimes flourishing at this time on the continent.

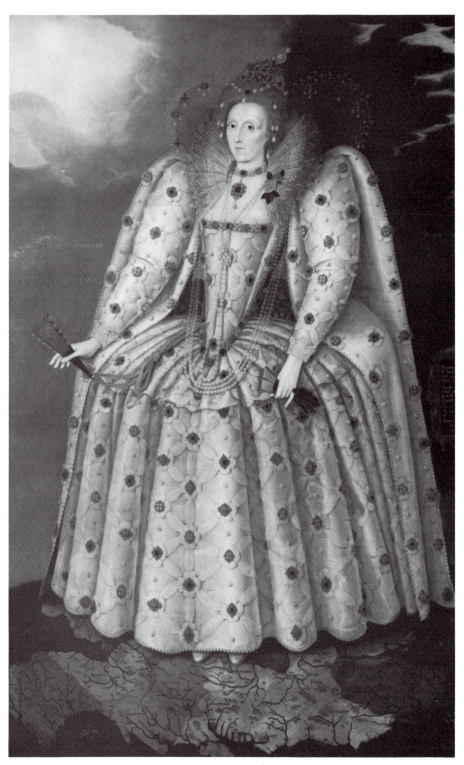

?Marcus Gheeraerts the Younger, the Ditchley Portrait of Elizabeth I (c.1592).

6 Painting and Imagery

MAURICE HOWARD AND NIGEL LLEWELLYN

Introduction

In considering the paintings and sculpture of Tudor England in terms of their basic materials, as images made from wood, stone and paint, it soon becomes clear that what, from a twentieth-century standpoint, is regarded as 'art' was not exactly what sixteenth-century English people thought of as 'image-making'. The portrait of Elizabeth I opposite helps us understand the differences between these two concepts. The Queen is shown life-size and standing in what at first appears to be a natural setting. The horizon can be seen at her feet and the sky above her head. But the convincing illusion of the natural world we might expect from figurative art does not survive beyond a second glance. The landscape turns out to be a map and the weather is quite unworldly. The ambiguities of the setting are soon transferred to the figure itself. Despite having been paid for by someone who knew her well, Elizabeth's portrayal is not concerned to replicate the physical reality of her body. The slenderness of the waist and the shape of the arms are anatomical impossibilities. Her feet are set firmly on the southern Midlands but fit awkwardly with the rest of her body. Any lingering doubts about the low priority given to naturalism in this picture are dispelled by the appearance of written texts on the surface of the canvas: not only the place-names on the map, but Latin mottoes, and to her left the words of a sonnet set in a decorative frame hanging artificially in ambiguous space.

'Artifice' is, in fact, a key concept in Tudor art, and more important for 'image-making' than our word 'art'. Despite recent experiments such as 'abstraction' which seemed to dispense entirely with subject-matter, and 'conceptualism', which rejected the idea that art resides in manufacturing objects, our sense of the art of the past remains relatively untroubled. We might expect English Renaissance art to take subjects, such as the person of the Queen, and, using certain conventions, render the person three-dimensionally in some accurate way on a two-dimensional surface. We might also expect Renaissance artists to be concerned to adjust this accuracy in an effort to make their creations more beautiful. If we know anything about the

Renaissance in Italy we might expect such adjustments to flow from a taste for classical antiquity.

All these concepts were foreign to the sixteenth-century English viewer, and if we attempt to see this 'art' in these modern senses of the word we would be misguided. Not only are the concepts different, so too were the institutions and the artists themselves. There was no National Gallery or Summer Exhibitions at Academies. There were very few collections of foreign art to act as examples which might influence taste, and none of these were public. There was no market for the sale of pictures in the modern sense. Artists were regarded as of the class of skilled craftsmen. Much of their work was ordered specially by the patrons, bought bespoke, not 'off-the-peg'. The way these artists went about image-making was also quite different. They regarded a theory such as linear perspective as a game played by a few learned geometricians, not as a rule to be obeyed – or even understood – by painters. The classical past was not a source of inspiration; it was a foreign world explored by scholars in whose intellectual and social class Tudor artists, with a few notable exceptions, did not have a place.

In some ways, then, 'Tudor art' is a contradiction in terms because the artists were very different from their modern counterparts. The modern view of the artist is as artificial a construction as the space in the Ditchley portrait.

We may also have a distorted view of Tudor patronage, another concept which needs handling very carefully in this context. The people who paid the artists were, for the most part, interested in using art objects in traditional ways, which were quite different from the expectations a modern artist might have of his or her audience. Most of the images to be discussed in this chapter were expected to transmit their message to the onlooker clearly and efficiently. There was considerable interest in ambiguity and symbolism in certain quarters, but suitability and propriety were more important than sensory pleasure or intellectual stimulation. Skill could be displayed but never at the risk of obscuring the image, which functions primarily as a transmitter of information about the subject-matter.

It is very clear, from the few accounts we have of Tudor reactions to the art of Renaissance Italy and elsewhere in continental Europe, that Tudor patrons were as impressed as we might be by manual virtuosity – the making of a whole figure from a single block of marble for example – but nervous of too accurate a replication of nature, such as the *trompe l'oeil* (or illusionistic) games of the Dutch or Italian masters. Protestantism, which dominated the ideology of most Tudor patrons, brought with it a deep mistrust of images which were too life-like and pictures rivalling the creativity of God were frequently condemned as 'scandalous'. Some Tudor reactions to foreign work seen on travels seem to us very naive; the travellers got excited by rich materials, great antiquity and sheer size. Novelty was greatly admired, but composition, *chiaroscuro* (contrast of light and shade) harmony and other aesthetic and theoretical qualities were usually left unnoted. Much continental art – most religious works for example – was not only misunderstood by English viewers but also unappreciated because it was inappropriate to English needs.

Most of the pictures which have survived from Tudor England are portraits of one sort or another. Given the way Tudor portraits were used by their audience and by their patrons – as records of social status, of character and, to some extent, of physiognomy – there was little room for the challenge of invention within perceived traditions of art, as was expected by the very different audience accommodated by Italian painters. Tudor artists were more obviously limited by the terms of their commissions, and artistic ingenuity was valued only within set limits. Licence was not given them for free expression, and artists were never encouraged to act in ways which have come to be seen as forming the pre-history of the Romantic artist's reputation: rebellious, restless, misunderstood and challenging codes of standard social behaviour. Thus there were vital social, institutional and conceptual differences between the art of Tudor England and that of Italy in the sixteenth century.

The divisions in this chapter will follow the contemporary social groupings: the Court, the Church, the gentry and the people who were ranked in a hierarchy which controlled the social lives of the artist's audience. Moreover, our account will not emphasise the innovations of individual artists in ways that were virtually unthinkable in Tudor England. The Tudor world was not completely ignorant of continental art after the break with Rome in the 1530s, but it was not altogether impressed by what it saw. In fact, it was more interested in other things. Tudor patrons were not generally intimidated by a system of values which featured 'classical' at one end and 'inferior art' at the other. They had images made of specific types, to function in particular public and private ways, within certain traditions and in the face of certain social and economic conditions. It is these purposes and circumstances of Tudor image-making that we discuss in this chapter.

Painting at Court

At the Court of the early Tudor monarchs, painting served in various ways to promote the image of the sovereign. As part of Court spectacle and pageantry, the visual arts were a means of demonstrating the power of the figure at the centre. The illusion of majesty, supported by the magnificence of display, offset any doubts about the reality of either the monarch's control or right to position. The head of the team of painters at Court was known from 1527 as the 'Serjeant Painter', though even he would spend very little of his time working on portable easel pictures. His work, and that of his subordinates, was mainly concerned with painting for occasion, decorating the temporary structures put up for particular receptions and festivities. Much time would be spent painting and gilding such objects as the King's tents and pavilions, banners and state barges, or three-dimensional images of the King's heraldic beasts, modelled in wood or papier-mâché; portraits or subject pictures were a secondary activity. Therefore, though payments are recorded for leading Court painters, much of their work was dismantled after use and no identifiable work by many of these individuals survives. The residue of 'painting at Court' from the Tudor period that we see in galleries and museums today would have formed only a small part of the busy activity of the Court painting workshop.

At Court, as in great houses, the chief contact that sixteenth-century people had with subject, or narrative, paintings in the domestic environment would have been not with panel paintings, but with hangings of all kinds; tapestries, often imported from the Netherlands, at the expensive end of the market, stained cloths at the cheapest. Before the Reformation of the 1530s, much of the imagery required was religious and, at Court, made for the occasion. For the funeral of Prince Arthur in 1502 there was painted a cloth of majesty with the 'grete image of our Lorde Jesus Cryste sitting upon the Raynebow'. Only a handful of narrative paintings on panel from the circle of royal patronage survives and there is not much evidence to suggest that they ever existed in very large numbers. Two famous paintings now at Hampton Court Palace showing significant events in the reign of Henry VIII encapsulate something of royal panoply. They show the events of 1520; the King riding with his entourage of courtiers towards the temporary palace erected for the Field of Cloth of Gold and his embarkation for Dover in the same year (see p. 278 and colour pl. 1). Also originally deriving from a Court commission, underlining Henry VIII's rivalry with Francis I of France, was a depiction of the Battle of Pavia in 1525, where the French King was captured by Imperial forces. Several versions of this composition are known to have existed and one hangs today at the Ashmolean Museum, Oxford.

With the Reformation of the 1530s there arose a demand at Court for paintings that were propagandist; they had to emphasise the new role of the King as head of the Church following the break with Rome. One such image survives in the Royal Collection, painted, perhaps surprisingly, by the Italian artist Girolamo da Treviso, showing the four evangelists stoning the Pope with the names of their gospels inscribed on the stones. Even this object may not have originally been a single framed panel picture for it is painted in grisaille (grey monochrome), suggesting that it may have formed one of a series inset into some form of temporary structure. In the National Portrait Gallery, London, can be seen the small but complex picture of Edward VI enthroned between the dying Henry VIII on the left, who points to his son to mark the transfer of power, and the Council on the right (colour pl. 6). Beneath the young King's feet, the Pope, beribboned by the words 'Idolatry' and 'Supersticion' and with the words 'All fleshe is grasse' on his cassock, is dragged from the scene by monks, banished from the dissolved monasteries of these years. Because, like so much of Tudor painting, the scene is emblematic and diagrammatic, spatial logic is abandoned and we read the scene episodically and in a fragmented way. There is little evidence that this kind of image made much headway outside the Court circle; or at least, not in painted form, for its message was known to the public at large via popular prints and woodcuts.

It is noticeable that a considerable number of the painters employed at the Courts of Henry VII and Henry VIII were foreigners. When we turn to the evidence of portraiture, a genre of painting for which large numbers of sixteenth-century examples survive, it would seem that, with the exception of the particularised skill of the miniature, the chief developments in Court portraiture were initiated by foreign painters. In the fifteenth century, the dominant mode of portrait painting throughout Western Europe outside Italy

had been set by the achievements of the Flemish school of painters, pre-
eminently Jan van Eyck, Rogier van der Weyden and their successors, whose
workshop styles were exported via the trade routes of Europe.

English travellers abroad often commissioned portraits from Flemish
painters; in the middle of the fifteenth century, the merchant Edward
Grymstone had his likeness taken by Petrus Christus, the pupil of Van Eyck,
a picture which survives on loan to the National Gallery in London. A
portrait (painter unknown) like that of Henry VI in the National Portrait
Gallery of *c*. 1530 demonstrates both the conservatism of style and the

Anonymous, Henry VI *(c.1530).*

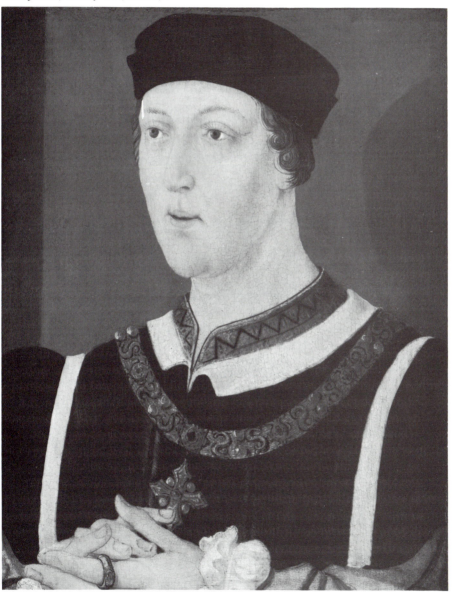

function of many portraits in the first decades of the sixteenth century. First, this image of the last Lancastrian king, believed by the Tudors to have been murdered at the instigation of their predecessor and rival, the Yorkist Richard III, was painted as one of a set of pictures of the Kings of England (ancient heroes, historical and legendary, were also popular) of the kind that proliferated both at Court and in the larger country houses of this period. Second, the format of this bust-length image, set in a very shallow space with the hands poised on the lower edge as if resting on the frame, would not have appeared old-fashioned to early sixteenth-century contemporaries, even though it is close to the sort of image that Van Eyck might have painted a century or so previously. Henry VII was painted by the Flemish artist Michael Sittow in much the same way and early portraits of Henry VIII are also very similar.

These small works, the form of which originated in the portraits of the donor included in fifteenth-century religious paintings, sought little more than to be highly veristic and allowed very little scope for the promotion of image-building, even if they were painted sometimes with great sophistication of skill and with subtle conditions of lighting. The Tudor propaganda machine required an image of the King that was more impressive and commanding, and one that could attract the attention of the spectator from a distance and in large public spaces. The particular recipe for this was brought to England by the work of Hans Holbein (1497/8–1543), a painter from Augsburg who had spent the early part of his working life at Basle.

At first, we might imagine that there was nothing unusual or propitious about Holbein's first coming to England in 1526, arriving as he did in the wake of many foreign painters. But the circumstances of his introduction to the English Court mark him out. Through the good offices of Peter Gillis, the town-clerk of Antwerp, he came recommended to Sir Thomas More, then Privy Councillor to Henry VIII, by the scholar Erasmus, whose portrait he had painted and who described him as 'insignis artifex', a notable painter. During his first stay, which lasted no more than two years, Holbein seems to have worked for different groups of patrons at Court not only the Royal Works themselves (for it is likely that he worked for the King on painted work for the Revels at Greenwich in 1527) but also the humanistic circle around More. Holbein's portrait of the astronomer and mathematician, Nicholas Kratzer, surrounded by instruments associated with his profession and his other interests, shows the artist already enlarging on the cramped format of the older, Flemish style, suggesting a multiple, rather than a single, view of the sitter's life (colour pl. 9).

A sense of the sitter's everyday surroundings took a further and quite major leap forward with the now lost group portrait of More and his family. The inventiveness of composition in this is recorded for us in later copies and in Holbein's preliminary drawing (colour pl. 2). Something of the quality of the lost work can be surmised from the single half-length portrait of More, now in the Frick Collection, New York. Holbein's success in particularising More's skin and the stubble of his beard among the fur and fabrics of his clothes and the curtain behind him testifies to his command of the medium of oil painting, established in the workshops of Flanders about a century before.

It was, however, during his second stay in England, from 1532 until his death in 1543, that Holbein painted his most celebrated pictures of Henry VIII's Court. He was never very highly rewarded, but enjoyed the distinction of being paid quarterly, raising his status above that of monthly-paid Court artists. Only one certain Holbein painting of the King survives, a small, half-length representation, but the artist succeeded in creating the image, known from copies of the full-length type, that has coloured the historical perception of Henry VIII ever since.

Nowhere was this more forcefully done than in his 1537 wall-painting for the Palace of Whitehall, destroyed by fire in 1698 and now known only through a copy and from a fragment of the artist's cartoon (a finished, life-size drawing prepared for direct transference to the wall surface). It showed the King, life-size, with his third wife Jane Seymour and his parents, Henry VII and Elizabeth of York, in a chamber richly decorated with Italianate 'antique' (as documents of the period describe it) ornament, a species of decoration associated with triumphs and military and dynastic celebration. The figures flanked a plinth with an inscription lauding the power of the Tudor royal house. Images of the sovereign, even full-length like this, were not totally unknown to contemporaries; a full-length series of the Kings of England was made for the great hall of Henry VII's Richmond Palace about 1500 and stained glass would also have depicted the King in this way. But

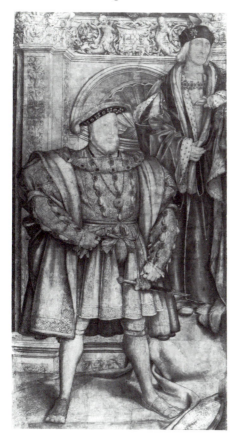

Hans Holbein, Henry VIII with Henry VII *(1536–7; copy, original destroyed by fire 1698).*

never before had the position of the current holders of power been isolated in this way from the historical past and projected so emphatically. Though there has been much speculation about the actual room in the lost Palace of Whitehall where this mural would have been seen, it undoubtedly decorated a room of audience or reception since its message was to make the King and the dynasty which he embodied ever-present. Both the Italianate setting and the message of the inscription, claiming the Tudors' direct power under God, must have struck spectators as a topical statement about political and religious changes.

In his wall-painting, Holbein presented Henry VIII less as a private individual than as the embodiment of dynastic power. The implicit tension between the public role of Court figures and their private selves emerges in Holbein's portraits of courtiers. In these works, Holbein took care to set outward signs of wealth and power against acute observations of individual physiognomy; the terse, fine line parting the lips, the three-quarter profile of a hooked nose, the scar on a neck. This detailing of the faces of his courtier sitters has led generations of artists and writers to comment on Holbein's ability to render the indefinable quality of 'character'. This lends a particular frisson to our contemplation of these works, because the historical information about many of these figures suggests their ruthlessness in pursuit of wealth and position; these were the 'new men' of Henry VIII's Reformation Court, opportunists and *nouveaux-riches*. Yet often their portraits deferred to the traditional place of portraiture as part of the subservience to a respect for religion. Sir Bryan Tuke held the important post of Treasurer of the King's Chamber at the time Holbein painted him. He is shown soberly, though expensively, dressed and the inclusion of information about his social position (*Miles*, the Latin word for knight), his age and his personal motto all speak of his public self. But in addition he wears a pendant cross with the five wounds of Christ and unobtrusively points with his left hand to an inscription from the Book of Job about the transience of life. Whilst this picture was painted at a time when the commissioning of religious works to aid private devotions was becoming proscribed, people still clearly had a concern for their personal salvation and took care to appear pious.

It is often said of Holbein that work for the English Court restricted him to portraiture and gave him less opportunity for the range of output he achieved during the pre-England years; for example, altarpieces or narrative cycles for the façades of houses. He certainly became part of the Tudor propaganda machine, providing not only portraits but designing artefacts for royal occasions and woodcuts for the new religious books promoted by the State. His reputation and his recipe for portrait painting cast a long shadow over his successors at Court. The role that Holbein had fulfilled for Henry VIII as chief image-maker of the sovereign appears to have been played by the Netherlander Guillim Scrots (who worked in England from 1545 to 1553) for Edward VI, and the Antwerp painter Hans Eworth (whose documented work in England dates from 1549 to 1573) for Queen Mary.

Another artist of the mid-century years around whom a small body of work can be identified is the German Gerlach Flicke, whose signed portrait of

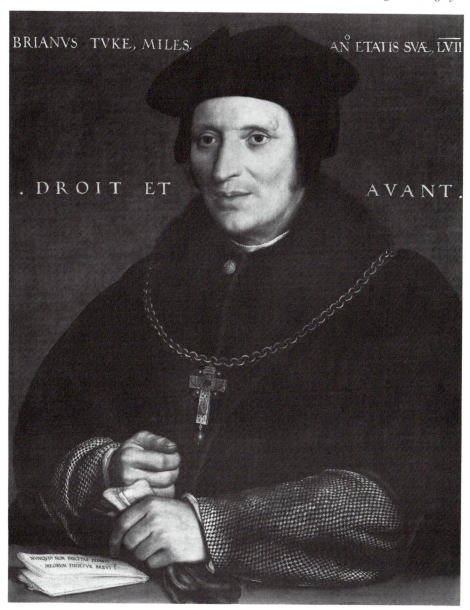

BRIANVS TVKE, MILES.   AN ETATIS SVÆ, LVII

. DROIT ET   AVANT.

NVNQVID NON PAVCITAS DIERVM
MEORVM FINIETVR BREVI !

Hans Holbein, Sir Brian Tuke *(1539–41)*.

Archbishop Cranmer probably dates from about 1546. Flicke seems to have
adapted his style to the principles of the Holbein tradition. Some might argue
that there has been a loss of quality here; the sitter appears more self-
conscious and more stiffly and artificially posed than Sir Bryan Tuke. An
explanation for this might be that Holbein's successors appear to have been
far less scrupulous than he was about careful preparatory drawing, as
evidenced by the remarkable series of Holbein portrait drawings in the Royal
Collection. But English contemporaries would have judged a portrait like this

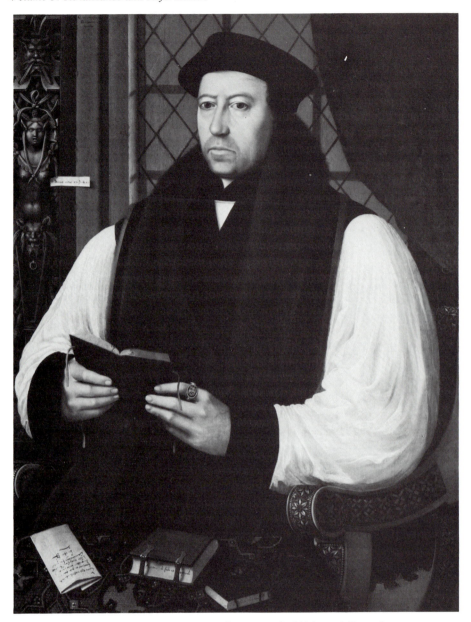

Gerlach Flicke, signed portrait of Thomas Cranmer, Archbishop of Canterbury (c.1546).

on the strength of its success in describing the essence of Cranmer's social position as the country's leading ecclesiastic and the nature of his interests and so would not have paid much attention to the stylistic niceties that we often discuss today. Flicke denotes Cranmer's position by mode of dress and by making prominent his episcopal ring, and denotes his interests in learning and attention to the word of scripture, by his books.

The portrait of the Archbishop is one of a group of mid-century works where high-born or politically successful figures at Court are shown as scholars. Contemporary with this is a portrait in the Royal Collection of the thirteen-year-old Princess Elizabeth, shown three-quarter length, holding a book in her hands and looking towards the viewer from a second book resting open on a lectern to the left. It is the earliest image we have of Elizabeth, whose depiction as Queen presents us with some of the most complex processes of image-making in the whole of Renaissance Court portraiture and provides the most interesting examples of the play between reality and non-reality in Elizabethan art.

The Court of Queen Elizabeth was different from that of her father, Henry VIII, in that spending on the visual arts was reduced to a minimum, whether on building and furnishing the royal palaces, on Court entertainments or the commissioning of pictures. Henry VIII became something of a legendary benefactor and liberal spender on the arts. Elizabeth was praised for her knowledge of painting, but no one eulogised her willingness to spend very much on it. Her portraits were carefully controlled as to their content and the timing of their appearance and it is a sign of their success that the series of images produced of the Queen had a profound impact; she got good ideological mileage out of them. From the first half of the reign, up to about 1580, there are some formal images, notably her Coronation portrait, now in the National Portrait Gallery. But there are also informal ones, sometimes with understated references to her personal virtues; these images were usually made as the preamble to successive protracted (and always ultimately abortive) negotiations for her marriage. Beyond about 1580, her portraits become the vehicles of the cult imagery that grew up around her and was celebrated by the active artistic patrons of the period, her courtiers, who vied with each other in building great houses and devising lavish entertainments to receive her.

So it was that even at the one annual feast day that was always celebrated at Court, the anniversary of the Queen's accession, the courtiers were the active participants. They became for the occasion the upholders of medieval and chivalric virtues in jousts and tournaments in which they upheld the honour and virtue of the Virgin Queen, who was herself the embodiment of quite depersonalised ideals of nationhood rather than the ageing woman behind them. At the Accession Day tilt of 1590, there was a special celebration in honour of the retirement of the Queen's long-serving Champion, Sir Henry Lee. A contemporary description of this event praises the Queen in a poem, beginning with the words 'Elizabeth, great Empress of the world, Britannia's Atlas, star of England's globe'. These metaphors emphasise the confident post-Armada world with England's territorial integrity seemingly protected and its values beginning to spread to the New World in the founding of the colony of Virginia. When, in 1592, Sir Henry Lee commissioned a portrait of the Queen for his house at Ditchley, something of the imagery of a knightly tournament is included in a picture clearly not meant to evoke the real presence of Elizabeth herself (see p. 222). Her face is portrayed as though a mask, her dress is based on, but deliberately an exaggeration of, the fashionable Court dress of the day, the setting symbolises her pivotal role as the upholder of the world of light in face of the danger of darkness. This picture may draw on the imagery of a moment, an occasion, and evokes a great figure whom everyone would have recognised; but its message is more to do with abstract ideas about the role and purpose of Elizabeth as monarch. Its physical presence was designed to bring distinction to the owner who was privileged to hang it in his house.

Though the position of Queen Elizabeth as a female head of both Church and State was peculiar to England, the sources of much of the imagery about her share ideas with the pictures of other European monarchs of the late Renaissance period. Though the identity of the painter of the 'Ditchley' portrait is not known for certain, it is likely that a foreign artist was responsible. But one form of painting which was quite the opposite of the idealised concept of the individual as found in the full-size portraits of Elizabeth, and one which was eventually developed by a distinguished school of native painters, was that of the miniature. In England, this type of painting originated at Court and for many years it was largely Court figures who were portrayed in this way. Perhaps the earliest known miniature to survive from the Court patronage circle is the 1525–6 painting of Henry VIII by Lucas Hornebolte, now in the Fitzwilliam Museum at Cambridge. Technically, the skill was developed from the work of manuscript illuminators; Levina Teerlinc, miniaturist and gentlewoman of the Court to Queens Mary and Elizabeth, was the daughter of the Flemish manuscript painter, Simon Benninck. The form was also practised and developed by Holbein.

Miniatures are personal objects; we know that they were sometimes locked in small cases and carried about the person, or kept amongst private possessions and therefore they are likely to have much more personal connotations or frames of reference than the more 'public' easel pictures. The name for these works did not initially come, as we might expect, from their size, but from their technical production, from *minium*, meaning white lead, the ground on which they were painted. The support is usually vellum, mounted on to bits of playing card to give it stiffness. Holbein's portrait of Henry VIII's fourth wife, Anne of Cleves, is one of two likenesses that he made of her in 1539 and it is preserved in a sixteenth-century carved ivory box, out of which is shaped the Tudor rose. Every detail of dress is discernible and, as usual in these miniatures, the image is brightened and made jewel-like by its setting against the deep blue background painted in pure lapis lazuli, or ultramarine. Whilst Holbein is a key figure in the development of the miniature, it seems that his technique of doing preparatory drawings, as he did for his larger portraits, was rather different from most miniaturists, including the most famous of all, the Englishman Nicholas Hilliard (*c.* 1547–1619) whose earliest work dates from 1571 (colour pl. 10).

The son of a goldsmith, Hilliard was skilled in the use of metallic pigments and is known to have painted from the life directly on to his prepared ground. In his treatise on the technique of miniature painting, *The Art of Limning*, Hilliard equates the meticulous skills of his work with those of the graphic arts rather than panel painting. He insists on the optimum conditions for working, including apparel of silk (to avoid transferring dust to the surface of the work in hand) and a large studio. He implies that the practice of miniature painting is on a higher level than those of painting and the crafts more generally, for the most important condition is 'cleanliness, and therfor fittest for gentlemen'. He painted Elizabeth and Court figures but, because he was not salaried by the Queen, he set up a London workshop and so extended the miniature trade to the wealthy merchant classes of the capital. His *Man Clasping a Hand from a Cloud* shows the extension of the miniature into the world of emblem and symbol and this has meanings not always possible fully to elucidate. Even for contemporaries, other than painter and

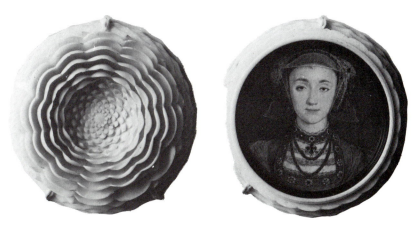

Hans Holbein, miniature of Ann of Cleves, in an ivory box carved with the Tudor Rose (1539).

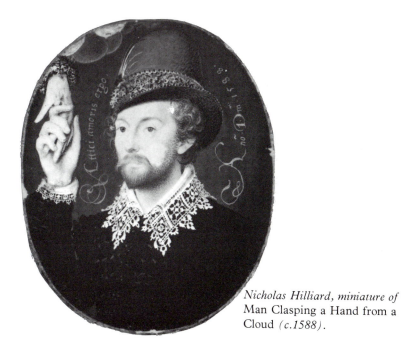

Nicholas Hilliard, miniature of Man Clasping a Hand from a Cloud *(c.1588).*

sitter, the personal allusions here may have been abstruse. But it is typical of the sort of concept of what art should do that was taken for granted in Court circles; a sense of using symbol and allegory to convey ideas. From prints we know that the clasping of hands was usually a reference to concord and plighted faith but, because the identity of this sitter has never been securely proved, we can only speculate about the deeper meaning of Hilliard's work. Where the identity of a particular subject painted in miniature is known the contrast it can present with a surviving full-length portrait of the same sitter often gives us a sharp insight into the private and public self-image which they projected into painting commissions.

Imagery in churches

The interiors of Tudor churches housed dozens of images. We can reconstruct the appearance of these places from written descriptions and early antiquarian drawings as well as from what remains. Despite the reforms to liturgical practice which took place in the mid-sixteenth century, the physical context for images at the death of Elizabeth was in most cases little changed from what it had been at the accession of Henry VIII almost one hundred years before.

Images of all kinds abounded: figures of St Christopher or representations of the Annunciation painted on the walls or over the chancel arch; heraldic coats-of-arms, the arms of the monarch especially encouraged by the law, brightly emblazoned; saints and biblical figures carved from wood or stone, such sculpture often polychromed and gilded and set amongst all sorts of decorative patterning. Inscriptions would have been prominent also, either painted or incised into panels of various sorts. The overall visual experience would have been richer than our modern expectation of church interiors. The illustrations show us something of the density of imagery that was once common. The mass of juxtaposed images would have been illuminated by what little natural light was allowed in through open doors or could penetrate the stained glass and by the flickering light of candles or torches.

There would have been little sense of open space. Wooden screens, gilded and decorated with figures, usually cut off the east end from the main body of the church. Examples of such furnishings made of oak can still be found in Devon and elsewhere in the West Country. Another screen, perhaps more splendid, might have been located at or behind the high altar. Carved stone images, always painted or gilded, would have acted as the focus of attention during the mass, decorated a shrine, a font or perhaps an Easter Sepulchre on the north wall of the chancel. All these would have been supplemented by painted images on wooden panels or by embroidered figures on wall-hangings. Most present-day Anglican churches are less cluttered than at any time in Tudor England. Indeed, it might require the imaginative leap triggered by a visit to a building of similar age in Italy to give us a more accurate idea of what religious art looked like in its original setting in sixteenth-century England.

But how did these images function and what expectations did Tudor church-goers have of them? As we have seen in discussions of Tudor art at Court and as we shall see in considering art in domestic settings, a key theme in understanding how all these images worked is to sense the tension, both positive and negative, between public and private demands.

In most communities the church was by far the biggest enclosed space accessible to the general population. It was not simply a place of devotion but, in effect, a public space. Under Elizabeth and the Anglican Settlement of 1560, this dual rôle for the church was formalised. Richard Hooker, the famous apologist for Anglicanism, expressed it thus:

It behoveth that the place where God shall be served by the whole church [i.e. the whole population] [shall] be a public place, the avoiding of privy conventicles . . . covered with pretence of religion.

His words remind us that the Elizabethan Church, as an institution, was 'Established' under the control of the State and of the Law. The fabric of the buildings themselves was expected to show a dignity and authority befitting the partnership between Church and State. It is clear from the records of the Diocesan law courts that the officers of the Church were obliged to engage in a constant battle to remind their flock of the sanctity of the place. Fights might break out over who deserved the best seats or over a boorish interruption of a sermon.

The images in the churches were not unaffected by the social life going on around them. Indeed, they owed their form directly to it, for the dominant principle of social organisation, hierarchy and the sense of degree, was also the principle which dominated church art, especially after the Reformation.

Prior to the reforms of the 1530s, English religious images have to be understood within the traditions of late medieval piety. This is the context for the image shown on p. 242. Orthodox teaching and liturgy presented religious images as intermediaries or aids to devotion. By concentrating upon an image, the spectator would be reminded of prayers taught or stories heard; the suffering of a martyred saint, the mystical purity of the Virgin, the majesty of the Creator. This prompt to the spectator's memory was perhaps accompanied by spoken, public statements of belief and supplemented by private devotions; an appeal made to a name-saint, for example, with each act using the image as a means of addressing the saint in Heaven. The tiny image of St John, less than eight inches in height, was designed to torment the conscience of the believer through its graphic representation of the severed head of the martyr. The Midlands were the great centre for the production of this sort of alabaster carving. The trade at Nottingham was especially widespread and lucrative. Images of this sort were exported as far afield as the Baltic and the southern Mediterranean along well-established trading routes.

The Reformation put an end to this trade and to the public use made of images as mediators between the worshipper and the divine. But it did not stop the work of the alabastermen or end the public's active interest in the creation of figurative imagery in churches. The main change was one which overtook subject-matter, that is, away from saints, representations of Mary and scenes of the Passion of Christ and towards carvings for funeral monuments and certain church furnishings. Reformers forbade traditional types of images. Puritans taught that the Second Commandment ('Thou shalt not make unto thee any graven image, or any likeness of anything that is in heaven above') was to be taken literally and held that the making and 'using' of any representation of the human figure was blasphemy. Anglicans agreed that idolatry, such as that practised with traditional images by papists, was to be stopped but argued in support of secular images, for example effigies and allegorical figures on tombs which they said would carry out a useful function by acting as examples of good behaviour.

While these definitions of idolatry were being argued over, there were sporadic, violent rejections of all images which resulted in their destruction. The most intensive periods of this were during the reign of Edward VI (1547–53) and early in the reign of Elizabeth. The terms of the Settlement of the late 1550s and succeeding Statute made legal the new secularised iconography of tombs which had gradually developed but forbade any images which could be taken as encouragements to idolatry. But the vulnerability of church images did not cease with this Settlement, and funeral monuments were later victims of damage too. They suffered at the hands of Puritan iconoclasts amongst the Parliamentarian forces active in the later 1640s and then more seriously as a consequence of nineteenth-century reforms in liturgy and taste. Neither side in the battle over the issue of taste could approve of Tudor tombs. To exponents of classicism, they were too crude or too disrespectful to Vitruvius (the 1st century BC writer to whom the classicals looked for guidance in the correct use of the orders of architecture); to those who supported pure, medieval Gothic as a 'national' style, they were corruptions. Many, less fastidious vicars found the great Elizabethan tomb-chests with their elaborate superstructures an encumbrance in the chancel and the monuments were often consigned to a corner behind the organ or beneath the tower. They were usually damaged, cut down or defaced in the course of these disruptions.

The Vernon tombs at Tong, in the West Midlands, are typical in this respect. The church was originally established to serve a college which housed a small religious community and supported charitable works. Early in the fifteenth century it was rebuilt in the local red sandstone and its patronage taken up by the Vernons, a Derbyshire family with extensive landholdings and a lineage reputed to go back to the Norman Conquest. Tong church quickly filled with their monuments and the new south chapel soon had to be built to house additions to the series. It is a good illustration of the way an act of Tudor piety can also function on a secular level. Tombs work wonderfully well as indices of social pretension and the desire to establish lineage in sixteenth-century England.

The archaic dress worn by so many of the effigies of this period act in a similar way by symbolising noble interests in medieval chivalry. We have already noted this interest as an aspect of Court patronage. These details of costume also helped to preserve continuity. The Vernon chapel at Tong was built by Sir Harry who is commemorated by a free-standing tomb-chest with an elaborate superstructure decorated with saints and bedesmen, the latter

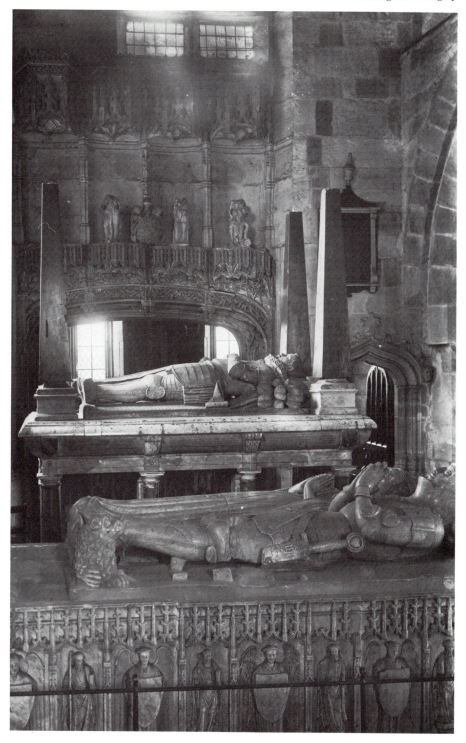

The Vernon tombs at the Church of St Mary with St Bartholomew, Tong, Salop (1600–10).

being mourning figures shown as if in attendance at a funeral. The photograph cannot show all the Vernon monuments but this view does give some idea both of the overcrowding that was to cause such problems by the eighteenth century, and of the damage sustained by individual tombs. In the middle distance we can make out the upper parts of a tomb erected in *c.* 1610. It marks the end of the long sequence of patronage by the family and in its original state it employed a design typical of English monuments *c.* 1600.

The tomb was built to commemorate Margaret Vernon, among others, and we can just see the effigy of her son, Sir Edward Stanley (d. 1632), recumbent in armour with hands clasped in prayer. His pose is very similar to that of his distant ancestor, Sir Richard Vernon (d. 1451), seen here on another tomb in the foreground. Changes have taken place between these two dates in the placing and form of the subsidiary figures and in the decoration, but the Stanley monument, despite damage to its fabric, rings a traditional note. This was exactly what was intended. The use made here of a tomb to reinforce the continuity of lineage through both its location and design was typical of the way in which Tudor images in churches worked.

As it is now constituted, the Stanley tomb comprises two registers. Above is an effigy and four obelisks, and below the slab (and not visible here) lie two more effigies to commemorate Sir Edward's parents. Originally the obelisks were positioned on the floor at the corners and four allegorical figures – probably representing virtues such as Fortitude and Justice – took their place next to the upper figure. What remains of these can be seen beyond the tomb on a shelf over a suppressed Tudor arch leading to a family chapel built in 1515. So, the allegories on the Stanley tomb replaced the rows of alternating saints and angels we can see on the fifteenth-century tomb-chest in the foreground.

The comparison offers an instructive example of how tomb imagery was adapted in recognition of the widespread post-Reformation nervousness about potentially idolatrous art. Justice, with her scales, was an easily recognised moral example but was clearly not intended to encourage worship. The non-figurative obelisks acted as symbols of eternity. Originally, they were topped off by little triangular pinnacles or 'pickes' as they were sometimes called in contracts. An early antiquarian drawing of the tomb also notes that Shakespeare was the author of the inscription we can just see on the curved edge of the tomb slab on which Stanley's effigy lies. Although the authorship has never been proved, the verse employs a reference to the 'sky-aspiring Piramide' and reminds the passer-by of the mortality suffered even by hard stone. There are countless versions of such moralising inscriptions on the tombs of this period right across Britain. They are the descendants of the traditional, late medieval *memento mori*, which reminded spectators of the inevitability of death and their final corporeal corruption.

Ironically, the fact that the Stanley tomb has been tampered with is a mark of its initial success. It was built on a large scale to make an impression. Sir Edward must have planned it before his own death – this was a common practice – and he was eager to match the social status he claimed – the Stanleys were Earls of Derby – to the scale of his monument. Size was one of the points of reference used in post-Reformation England to establish strong ties between the images erected in the churches and the social order which supported the Elizabethan State. The construction of a family chapel, often closed off from the church itself and not the property of the parish, was another means of using funeral monuments to demonstrate the hierarchy of the social order.

Size and location were two of the most important of the several scales which controlled both the patronage of Tudor tombs and the public reaction to them. Another important hierarchy influenced the choice of materials so that the very fabric of the images set up in the churches was determined by the structure of society itself. The tomb of one of Stanley's ancestors at Tong (d. 1517) was built of alabaster, a highly prestigious substance but not of the very highest rank. This place was occupied by bronze, cast and then gilded, a technique which was only used on the tombs of princes. The most notable cases of such works were those undertaken for the Court by the Florentine sculptor Pietro Torrigiano (1472–1528) and especially the monument to the founders of the Tudor dynasty, Henry VII and Elizabeth of York, in Westminster Abbey. This great project was started by their son, Henry VIII, soon after his own accession and seems to have been finished by 1519. Contemporary comment praised it for its skilful craftsmanship and the appropriateness of its materials. Modern art history has accorded it high status because of its use of Italianate decoration, signs of Renaissance style such as *putti* (naked cherubs) and other ornamental motifs. But Tudor contemporaries would not perhaps have found it so extraordinary as it was compatible with the tradition established by the gilt bronze tombs of earlier kings in the Abbey. Among the banners and crowded wall sculptures of the Henry VII Chapel it has little in common with contemporary commissions for tomb sculpture in the Florence of the Medici.

Hardly any Tudor tombs in bronze exist and most were in alabaster, the geological properties and availability of which made it the most popular material for statuary of superior quality. Though not durable enough for external use, in dry conditions the hardness and fine grain of alabaster allowed the carver to achieve a high polish, fine detailing and some deep cutting under the surface. After carving and polishing, the surface was primed with a sealer and then painted. Towards the end of the century, alabaster was still being carried to London where the best tomb-makers were based from the 1570s, but the purest, whitest seams were gradually worked out, leaving imported, foreign marble as the most prestigious stone in use by the early 1600s. Seams of red or reddish brown discolouring can often be seen on effigies and tomb-chests of this period.

Provincial patrons had tombs made from local materials of various sorts when they were not prepared to bring in expensive alabaster carvings. Limestone was rarely hard enough to take much detail but could sometimes be shaped into column shafts or used to form the core of effigies or other figures. Some details and sometimes whole tombs were carved from an oak block which would then be painted to resemble stone. There is a group of oak effigies in the north east of about 1530 (Thornhill in West Yorkshire and Staindrop, in County Durham, for example) and another group of tombs

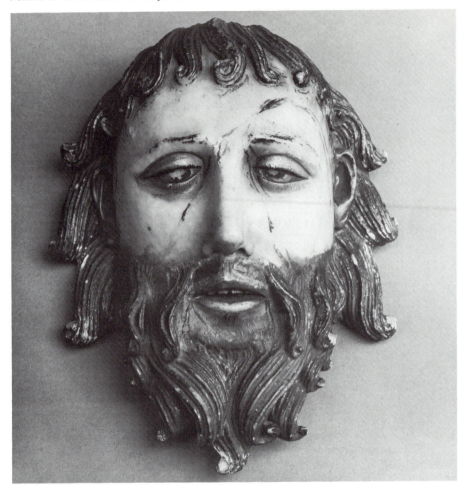

St John the Baptist, *alabaster (c.1500)*.

made entirely of wood in Worcestershire (Stockton-on-Teme, Wickenford, etc.) dating from the 1590s.

As we might expect, there was considerable regional variation in the materials used to make more modest tombs: terracotta in East Anglia; clunch in Kent and parts of the Midlands; black, Catacusan 'marble' in Cornwall; slate for inscription slabs all over the country; sometimes even granite. Fancier items, especially those made in London, used selected foreign materials in colourful combinations: touch-stone for inscription slabs; a German limestone called Rance, often used for the column shafts on the architectural surround; green, spotted Serpentine; freestone from Caen.

All this carved work was brought into the churches from outside. They were therefore places of assembly for the images, not sculptural workshops in the medieval tradition. At the upper end of the market, tombs might have to be carried many miles. Under Elizabeth, patrons wishing to establish their reputations by exploiting the sense of degree implicit in the tomb market employed prestigious London masons. The Stanley tomb at Tong is an example of this and contrasts with the earlier monuments in the church. These might have been brought in from Burton-on-Trent, but not from Southwark on the south bank of the Thames which was where many immigrant carvers settled and which formed the centre of the London trade.

Some of the best London masons were able to specialise in funeral monuments, but the provincial carvers relied upon a more general trade. There is evidence that the images turned out by the provincial workshops included engraved brasses, domestic carvings in wood, such as fine overmantels for fireplaces, newel posts and even garden ornaments, as well as tomb effigies. Once contracted, work was undertaken in the shop and then carried to the site for assembly and finishing off. The transportation of such bulky, fragile and heavy items as funeral monuments in Tudor England presented both patrons and artists with special problems and therefore contributed to the financial realities of tomb patronage in a way which our concept of taste does little to register. Water was used for the carriage of the sections of tombs whenever possible and what remained of the journey when the navigable water ran out was made by ox-cart over poor roads. The tomb-makers would usually ride down from London to supervise the final installation, a task which might take several weeks and demand extensive, structural alterations to the fabric of the church.

In early Tudor England, most church images were designed to show the piety of the user. In later Tudor England they were taken as indices of social status and subjected to the rigid control of a set of rules about the perceived hierarchy of society. Secular subject-matter replaced scenes of devotion or biblical narratives. The new types of secularised images commemorated worthy members of the common weal, that is, those who took part in the political and social hegemony established by the Anglican Settlement. Great energy was poured into the development of a vocabulary from which acceptable tomb images could be assembled and erected in the churches. The new, post-Reformation monuments had effectively to commemorate the secular status of the subject and make conventional, but now Protestant, gestures towards his or her piety. The new tombs used long-established forms, such as the recumbent figure on the tomb-chest, but integrated these into iconographic programmes which established the record of the good works of the patrons for whom they were made. These might include their service to sovereign and country, their consolidation of their lineage, their scholarship, wifely fidelity and especially their charity.

The new vocabulary of church images had also to be adaptable for use by a wider range of social classes than was the case before the Reformation. Those traditionally commemorated – the *nobilitas major*, or higher nobility – had included both the senior aristocracy and leading church dignitaries. After the Reformation, the latter group changed its composition as the great abbots and heads of other religious houses no longer existed, leaving only the two archbishops, the twenty-four bishops and the deans of the thirty or so cathedrals, all of whom might be commemorated by tombs. By the end of the century, a far greater number of tombs than in medieval times were being erected to people among the groups contemporary commentators called the 'minor nobility'; knights, esquires (usually the younger sons of knights), gentlemen, lawyers, academics and the ranks of the lesser clergy (colour pl. 7).

The minor nobility had their own types of images, some of which had to be newly invented and some of which could be adapted from extant forms. By returning to the Vernon tombs at Tong we can demonstrate the origins of one of these types which was to become very widespread by the late 1500s. Great men had great tombs, but clerics and scholars such as Arthur Vernon (who died in 1517) were commemorated more modestly. On the floor of the family chapel is an engraved brass plate and up on the wall is a small stone half-effigy in a simple frame. The inscription on the brass reminds us of pre-Reformation piety since it is an exhortation in Latin to the passer-by to pray for the soul of the departed: *Orate specialiter pro anima* . . . It was exactly this sort of Latin wording, in the language of educated Tudor people, which encouraged the images to be used as a mediator between the living and the soul of the dead and was to be outlawed after the 1530s. Arthur Vernon's will, completed in September 1516, shows that he made careful but modest preparations for his tomb:

. . . and to have a stone what myn executours think best for me, and my picture drawen thereupon, and for the making of my stone I bequeth xxx sh. [thirty shillings]

This reference to a stone with an incised effigy suggests a cheap floor slab but this did not suit his ambitious Vernon executors. They were perhaps encouraged to be more generous by the space now available in the new family chapel, but we should also remember that the ceremony of burial and the process of commemoration were in themselves acts of pious display and that the practice of tomb patronage was traditional. Arthur Vernon's plea in his will was a gesture of traditional modesty, whilst the patronage of his executors was one of social expediency.

The two monuments illustrated here show something of the enormous range of post-Reformation funerary sculpture in this country and also offer something of a contrast. One is small in size, pictorial, set up on a wall and records the short life of someone in a profession new to the ranks of the tomb subjects. The other is a huge wall-tomb, heraldic and designed to represent a local landowner. Both tombs include representations of their subjects in the form of a small, kneeling figure and a recumbent effigy, but we should take great care over too liberal a use of our modern term 'portrait' in relation to Tudor tombs. The details of the commemorated person's physiognomy and personality may have had significance for their relations but these monuments were designed to satisfy much longer term interests. Tudor tomb subjects are 'represented' but not necessarily 'portrayed', and it is worth recalling that in the many cases where tombs were erected prior to the subject's decease the tomb patrons may well have prayed regularly alongside their own effigies.

History records little about Matthew Godwin but his tomb tells us that he had achieved great prominence as a musician by his early death, aged seventeen, in 1586. The inscription on his simple memorial tablet in the north aisle at Exeter Cathedral notes his holding of posts in music both there and at Canterbury. The tomb takes the form of a scene showing Matthew praying before an organ surrounded by other symbols of his skill in music:

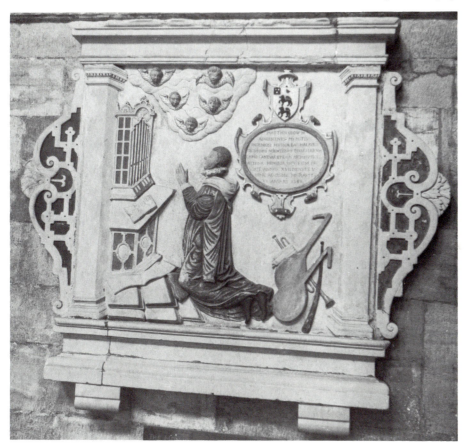

The tomb to Matthew Godwin (d.1586), in Exeter Cathedral.

lutes, a trumpet and a cornet. These details are carved in low relief rising out
of a plain, white freestone base. Above the subject a group of cherubs awaits
his soul on its journey into the cloudy heavens and the inscription, in
scholar's Latin, hangs in an oval frame with an armorial decoration above it.
The flanking pilasters are treated with a crude perspective to give an
impression of interior space seen from without. All the narrative detail would
have been picked out in colour and gilt.

The illustration on p. 246 shows a monument designed to make a quite
different impression. The tomb of Richard Harford (d. 1576) and his wife,
Martha Fox, stands in the chancel of Bosbury Church in Herefordshire
opposite to that of his father John Harford (d. 1559). Richard was patron of
both tombs and they dominate the east of the church, of which the family
were patrons. John's tomb is the earlier and dated 1573 and it is known that
Richard's was completed by mid-1575. John's tomb has caught the eye of the
art historians for its careful use of Italianate architectural detail and for
another sign of sophistication, a rare signature denoting it the work of a local
carver, John Gildon. Gildon was based in Hereford and active in the area
through the 1570s and 80s.

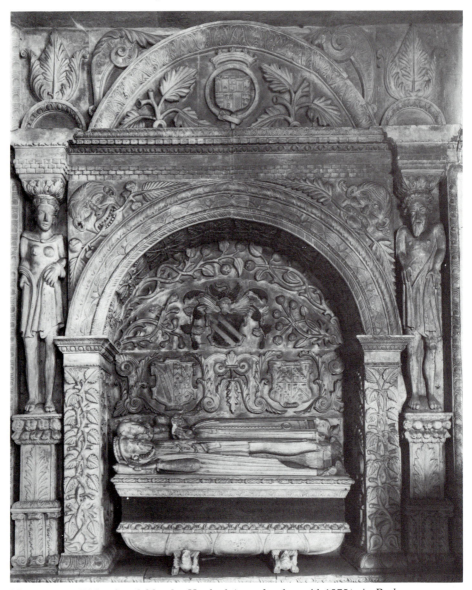

Monument to Richard and Martha Harford (completed c. mid-1575), in Bosbury Church, Hereford and Worcester.

But in terms of the history of Tudor images it is Richard's tomb which is more typical, despite its offences against classical taste and the apparent inconsistencies of its patronage. Richard's tomb, about three metres high, is set into the wall of the church and juxtaposes two standard compositional devices; the triumphal arch and the sarcophagus supporting recumbent effigies. A free-standing tomb-chest, of the type shown in the Vernon tombs, has been set into a niche in a side wall and topped off by a grand architectural frame. The tomb is carved from high quality freestone, not local in origin, and still retains traces of the extensive layer of pigment which would have decorated it and elaborated the figure carving. Religious symbolism is virtually nonexistent although heraldry is prominent in the tomb programme. It has been suggested that the flanking male and female figures possibly represent Adam and Eve, but the fact that the meaning is not clear militates against a specific, religious identification. It is more likely that they are descendants of the bedesmen or mourners familiar from medieval tomb sculpture, here transmuted into structural attendants not dissimilar to the caryatids of the classical tradition. The rest of the surface decoration is related to the fancy ribbon and strapwork common in interior decoration of this period, over fireplaces and on plaster ceilings and friezes.

Looking at funeral monuments in parish churches today, we often want to get to know something of the deceased as people; it is one way of coming to terms with the past. Between the static and apparently sleeping effigies of the Middle Ages and the later, grief-laden figures of the Romantic age of the late eighteenth and early nineteenth centuries, tombs of the Tudor period might seem to show effigies with some sense of life and a framework of personal reference to help us do this; the figures sometimes kneel, are propped on one elbow, are reading a book, or are attended by tiny rows of their children in prayer. But the architectural framework of so many of these monuments, their lavish use of colour in marble and paint (often garishly restored in recent times), the usually expressionless features and especially their dignified and often worldly inscriptions, all speak of a perceived order that keeps those commemorated distant from us. Today, it is alien to us, whether practising Christians or not, to imagine an Anglican church as a likely setting for the celebration of social status. The patrons of Tudor tombs, however, would have expected that the size of their monuments, and the splendour and position in the church of their monuments would make just such a point about their wealth and rank to contemporaries of all classes who worshipped there.

Painting in great houses

The houses of all the wealthier people of Tudor England, from the aristocracy to the merchant classes, would have contained much painted and other imagery, though not predominantly in the form of portable pictures of the kind we know today. Evidence suggests that there were not always the sharp distinctions made between different kinds of imagery that we might expect; inventories frequently use the words 'picture', 'table' and 'image' but it is not always clear whether it is a painted work or a piece of sculpture in wood, alabaster or other material that is being referred to. People would have expected to see imagery, with narrative subjects, in various places in the room of a house, perhaps worked into the design of plaster ceilings (by the end of the century, replacing the simple rib patterns of the early years) and on the larger fittings of the room, like cupboards or chests. Fireplaces were particularly suitable for figural subjects in low relief, and during the reign of Elizabeth they came to dominate the great rooms of the house and bear the concentration of decoration and expense.

The most common experience of seeing narrative imagery would have been through wall-paintings and, more especially, wall-hangings. At Court and in the houses of the very great and powerful, these might be imported tapestries from Flanders, but more prevalent were cheap painted cloths which are recorded extensively in contemporary inventories. Due to their cheapness and frailty, practically none of these survive. Even the rooms of higher servants in great houses might have hangings of buckram, though these were often painted in a single colour or decorated with simple floral or geometric patterns. The subject-matter of hangings with narratives is important, because it reveals the abiding interest in the chivalric themes of the medieval past and the way in which, as religious painting became suspect and idolatrous after the 1540s, certain Old Testament themes which had always been popular were clearly safe because of their association with military heroism or moralistic advice to the onlooker. Hence these biblical scenes often appear cheek by jowl with similar stories from classical history and legend. In the house of Lord Darcy in 1518–19 there were tapestries depicting St George and St Christopher, others showing the stories of King David, Abigail and Achilles and, still permissible at this period, a hanging showing the birth of Christ. In the 1575 inventory of Lacock Abbey, the dissolved nunnery that had been turned into a private house by Sir William Sharington after 1540, the parlour contained hangings of the story of Samson and the Great Chamber six hangings of the story of Jephthah from the Book of Judges. Other rooms contained hangings of flowers and birds.

It is noteworthy that sixteenth-century inventories record so many painted hangings, remedying our otherwise false impression from the comparatively few tapestries that have survived in houses of this period. It is also interesting that those carrying out the inventory by walking around the house, often at the time of the drawing up of the owner's will, or after his or her death, could easily recognise the visual rendition of biblical and classical subjects, known primarily to these people through the written and spoken word. To us the subjects might be quite obscure.

Rare examples of what this imagery was like are the surviving wall-paintings at (or from, because some have been removed) Hill Hall, in Essex, a house rebuilt by Sir Thomas Smith, Privy Councillor and frequently an ambassador to France, in the 1560s and 1570s. One room was decorated with the story of Cupid and Psyche; the images here are surrounded by fictive borders of fruit and flowers and they have edges painted to look like fringes, mimicking wall-hangings. We know that the compositions of this series were derived from Flemish prints of the story. The biblical scenes of another room such as the *King Hezekiah entering the Temple* show how relatively crudely they were painted and how, through costume and headgear, they reveal a taste for the exotic mixed with an approximate and non-archaeological perception of classical and historical forms of dress. If this represents the upper end of the market for images like these (for Smith held high Court office and was one of the most learned and well-travelled men of his day), then we must expect that the general run of hangings and wall-paintings of this sort were very often in a naïve and robust style.

By mid century the keeping of small portable objects for religious devotion

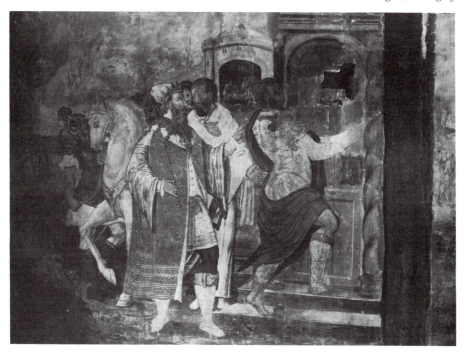

Wall-painting of King Hezakiah Entering the Temple, *Hill Hall, Essex (1570s)*.

was coming under suspicion and the instances of these objects in inventories were increasingly rare. This was especially true of images of the central, spiritual themes of the Christian faith. At his house at Easton Neston, in Northamptonshire, in 1540, Richard Fermor had a stained cloth depicting the Holy Ghost and at Markeaton in Derbyshire in 1545, one Vincent Mundy had a small canvas hanging of the 'Salvator Mundi', or Christ with his hand raised in blessing. Images like this were proliferate, not just or even primarily in painted form, but as small pieces of wood sculpture, or perhaps crudely carved on the lids of boxes containing holy books or other objects. After the 1530s, they disappeared or became secreted away from the private chapels and closets where owners kept their valuables in the great houses of England. It is generally assumed that a greater number of framed portraits took the place of these works in the domestic environment, but what do we know of the existence of painting in houses?

Certainly there is little evidence that even the very wealthy in any sense 'collected' framed paintings for their quality or for their rarity because they happened to be by a particular artist. The valuation put on pictures was usually by size and they were rarely estimated to be worth anywhere near the sums attached either to the larger pieces of furniture in the house, or to important items of clothing made from expensive materials. It was also important whereabouts in the house portraits were seen and admired. Documents suggest that hall and downstairs parlour were the most likely places in middle-sized houses. Great houses might have other large rooms for the display of such things.

It has already been noted in considering the early Tudor painting of Henry VI that sixteenth-century people sometimes commissioned portraits in sets. Inevitably, the overall quality, in the way later ages would judge it, was bound to be low. For portraits of the fifteenth-century Kings of England standard types could be copied, but for ancient and early medieval figures a basic pattern of common physiognomy would be adopted, adjusting little more than dress and age to create different figures. We associate these sets of images and portraits with long galleries and imagine them displayed there. It is true that by the end of the sixteenth century there were galleries hung with rows of portraits, but it would be wrong to think that this was the cause of the development of the long gallery in the first place or that this became their primary function. Galleries were also places of recreation and, being usually high in the house, served as prospect rooms. The Duke of Norfolk had twenty-eight 'vysenamies [likenesses] of divers noble persons' in his gallery at Kenninghall in Norfolk, when that house was inventoried for the King at the attainder of the Duke at the beginning of 1547. At Leicester House, in London, the 'high gallery' in 1590 included a portrait of the King of France and also fanciful images of classical and legendary figures such as Penelope and Julius Caesar.

The Brown Gallery at Knole in Kent is a later example of a gathering of portraits, for the pictures here seem to have been commissioned about 1630. This is an important surviving example of a practice that was quite well established by the later years of Queen Elizabeth. The crowding of images here would also have been quite usual (though we do not know how close this is to the original arrangement); just as we might find it odd to find Elizabethan tombs crowded together in a small chapel space, as discussed above, so here we are conscious that sixteenth-century people would not have thought in terms of isolating objects such as these. Nor was it strange, as shown by the long gallery at Hardwick Hall, to hang paintings on top of wall coverings, even expensive tapestries. Rather, the close gathering of worthies from the past alongside images of the great families of the present suggested a security and continuity to the contemporary sense of history and the owners of these objects' present place in the world. By 1600, a copy of the latest 'official' image of Queen Elizabeth might well be the climax of a series of portraits in the greatest houses.

As in Court portraiture, the sort of portrait that patrons commissioned of themselves varied in format. New fashions and standards were established. A typical half-length image is the portrait of Sir Richard Drake (p. 252), now in the National Maritime Museum. Like the portrait of Sir Bryan Tuke, we are given here the sitter's age and a personal motto, 'Tous jours prest a servir' (Always ready to serve). The date at which it was painted (1577) is also inscribed, along with his coat-of-arms. Even forty years after the Tuke portrait we find little advance in the concept of spatial depiction; if anything, the average Elizabethan portrait is a retreat from some of the spatially conceived works of mid-century. Portraiture had settled into a formula for the conveying of information and at the same time was remaining on the safe side of the charge that was often thrown at images in the age of religious iconoclasm, namely that the making of something that approximated reality

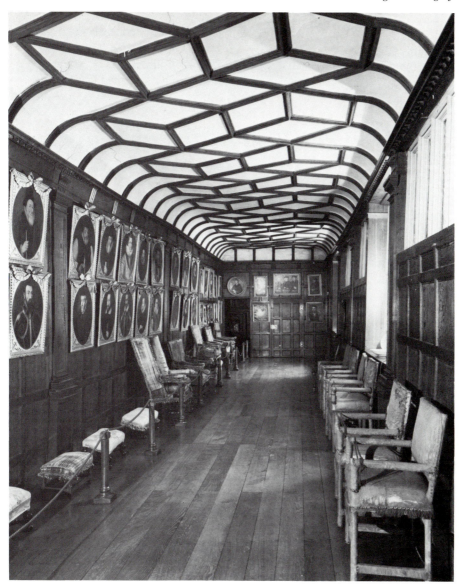

The Brown Gallery, Knole, Kent; panelling and ceiling c.1600–10.

too closely was somehow dangerous and encroached on the preserve of God, the only true maker of earthly things. Today we are drawn to the surface of these works in art galleries and country houses to admire their meticulousness and sense of pattern, the reflections on polished armour and dazzling jewels. Recent discussion of these images has compared them to icons. Certainly the point is missd if there is an expectation of perceiving these subjects in some definable space in which they could be expected to move. This is especially true of the full-length format.

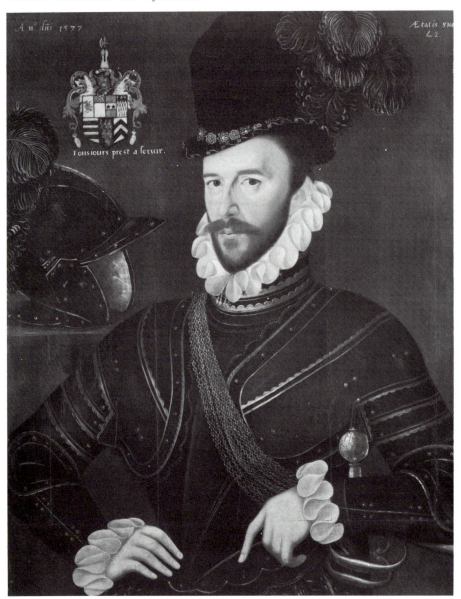

Anonymous, Sir Richard Drake *(1577)*.

The full-size, full-length format, hitherto very rare and hardly ever used
for portable panel paintings, became much more popular from about the
middle of the sixteenth century. But it was a type usually reserved for the
very highest classes, partly because of the space needed for display. A
portrait such as that of Frances Sidney, Countess of Sussex, of about 1565,
is a typical but particularly splendid example. She is not shown in a
perspectivized setting; what is clearly significant here is the splendour of her
apparel and the ermine which signifies her rank. She was to have one of the

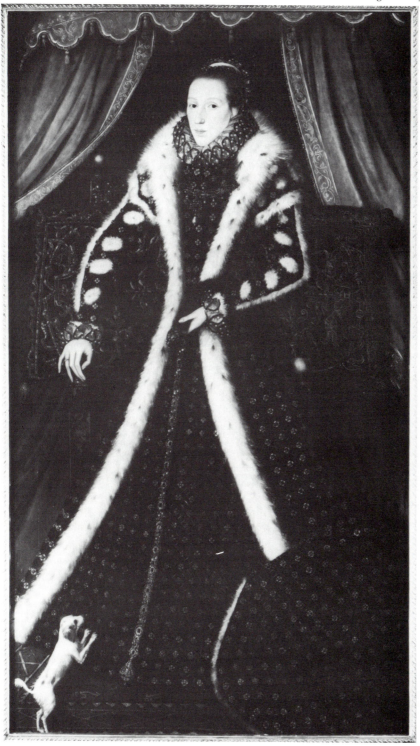

Steven van de Meulen, Frances Sidney, Countess of Sussex, *commissioned for the hall of Sidney Sussex College, Cambridge (c.1565).*

finest and most elaborate tombs in the great series of monuments to high-born Elizabethan and Jacobean women in the small chapels off the aisles to the royal chapels at the east end of Westminster Abbey. Though this picture is typical of many similar images made for country houses, it was actually commissioned for the hall of the college that the Countess founded, Sidney Sussex, at Cambridge. In the context in which this picture was seen, and indeed is still seen, the Countess of Sussex, rather like Queen Elizabeth in the 'Ditchley' portrait, is a symbol of something, in this case the beneficence and concern for learning of the wealthy and powerful individual. In this setting, her portrait is virtually synonymous with the heraldic device of the college. The splendour therefore, the flatness of the image, is particularly appropriate. Too life-like a treatment might have obscured the symbol.

This concern of the painter to realise the particular guise or role that the sitter is playing was not to change fundamentally in the next century, though the range of possibilities was to widen considerably. New aristocratic interests in collecting antique sculpture and continental paintings were explored as the means of expressing character. The possibilities of expressing high birth and position by a grace of bearing instead of more direct signals such as stiffness of pose and mottoes and heraldry were experimented with. It was the need of these new avenues of portrait depiction for a firmer grasp of perspective and for fluency of brushwork, rather than these techniques for their own sake, that was to characterise the revolution in portraiture brought about by a new wave of foreign artists in the early seventeenth century, led by Mytens and Van Dyck.

Imagery and urban life

This account of painting and imagery in Tudor England has shown how patrons commissioned art which would function in both public and private ways. The most public spaces of all where visual imagery might have its most profound effect were the streets and open places in the towns. The government of the 1530s was sufficiently concerned about the state of decay of the urban environment that Acts of Parliament were passed to revitalise the building trade and make cities and towns more prosperous and populous. In this environment, the visual image was to become a vital means of communication second only to word of mouth. As already established in this chapter, important Tudor people, especially the monarch, had themselves portrayed with some attention to physiognomy but more to the reinforcement or the creation of a powerful image. On more modest levels, images existed which were designed to communicate to the less well-educated people 'on the street'. Little of this imagery fits our modern category of 'fine art', and for this reason much of it has been lost. But it has also suffered because like much Court art it was never intended to be anything other than ephemeral and temporary.

Heraldry played a key role in communicating the presence and status of armigerous persons moving along the crowded streets or through the countryside. We can assume that most onlookers would have been familiar

with the colours of the local magnate and the form of his or her heraldic
device. Such a device would quite likely decorate local buildings such as
alms-houses or inns. It would also be displayed on the uniform worn by the
lord's servants as they collected rents or enforced the law. Amongst the
gentry a familiarity with the imagery of emblazons, quarterings and the rest
was more essential to their social training than a taste for the Old Masters or
ancient sculpture. Heraldic images became really important on great state
occasions or when great lords, princes or prelates were travelling. The
engraving records a procession of heralds at one of the most splendid of all
late Tudor events: the funeral of Sir Philip Sidney (1544–86), who was
accorded the status of a national hero after his death in battle. The scale of
the procession and the popular interest is evidenced by the series of no less
than thirty-four engraved plates published early in the following year by the
Dutchman Theodore de Bry to mark the occasion. The artist was mostly
concerned to transmit a good deal of technical detail about the heraldic
devices worn and carried and he added explanation by means of Latin
captions. We are not given much idea about the social and topographical
setting for what must have been an extraordinary sight, for this is less
important than the sense of 'occasion' created by heraldry. During the course
of the century even people of lesser rank were given funerals attended by
heraldic imagery.

Civic pageants of various sorts were traditional in the English calendar.
Despite the Reformation, which to some extent reduced the scope of the
church for magnificent display, the clergy with their servants and musicians
would still have processed on holy days. The civic authorities were also fully
conversant with the propaganda potential of pageantry and display. In
manufacturing towns the guilds would process at regular intervals, such as
the name-day of their patron-saint, or on special days such as coronations or
commemorations of such events as the defeat of the Armada. On all these
occasions, images played an important role. In symbolic and allegorical forms
they were set on floats, carried on poles, borne on litters and embroidered or
painted on to cloth for use as banners.

These events were celebrated with particular expense in London. The City
livery companies competed with one another in designing elaborate floats and
carriages for the annual Lord Mayor's procession. Some of the designs for
these survive at the Guildhall Museum and elsewhere and show full use
being made of rich allegory and striking figurative images. Other important
cities, like Coventry, York, Bristol and Norwich, celebrated on a slightly less
grand scale. The illustration on p. 256 shows one of the many scenes
prepared when John Leman, a fishmonger, became Lord Mayor. The lemon
tree in the centre is a typical piece of word-play on his name and to the left
the pelican sacrifices her own blood to feed her brood – a caring gesture
which Leman will emulate in his work for the City. Beneath the tree sit
personifications of the five senses which will be revived by its sharp fruit as
will the commercial prosperity of the place under the new Mayor.

The triumphal entries peculiar to London were the most elaborate of all
civic pageants and in their use of images they owed a good deal to continental
precedent. Here too, visual and verbal images were closely combined. For

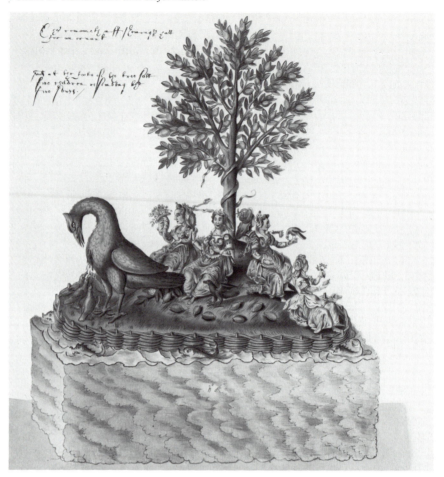

Unknown artist, allegory featuring a lemon tree devised for the Lord Mayor's procession of John Leman. Illustration to the text of Anthony Munday's pageant, Chrysanaleia: The Golden Fishing *(1616).*

example, the coronation entry of Anne Boleyn (1533) was later retold by Shakespeare in *Henry VIII*. For many entries of the Elizabethan period, short explanatory texts were published to act as commentaries on the series of triumphal arches or tableaux around which such events were usually organised. The notables would move from one group of images to another and they would be supplemented by poetic and musical accompaniments.

Elizabeth I was especially keen to use such shows to celebrate the various symbolic manifestations of her power. Visual images of her were strictly controlled and central to the programmes of the larger events. The spoken word was of more importance on those lesser occasions so often arranged in the course of the Queen's 'progresses', as recorded at Kenilworth in 1575 and Elvetham in 1591.

Elizabeth was not only head of State but also the head of the Church and the visual propaganda displayed about her in public had to support both these roles. Popular religious imagery of a more modest sort had been

produced during the turmoils of the Reformation and the subsequent, brief
Marian reaction. The most famous account of the persecutions of Protestants
was John Foxe's *Book of Martyrs*, originally an enormous Latin text which
was probably started in about 1552 and published in parts, in various
editions and translations from 1554 onwards. Foxe's aim was to expose the
persecutions and 'horrible troubles . . . wrought by the Romish prelates'
(1653 title-page) and of special interest here are the woodcut illustrations
which were used to supplement the text. The example of Edmund Bonner,
Bishop of London under Queen Mary, ardent papist and career politician,
beating heretic prisoners with his own hands. The scene is set in the Bishop's
orchard and the crude but powerful image is clearly intended to expose
Bonner as a coarse-grained bigot, just as he is depicted in Foxe's long tract.
In his enthusiasm to administer the corrective treatment he thinks necessary,
Bonner dispenses with the social propriety which distinguished people of high
rank in Tudor England. He has shed his cloak to take an active part in the
punishment and has thus exposed his corpulent frame and bulging cod-piece,
signs of the sensual preoccupations for which the Catholic hierarchy were so
often pilloried by their Protestant adversaries. His name and religion are
signalled by a small abbreviated caption – the only text on the image – and
his tonsured head. Behind him, servants come with more scourges. To the
right a gentleman cannot bear to witness the scene and two more priests
discuss the hard path that must be trodden to achieve salvation.

As we have seen in the cases of the funeral monuments and processions,
these opportunities for the display of images became accessible to a wider

'Bishop Bonner beating a prisoner', woodcut, from Foxe's Acts and Monuments
(1563).

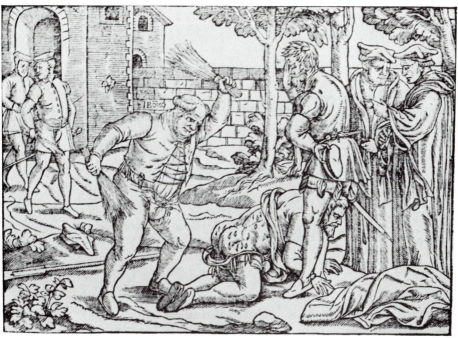

social range as the sixteenth century wore on. The same was true of popular portraits printed, which formed the frontispiece to a book or were sold occasionally from the printer's shops as were pamphlets, chap-books and other ephemera. A case in point is Wierix's engraved portrait of Robert Dudley, Earl of Leicester which was published in *c*. 1586 to mark the appointment of Elizabeth's favourite as her commander in the Netherlands.

The example of the genre shown here is of the herbalist and surgeon John Gerard; this was engraved by William Rogers (active *c*. 1589 – *c*. 1604) for the frontispiece of Gerard's famous *Herball* of 1597. The image comprises a

William Rogers, engraving of John Gerard for the frontispiece of Gerard's Herball *(1597–8).*

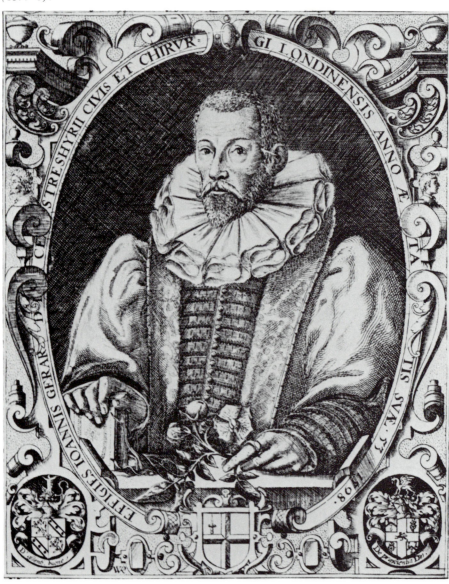

combination of motifs typical of later Tudor art. Gerard is shown half-length, dressed in the gown and ruff of a scholar. His field of expertise is symbolically suggested by the book and the plant specimen he holds. Around him, mingling with the then fashionable strapwork decoration, is the means of placing him within the social hierarchy. As was usual on a Tudor portrait, whether a grand painting or a popular print, the following information is given: name and place of birth (Cheshire), age and occupation. His origins are recorded by coats-of-arms and thus with use of artifice Gerard's fame is established by the portrait. The music of Matthew Godwin, the exploits of Richard Drake and the curiosity of John Gerard have led them all to be commemorated by the various means available in Tudor England to honour their achievements by rendering their likenesses in art.

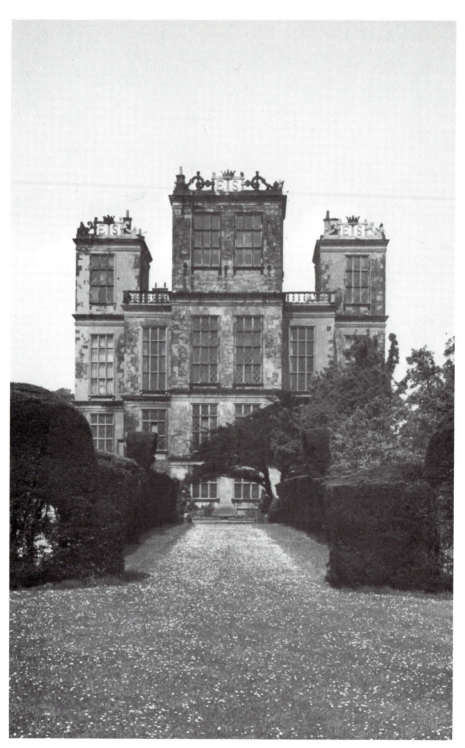

Hardwick Hall, Derbyshire, from the south (1590–8).

7 A Tudor House: Hardwick Hall

MALCOLM AIRS

The glittering façades of Hardwick Hall placed high up on an eminence overlooking the Derbyshire countryside provide an architectural experience of unforgettable beauty and romance. There is a consistency and an air of self-confidence about its design which make it difficult to dispute Sir Roy Strong's conclusion that the house is 'the crowning jewel of the age' or the belief of Sir Sacheverell Sitwell that the High Great Chamber is 'the most beautiful room, not in England alone, but in the whole of Europe'.

In evoking such enthusiastic praise Hardwick epitomises many of the qualities that were characteristic of the English country house in general in the late Elizabethan period. The disciplined way in which it combines a compact plan two-rooms deep with an appearance of great height; the intricate sequence of symmetrical projections on all four elevations which create a changing pattern of light and shade across the plain surfaces of the walls; and the highly decorated emphasis on the roof were the basis of an architectural achievement fully comparable with the other exciting cultural innovations of the time. Equally characteristic of the period is the wealth of allegory and symbolism which almost overwhelms the decoration of the interior and which finds an obscure delight in presenting the plan as a conjunction of two Greek crosses separated by the central rectangle of the hall. It is much more difficult for the modern observer to respond with quite the same enthusiasm or comprehension to this sort of artifice as the contemporaries of the builder must once have done. Nevertheless, its importance in the original scheme must be recognised and explained.

Hardwick Hall was built by a remarkable woman whose successful rise up the social scale provides a fascinating insight into the opportunities for advancement that were available to shrewd and talented individuals in the fluid conditions of Tudor society.

Bess of Hardwick was born in the 1520s into an impoverished minor gentry family. Her fortune was made by a sequence of marriages each more lucrative than the last. Her second husband, Sir William Cavendish, had been one of the commissioners for the Dissolution of the Monasteries. He fathered her six children who survived infancy and he bought her the estate at Chatsworth where she built her first house. Her fourth husband, George Talbot, 6th Earl of Shrewsbury, elevated her into one of the oldest and richest families in the land and enabled two of her children to marry two of his in an alliance which founded the dukedoms of Devonshire, Newcastle and Portland. It was the bitter deterioration of this marriage which directly led to the construction of Hardwick Hall. By 1583 Bess and her husband were barely on speaking terms and were living apart. Shrewsbury claimed that Chatsworth belonged to him under the terms of their marriage settlement and Bess therefore returned to her ancestral home at Hardwick which she had purchased with her own money from the bankrupt estate of her brother James. Between 1588 and 1590 she busied herself with the construction of the large and eccentric house, now in ruins and known as the Old Hall.

When Lord Shrewsbury unexpectedly died in 1590 her position was immediately transformed. She recovered complete control of all her lands and became almost overnight one of the richest people in England. Within a month the foundations had been dug for a new and altogether grander house only a short distance away from the Old Hall. The work, which is amply illustrated by the surviving building accounts, continued simultaneously on both projects until the virtual completion of the New Hall in 1598. The construction was entirely financed out of current revenue and it is this factor, coupled with the limited availability of sufficient highly skilled craftsmen capable of executing the fine decorative finishes, which accounts for the length of time taken over the work.

Bess took a very close personal interest in the building and the dry accounts are frequently enlivened by characteristic acts of generosity to her workmen and their families, such as the £2 she gave to a mason's wife in 1596 'in respect of her husband's device of sawing blackstone to buy her a gown withal' and the same sum which she presented to another mason in 1592 'against his wedding'. She was rewarded by remarkable loyalty on the part of her favoured craftsmen, some of whom had been associated with her building works from as far back as Chatsworth in the 1550s.

The overall supervision of the building was entrusted to John Balechouse, a painter, possibly of Flemish origin, and one of the craftsmen who had worked at Chatsworth. He was a member of the permanent household and was granted a rent-free farm in addition to his annual salary. Abraham Smith, the plasterer and stone carver who was responsible for the frieze in the High Great Chamber, and Thomas Accres, the marble mason who created many of the chimneypieces, were permanently employed on the same basis. The other skilled craftsmen, such as the two brothers John and Christopher Rodes, who erected most of the masonry, were employed by contract for specific parts of the work, whilst the ordinary craftsmen and the labourers were paid a daily wage and provided with their food and drink.

By the end of the sixteenth century, this mixed method of employment was the common way of organising the necessary workmen when building a country house of any size. The composition of the labour force also conformed to the general pattern, with the labourers and the common craftsmen drawn from the immediate vicinity of the house and the skilled men attracted from further afield, often coming in groups from a comparable project which was nearing completion. In the case of Hardwick, some of the craftsmen, such as both the Rodes and Thomas Accres, had been working for Sir Francis Willoughby at Wollaton Hall in Nottinghamshire which was building between 1580 and 1588. Much of the materials for Hardwick were also found locally and the quarry which provided most of the stone can still be made out in the rough ground close to the drive leading up to the house.

On the basis of a single entry in the accounts and some closely related drawings it is generally accepted that the design for Hardwick was made by Robert Smythson. Although a trained mason and a highly-regarded superviser, there is no evidence that he took any direct part in the works and it is likely that his role was limited to the provision of the plans for the overall conception of the building with much of the decorative detail being the separate responsibility of the executant craftsmen such as Accres and Smith. This was a common method of working by this date and there is evidence both from the accounts and from the fabric itself of some fairly radical alterations to the design of Hardwick as the work proceeded. For example, the open colonnades on the two principal elevations were originally intended to extend around the complete building, but they were omitted from the north and south ends at a late stage after the walling had been prepared to receive them and the towers, which are such a prominent feature of the design, were raised by a further five feet in 1594, apparently at the instigation of John Balechouse.

Smythson was an important and well-documented figure in Elizabethan country house design. He had worked as a mason and contractor on Longleat House in Wiltshire and had moved up to the Midlands in 1580 to design and supervise the building of Wollaton Hall. He made his home at Wollaton and established an extensive practice in the area, designing houses for a large number of patrons principally drawn from the Talbot and Cavendish circle. His reputation must have been fully established in the years immediately following the completion of Wollaton in 1588 and it was no doubt the success of this highly-regarded house which led to the commission for Hardwick.

Robert Smythson's preliminary design for Hardwick Hall.

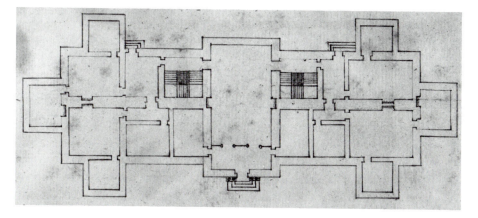

Both houses share the same emphasis on an elevated hill-top position with glittering multi-fenestrated elevations and they are both characterised by symmetrically disposed projecting towers which articulate the planes of the walls in a sequence of constantly changing vistas.

Hardwick, however, is an infinitely more satisfying design with few of the decorative excesses and fantastic flourishes which coarsen Wollaton. Its masonry is comparatively plain and smooth and it relies on the massing of the towers and its perforated sky-line for its full architectural effect. The surface decoration is confined to the massive columns in the centre of the east and west elevations and the strong horizontal string courses which divide the storeys. The roof of the main range is crowned by a simple classical balustrade which sets out its basic rectangular form and emphasises the more subtle geometrical figures created by the taller projecting towers. The elaborate cresting on these towers which supports the initials ES and which are repeated on all three public faces are the only concession to blatant display.

Yet, despite its decorative reticence, the house was conceived in a thoroughgoing spirit of public advertisement which was meant both to impress and amuse all those who saw it in a variety of different ways, some of which are no longer obvious to modern eyes. It proclaimed the social standing and the wealth of its builder, but it was also an announcement of her intellectual achievements and the sophistication of her taste. The initials, of course, stand for Elizabeth Shrewsbury. They are placed at the very top of all six towers in such a position that it would be impossible to be in any doubt as to who was responsible for the erection of such a striking edifice.

West front, Hardwick Hall.

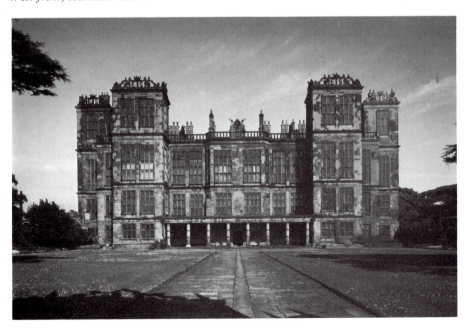

The S for Shrewsbury and the coronet which surmounts the initials is of paramount importance in establishing her rank in society. The daughter of humble John Hardwick had returned to her birthplace as the Countess of Shrewsbury and the magnificent mansion that she had erected was a deliberate and tangible monument to this staggering social achievement. More than any vulgar display of expensive ornament, the vast area of glazed windows which punctuate the plain surfaces of the walls and which inspired the familiar jingle, 'Hardwick Hall, more glass than wall', unmistakably demonstrates her enormous wealth. Glass was still a luxury item which most builders treated with a degree of economy. The profligate fashion with which it covers every elevation at Hardwick is an awe-inspiring indication of the economic power that her new status commanded.

The windows at Hardwick also play a more intellectual part in the response that was expected of the educated visitor to the house. Each successive storey is marked by windows of increasing height as a deliberate expression of the ascending hierarchy of the rooms within. The ground floor is largely given over to service rooms and is lit by windows only two lights high. The family rooms on the first floor have three-light windows, but the state apartments on the top floor are flooded with light from windows which are a full four lights in height. Their importance is underlined by the sequential reduction in the height of the windows to the tower pavilions above.

The simple architectural statement of the formal social hierarchy that could be anticipated on entering the house would have been recognised by contemporaries as a neat device, but it was not achieved without a measure of deceit. Mezzanine floors horizontally divide some of the windows and the High Great Chamber is not placed within the central canted projection (that is, with angled rather than straight sides), as the arrangement of the principal elevation would suggest, but is set to one side where it can take advantage of the extra space provided by one of the great towers. These minor discrepancies would have been barely perceptible inside the building and were of little consequence. The important thing was to appreciate the basic message conveyed by the design of the principal elevations. The levels at Hardwick symbolise the divisions in society at large and to be invited into the rooms at the very top implied a distinct status on the part of the visitor which was rewarded by a journey of great visual excitement.

The entrance to the house is through the colonnade in the centre of the west elevation. It leads into a two-storeyed hall which was merely the point of departure in a ceremonial procession, rather than the pre-eminent domestic space which it would have been in the Middle Ages. The stone staircase, which is one of the most daring architectural features of Hardwick, is placed off the far end of the hall. It is totally devoid of ornament yet full of drama and surprise as it winds its serpentine way through half landings and right-angles past the family quarters on the first floor to the important state rooms at the top of the house. Like other comparable houses of the period, Hardwick was built with royalty in mind; either to receive the Queen herself on progress or, more deviously, to provide a suitable base for the claim to the throne of Lady Arabella Stuart, Bess's own grand-daughter, which was still

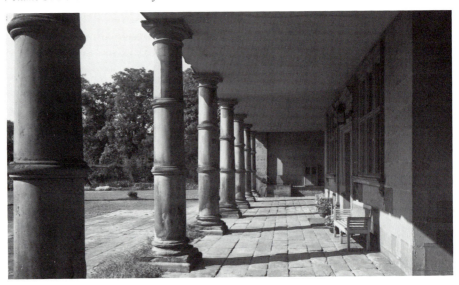

Colonnade, West front, Hardwick Hall.

being seriously entertained in the 1590s. The state rooms, therefore, were conceived on a truly regal scale and decorated with appropriate symbols of their purpose. The sequence of High Great Chamber, Withdrawing Chamber and Best Bed Chamber are deliberately redolent of the palatial progress from a Presence Chamber through the Privy Chamber into the Royal Bedchamber.

In the event, Queen Elizabeth never visited Hardwick, but had she done so she would have readily recognised the allusions that had been created in her honour, especially in the decoration of the High Great Chamber. The royal coat of arms is placed in a position of prominence over the fireplace and the great painted plaster frieze which runs around the room celebrates the story of Diana, chaste goddess of the hunt, as an allegory of the Queen's particular qualities. The trees modelled in relief symbolise her virtue, whilst the elephants which gravitate towards her are emblematic of her virginity. Other scenes, such as the Cavendish roebuck chasing away the predatory beasts of the forest, are designed to involve Bess herself in this symbolic drama and to demonstrate her loyalty to the throne. The Brussels tapestries which hang below the frieze were purchased in 1587 and the proportions of the whole room were designed around them. In depicting the story of Ulysses, they continue the mythological themes which pervade the decoration of the whole house and enabled Bess to identify with Penelope, his virtuous wife, whose fidelity was symbolised by her prowess at the loom.

The aptness of this image would not have been lost on the spectator for Hardwick contains a greater wealth of embroideries and hangings than any other contemporary house in Europe, many of them made by Bess herself. They survive all over the house and in their original condition would have filled the rooms with colour as a splendid and luxurious background to the sparse arrangements of furniture. Nowhere is this more true than in the long gallery which runs along the full length of the top storey behind the state rooms. This is the largest surviving gallery in any house of the Elizabethan period. The vast collection of portraits which it was designed to display hangs from a backdrop of tapestries along all the wall surfaces in a gesture of supreme extravagance, which would have been heightened by the contrast with the three small tables, three chairs and the handful of stools and forms which comprised the only items of furniture in 1601.

A gallery was one of the important new architectural developments of the late-sixteenth century and its opulence and size rapidly became something of the ultimate status symbol. It had both a practical and a spiritual purpose. It was a room of recreation where exercise could be taken in bad weather and views of the surrounding countryside could be enjoyed from the high windows; but it was also a place for contemplation of a very specialised kind, prompted by the paintings and the decoration with which it was adorned. At Hardwick all the paintings are portraits depicting royalty, family and influential friends. They are displayed as an overt demonstration of the dynastic achievement of Bess and her lineage, her intimate association with royalty, and the power and influence of her connections. In a sense they are a biographical statement of her social triumph set out in tableau form for the edification of both her guests and her descendants. But they are also a reminder to Bess herself of her origins and her good-fortune, and the responsibilities that were implicit in her exalted position were spelt out over the two fireplaces which heated the room and which contain the symbolic figures of Justice and Mercy.

Unfortunately, Hardwick provides little evidence for any arts other than those of architecture and needlework. Bess was an elderly woman when she entered into residence. She had no permanent musicians on her staff nor are any musical instruments noted in the inventory of 1601. Nevertheless, she clearly enjoyed music – the household chaplain and three other amateur musicians played her into the new house on 4 October 1597; in September 1599 she was entertained by the Nottingham waits, the Earl of Rutland's musicians, and those of the Earl of Essex. In 1600 the Queen's Players presented theatricals in the house. But these were merely incidental diversions rather than any evidence for consistent patronage and hardly merit special attention. Similarly, the walled enclosures of the garden layout survives, but details of the planting, which would be of great interest, are now lost.

It is singularly fortunate that such an important house as Hardwick has been so very little altered since the sixteenth century. The architecture, the decoration, the layout of the rooms and many of the tapestries and paintings survive as the builder envisaged them and form a cultural unity which is without precedent in England. Together they provide a unique opportunity to attempt an understanding of how the contemporary mind created and responded to a complex iconography which has totally vanished from our modern artistic perception. The fabric and the artefacts give only an imperfect glimpse, but without them our appreciation of the cultural aims and achievements of the Elizabethan age would be infinitely poorer.

A poster for the first English lottery (1567); prizes included sets of tapestry, plate and money.

8 The Crafts and Decorative Arts

PHILIPPA GLANVILLE

Introduction

In the sixteenth century for the first time, it is possible to describe the decorative art of the English in more than general terms; there is a profusion of written details as to the material culture of a wide cross-section of society (primarily in probate inventories) both for king and courtiers and for humble citizens, and a wealth of objects, also from the most luxurious articles commissioned by aristocrats to the humble pots and treen made for the poor. These objects, whether tapestries, jewels, armour or plate, can be enjoyed in museums or in such furnished houses of the period as Hardwick, Compton Wynyates, the Vyne or, representing a lower social level, the late medieval parson's small house at Alfriston, Sussex, the first property to be taken over by the National Trust.

Recent studies have focused on fresh areas of interest, for example the role of bastard feudalism in dictating the choice of family badges as ornament for jewels, plate and textiles. Again, it is now accepted that late medieval traditions in ornament survived and indeed thrived alongside the newly-introduced Renaissance and Mannerist forms, the latter characterised by exaggeration, distortion and dramatic effects. The transformation of English decorative art from a pan-European Gothic tradition, drawing on common themes, whether Biblical or classical, to a distinctive native version of Mannerism, is familiar enough. How that change was fuelled is emerging from detailed studies of engraved ornament, from biographies of craftsmen which draw out their family links and from the discovery of networks of patronage.

The English dependence on imported techniques to stimulate native production in textiles, glass-making, ceramics and metalworking has been demonstrated both through excavations of glasshouse, kiln and foundry sites and through a fresh, more analytical approach to the documentary sources. The object-centred emphasis, which sprang naturally from collectors' needs and interests, has been widened, and almost every aspect of the history of English decorative art has felt the benefit. The technical analyses are illuminating the study of silver, of armour and of paintings, and helping to identify the fakes which inevitably, over the past 150 years, have crept into acceptance and so distorted our view of the period. Because of their antiquarian appeal, and their associations with colourful historical figures, most important Tudor objects have been known for many years; the Howard Grace Cup for example, an early Renaissance piece of outstanding importance, had been shown at the Society of Antiquities twice before 1770. The Bed of Ware was already a tourist attraction in the early seventeenth century; quite apart from its extraordinary size and even without its hangings or bedding, its painted carving and inlay still make it an extraordinary evocation of its time.

With the analysis of documents such as the Jewel House Inventory of 1574, published in 1955, new identifications of objects have become possible. Two pieces from Henry VIII's Jewel House, a crystal and gold cup designed by Holbein and a Paris-made clock salt, were identified for the first time within the past twenty-five years – as the main piece of table ornament, the salt often took fantastic forms. Tudor art has been popular with some collectors at least since the mid-eighteenth century, when a small circle which included Horace Walpole and John Chute of the Vyne competed for Tudor paintings, tapestries, manuscripts and objects with historical associations. Wolsey's cardinal's red hat was at Strawberry Hill, plus 'Katharine Parr's jug'. This little ale pot of white striped Venetian glass has English silver-gilt mounts which are enamelled with the arms not of Queen Katharine, but of her less well-known uncle (now at the Museum of London).

Other discoveries, equally significant if less glamorous, have come as a result of improved archaeological techniques and opportunities. The site of Baynards Castle, the Thameside palace, was exposed during the wholesale redevelopment of the waterfront in the city in the 1970s. The other royal palaces around London were excavated in a conscious research programme for the *History of the King's Works* at about the same time. The rubbish pits at Nonsuch, Richmond and Whitehall and the water system at Greenwich yielded tightly-dated deposits of ceramics, glass and architectural ornament, such as the gilded lead leaves at Greenwich which originally decorated the painted papier mâché ceiling of Henry VIII's Banqueting House there.

At Whitehall Palace the ground under Henry VIII's newly-built tennis courts was levelled off in 1530–2 with cartloads of pottery, almost a ton of it, from Wolsey's pantries across the road, giving a secure date for the first time to many different types of early Tudor ceramics, from redware storage jars and pancheons to stoneware drinking pots from the Rhineland. Tin-glazed earthenware and glass bottles from the cesspits of Nonsuch, which belong to the building phase (*c.* 1540–5), again gave an invaluable base date for comparable pieces in museums or fragments from glasshouse sites. But these palace sites were most informative about the material culture of the court, a section of society already fairly well-documented.

Marine archaeology has enabled us to recover from the sea the goods and chattels of a lesser order in society. The wreck of the *Mary Rose*, Henry VIII's reconditioned warship which went down in the Solent off Portsmouth on 19 June 1545, is a time capsule of the middling sort, of men to whom pewter was a luxury. These men used wooden tankards, plates and spoons in their everyday lives, items supplied by the thousand by the turners for a few shillings a hundred. Leather, wood and other organic materials rarely survive in the soil and were rarely, unlike pewter or plate, preserved as heirlooms for their value or associations. In the anaerobic silt of the Solent, weapons, clothing, tableware, musical instruments and personal accessories have been preserved to a miraculous degree. Such items as a wooden shawm (a wind-instrument like an oboe), still in its case, slashed leather jerkins and an archer's leather wristguard punched with the Tudor arms, a fashionable woollen cap with a coloured silk lining and a silk velvet hat with ribbons, as worn by the Barber-Surgeons in Holbein's portrait of Henry presenting the Company with its charter in 1540, evoke the material culture of working men, the sailors and officers of the Navy. Decoration on these practical, everyday objects is limited to the royal arms, an IHS on a leather pouch or the arms in a Garter stamped on the pewter of the Lord High Admiral, John Dudley Viscount Lisle.

Colourful painted tin-glazed earthenware from the kilns in Antwerp was not nearly as common as its presence in our museum showcases would suggest. Far more common were the coarse earthenwares fired at kilns in Surrey or in Essex near Harlow. Sturdy drinking vessels of stoneware, the fabric impervious (unlike the locally glazed earthenwares) to the effect of vinegar, came by the thousand annually from the Rhineland. A curious

Domestic items recovered from the Mary Rose *(sank 1545).*

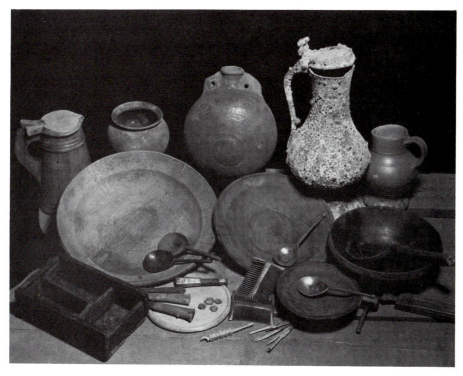

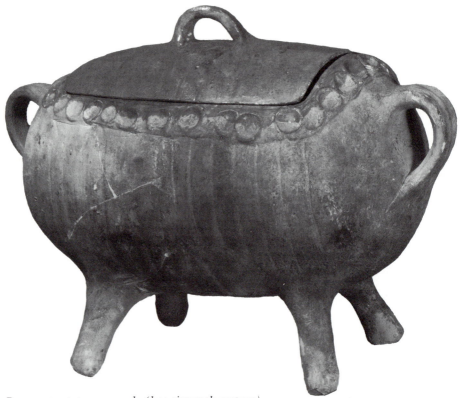

Pottery stewpot or casserole (late sixteenth century).

English idiosyncrasy was the taste for mounting these cheap little pots with expensive mounts of silver-gilt (gilded silver). The taste can be perceived at court in the 1530s and from there disseminated rapidly through society. From the 1560s stoneware pots with silver-gilt mounts are recorded from Exeter and Norwich, as well as London, and Goldsmiths' Company wardens on their searches of smaller provincial towns found that goldsmiths there stocked them too. This inexplicable fashion disappeared abruptly before 1600, perhaps because the class which had enjoyed the use of these objects had transferred its collective affections to the tankard, also a novelty of the mid-sixteenth century which had appeared first at court, to be copied widely by 1600. It may be also that the disappearance of the stoneware pot as a status symbol was an indication of that general rise in prosperity and in conspicuous consumption which was so much a feature of those in Elizabethan society prospering from the effects of the price rise.

The market for consumer goods, which was expanding so rapidly in the sixteenth century and whose effects can be seen in the probate inventories of the middle, as contrasted with the later years of the century, transformed English industry. Sir Thomas Smith complained in 1549 of the 'inestimable treasure' flowing abroad for the purchase of non-essentials such as glasses as well looking as drinking . . . dials, tables, cards, balls, puppets, penhorns, inkhorns, toothpicks . . . brooches, agates, buttons of silk and silver, earthen pots . . . hawks bells . . . and a thousand like things that might either be clean spared or else made within the realm,

a complaint whose truth is borne out by the portbooks and other contemporary records of imports.

In shipping the Elizabethan era saw a positive leap forward; English shipbuilding expanded dramatically, as did the native carrying trade, both coastal and long distance into the Mediterranean, the East Indies and the Americas. The trigger was, as Hakluyt expressed it in 1599, to find new markets after the 1551 slump of Antwerp and its later sack disrupted traditional trading patterns: 'our chiefe desire is to find out ample vent of our woollen cloth'. New export commodities, such as pewter, were beginning to break down the virtual monopoly of cloth, and the imported luxuries, such as carpets, silks, cotton, spices and, at the end of the century, porcelain, fed an expanding market among English consumers. By 1600 these goods were no longer being carried by the traditional shippers – the Genoese, Venetians or Flemings – but in English bottoms; both the small coastal hoys and the larger ocean-going craft of more than a hundred tons were being built in ever-increasing numbers. This was attributable to Cecil's policy of restricting foreign carriers and making Wednesday an additional fish-day 'for the maintenance of the navye'. So effective was this policy that Philip II complained about the losses of the Flemish shippers; between 1571 and 1576 at least fifty-one ships of more than a hundred tons burthen were built. By 1600 virtually all the cloth carried to the Baltic travelled in English ships and the Levant Company (formed in 1592 by a merger of the Turkey and Venice Companies) had a generous share of the lucrative Medterranean trade. Whatever the economic fluctuations of the later years of Elizabeth's reign, the English mastery of the seas ensured a steady flow of luxuries, whether the fruit of privateering (Drake's 1577–80 expedition was said to have yielded Indian goods and spice worth one and a half million pounds) or of legitimate trade. The presence of thirty-two Turkish carpets at Hardwick in 1601 can be seen as a direct result of the English maritime achievement.

England in 1500 was a technologically backward country, dependent on its neighbours across the Channel, particularly the Low Countries, for manufactured goods. The English appetite for Low Countries' wares, no novelty at the beginning of the sixteenth century, was stimulated by Henry VIII's energetic personal diplomacy. A retinue of 5,000 men and some women accompanied him to the Field of the Cloth of Gold. Smaller groups on diplomatic missions criss-crossed the Channel and bought anything from tapestries to jewellery in Bruges and Antwerp. William Paget, when building his Middlesex palace in the 1540s, imported the fireplaces, the floor tiles and some of the woodwork from Antwerp. Another of Henry VIII's new men, William, Lord Sandys (d. 1540) who was Treasurer in Calais from 1517, ordered the stained glass for his chapels at the Vyne and in Basingstoke from Bernard van Orley and Pieter Coeck, glass painters in Flanders (present-day Belgium), and the decorative tin-glazed floor tiles for the chapel from potters in Antwerp, in the early 1520s. Sir Richard Weston (d. 1542), who built

Sutton Place, a man who had spent many years travelling in northern France in pursuit of the diplomatic interests of the English king, incorporated into the courtyard facade terracotta panels from moulds undoubtedly imported from France.

The clearest example of this early Tudor dependence on, and emulation of, French contemporary decoration was Henry VIII's palace at Nonsuch (demolished in Charles II's reign), consciously copying the decorative motifs and even the materials of Francis I's new palace at Fontainebleau, on which the Italian artists Rosso and later Primaticcio were working in the 1530s. Henry's ambassador, Sir Henry Wallop, sent back to the King vivid accounts of Francis's innovations. Eventually Henry brought over to England not only workmen such as Nicholas of Modena, an Italian stuccoist who had worked under Primaticcio, but also specifically French decorative techniques, such as the panels of carved and gilded slate which ran as vertical framing to the great plaster reliefs in the inner courtyard at Nonsuch. The decorative scheme too was derived from contemporary French interpretations of high

Tin-glazed (Delft) plate in praise of Elizabeth I (1600).

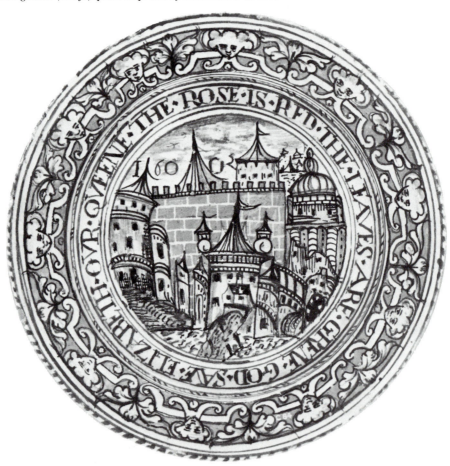

Renaissance motifs, such as strapwork and swags of fruit. But the whole composition was dominated by a more than life-size figure of Henry himself in classical dress, a conceit which would not have been acceptable to the more purely classical lay-out of the decoration at Fontainebleau.

This disjunction of scale and of ornament, and the insertion of ornament of some personal or heraldic significance was typical of the English response to imported designs. Personal badges, devices or the whole coat of arms predominate in every descriptive list of plate or tapestry. However, because of the process of gift exchange and the lack of prejudice against either giving or receiving second-hand items, it is not at all surprising to find sets of tapestries, for example, woven with the badges of Henry VII among the possession of Sir Richard Weston at Sutton Place, or conversely plate in the King's Jewel House at the Tower with the badges of Cardinal Wolsey, Edward Seymour or other members of the Tudor aristocracy unfortunate enough to lose their possessions and eventually their heads.

Although the new industries established in the second half of the sixteenth century were not to be of enormous economic significance before the seventeenth century, their products illuminate the native tastes of the English; a plate in the Museum of London, which is made of tin-glazed earthenware and presumably emanated from a London kiln, perhaps that of Johnson in Aldgate, depicts the city and the Thames in the foreground. It is clearly an example of civic pride but the border is a direct lift from a sheet of engraved ornament. The tapestries produced at the Sheldon factory discussed below show a similar marriage of local preoccupations with imported ornament.

Another new industry, the making of fine glass, was established by the Italian Jacob Verzelini in Crutched Friars in the City in 1572. The Glass House had been established five years before by Jean Carré from Antwerp, who came with the intention of making Venetian style *cristallo*, particularly drinking glasses. Verzelini obtained a patent giving him a monopoly of the making of crystal glasses for twenty-one years, on the condition that he taught his craft to native Englishmen. This was a requirement attached to many of the skills brought over by aliens, particularly those working in the New Draperies, that is the making of fine woollen cloth, the bays and says (light cloths) which were to prove so profitable in the seventeenth century. Venetian or *façon de venise* glass had been popular in England at least from 1500; Henry VIII had a collection of 600 glasses in 1542, objects as large as a table fountain and a cistern plus sets of sweetmeat glasses with gilded and painted decoration. Later in the century, the Earl of Leicester had at Kenilworth an equally rich range of dessert glass, also gilded and painted. But the rubbish pits of Southampton, Exeter and Norwich show that the merchant elite of these towns, and of London too, also enjoyed coloured, decorative, imported glass.

The shape of Verzelini's glasses and, to some extent, the diamond-engraved decoration was paralleled by contemporary silver and pewter drinking vessels. Horizontal bands on the bowl enclosed strapwork panels with dates, initials and love-knots, and inscriptions. Several of the glasses have engraved around the base of the bowl rudimentary lobes, reminiscent of those embossed on contemporary silver. The glasses are associated with members of the bourgeoisie and gentry and various livery companies, and are engraved with initials or cyphers, suggesting that their appeal lay not at court level but in those prospering classes who were anxious to enjoy novelties, and were not sufficiently well-travelled to be able to discriminate between the London-made product and the higher quality Venetian original.

Until the Reformation, traversing Europe offered no real difficulties. Artists and craftsmen from Flanders, Germany or France travelled down into Italy to see and learn as Dürer did, and disseminated their experience on their return for the benefit of their patrons. Although English craftsmen did not share this tradition of travelling to gain experience and pick up new variants in design, new themes in ornament crossed the Channel rapidly both in the form of sheets of engraved ornament and in the heads of those aliens who played so disproportionate a role in the luxury trades in England. Early in the century imported woodblock prints of birds, monkeys and other beasts were copied by engravers of plate, as on the Ralph Davy coconut cup at the Vintners Company (1518) or the standing cup at Charlecote (1524). From the 1550s a flood of engraved ornament poured from the printing shops of Antwerp and Paris. Some, like the *Architecture* of Vredeman de Vries, reinterpreted classical motifs in an inchoate medley which became a source book for stone carvers and decorative painters. Influential compilations of designs were published by Androuet du Cerceau in Paris; his many prints of moresque ornament, of grotesques derived from Cornelis Bos and Aeneas Vico and of strapwork derived from Rosso's work at Fontainebleau had a wide circulation and one of his Mannerist furniture designs of about 1560 was the source for the sea-dog table at Hardwick.

Certain long-established pictorial themes continued to be popular, particularly Biblical ones such as Jonah and the Whale, chosen as the subject of wall-paintings at the Carpenters Company Hall early in the century. The Goldsmiths Company commissioned a set of tapestries in Flanders with the story of St Dunstan, their patron; unfortunately in the extreme Protestant climate of the early 1550s the subject was, like the popular devotion to St Thomas à Becket, condemned. The marine theme of Jonah and the Whale, which was peculiarly suited as a subject for the silver mounts of exotic shells, survived the Reformation. Handsome nautilus shell cups mounted in silver-gilt, on which the sea-monster's open jaws encircle a tiny figure of Jonah, can be seen at the Fitzwilliam and Victoria and Albert Museums. The association between marine imagery and the liquid to be contained in the vessel extended to ewers and basins too, which were chased with plaques of sea monsters, copied from imported brass or lead models.

Whatever the cross-Channel source of the subject-matter of textiles, cushions, standing cups or carved screens, one native element, heraldry, usually predominated. The English stress on family descent expressed itself through an obsessive repetition of badges, crests and arms, often inserted with little understanding of the integrity of the original engraved design. One longstanding subject, popular in many media, was that of the Nine Worthies, which had already appeared in civic pageants in the mid-fifteenth century and retained its popular appeal although it had to be handled with due attention to current politics. When the Gracechurch Street conduit was redecorated for the coronation procession of Queen Mary in 1553, the painter included Henry VIII and Edward VI among the Nine Worthies, depicting Henry holding a book entitled *Verbum Dei*. This Protestant reference, however veiled, inevitably attracted Bishop Gardiner's hostile interest and the unfortunate painter was forced to substitute a pair of gloves. The Nine Worthies recur as the subject for Elizabethan wall decoration and three of them are depicted, along with four emblems, in the painted glass panels set into the Vyvyan Salt (1592, Victoria and Albert Museum).

Arms and armour: the Greenwich Armoury

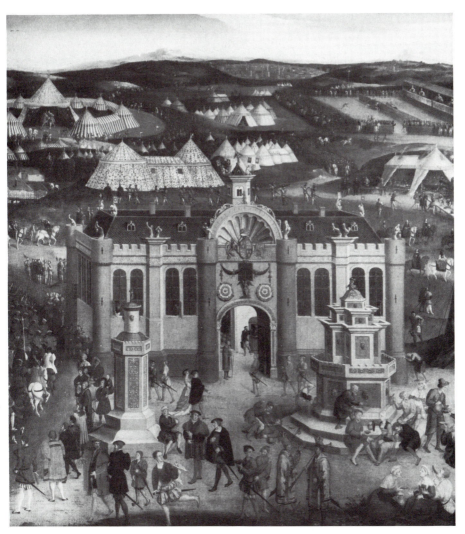

Detail from ?Johannes Corvus's The Field of the Cloth of Gold *(c.1520).*
Reproduced by Gracious permission of Her Majesty The Queen.

Among the most spectacular and familiar Tudor objects are the magnificent armours for horses and men displayed in the White Tower at the Tower of London. These armours, mostly made for Henry VIII, have been a central element in Britain's first and greatest showpiece, the Tower Armouries, since the sixteenth century, and attracted admiring comments from such European visitors as Thomas Platter and Paul Hentzner in the 1590s.

Magnificence signified power to the Renaissance monarch; rich suits of armour were essential both for warfare and for the ceremonial parades in pursuit of diplomatic ends, like the meeting of Henry VIII and the Emperor Maximilian in 1513 or Henry and Francis I at the Field of the Cloth of Gold in 1520; and also for the seasonal programmes of jousts and tilts which played so essential a part in court entertainment. Before Henry VIII's accession, the best armours and weapons were imported, either from Burgundy or from south Germany or Milan. The native Armourers' Company occupied itself with making and retailing mail, padded undercoats, brigandines (to protect the legs) and lower quality helmets, sallets (light head-pieces) and the like.

In pursuit of his conscious and vigorous policy of presenting himself as a fully European prince, a programme which flowed into every aspect of his surroundings from his books and music to his passion for chivalric pageantry, Henry quickly invited foreign armourers to London. The armours that they made, or those he received as gifts from Maximilian made in the Innsbruck workshops, reflected Henry's passionate obsession with the badges of his dynasty, again a ubiquitous feature of his surroundings; on his engraved and silver-gilt parade armour made about 1515, Tudor roses on double stems entwined with the pomegranate badge of Catherine of Aragon cover every inch of the suit, including the helmet. The addition of figures of St George and St Barbara on the breast and back of the suit remind us that both contemporary artists and patrons saw no incongruity in combined themes drawn from religion and from heraldry, although by the middle of the century the latter was to predominate along with emblems and devices. This suit neatly demonstrates the many cross-Channel sources from which the English court was drawing its finest works of craftsmanship, and its heavy dependence on aliens working in England; the armour with its fluted skirt has some typically Italian features and is attributed to Filippo de Grampis and Giovanni Angelo de Littis, Italians working at Greenwich, while the horse armour appears to be Flanders work. Both were decorated by Paul van Vrelant of Brussels, either in his Flanders workshop or in London where he held a court appointment.

As early as 1511 Henry had brought Italian and Flemish armourers to London and the latter probably made the skirted foot combat armour of about 1512, although this suit again has a composite origin since the helmet is Milanese. In 1515–16 Henry set up the Royal Armourers at Greenwich Palace under the direction of the Flemish Master Armourer, Martin van Royne. During his long Mastership (he handed over to his successor, the German Erasmus Kyrkenaar, about 1540) he continued to make armour both for Henry and as royal gifts for favoured members of the court and foreign ambassadors. In 1527 a particularly grand new suit appeared for the first time. As the chronicler Hall commented, 'A new harness all gilt of a strange fashion that had not been seen' was worn by the King at the Shrove Tuesday jousts at Greenwich. Comparable with this, which has not survived, is the suit called that of Geliot de Genovillac. This all-gilt Greenwich suit which is dated 1527 is now in the Metropolitan Museum of Art, New York.

Later in the century the Royal Armourers turned their attention to supplying suits for members of the Elizabethan court; the Jacope Album of watercolours in the Victoria and Albert Museum recalls the splendour and beauty of suits which, blued, damascened, gilded and engraved, have not survived or are now so over-cleaned, rubbed and skinned as to be only a shadow of themselves. These became more fantastical as the Elizabethan cult

A watercolour from the Jacope Album showing the Earl of Leicester carrying the Badge of the Ragged Staff, with the Bear and Ragged Staff engraved on the elbow-crook of his armour (c.1565).

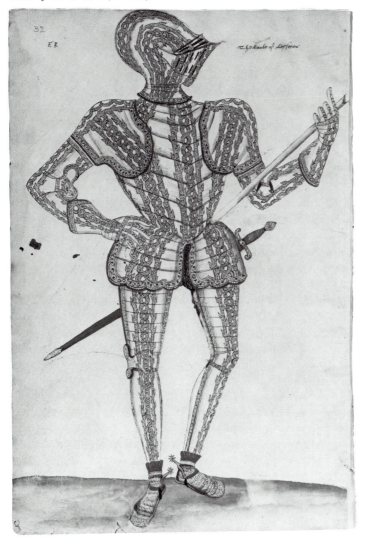

of chivalry evolved. The tilt armour of Robert Dudley, Earl of Leicester is engraved all over with his badge of a flaming star (*c.* 1565); while Hilliard's miniature of George Clifford, Earl of Cumberland, who succeeded Sir Henry Lee as Queen's Champion at the tilt on 17 November 1590, depicts him as Knight of Pendragon Castle, a figure from Arthurian romance. His elaborate costume, full of allegories, combines a jewelled surcoat embroidered with olive branches and celestial spheres over a blackened armour inlaid with gold stars (see p. 19; also colour pl. 8).

The outward magnificence of these suits did not preclude their being carefully engineered and constructed means of defence, tailored to the owner, carefully hinged and shaped over the feet and along the arms to allow the full play of the muscles in fighting. The best Greenwich armours remain outstanding examples of technical achievement. However, it must be said that the armourers working in England, whether German or Italian or Flemish, never acquired the technical secrets of the Augsburg armourers. Conrad Seusenhofer of Augsburg was induced by Maximilian to settle in Innsbruck and produce armours for the Emperor. The ram's horn helmet in the Tower is a solitary survivor, much altered later, of one of those suits sent to Henry VIII.

A series of tests on armours of different nationalities in the Tower and elsewhere have shown that while all are of steel, the degree of hardening varies enormously; some had been merely air-cooled, others partially hardened by slack-quenching and others fully hardened and tempered. The last technique was the secret of the Innsbruck armourers, and without this technical knowledge it was not possible to produce case-hardened armour and then to decorate it with gilding, since the heating required to fix the gilding would undo the hardening effected by the quenching process. Because Henry's armourers were denied access to this knowledge the Greenwich armours, although incomparably stronger than the normal run of munitions armour which would have been of iron or low carbon steel without any hardening, were still not up to the Imperial standard.

It is a far cry from these splendours at court to the practical everyday arms and armour with which Englishmen generally were equipped when the muster was summoned. The participants were issued with a motley selection of equipment old and new, London-made or imported by the barrel load from Flanders. The county or civic authorities to whom the muster demands came from London, shared out the duty among the leading gentry and yeomen in each parish, or in the case of London and the other major towns required the livery companies each to produce its quota of armed men. In 1569, for instance, the parish of Yoxhall, Staffordshire was rated to supply 'Pikemen three: Bilmen five: Harquebus nine'. Billmen carried six-foot long halberds or bills which were shorter and more wieldy than pikes and wore breast plates or corselets 'with light Millain murians (morions or helmets) the forepart ought to be proof of the calibre'. This recommendation as to the quality and hardness of the metal, given by Sir Francis Williams in his *Brief Discourse of Warre* (1590) is a reminder that the Armourers' Company was by the end of the century testing locally-made breast-plates and helmets for their resistance to both pistol shot and to sword blow, and marking pieces so tested with a proof mark, a crowned 'A', a further symptom of that Elizabethan interest in regulating the products of their new or newly invigorated industries.

In 1542 Norwich was called on to supply forty 'fullest and most apte and able men', nineteen archers with harness, bows, arrows, swords and daggers and twenty-one billmen similarly equipped for the invasion of Scotland, a demand reiterated the following year when the billmen and archers demanded for the French campaign were to be issued with uniform blue cloth coats guarded or striped with red, and hose of one leg red and one blue with a red stripe, so as to distinguish one contingent from another. Their equipment was not expensive; Dutch muskets with rests and bandoliers cost only £1 each and harquebuses or calyvers complete with flasks and touchboxes eight shillings apiece. Judging from the parish armouries that have survived (the remnants of one from Essex are in the Museum of London and another is in the Castle Gate, Winchester), the quality of these collections was poor and their appearance motley. A calyver cost in 1588 10 shillings and a morion 5 shillings and 10 pence. These were simple head coverings made of two plates soldered together, rather than the handsome single sheet, forged in one, of the best Greenwich helmets. The equipment of an archer was of course cheaper; yew bows retrieved from the wreck of the *Mary Rose*, which went down in 1545, are 6 foot 4½ inches long. The bow cost 2 shillings and 8 pence, bow strings 6 pence a dozen, and arrows 22 pence a sheaf. Among the equipment recovered from the *Mary Rose* is a wooden disc pierced with holes in which the arrows were stored until needed.

Somewhere between these two extremes, the humble citizen issued by the parish council with his plain and no doubt battered and old-fashioned corselet and morion and the nobleman in his Greenwich suit, came the English squirearchy, people who took pride in their equipment and saw military exercises, or indeed the pursuit of war, as being wholly appropriate to the upbringing of a gentleman. Their armour was among their most valued possessions, specified in their wills by men like Henry Cornysh Esquire of Glastonbury who in 1552 left to his son his complete armour, including a gilt saddle of black velvet with trapper gilt, a tonke (a small hand-gun), a dagger, stirrups, spurs and 'a hand gun sutable gilt with a morreyn [a light helmet] of black velvet, a shanfreyn [a part of the armour], four hand guns, four ship pieces with all my other furniture for the war, plus four crossbows and three longbows'.

The repeated mention of gilding is characteristic of the English taste for decoration in their arms; daggers recovered from the foreshore of the Thames, while wholly practical as weapons, are elaborately decorated around the hilt and pommel and have damascening on the blade. Stubbes, in his *Anatomy of Abuses* (1583), referred indignantly to swords, rapiers and daggers which were

gift twice or thrice over the hilts with good angel gold: others at the least are damasked, varnished and engraven marvellous goodly, and lest anything should be wanting to set forth their pride, the scabbards and sheaths are of velvet or the like.

This splendour was not peculiar to England; a sword of Landsknecht type, double-edged and with applied gilt cable ornament, has the Imperial eagle

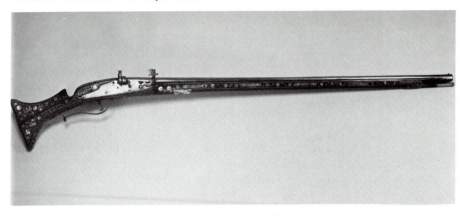

Musket, jewelled and inlaid with bone and ivory (c.1600).

engraved on a gilt escutcheon on the collar. Found in the foreshore under New Scotland Yard, it was presumably lost by one of Charles V's entourage on his visit to London in 1522.

Swords were not confined to military exercises but were very much part of a gentleman's everyday dress, and in cities the servants of the merchants also carried short swords, as may be seen in the family group depicted in Braun and Hogenberg's map of London, 1572. These short swords or baselards were London-made, unlike the handsome damascened blades of the gentry which were imported from Spain and fitted with hilts in England. The duties of men of military age were as much ceremonial as aggressive, on state visits they paraded, fully equipped, to honour and to impress (it was hoped) the foreigners; at the state funeral of Sir Philip Sidney, as recorded in Theodore de Bry's engraving, soldiers trailing pikes or carrying muskets dominated the procession to St Paul's Cathedral. Their equipment was expensive and highly decorative, like the silver caliver with a dragon's head on the mouth with matching flask and touch box, and the gold-lace trimmed sword-rest which Peter Peterson of Norwich left in 1603. A comparable set of weapons formerly belonging to the Raymond family of Belchamp Hall is in the Victoria and Albert Museum, the bone and horn inlay reproducing typical Mannerist scroll work and fantastic animals.

Gunnery was another field in which England was striving to catch up with Europe in the early years of the sixteenth century. Henry VIII persuaded Peter Baude the armourer to settle here both to make cannon and to teach the art to Englishmen. Guns recovered both in the nineteenth century and more recently from the *Mary Rose* demonstrate that Henry VIII's navy was equipped with a very heterogeneous collection of ordnance, from the bronze cannon of Peter Baude, one made as recently as 1543, to the crude stave-built iron guns which were intended to fire stone shot at short range. Single-shot wrought iron guns provided an alternative means of armament so that the ship was fully equipped for both long range and short range action.

The finest of the *Mary Rose* guns was made by Robert and John Owen in 1537 at their Houndsditch foundry. The bronze gun is over ten feet long and has two inscriptions, one naming the makers and the other referring to

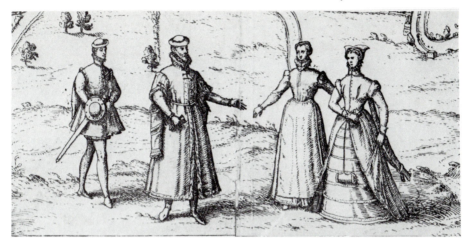

Family group showing a merchant and his wife, with their maidservant and manservant, depicted in Braun and Hogenberg's map of London (1572).

Henry's title as Defender of the Faith and head of the English Church, a new and proud claim. His Tudor Rose crowned and in a garter is also cast on to the gun. English mastery of the technology of casting in iron improved enormously during the sixteenth century and by 1600 foundries in the Sussex Weald were producing not only cannon but firebacks and grates, in response to the increased domestic comfort which characterised English living standards.

Goldsmiths and society

Many a peasant here keeps greater state and a better table than the nobility in Germany. He must be a poor peasant indeed who does not possess silvergilt salt cellars, silver cups and spoons.

(Von Wedel, on his visit to England in 1584.)

The enormous significance of silver and gold to Tudor society is sometimes overlooked, perhaps since, unlike textiles, silver has not survived in large quantities. Visitors to museums or cathedral treasuries see only the pathetic vestiges of past glories, objects both comparatively light in weight and plain in their design and so gain little sense of the great size and elaboration of the plate formerly in use, for example at the court of Henry VIII, among the nobility and in the homes of the great merchants of Elizabethan London. Henry VIII was known throughout Europe for his love of plate and jewels and his Jewel House was one of the richest of its time. Two solitary remnants from Henry VIII's time are a crystal bowl in gold and enamelled mounts whose design is attributed to Holbein (now at the Schatzkammer, Munich) and a French-made clock salt set with shell cameos (Paris 1533–4, now Goldsmiths' Company) along with the medieval Royal Gold Cup, Paris work of the late fourteenth century, which James I presented to a Spanish Count in 1604 (British Museum). But these are exceptional court pieces.

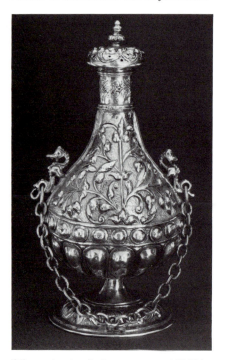

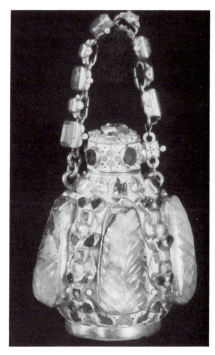

Gilt casting bottle for rosewater (1553).

Pomander of enamelled gold, set with rubies, topazes and diamonds (c. 1600).

What survives is much more characteristic of the mainstream of English taste, the kind of objects which would have been exhibited in the goldsmiths' shops in Cheapside, those shops on whose rich stocks of plate foreign visitors, whether French, Italian or German, commented so enthusiastically. There are rich collections in the livery companies, colleges and some ancient civic corporations of England, but on the whole these pieces are standard types, decorated with motifs drawn from the common repertoire of Antwerp Mannerism as mediated through English preferences and in no way unusual in their time. But only in the Kremlin Armouries, Moscow, among the English silver held since the seventeenth century by the Russian State, is there silver truly indicative of that in use at the Tudor Court. Some of the massive and elaborately-decorated water pots and flagons in Russia were diplomatic gifts, sent by the Crown or by the Muscovy Company in hope of securing trade monopolies, others were purchased by the Tsar in London in the late 1620s when Charles I, desperate for money, was weeding out old plate from the Jewel House.

At Court, silver, silver-gilt or at the best gold pervaded every aspect of the monarch's surroundings. Gold lace and spangles decorated the bed hangings, silver cups surmounted the bedposts, and the Earl of Pembroke in 1564 gave Elizabeth a massive silver dressing set complete with earpicks, tooth and shoe brushes, pincers, scissors, and so on, all of the precious metal. Her gold and silver chess set was another marvel and another gift from an Earl, purchased from the goldsmith Handford of the Black Swan in Cheapside. This chess set was noted by Paul Hentzner, among other visitors to Greenwich, and was clearly one of the treasures of the Palace. But the Jewel House was already extraordinarily rich, not only in gold and silver-gilt, but in mother of pearl, crystal, alabaster, agate and other hardstones; many of the pieces were gem-set, or hung with pearls, diamonds and emeralds.

A reminder of this taste for setting precious stones on vessels and for mounting up exotic materials, is the Howard Grace Cup (Victoria and Albert Museum). The Cup is an ivory bowl with a silver-gilt foot, rim and cover which still retains coarse pearls and a few garnets, although these may be replacements. The ivory cup, traditionally called Thomas à Becket's, may have been left by a member of the Howard family to Queen Catherine of Aragon in 1513; the mounts are London work of 1525 and show a curious mixture of Gothic form and Renaissance decorative motifs, for example in the cast borders of antique heads, sheaves and scrolling foliage around the foot and cover. The gold and crystal cup attributed to Holbein mentioned above is also gemset, as is the great standing cup and cover given by Lady Margaret Beaufort to Christs' College Cambridge in 1509. This is engraved with her badges of the portcullis and marguerite, another characteristic of early Tudor plate, and the foot of the cup is formed as a Tudor rose. Heraldry pervaded every aspect of Tudor decorative art and particularly its plate.

The contents of the Jewel House altered many times during the sixteenth century. There were about a thousand sets or entries in the Jewel House in 1533 and again about a thousand in 1574. But in those forty years enormous shifts in Tudor society, both in Church and in state, affected the contents of the Jewel House, as did the dramatic change in style from the purity of the early Renaissance to the grotesques and strapwork of Antwerp Mannerism. Confiscations from the estates of deposed noblemen were a rich source. Already by 1533 the Jewel House contained almost a hundred pieces of plate with the friars' knots, the badge of Francis I, plate confiscated from Wolsey which had been presented to him by the French king on his diplomatic visits to France in the 1520s. These confiscated pieces were melted and refashioned or at least the offending badges, like those of Wolsey himself, were removed. The Duke of Northumberland sacrificed 10,000 ounces of plate from his London house in 1553, some of which was absorbed into the Jewel House, but most sent to the Mint. Edward Seymour, Protector, Earl of Somerset whose plate bills survive at Longleat and who had spent lavishly on silver in the 1540s, was to lose all his possessions, and indeed his head, in 1552. But much of his plate survived and was still to be found in Elizabeth's Jewel House in 1574, no doubt because as a connoisseur of goldsmith's work, his pieces were particularly handsome and his phoenix badge not offensive to a queen who was herself fond of that device.

All this splendour did not simply lie in the Jewel House in dark closets but was brought out as an essential element of the panoply of state on great occasions. It was intended to dazzle the beholder and indeed visitors to London were often shown the contents of the Jewel House, or a selection of the contents, as part of the process of impressment. When Westminster Hall was dressed for the disguising and other revels at the time of Catherine of Aragon's arrival in England to marry Prince Arthur, the Hall was not only hung with 'pleasant Clothes of Arras' but

in its upper Part a royall and a great Cupboard was made . . . in it were sett Seven Shelves or Haunches of a goodly height, furnished or filled with so goodly and rich treasure of plate as could be seen, great part whereof was gould and all the remnant of silver.

This great display was repeated and amplified for every one of the international state occasions which punctuated the reigns of Henry VII and Henry VIII. An important part of the occasion was the subsequent void or banquet in which a very large number of royal servants, earls, barons, knights, and esquires wearing collars and chains of gold, carried in silver-gilt spice plates and cups, followed by guards with pots of wine to fill up the cups;

the number of the said spice plates and cups were goodly and marvellous and yet the more to be wondered for that the cupboard was nothing touched but stood complete garnished and filled, seemingly not one diminished.

This was an important part of the expression of regality and prodigality, in that the King must appear to be so wealthy that the plate on display did not have to be called upon for practical use. In order to achieve this effect, plate was hired from the livery companies and from the Lord Mayor and indeed from the goldsmiths' shops.

No opportunity for display was omitted. At the state christening of Cecilia Vasa's child, Edward Fortunatus, at the Chapel Royal Westminster in 1565, a massive display of plate was laid out on the communion table including a fountain and basin of mother of pearl and gold, another of gilt, a basin garnished with precious stones, crystal candlesticks, bowls of coral and crystal and a cup of agate, gold candlesticks and two ships (for incense presumably) of mother of pearl, all lent from the Jewel House for the occasion. The Jewel House was also the source of the diplomatic gifts which were expected by all ambassadors to the English Court. When Margaret was married to James of Scotland, her father Henry VII sent to the Archbishop of Glasgow, who led the Scottish legate to England, a cupboard of plate consisting of a gold cup, six standing pots, twenty-four drinking bowls with covers, a basin and ewer, and a chafing dish.

Who made all this splendid plate? And who was responsible for its design? We know that, as in so many other aspects of the decorative arts, the finest craftsmen were almost certainly aliens, familiar with the newest fashion and perhaps capable of higher quality work, for example chasing, than their English counterparts. The practice of the *wanderjahre* was widespread, journeymen travelling from one city to another to acquire ideas and refine their skills. These workmen remain shadowy figures, known only from references in the royal accounts or from the lists of names of aliens licensed to work by the Goldsmiths' Company. A list of those so licensed between 1527 and 1562 contains 232 names, most from Flanders or the duchies of Julich and Cleves, with a few Frenchmen who were probably specialists in diamond cutting, gem setting or engraving. Many other goldsmiths occur in the lists of those aliens receiving letters of denization, giving them permission to reside in the country; and in 1567 and again in 1593 a series of returns were made of aliens resident in the City of London ward by ward, which in some cases give occupations.

Unfortunately, because the workmen would almost always have had to have their work marked by an English master, it is not possible to tie down even plate of exceptional quality, such as those pieces with the mark of a bird which appear to be of Jewel House quality, to a given named alien. This goldsmith, who made the so-called Queen Elizabeth salt in the Jewel House (bought by Charles II) was clearly familiar with the designs of the Nuremberg goldsmith Peter Flotner and copied his plaquettes of the Virtues both on the Tower salt and one of 1572 at the Vintners' Company.

Designs which originated in the workshops of Antwerp or Nuremberg were rapidly disseminated through Europe and across the Channel in the form of printed sheets of engraved ornament or, more conveniently for the goldsmith, as lead or brass models or casting patterns. These base metal patterns were convenient to send to patrons too; Viscount Lisle in Calais, ordering a carcanet for his wife, had a lead pattern of it sent from a London goldsmith for her approval, and sample patterns of jewels offered to Henry VIII were sent to London from Antwerp. Goldsmiths valued their patterns highly and sometimes specified them in their wills; in 1603 Peter Peterson, a leading Norwich goldsmith, left his 'tooles and patterns of lead belonging to my science' to his nephew, also a goldsmith; they were kept not in the workshop but for greater security 'in my great iron chest now standing in my little hall'.

There were goldsmiths in almost every town; from time to time the Goldsmiths' Company swept through the provinces searching out shops and visiting their booths at the great regional fairs at Stourbridge, Cambridge and so on to check their stocks. Several towns, notably Exeter, Norwich and Chester, set up offices and adopted the London hallmarking policy in the 1560s and 1570s, an indication of the local demand for plate. Spoons and the Elizabethan communion cups illustrate the bulk of their work, but the provincial goldsmiths, who had often served their apprenticeships in London were supplying other items too. At Beccles in 1593 one had stoneware pots with silver gilt mounts, beakers and salts. The goldsmiths of Exeter and Norwich are particularly well-documented; the West Country and East Anglia were both prosperous regions, whose silver paralleled that made in London in decoration and form.

The style of English silver in the sixteenth century went through three distinct phases. At the accession of Henry VIII late medieval ornament still predominated, although in the Low Countries the influence of the Renaissance was already significant in sculpture and painting. References to plate with 'anticke worke', naked boys and scroll work occur in England at court level before 1520, an indication that the new ornamental motifs were becoming familiar. The Howard Grace Cup and another standing bowl at All Souls, Holbein's drawings of Tudor Court plate from the mid-1530s and the few surviving pieces such as a standing cup at Cirencester Church with an acanthus-clasped knob, another cup in a City church (St Margaret Pattens) show that the fairly pure early Renaissance style was well-established.

But from the late 1540s there was a dramatic change in the appearance of English silver, under the impact of designs emanating from Antwerp. Clusters of fruit and fat gourds, suspended in strapwork panels, grotesque half-human figures, dissonance of scale and a lively appetite for marine motifs characterised the new northern European style, which found its greatest expression in the plasterwork and statuary by Primaticcio for Francis I at Fontainebleau and was imitated by Henry VIII at Nonsuch in the early 1540s. This new style, termed Antwerp Mannerism, was disseminated both through books of designs by Cornelis Bos, Pieter de Cocke and Vredeman de Vries and by those alien craftsmen who were attracted to London by its reputation for prosperity or impelled to travel abroad by their religious convictions.

There was not to be another major change in the design of plate before the early seventeenth century and it appears that English silver stagnated. The flat strapwork, which depended for its effect on the contrast with high relief embossing and chasing, became standardised and the designs stereotyped.

Alongside these strapwork and fruit motifs, the Elizabethan goldsmith also satisfied a demand for Gothic forms such as the standing cup in the shape of an apple, melon or gourd, a form which Dürer had recorded (but not invented, as sometimes claimed) early in the century.

The arabesque or moresque was another quite unrelated ornament, popular both on plate and in decorative painting on furniture from the 1530s, which was derived ultimately from Turkish interlacing leaf scrolls. In the later sixteenth century this 'Rabask' work deteriorated into the simple bands of scrollwork often found engraved on Elizabethan communion cups; a set of designs published by Thomas Geminus in 1548, *Morysse and Damashin renowned and encreased very profitable for Goldsmythes and Embroiderers*, plagiarised earlier publications in Paris by Pellegrino.

The translator of von Wedel's account of his visit to England should have substituted 'yeoman' for 'peasant', a term more suited to the rigidly demarcated class system of Germany than to the fluid mobility characteristic of English society. But as a general comment this has considerable force. While von Wedel may have exaggerated, or indeed have been repeating an impression garnered from earlier travel writers, the same comment was made also by Polidore Virgil rather more than half a century earlier. It is reinforced by the well-known description by William Harrison, the Essex rector, of the general increase in domestic comfort and luxury among the yeomen and gentry of his native county. When these comments are set beside the plate recorded in inventories and wills it is clear that many Englishmen, probably a far higher proportion than today, enjoyed the regular use of silver, if not in their private then in their corporate lives. There was no real alternative; pewter was of course much cheaper but was declining in status in the sixteenth century as the wealthy turned to silver. Porcelain was only appearing in the last decade of the century and was confined to the buffet or the banqueting house for dessert use.

To own plate was both essential and a basic attribute of status, and whatever social group is examined, first drinking vessels, then plates, then

washing utensils of silver were becoming far more widespread in the
sixteenth century. Many Englishmen belonged to corporate bodies; they were
liverymen of craft companies, brethren of Trinity House, Fellows of a college
or Inn of Court, or members of a civic corporation. To mark entry to the
senior ranks of a society, whether college, Inn of Court, guild or civic body, a
gift of plate was customary and a generally recognised tariff operated, so that
the freemen of Ludlow, Exeter or Norwich, for example, were expected to
present spoons on their admission to the freedom. These spoons were of a
prescribed weight and finish. Livery companies too demanded uniformity in
these tokens of admission to their freedom; for 150 years at least the
Innholders' Company accumulated spoons each year which had identical
terminal figures of St Julian, their patron saint. A model spoon was kept in
the Hall and copied.

Once reaching a more elevated level of responsibility, the Master, President
or Mayor was expected to give at least a cup, salt, ewer or basin or, more
often, to leave money to enable the institution to buy something in his
memory. Such pieces were often inscribed EX DONO and were engraved as a
matter of course with the original donor's arms, although his connection
might have been somewhat indirect. Since both inscription and coat of arms
were normally copied onto any replacement plate, the memory of the donor
could be preserved indefinitely. A set of two dozen trencher plates, a
symptom of the rising prosperity and self-confidence of the City of London,
was presented for the Lord Mayor's use in the 1580s by Dame Elizabeth
Nicholas, widow of a former Lord Mayor. These, melted down and
refashioned several times, now are transmogrified into part of a dinner service
by De Lamerie and are still in use at the Mansion House, with Lady
Nicholas's arms and an inscription recording the occasion of her gift.

Occasions for a full gift-exchange, a ritual in which the lesser humbly
solicited the favour of the greater power by presenting plate, were frequent.
For the King on progress, at royal entries and annually at New Year, gifts
flowed in from all members of the Court and from many institutions outside.
In return the King gave the donor a chit on the Jewel House to choose a
piece of plate commensurate with his rank. William Husee, London agent of
Lord Lisle, governor of Calais, in the 1530s, has left a vivid description of
Henry VIII's personal attention to the quality of his New Year's gifts; the
King, leaning against a cupboard, commented on each as the donor handed it
to the Master of the Household.

Henry's interest in matters artistic extended to every aspect of his life. His
agents purchased plate for him in Antwerp, then the centre of innovative
design and craftsmanship, and the Jewel House was noticeably well stocked
with handsome and elaborate plate 'in the antique fashion' by the time of his
death. Under Mary and Elizabeth the contents of the Jewel House received
less personal attention from the monarch and pieces came in as the result of
the process of gift exchange or confiscation and not of conscious choice on
the part of the monarch. Great court officers also shared this New Year's
bounty. The Earl of Pembroke, for example, in 1562 received a handsome
cup with a pyramid or steeple cover from the Merchant Staplers, no doubt in
hopes of some favour in the year to come. And in the early 1600s the

extravagant Earl of Rutland was desperately wooing significant members of the Court hierarchy, including the Earl of Northampton, with extravagant gifts such as a mermaid ewer with an accompanying basin formed as a shell, a typical Mannerist conceit. He needed to regain a place at Court and overcome his handicap of being a professed Roman Catholic.

This ritual of the presentation of plate was part of the essential cement holding Tudor society together. Robert Herrick, alderman of Leicester, gave a telling glimpse of the reality behind the process of gift exchange in a letter of June 1616. Instructing his brother Sir William the goldsmith in London as to the ceremonious gift of a silver-gilt cup to the newly appointed Chancellor of the Duchy of Lancaster, Sir John Daccombe, he asked 'that the bearer be with you in the delivering as though he brought it of purpose from Leicester'. In the event, Sir John preferred a silver basin which cost £13 'to signify the town's love and affection for his honour'.

The raw material of silver, unlike other forms of decorative art, retained its intrinsic value and silver has been ruthlessly transmogrified in each generation, either because it was battered, bruised and considered 'unfit for service', or to bring it up to date. The phrase 'in the new fashion' occurs again and again in references to plate. Particularly from the 1560s or so when the overwhelming impact of Antwerp Mannerism was swamping virtually every aspect of ornament in England, plate in an older style was vulnerable and likely to be sent to the melting pot. There were new uses for silver too. With the increasing prosperity of the English gentry and the merchant elite, silver ewers and basins, tankards, and flagons, and trencher plates were becoming more common at this level in society. At Kingston upon Hull an early gift of plate to the town was his 'best standing gilted pece' left by Alderman Jeffray Thruscross in 1520; by 1604 this cup still had pride of place in the civic list but the list was much longer, the twenty-five items including that significant indicator of luxury and ostentation, a ewer and basin.

More came flooding in to this and other civic collections until the losses of the 1640s. Norwich had a splendid civic collection by 1600, including several cups by local goldsmiths and again a ewer and basin. Because of the great prestige attached to the ewer and basin they were both carefully designed and often very heavy and they represented a considerable expense. The symbolism of the ornament was marine, in keeping with their function. A ewer in the Victoria and Albert Museum is modelled as a mermaid, whose nipples are pierced to allow the rosewater to flow and then to be caught in the basin which is in the shape of a mussel shell. A standard design for ewers and basins incorporated plaques chased with dolphins and other marine subjects. The ewer and basin weigh over ninety ounces and probably cost well over £50, including both the metal at 5 shillings an ounce and the fashion, at as much again, which is far more than a cup or salt, which could weigh as little as five or ten ounces and cost only £2–3. Institutions, or indeed private individuals, making the leap from pewter to silver for their ewer and basin were making a considerable statement as to their prosperity and expectations.

The high status evoked by silver was something every corporate body

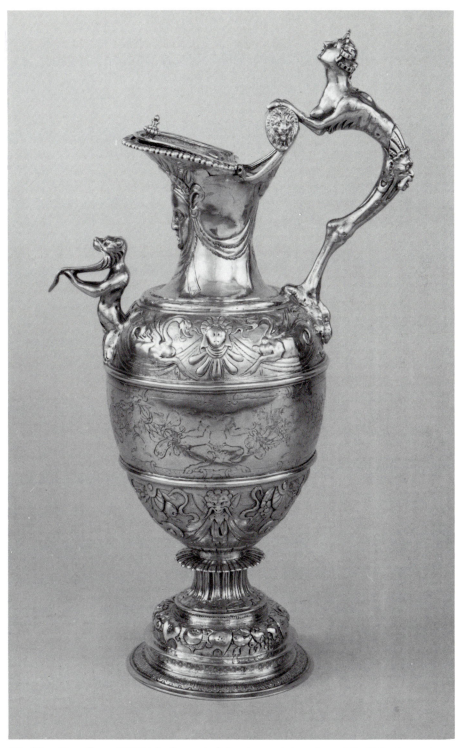

The Wyndham Ewer (1554) is the most elaborate surviving piece of English silver using a Mannerist motif.

wanted to share, so the Wards of the City of London, sharing out such mundane unpaid local duties among their householders as the post of scavenger or street cleaner were prepared to convert the money fines paid by reluctant citizens into handsome drinking vessels. St Giles Cripplegate in London retains beakers acquired as fines in the first decade of the seventeenth century.

A high proportion of the surviving goldsmiths' work of the sixteenth century consists of mounted exotica such as ostrich eggs, ivory, porcelain, agate and other hardstones such as serpentine, porphyry or alabaster and crystal, plus mother of pearl and nautilus and other shells from the Far East. Some of these were 'naturall and artificiall' rarities, set out in rooms designated for display, along with clocks and other mechanical wonders in embryonic museum collections or cabinets of curiosities. Other mounted objects were made for the buffet, such as a ewer and basin of agate at Belvoir belonging to the Earl of Rutland (1579) or a set of porcelain basins and bottles, formerly at Burghley House. All these pieces had gilded mounts. White silver was confined to practical tablewares, such as serving dishes, platters, 'saucers' (literally for sauce) and trencher plates.

A substantial quantity of gold in the form of cups, salts and spoons circulated at Court level, often as ceremonious gifts at New Year, or to ambassadors. Gold lent itself both to beautifully detailed chasing and to heraldic and pictorial enamelling, which could not conveniently be carried out on silver. It is perhaps hardly surprising that gold vessels belonging to the Earl of Pembroke, or indeed to Queen Elizabeth herself, were more often ornamented with armorials, badges or crests than chased with fashionable Mannerist fruitage, monsters, or naturalistic birds and marine subjects, although there were fantasies such as the gold salt 'like a Globe standing upon two naked men with the historie of Jupiter and Pallas' which Sir Francis Drake gave to the Queen in 1581 to commemorate his circum-navigation of the world.

The interior

Certes in Noblemen's Houses, it is not rare to see abundance of Arras, rich hangings of tapistrie . . . likewise in the houses of knights, gentlemen, merchantmen, and some other worthy citizens . . . great provision of tapistrie . . . Inferior artificers and manie farmers . . . garnish their cupboards with plate, their joined beds with tapistrie and silk hangings and their tables with carpets.

(William Harrison, *Description of England*, 1577)

To reconstruct the appearance of a Tudor interior it is not the woodwork, more or less underdecorated and crude as it was, but the textiles which are essential. Every horizontal surface was concealed – stools and window-sills with cushions, cupboards and buffets with plain woven cloths and damask runners at mealtimes, the tables again with cloths, or in wealthier homes carpets over cloths which were further protected with linen when the meal was in progress (colour pl. 5). On the walls hung sets of tapestries (Arras) or in lesser homes painted cloths. Beds were dressed more richly than any other piece of furniture, with gold or silk-trimmed valances and testers and heavily embroidered coverings. Taken as a whole, beds, often with painted and gilded head boards and posts, plus their textiles, were by far the most valuable item in any probate inventory, apart from the plate. By 1600 window curtains of wool were no longer a novelty and were becoming important in the decorative scheme, sometimes made up of designs and colours to match the other furnishings, as at Ingatestone Hall. Harrison's description of the social penetration of textiles is borne out by the inventory evidence both from rural counties and towns such as Coventry and Exeter.

These textiles were valued not only because they were decorative but also because of their high cost. All the most luxurious fabrics were imported – velvets from Lucca, satin and silk from other Italian centres such as Naples or Florence, ribbons from Spain, fine linen from Brittany and the Low Countries and above all tapestries from a number of centres but primarily Brussels and Antwerp.

'Tapestries, and painted linens which are well done and on which are magnificent roses embellished with fleur de lis and lions': Etienne Perlin's comment in 1558 is borne out by contemporary descriptions of wall coverings. Tapestries and cheaper painted imitations were virtually universal in public rooms at least and were displayed outside too on state occasions. In the engraving of Edward VI's coronation procession through the City, the goldsmiths along Cheapside have hung out tapestries from their upper windows; and at the Field of the Cloth of Gold Francis I hung his temporary banqueting hall with his newly-woven set of the Continence of Scipio. Along with plate, sets of tapestry were the major prizes in the Crown lottery of 1567. One, the Judgement of Solomon, is the centrepiece of the broadsheet promoting the lottery.

The sixteenth century was the golden age of the pictorial tapestry; the finest, of silk, wool and gold thread, were woven in Flemish workshops, a process which took many months, after designs (cartoons) commissioned from leading artists such as Raphael or Guilio Romano. The Pope in 1515 placed an order with the Brussels tapestry-maker Pieter van Aelst for a famous High Renaissance masterpiece, the Acts of the Apostles for the Sistine Chapel; this order, which took five years to complete, copied cartoons by Raphael (seven of the cartoons are in the Victoria and Albert Museum). Henry VIII, who had inherited rich sets of tapestries, was an insatiable collector and wished to be the equal of any prince in Europe, in this as in other aspects of his life style. In 1550 there were 436 tapestries at Hampton Court and survivors from several of his orders are still hanging there, notably in the Great Hall a spectacular set woven by William Pannemakers of Brussels about 1540; these panels, depicting the History of Abraham after cartoons by Bernard van Orley, neatly demonstrate the international demand for Brussels work. Copies of this set were ordered also for the Emperor and for the King of Spain.

Cardinal Wolsey is known to have ordered twenty-one sets of hangings in 1521 alone, of which 132 pieces were intended for Hampton Court and the rest for his palace at Whitehall. John Skelton attacked both the richness and the licentious subject-matter, 'with wanton wenches winking', of his 'Arras of rich array'; but these were at the time an essential adjunct of power for international diplomats, whether churchmen, or not. Since Henry acquired most of Wolsey's property on his fall, it is hardly surprising to find overdoor panels and borders at Hampton Court woven with his devices of a crystal pillar, a griffin and a cardinal's hat, plus his motto 'Dominus michi adiutor'. Some of the seven sets of David and Bathsheba later owned by Henry VIII were no doubt among his 'voluptuous pleasures'.

Because of their splendour and cost, tapestries were treasured and handed on; 'story' sets left in 1509 by Lady Margaret Beaufort, mother of Henry VII, included one, 'The Story of Nabugorodonosor' (Nebuchadnezar) which had been ordered originally by Edward IV in 1468. This, with 'The Story of Parys, Elyn and Moyses' (a very popular subject in the sixteenth century), was apparently repurchased by lady Surrey, Edward IV's daughter, on Lady Margaret's death. These, and her other pictorial sets, had standard classical, historical or biblical themes: Hercules, Hannibal, King Robert of Sicily, Samson and so on. But there were also special orders, personalised with the ubiquitous badges of the early Tudor Court, such as the 'Verdours' woven with her portcullis and the red rose.

Catherine of Aragon's Wardrobe at Baynards Castle in 1535 also included several with the royal arms, as well as Jason, Hercules and the Old and the New Law. Her finest set of 'Velvett Fygurye' was a relic of happier days, gaily squared in red and green and embroidered with the arms of England and Spain under an imperial crown, with a border of her pomegranate badge interspersed with roses and fleurs de lis. The heraldic message was omnipresent in every aspect of Tudor decorative art at Court level.

The English did not merely send their orders for tapestry across the Channel; in this, as in other luxury manufacturers, individuals attempted to establish a native industry. Although the early history of arras-making in England is obscure, there were certainly weavers attached to the King's Wardrobe capable of weaving armorial borders and single panels at least; in the second half of the century (about 1560) William Sheldon, a Worcestershire squire, brought over Flemish weavers and set up the first English manufactories at Barchester in Warwickshire, and Bordesley in Worcestershire. The managers had close links with arras workers in the Great Wardrobe and stimulated a healthy regional demand for their products.

Orders woven at Barchester included both standard Flemish themes, such as the Prodigal Son, Judah and stories from Ovid, and special orders, such as the seventeen small armorial panels supplied to Bess of Hardwick in 1592; these were attached to large Brussels-woven panels. A pair of larger tapestries are woven with the arms of Robert Dudley, Earl of Leicester, as the central feature on a rich background with peacocks and delicate flowers. Outside a double border of Renaissance ornament are panels with scenes from the Flood. The most famous of the Sheldon tapestries are the sets of county maps, based on Christopher Saxton's recently-published atlas, which were apparently woven for Ralph Sheldon's new house at Weston in 1588. These express several Elizabethan characteristics, sturdy regional pride, interest in topography and a conscious rejection of imported themes. The bulk of the Sheldon weavers' output, apart from the special armorial orders from local families, took the form of small panels, used as cushion covers and the like.

The wills of the sixteenth century are rich in references to textiles which were rated in the testator's mind only slightly less highly than his plate. George Talbot, Earl of Shrewsbury in 1538, left his wife 'hole sets of hangings'; their subjects, Helen, Moses, shepherds and Moors, are the themes popular at the turn of the fifteenth and sixteenth centuries, and they were probably at least as old as this. No hint of Renaissance ornament here, nor in his sets of bed-hangings of cloth of gold and velvet with matching counterpoints.

Because of their high value and the low cost of labour to carry out alterations, there was a flourishing secondhand market in all textiles. At the time of the sales of church goods in the early 1550s, purse makers, saddlers and other dealers in fashionable accessories were prominent among the purchasers of the rich late Gothic altar frontals and vestments disposed of by London's churchwardens. The goods that changed hands could be cut up, re-embroidered and have new borders added, in the case of tapestries, with the new owner's arms. In 1553 the robes of estate of the Duke of Northumberland, which were magnificent in gold-trimmed crimson velvet, were found in the hands of a London skinner, probably to be used as linings for fur garments.

Matching chamber textiles and upholstery were by now customary in Court circles at least. In 1562 the Earl of Pembroke's London house, Baynard's Castle on Thames waterfront, had several chambers in which the bed-hangings, upholstered furniture and window curtains were all the same 'sute'. With the exception of decorative cabinets and musical instruments, furniture made only a small contribution; the values quoted in inventories are always low, and indeed the absence of some essential items from some houses, where they must have been present but too crude to attract the attention of the appraiser, is evident. At Sutton Place in 1542, Sir Richard Weston apparently had no chairs at all!

Furniture was very rarely bequeathed, with the exception of bedsteads, although occasionally a table or a cupboard is quoted as an heirloom in North Country wills, but these were no doubt massive constructions of locally-made oak with little more than the minimum of ornament. Items of furniture that were listed, such as spruce chests, Flanders coffers or 'a little table of walnutree', were valued as personal possessions. These were often covered with velvet and lined with painted and gilt paper, like the delicate and luxurious box in the Victoria and Albert Museum, which represents a vanished class of objects quite unlike the large coarsely carved court cupboards so often considered typical of Tudor furniture. Many of the latter are now recognised as being Jacobean and provincial, so there is a positive gap in our picture of the better Tudor furniture. At Court level, however, there were elaborate pieces, such as the tables carved in stone for the banqueting house of Sir William Sharington at Lacock Abbey and those in the presence chamber at Hardwick with their seadog feet.

There are also a few beautiful, but mostly imported, musical instruments; the 1540 list of the contents of the Palace of Westminster includes several with the fashionable 'Rabask' or moresque work, and Paul Hentzner commented on a musical instrument 'made all of glass, except the strings' at Hampton Court in 1598. A virginal of about 1600 is set with coloured glass painted with Ovid's *Metamorphoses* (Victoria and Albert Museum). Another instrument in the Museum is a combined harpsichord and organ (claviorgan) made by the Fleming Lodewyk Theewes at his Southwark workshop. This was made in 1579 for the Roper family. On it gilded and painted Mannerist strapwork, hung with fruit clusters, encloses a cartouche of Orpheus playing to the wild beasts.

Unlike goldsmithing, sculpture, painting or potting, furniture-making was not a skill that attracted alien immigrants. Only thirty-odd are recorded in London between 1511 and 1550. Even in 1593 only a handful of aliens, joiners, turners and carpenters were identifiably associated with supplying furniture. As the major expense and impact came from the upholstery and trimmings, this is perhaps not surprising, although panels of inlay appear on English-made chests and even on the Great Bed of Ware (*c.* 1590) which otherwise is richly carved and painted. Their design was taken from imported pattern books such as those by Hans Vredeman de Vries.

In the full and detailed inventory of a wealthy Exeter merchant, William Chappell, in 1580, the contents of the well-furnished and fashionable first-floor chamber in his town house were worth well over £100, of which the furniture represented less than ten per cent in value (two bedsteads, a cupboard, a table, four stools and various chests and boxes). The hangings alone, of 'Painted Canvas of the Storie of Joseph, and Courtaines of redd and grene saie before the windowe' and the two sets of bed-hangings of red and green with a fringe and blue and yellow taffeta sarcenet with a silk fringe were worth far more. His set of gilt crewelwork chair and stool with silk fringes, and the wroughtwork cupboard cloths, damask towels and blackwork drinking cloths, plus the six yards of wroughtwork fringe to set about a cupboard, added up to an extremely richly-textured interior, in which most of the richness and almost all the value lay in the imported textiles.

Dress and clothing

William Chappell's clothing was also worth a considerable sum, £37; the most significant and most valuable items were his six fur- or satin-trimmed or faced gowns and six cassocks or undergarments of damask. These included his scarlet aldermanic gown, 'faced with Ffoynes and furred with Squirrels', and its cloak and velvet tippet or hood. Livery gowns were the standard wear for men below the noble class. Their colour was often dictated by member-ship of a particular organisation, and the livery companies of London, for example, periodically changed the colour of their livery gowns and hoods, issuing livery men with a new set at considerable expense.

The Crown tried repeatedly from the 1460s until the 1590s to enforce sumptuary laws which would serve the dual purpose of maintaining social distinctions, distinguishing the aristocracy (exempted from the regulations) from the lower orders and protecting native industries against violent swings in fashion. These were perceived to be a peculiarly English problem, 'The monstrous abuse of apparel almost in all estates but principally in the meaner sort' which was referred to in the 1562 proclamation against 'the abuses in hose and the wearing of swords and rapiers'. There was, of course, also an element of public order in the wish to restrict the wearing of swords to the gentry and above.

Apparel denoted status, a principle exploited by the well-dressed rogues and swindlers who haunted St Paul's Churchyard and attracted their victims by the magnificence of their dress, purporting to be gentlemen, 'they are dressed in silk, gold and jewels with three or four servants in gay liveries', as

Satin cloak, leather hat and gloves embroidered with silk (late sixteenth century).

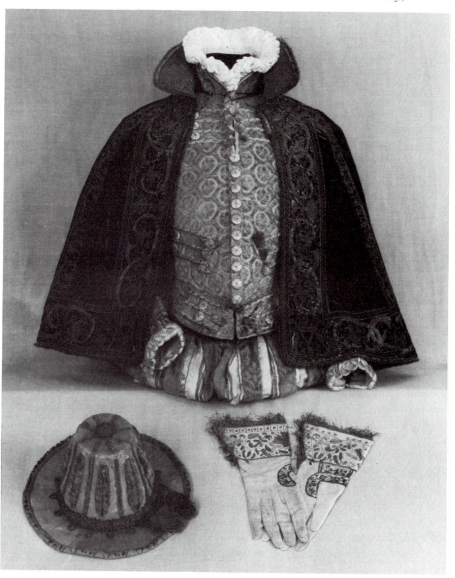

the *Manifest Deception of Dice-Play* (c. 1552) describes them. The Act of 1533, which listed a series of provisions for both laymen and priests, designated twelve classes of society; yeomen and above for instance could wear silk, a generous privilege which from their inventories they clearly exploited, although this was withdrawn in 1555, when the wearing of silk was restricted to the heirs of knights or men who could spend £20 a year.

A description of the apparel of the mayors, aldermen, sheriffs, bailiffs and their wives in Southampton in 1576 demonstrates the elaboration, cost and attention to detail considered important at the time. The mayor and aldermen in the winter wore scarlet fur-trimmed gowns and velvet jackets and doublets, the latter with silver buttons, while their wives wore scarlet gowns also trimmed with fur and considerable quantities of goldsmiths' work, 'partlettes for there neckes or velvet with buttens of gold enamyled', plus silver-gilt 'harnes gerdelles' which were set with stones and pearls and enamel, plus a neck chain of gold, bracelets and rings. The requirements for sheriffs and bailiffs and their wives were equally specific and only slightly less grand.

Dress fabrics were expensive, at least the fashionable and luxurious fine wools, linens, satin, damask, velvet or silk, and there was a thriving secondhand market in luxury items of clothing. Some passed by will; fur-trimmed livery gowns frequently occur in merchants' inventories; others were gifts to body servants, a customary perquisite. Others were stolen; the Assize records for the Home Counties, especially Middlesex which impinged so closely on the Metropolis, are full of references to thefts from closets, bedchambers and washing lines. Goldsmiths were prepared to buy gold or silver lace and other trimmings by weight to recover the precious metal.

The luxurious clothing just discussed was not accessible to the bulk of the population, who wore coarse linen, canvas or wool. One new area in which English workers were to dominate Northern European textile production by the end of the century was knitting. At the beginning of the period knitting was a peasant craft, whose products were coarse, largely practised for family use only, although knitted caps, socks and vests found in Moorfields outside the walls of London and the inclusion of knitted articles as a commonplace in a statute of 1488 indicate that there was a domestic market. Citizens wore flat woollen caps, sometimes with earflaps and coloured linings or decorative pinking, headgear so evocative of their social origins that they became a cliché to Jacobean playwrights such as Dekker; the City of London recapitulated the regulations on apprentice-dress in 1582, emphasising the woollen cap as virtually the uniform of urban youth.

By 1600 woollen stockings knitted by the English were finding a ready sale in France, Holland and Flanders. The knitters of Norwich even exported stockings to Rouen, a major knitting centre itself. Some were of fine wool, others of cotton and there were even knitted silk stockings to rival those formerly imported from Spain and Naples. William Lee's invention of the knitting frame is one of Elizabethan England's technical achievements. He had close links with the Huguenot silkweavers in London after 1589; there were over 250 strangers engaged in weaving, plus another fifty or more in associated trades.

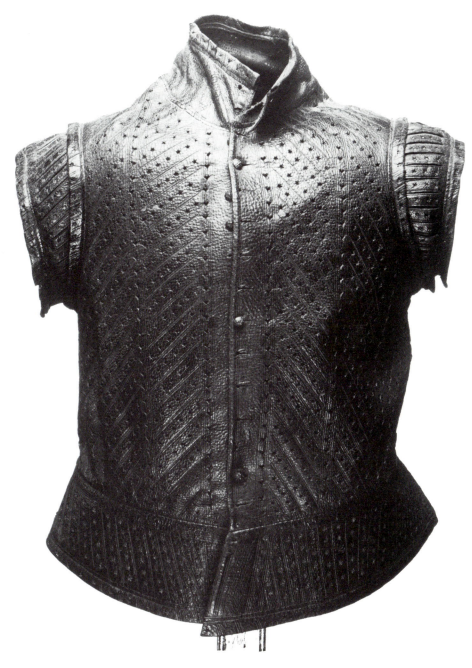

Boy's leather jerkin with 'pinked' ornament (late sixteenth century).

Knitted stockings constituted a completely new fashion; the late medieval nether garment had consisted of cloth hose, cut on the cross and seamed, which were held up by cross gartering or laced, or sewn all in one with the breeches. By the accession of Elizabeth, the breeches had become a garment in their own right, often slashed or pinked with fabric of another colour, and the nether hose or stockings were also treated decoratively, perhaps dyed a bright colour or knitted with decorative clocks, even incorporating silver or gold wire. When Mary Queen of Scots went to her execution, she wore not one, but two pairs of stockings, the outer of blue worsted embroidered with silver silk and then next to the skin a fine, white jersey pair. Phillip Stubbes inevitably railed against this new fashion

to such imprudent insolvency and shameful outrage it is now grown, that every almost will not stick to have two or three pairs of these silk nether stocks though the price of them be 20 shillings or more as commonly it is.

Judging from the Elizabethan books of rates, stockings were still a considerable luxury. In 1584 a pair was still a fitting present for the Queen at New Year, and pairs of silk stockings associated with her are preserved at Hatfield and Lanhydrock, Cornwall.

Part III
Appendix: Further Reading and Reference

MICHAEL LESLIE

Contents

Abbreviations

BM   *Burlington Magazine*
JWCI   *Journal of the Warburg and*
        Courtauld Institutes
NY   *New York*
WS   *Walpole Society*

Introduction

This reading list aims to provide an introduction to the bibliography of arts covered in this volume. Some sections, such as that on Literature and Drama, are longer than others, such as Crafts and Decorative Arts; this does not imply a value judgement but merely reflects the availability of secondary material. For reasons of space, the list avoids citing articles in periodicals where possible.

Many of the books listed illuminate aspects of the art and culture of the sixteenth century besides those with which they are ostensibly concerned. Some are gathered in the first section, Cultural and Social Setting; but the reader is advised to use the bibliography as a whole, as well as referring to particular sections.

Under each main section heading, any general studies appear first, followed by other works, arranged under appropriate, alphabetically-ordered sub-headings.

In three sections, Literature and Drama (VI. 2), Music (VII. 2) and The Visual Arts (IX. 4) brief artist biographies and bibliographies are given after the list of general studies. In other arts, such as Architecture and Crafts and Decorative Arts, this pattern is inappropriate as the information does not exist, because in this period little emphasis was placed upon the individual artist. In sections with artist bibliographies, the general books are numbered; and important references to individual artists in general books are indicated by the combination of the number of the section and the number of the entry (e.g., VII. 57 = Music 57 Wulstan, D., *Tudor Music* (1985)).

The place of publication, unless otherwise indicated, is London.

I   Cultural and Social Setting

1   General history
Allen, J.W., *History of Political Thought in the Sixteenth Century* (1928; rev. ed, NY, 1957)

Appleby, A.B., *Famine in Tudor and Stuart England* (Liverpool, 1978)
Aydelotte, F., *Elizabethan Rogues and Vagabonds* (Oxford, 1913)
Bamborough, J.C., *The Little World of Man* (1952)
Battisti, E., *L'Antirinascimento. Con una appendice di manoscritti inediti* (Milan, 1962)
Beier, A.L., *Masterless Men: the Vagrancy Problem in Britain, 1560–1640* (1985)
The Problem of the Poor in Tudor and Early Stuart England (1983)
Beier, A.L. and Finlay, R., *The Making of the Metropolis: London 1500–1640* (1985)
Bernard, G.W., *The Power of the Early Tudor Nobility. A Study of the Fourth and Fifth Earls of Shrewsbury* (Brighton, 1985)
Bindoff, S.T., *Tudor England* (Harmondsworth, 1950)
Bindoff, S.T., Hurstfield, J. and Williams, C.H. (eds.), *Elizabethan Government and Society* (1961)
Black, J.B., *The Reign of Elizabeth, 1558–1603* [Oxford History of England, vol. VIII] (1956; 2nd edn, Oxford, 1959)
Bowden, P.J., *The Wool Trade in Tudor and Stuart England* (1962)
Burke, P., *The Renaissance Sense of the Past* (1969)
Byrne, M.St C., *Elizabethan Life in Town and Country* (1925; rev. edn, 1961)
Byrne, M.St C. (ed.), *The Lisle Letters*, 6 vols. (Chicago, 1981). One-volume abridgement, 1983.
Camden, C., *The Elizabethan Woman: a Panorama of English Womanhood 1540–1640* (1952)
Campbell, M.L., *The English Yeoman under Elizabeth and the Early Stuarts* (New Haven, Conn., 1942)
Caspari, F., *Humanism and the Social Order of Tudor England* (1954; reissued Chicago, 1968)
Clapham, J.H., *A Concise Economic History of Britain* (Cambridge, 1949)
Clark, G.N., *The Wealth of England, 1496–1760* (1946)
Clark, P., Smith, A.G.R. and Tyacke, N. (eds.), *The English Commonwealth 1547–1640* (Leicester, 1979)
Clark, P. and Slack P. (eds.), *Crisis and Order in English Towns, 1500–1700: Essays in Urban History* (1972)
Coleman, D.C., *The Economy of England, 1450–1750* (1977)
Industry in Tudor and Stuart England (1975)

Cowan, I.B. and Shaw, D. (eds.), *The Renaissance and Reformation in Scotland: Essays in Honour of Gordon Donaldson* (Edinburgh, 1983)

Davies, C.S.L., *Peace, Print and Protestantism, 1450–1558* (1977)

Dickens, A.G., *Thomas Cromwell and the English Reformation* (1959)

Dodd, A.H., *Life in Elizabethan England* (1961)

Donaldson, G., *All the Queen's men: Power and Politics in Mary Stewart's Scotland* (1983)

Scotland – James V to James VII (Edinburgh, 1965)

The Scottish Reformation (Cambridge, 1960)

Dowling, M., *Humanism in the Age of Henry VIII* (1986)

Dunham, W.H. and Pargellis, S.M. (eds.), *Complaint and Reform in England, 1436–1714. Fifty Writings of the Time on Politics, Religion, Society, Economics, Architecture, Science and Education* (NY, 1938)

Elton, G.R., *The New Cambridge Modern History II: the Reformation 1520–1559* (Cambridge, 1958)

England under the Tudors (1955; 2nd edn, 1974)

Reform and Reformation: England 1509–1558 (1977)

Elton, G.R. (ed.), *The Tudor Constitution: Documents and Commentary* (Cambridge, 1960)

Esler, A., *The Aspiring Mind of the Elizabethan Younger Generation* (Durham, NC, 1966)

Ferguson, A.B., *The Articulate Citizen and the English Renaissance* (Durham, NC, 1965)

Clio Unbound: Perception of the Social and Cultural Past in Renaissance England (Durham, NC, 1979)

The Indian Summer of English Chivalry: Studies in the Decline and Transformation of Chivalric Idealism (Durham, NC, 1960)

Fletcher, A.J., *Tudor Rebellions* (1973; 3rd edn, 1983)

Fletcher, A.J. and Stevenson, J. (eds.), *Order and Disorder in Early Modern England* (Cambridge, 1985)

Greenleaf, W.H., *Order, Empiricism, and Politics: Two Traditions of English Political Thought* (1964)

Haigh, C. (ed.), *The Reign of Elizabeth I* [Problems in Focus series] (Basingstoke, 1984)

Hexter, J., *Reappraisals in History* (Evanton, 1961)

Hibbert, C., *The Grand Tour* (1987)

Hoskins, W.G., *The Age of Plunder: King Henry's England, 1500–1547* (1976)

Houlbrooke, A., *The English Family 1450–1700* (1984)

Howard, C., *English Travellers of the Renaissance* (1914)

Hurstfield, J., *Freedom, Corruption and Government in Elizabethan England* (1973)

The Queen's Wards: Wardship and Marriage under Elizabeth I (1958)

Ives, E.W., *Anne Boleyn* (1986)

James, M.E., *Change and Continuity in the Tudor North. The Rise of Thomas, first Lord Wharton* (York, 1965)

Jardine, L., *Still Harping on Daughters: Women and Drama in the Age of Shakespeare* (Brighton, 1983)

Jones, W.R.D., *The Tudor Commonwealth 1529–1559: a Study of the Impact of the Social and Economic Developments of mid-Tudor England upon Contemporary Concepts of the Nature and Duties of the Commonwealth* (1970)

Jordan, W.K., *Philanthropy in England 1480–1660: a Study of the Changing Patterns of English Social Aspirations* (1959)

Joseph, B.L., *Shakespeare's Eden: the Commonwealth of England 1558–1629* (1971)

Judges, A.V., *The Elizabethan Underworld: a Collection of Tudor and early Stuart Tracts and Ballads telling of the Lives and Misdoings of Vagabonds, Thieves, Rogues, and Cozeners, and giving some Account of the Criminal Law* (1930)

Kantorowicz, E.H., *The King's two bodies: a Study in Medieval Political Theory* (Princeton, 1957)

Kinney, A.F. (ed.), *Elizabethan Backgrounds: Historical Documents of the Age of Elizabeth I* (Hamden, Conn., 1975)

Lee, S. and Onions, C.T. (eds.), *Shakespeare's England: an Account of the Life and Manners of his Age*, 2 vols. (Oxford, 1917)

Lipson, E., *Economic History of England. Vols. II – III: the Age of Mercantilism* (1931; 3rd edn, 1943)

Lockyer, R., *Tudor and Stuart Britain 1471–1714* (1964)

MacCaffrey, W.T., *Queen Elizabeth and the Making of Policy 1572–1588* (Princeton, 1981)

The Shaping of the Elizabethan Regime (Princeton, 1968)

McConica, J.K., *English Humanists and Reformation Politics under Henry VIII and Edward VI* (Oxford, 1965)

Macfarlane, A., *Witchcraft in Tudor and Stuart England: a Regional and Comparative Study* (1970)

McLaren, A., *Reproductive Rituals: Perceptions of Fertility in England from the Sixteenth Century to the Nineteenth Century* (1984)

McRoberts, D. (ed.), *Essays on the Scottish Reformation* (Glasgow, 1962)

Marshall, R., *Queen of Scots* (Edinburgh, 1986)

Moody, T.W., Martin, F.X. and Byrne, F.J. (eds.), *A New History of Ireland. Vol. III: 1534–1691* (Oxford, 1976)

Morris, C., *Political Thought in England. Tyndale to Hooker* (1953)

Neale, J.E., *Queen Elizabeth* (1934)

Neale, J.E., *The Elizabethan House of Commons* (1949)

Elizabeth I and her Parliaments, 2 vols. (1953–7)

Queen Elizabeth (1934)

Nichols, J., *Progresses and Public Processions of Elizabeth I*, 3 vols. (1788–1805; 1823)

Palliser, D.M., *The Age of Elizabeth: England under the Later Tudors, 1547–1603* (1983)

Pinchbeck, I. and Hewitt, M., *Children in English Society. Vol. I: from Tudor Times to the Eighteenth Century* (1969)

Platt, C., *Medieval England. A Social History and Archaeology from the Conquest to AD 1600* (1978)

Pound, J.F., *Poverty and Vagrancy in Tudor England* (Harlow, 1971)

Prior, M. (ed.), *Women in English Society 1500–1800* (1985)

Quinn, D.B., *England and the Discovery of America 1481–1620* (1974)

Raleigh and the British Empire (1947)

Quinones, R., *The Renaissance Discovery of Time* (Cambridge, Mass., 1972)

Raab, F., *The English Face of Machiavelli: a Changing Interpretation, 1500–1700* (1964)

Ramsey, P., *Tudor Economic Problems* (1963)

Ramsey, P. (ed.), *The Price Revolution in Sixteenth-Century England* (1971)

Read, C., *Lord Burghley and Queen Elizabeth* (1960)

Mr Secretary Cecil and Queen Elizabeth (1955)

Mr Secretary Walsingham and the Policy of Queen Elizabeth, 3 vols. (Oxford, 1925)

Rosenberg, E., *Leicester: Patron of Letters* (NY, 1955)

Rowse, A.L., *The England of Elizabeth: the Structure of Society* (1950)

Russell, C., *The Crisis of Parliaments: English History 1509–1660* (1971)

Salgado, G., *The Elizabethan Underworld* (1977)

Salgado, G. (ed.), *Cony Catchers and Bawdy Baskets: an Anthology of Elizabethan Lowlife* (Harmondsworth, 1972)

Sharpe, J.A., *Crime in Early Modern England 1550–1750* (1984)

Siebert, F.S., *Freedom of the Press in England, 1476–1776* (Urbana, 1952)

Skinner, Q., *Foundations of Modern Political Thought. Vol. I: The Renaissance; Vol. II: The Reformation* (Cambridge, 1978)

Smith, A.G.R., *The Emergence of a Nation State: the Commonwealth of England, 1529–1660* (1984)

The Government of Elizabethan England (1967)

Smith, A.H., *County and Court: Government and Politics in Norfolk 1558–1603* (Oxford, 1974)

Spufford, M., *Contrasting Communities: English Villagers in the Sixteenth and Seventeenth Centuries* (1974)

Starkey, D., *The Reign of Henry VIII: Personalities and Politics* (1985)

Stone, L., *The Causes of the English Revolution 1529–1642* (1972)

The Crisis of the Aristocracy, 1558–1641 (Oxford, 1965)

The Family, Sex and Marriage in England 1500–1800 (1977)

Stone, L. (ed.), *Social Change and Revolution in England, 1540–1640* (1965)

Talbert, E.W., *The Problem of Order. Elizabethan Political Commonplaces and an Example of Shakespeare's Art* (Chapel Hill, 1962)

Taylor, E.G.R., *Late Tudor and early Stuart Geography 1583–1650* (1934)

Tudor Geography 1485–1583 (1930)

Thomas, K., *Man and the Natural World: Changing Attitudes in England 1500–1800* (Harmondsworth, 1983).

Trevelyan, G.M., *English Social History* (NY, 1942)

Trevor-Roper, H., *Renaissance Essays* (1985)

Wernham W.B. (ed.), *New Cambridge Modern History. Vol. III: The Counter-Reformation and Price Revolution, 1559–1610* (Cambridge, 1968)

Williams, P., *The Tudor Regime* (Oxford, 1979)

Wilson, D., *Sweet Robin* (1981)

Wilson, *Entertainments for Elizabeth I* (Woodbridge, 1980)

Wormald, J., *Court, Kirk, and Community: Scotland, 1470–1625* (1981)

Wright, L.B., *Middle-class Culture in Elizabethan England* (Chapel Hill, 1935)

Wright, L.B., and Lamar, V.A., *Life and Letters in Tudor and Stuart England* (Ithaca, 1962)

Wrightson, K., *English Society, 1580–1680* (1982)

Yates, F.A., *Astraea: the Imperial Theme in the Sixteenth Century* (1975)

Youings, J., *Sixteenth-Century England* (1984)

2 Bibliographies

Elton, G.R., *Modern Historians on British History, 1485–1945: a Critical Bibliography 1945–1969* (1970)

Levine, M. (ed.), *Tudor England, 1485–1603. A Bibliographical Handbook* (Cambridge, 1968)

Read, C. (ed.), *Bibliography of British History: Tudor Period, 1485–1603* (2nd edn, Oxford, 1959)

3 Culture

Allen, D.C., *The Star-Crossed Renaissance: the Quarrel about Astrology and its Influence in England* (Durham, NC, 1941)

The Legend of Noah: Renaissance Rationalism in Art, Science and Letters (Urbana, 1949)

Anglo, S., *Spectacle. Pageantry and Early Tudor Policy* (Oxford, 1969)

Babb, L., *The Elizabethan Malady: a Study of Melancholia in English Literature from 1580–1642* (East Lansing, 1951)

Baker, H., *The Dignity of Man: a Study of the Idea of Human Dignity in Classical Antiquity, the Middle Ages, and the Renaissance* (Cambridge, Mass., 1947; repr. as *The Image of Man*, 1961)

Burke, P., *Popular Culture in Early Modern Europe* (1973)

Bush, D., *The Renaissance and English Humanism* (Toronto, 1939)

Buxton, J., *Elizabethan Taste* (1963)

Sir Philip Sidney and the English Renaissance (1954)

Castiglione, B., *The Book of the Courtier*, tr. Sir Thomas Hoby (1928; repr. with an introduction by J. H. Whitfield, 1974)

Dunlop, I.G.D., *Palaces and Progresses of Elizabeth I* (1962)

Einstein, L., *The Italian Renaissance in England* (NY, 1902)

Elyot, Sir Thomas, *The Book of the Governor* (1962)

Gombrich, E.H., *Symbolic Images: Studies in the Art of the Renaissance* (Oxford, 1972)

Impey, O. and MacGregor, A. (eds.), *The Origin of Museums: the Cabinet of Curiosities in Sixteenth- and Seventeenth-Century Europe* (Oxford, 1985)

Kendrick, T., *British Antiquity* (1950)

Kipling, G., *The Triumph of Honour: Burgundian Origins of the English Renaissance* (The Hague, 1977)

Klibansky, R., Panofsky, E. and Saxl, F., *Saturn and Melancholy: Studies in the History of Natural Philosophy, Religion, and Art* (1964)

Sypher, W., *Four Stages of Renaissance Style: Transformations in Art and Literature 1400–1700* (1955)

Taylor, E.W., *Nature and Art in Renaissance Literature* (NY, 1964)

4 Education and literacy

Arber, E. (ed.), *A Transcript of the Registers of the Company of Stationers of London, 1554–1640* (1875–94)

Baldwin, T.W., *Shakespeare's 'Small Latine and Lesse Greeke'*, 2 vols. (Urbana, 1944)

Bennett, H.S., *English Books and Readers 1475–1557, from Caxton to the Incorporation of the Stationers' Company* (1965; 2nd edn, Cambridge, 1966)

English Books and Readers 1558–1603, Being a Study in the History of the Book Trade in the Reign of Elizabeth I (1952)

Blagden, C., *The Stationers' Company: a History, 1403–1959* (1960)

Bolgar, R.R., *The Classical Heritage and its Beneficiaries* (Cambridge, 1954)

Charlton, K., *Education in Renaissance England* (1965)

Cressy, D., *Literacy and the Social Order: Reading and Writing in Tudor and Stuart England* (Cambridge, 1980)

Cressy, D. (ed.), *Education in Tudor and Stuart England* (1975)

Curtis, M., *Oxford and Cambridge in Transition, 1558–1642: an Essay on Changing Relationships Between the English Universities and English Society* (Oxford, 1959)

Eisenstein, E.L., *The Printing Press as an Instrument of Change*, 2 vols. (Cambridge, 1979; single-volume paperback edn, 1980)

Grafton, A. and Jardine, L., *From Humanism to the Humanities: Education and the Liberal Arts in Fifteenth and Sixteenth-Century Europe* (1987)

Greg, W.W. and Boswell, E. (eds.), *Records of the Court of the Stationers' Company, 1576–1602 – from Register B* (1930)

Jayne, S., *Library Catalogues of the English Renaissance* (Berkeley, 1956)

Kearney, H.F., *Scholars and Gentlemen: Universities and Society in Pre-Industrial Britain 1500–1700* (1970)

McConica, J.K. (ed.), *The Collegiate University*, vol. III of *The History of the University of Oxford*, ed. T. H. Aston (Oxford, 1986)

O'Day, R., *Education and Society 1500–1800: the Social Foundations of Education in Early Modern Britain* (1982)

Prest, W.R., *The Inns of Court under Elizabeth I and the Early Stuarts* (1972)

Simon, J., *Education and Society in Tudor England* (Cambridge, 1966)

Spufford, M., *Small Books and Pleasant Histories: Popular Fiction and its Readership in Seventeenth-Century England* (1981)

Thomas, K., *Rule and Misrule in the Schools of Early Modern England* (Reading, 1976)

Watson, F., *The English Grammar Schools to 1660: their Curriculum and Practice* (Cambridge, 1908)

Woodward, W.H., *Studies in Education during the Age of the Renaissance, 1400–1600* (Cambridge, 1906; repr. 1967)

Wormald, F. and Wright, C.E. (eds.), *The English Library before 1700: Studies in its History* (1958)

5   *Emblems, imprese, and art/literature relations*

Clements R.J., *Picta Poesis: Literary and Humanistic Theory in Renaissance Emblem Books* (Rome, 1960)

Daly, P.M., *Literature in the Light of the Emblem: Structural Parallels Between the Emblem and Literature in the Sixteenth and Seventeenth Centuries* (Toronto, 1979)

Farmer, N.K., *Poets and the Visual Arts in Renaissance England* (Austin, 1984)

Gent, L., *Picture and Poetry 1560–1620: Relations between Literature and the Visual Arts in the English Renaissance* (Lemington Spa, 1981)

Hagstrum, J.H., *The Sister Arts: the Tradition of Literary Pictorialism and English Poetry from Dryden to Gray* (Chicago, 1958)

Yates, F., *Astraea: the Imperial Theme in the Sixteenth Century* (1975)

Young, A., *Tudor and Jacobean Tournaments* (1987)

See IX. 43, 56, 67

6   *Philosophy and history*

Allen, D.C., *Doubt's Boundless Sea, Skepticism and Faith in the Renaissance* (Baltimore, 1964)

Cassirer, E., *The Individual and the Cosmos in Renaissance Philosophy*, tr. M. Domandi (Oxford, 1963)

The Platonic Renaissance in England, tr. J. P. Pettegrove (1953)

Cassirer, E. *et al.* (eds.), *The Renaissance Philosophy of Man* (Chicago, 1948)

Craig, H., *The Enchanted Glass: the Elizabethan Mind in Literature* (NY, 1936)

Davies, S. (ed.), *Renaissance Views of Man* (Manchester, 1978)

Ellrodt, R., *Neoplatonism in the Poetry of Spenser* (Geneva, 1960)

Fox, L. (ed.), *English Historical Scholarship in the Sixteenth and Seventeenth Centuries* (1956)

Fussner, F.S., *The Historical Revolution: English Historical Writing and Thought, 1580–1640* (1962)

Tudor History and the Historians (NY, 1970)

Haydn, H., *The Counter-Renaissance* (NY, 1950)

Huizinga, J., *The Waning of the Middle Ages*, tr. F. Hopman (1924; Harmondsworth, 1979)

Levy, F.J., *Tudor Historical Thought* (San Marino, Cal., 1967)

Lewis, C.S., *The Discarded Image: an Introduction to Medieval and Renaissance Literature* (Cambridge, 1964)

Lovejoy, A.O., *The Great Chain of Being: a Study of the History of an Idea* (1936; 2nd edn, Cambridge, Mass., 1964)

McKisack, M., *Medieval History in the Tudor Age* (Oxford, 1971)

Ong, W., *Ramus: Method and the Decay of Dialogue from the Art of Discourse to the Art of Reason* (Cambridge, Mass., 1958)

Rivers, I., *Classical and Christian Ideas in English Renaissance Poetry: a Students' Guide* (1979)

Yates, F.A., *Giordano Bruno and the Hermetic Tradition* (1964)

The Occult Philosophy in the Elizabethan Age (1979)

7 Religion

Anglo, S. (ed.), *The Damned Art. Essays in the Literature of Witchcraft* (1977)

Blench, J.W., *Preaching in England in the Late Fifteenth and Sixteenth Century: a Study of English Sermons, 1450–1600* (Oxford, 1964)

Bossy, J., *The English Catholic Community, 1570–1850* (1975)

Bruce, F.F., *The English Bible: a History of Translations from the Earliest English Version to the New English Bible* (1961; 2nd edn, 1970)

Cambridge History of the Bible, vol. II, ed. G. W. H. Lampe (Cambridge, 1969); vol. III, ed. S. L. Greenslade (Cambridge, 1963)

Chandos, J. [McConnell, J.L.C.] (ed.), *In God's Name. Examples of Preaching in England from the Act of Supremacy to the Act of Uniformity, 1534–1662* (1971)

Collinson, P., *The Elizabethan Puritan Movement* (1967)

The Religion of Protestants: the Church in English Society, 1559–1625 (Oxford, 1982)

Coolidge, J.S., *The Pauline Renaissance in England. English Puritanism and the Bible* (Oxford, 1970)

Cross, C., *Church and People 1450–1660: the Triumph of the Laity in the English Church* (Hassocks, 1976)

Dickens, A.G., *The English Reformation* (1964)

Dures, A., *English Catholicism 1558–1642: Continuity and Change* (1983)

Firth, K.R., *The Apocalyptic Tradition in Reformation Britain, 1530–1645* (Oxford, 1979)

George, C.H. and K., *The Protestant Mind of the English Reformation, 1570–1640* (Princeton, 1961)

Haller, W., *Foxe's 'Book of Martyres' and the Elect Nation* (1963)

The Rise of Puritanism: or, the Way to the New Jerusalem as Set Forth in Pulpit and Press from Thomas Cartwright to John Lilburne and John Milton, 1570–1643 (NY, 1938)

Haugaard, W.P., *Elizabeth and the English Reformation: the Struggle for a Stable Settlement of Religion* (Cambridge, 1968)

Heal, F., *Of Prelates and Princes. A Study of the Economic and Social Position of the Tudor Episcopate* (Cambridge, 1980)

Heal, F. and O'Day, R. (eds.), *Church and Society in England: Henry VIII to James I* (1977)

Continuity and Change: Personnel and Administration of the Church of England, 1500–1642 (Leicester, 1976)

Holden, W.P., *Anti-Puritan Satire, 1572–1642* (New Haven, 1954)

Hughes, P., *The Reformation in England*, 2 vols. (1950; 5th edn, 1963)

Knappen, M.M., *Tudor Puritanism: a Chapter in the History of Idealism* (Chicago, 1939)

Knowles, D., *The Religious Orders in England. III. The Tudor Age* (1959; 2nd edn, Cambridge, 1979)

Morgan, I., *The Godly Preachers of the Elizabethan Church* (1965)

O'Day, R., *The Debate on the English Reformation* (1986)

The English Clergy: the Emergence and Consolidation of a Profession, 1558–1642 (Leicester, 1979)

Partridge, A.C., *English Biblical Translation* (1973)

Pearson, A.F.S., *Church and State: Political Aspects of Sixteenth-century Puritanism* (Cambridge, 1928)

Phillips, J., *The Reformation of Images: Destruction of Art in England 1535–1660* (Berkeley, 1973)

Roberts, J.R. (ed.), *A Critical Anthology of English Recusant Devotional Prose, 1558–1603* (Pittsburgh, 1966)

Scarisbrick, J.J., *The Reformation and the English People* (Oxford, 1984)

Southern, A.C., *Elizabethan Recusant Prose, 1559–1582: a Historical and Critical Account of the Books of the Catholic Refugees Printed and Published Abroad and at Secret Presses in England, with a Bibliography of the Same* (1950)

Thomas, K., *Religion and the Decline of Magic: Studies in Popular Beliefs in Sixteenth- and Seventeenth-century England* (1971)

Walker, D.P., *The Decline of Hell. Seventeenth-century Discussions of Eternal Torment* (1964)

Walzer, M.L., *The Revolution of the Saints. A Study in the Origins of Radical Politics* (1966)

Watkins, O.C., *The Puritan Experience* (1972)

8 Rhetoric

Howell, W.S., *Logic and Rhetoric in England, 1500–1700* (Princeton, 1956)

Kennedy, G.A., *Classical Rhetoric and its Christian and Secular Tradition from Ancient to Modern Times* (Chapel Hill, NC, 1980)

Lanham, R.A., *A Handlist of Rhetorical Terms. A Guide for Students of English Literature* (Berkeley, 1968)
The Motives of Eloquence: Literary Rhetoric in the Renaissance (New Haven, Conn., 1976)
Murphy, J.J., *Renaissance Eloquence: Studies in the Theory and Practice of Renaissance Rhetoric* (Berkeley, 1983)
Sonnino, L.A., *A Handbook to Sixteenth-century Rhetoric* (1968)
Vickers, B.W., *Classical Rhetoric in English Poetry* (1970)

9 Science

Butterfield, H., *The Origins of Modern Science 1300–1800* (1951; 2nd edn., 1957)
Copeman, W.S.C., *Doctors and Disease in Tudor Times* (1960)
Debus, A.G., *The Chemical Philosophy: Paracelsian Science and Medicine in the Sixteenth and Seventeenth Centuries*, 2 vols. (NY, 1977)
Man and Nature in the Renaissance (Cambridge, 1978)
French, P.J., *John Dee: the World of an Elizabethan Magus* (1972)
Garrison, F.J., *An Introduction to the History of Medicine* (1913; 4th edn, 1929)
Hall, M.B. [Boas, M.], *The Scientific Renaissance 1450–1630* (1962)
Heninger, S.K., Jr, *The Cosmographical Glass: Renaissance Diagrams of the Universe* (San Marino, Cal., 1977)
A Handbook of Renaissance Meteorology, with Particular Reference to Elizabethan and Jacobean Literature (Durham, NC, 1960)
Touches of Sweet Harmony: Pythagorean Cosmology and Renaissance Poetics (San Marino, Ca., 1974)
Hill, C., *Intellectual Origins of the English Revolution* (Oxford, 1965)
Johnson, F.R., *Astronomical Thought in Renaissance England: a Study of the English Scientific Writings from 1500 to 1645* (Baltimore, 1937)
Kocher, P.H., *Science and Religion in Elizabethan England* (San Marino, Ca., 1953)
Maclean, I., *The Renaissance Notion of Women. A Study in the Fortunes of Scholasticism and Medical Science in European Intellectual Life* (Cambridge, 1980)
Nicolson, M., *Science and Imagination* (Ithaca, 1956)
Shumaker, W. and Heilbron, J.L. (eds.), *John Dee on Astronomy: 'Propaedeumata aphoristica' (1558 and 1568). Latin and English* (Berkeley, 1978)
Shumaker, W., *The Occult Sciences in the Renaissance: a Study in Intellectual Patterns* (Berkeley, 1972)
Smith, A.G.R., *Science and Society in the Sixteenth and Seventeenth Centuries* (1972)
Taylor, E.G.R., *The Mathematical Practitioners of Tudor and Stuart England* (Cambridge, 1954)
Wightman, W.P.D., *Science and the Renaissance: the Emergence of the Sciences in the Sixteenth Century*, 2 vols. (Edinburgh, 1962)

II Architecture

Airs, M., *The Buildings of Britain: Tudor and Jacobean. A Guide and Gazetteer* (1982)
The Making of the English Country House, 1500–1640 (1975)
Allsopp, B., *A History of Renaissance Architecture* (1959)
Barley, M.W., 'Rural housing in England, 1500–1640'. *The Agrarian History of England and Wales* (gen. ed. H. P. R. Finberg) vol. IV, 1500–1640, ed. J. Thirsk (Cambridge, 1967), chap. 10, pp. 696–766
Blomfield, R., *A Short History of Renaissance Architecture in England, 1500–1800* (1900)
Brunskill, R., *Traditional Buildings of Britain* (1981)
Brunskill, R. and Clifton-Taylor, A., *English Brickwork* (1977)
Castle, S.E., *Domestic Gothic of the Tudor Period* (NY, 1927)
Clifton-Taylor, A., *English Stone Building* (1983)
The Pattern of English Building (1962; 2nd edn, 1972)
Colvin, H.M. (ed.), *The History of the King's Works*, vol. III, *1485–1660* Part 1 (1975); vol. IV, *1485–1660* Part 2 (1982)
Cook, O., *The English House through Seven Centuries* (1968)
Dugdale, G.S., *Whitehall Through the Ages* (1950)
Dutton, R., *The English Interior 1500–1900* (1948)
Field, H. and Bunney, M., *English Domestic Architecture of the Sixteenth and Seventeenth Centuries* (1905; rev. 1928)
Garner, T. and Stratton, A., *The Domestic*

Architecture of England during the Tudor Period, 2 vols. (1908–11; 2nd edn 1929)

Girouard, M., 'Elizabethan architecture and the Gothic tradition', *Architectural History*, VI (1963), 23–40
Robert Smythson and the Architecture of the Elizabethan Era (1966; 2nd edn published as *Robert Smythson and the Elizabethan Country House* (New Haven, 1983))
Life in the English Country House (New Haven, 1978)

Gloag, J., *The English Tradition in Architecture* (1963)

Gotch, J.A., *Architecture of the Renaissance in England* (1894)
Early Renaissance Architecture in England (1901; 2nd edn 1914)

Gravett, K.W.E., 'Smaller houses under the Tudors – a period of transition', *Proceedings of the Royal Institute of Great Britain* **43** (1969) 161–9

Hall, R. de Z. (ed.), *A Bibliography on Vernacular Architecture* (Newton Abbot, 1972)

Harvey, J., *English Medieval Architects: a Biographical Dictionary down to 1550* (2nd edn, Gloucester, 1984)
The Perpendicular Style (1978)

Hoskins, W.G., 'The rebuilding of rural England, 1570–1640', *Past and Present* **4** (1953), 44–89

Howard, M., *The Early Tudor Country House: Architecture and Politics 1490–1550* (1987)

Jourdain, M., *English Decoration and Furniture of the Early Renaissance* (1924)
English Decorative Plasterwork of the Renaissance (1926)
English Interior Decoration 1500–1830 (1950)

Kidson, P., Murray, P. and Thompson, P., *A History of English Architecture* (Harmondsworth, 1965)

Knoop, D. and Jones, G.P., *The Sixteenth-Century Mason* (1937)

Lees-Milne, J., *Tudor Renaissance* (1951)

Lloyd, N., *A History of English Brickwork* (1925; 2nd edn 1935)
A History of the English House (2nd edn, 1949)

Mercer, E., *English Art 1553–1625* (Oxford, 1962), *Oxford History of English Art*, vol. VII
English Vernacular Houses (1975)

Michelmore, D.J.H. (ed.), *A Current Bibliography of Vernacular Architecture 1970–1976* (York, 1979)

Papworth, *The Renaissance and Italian Styles of Architecture in Great Britain* (1883)

Pevsner, N., *et al*, *The Buildings of Britain* (Harmondsworth, 1951–74)
The Planning of the Elizabethan Country House (1960)

Richardson, C.J., *Observations on the Architecture . . . of Queen Elizabeth and James I* (1837)

Salzman, L.F., *Building in England down to 1540: a Documentary History* (1952; rev. 1967)

Shaw, H., *Details of Elizabethan Architecture* (1839)

Small, T. and Woodbridge, C., *English Brickwork Details, 1450–1750* (1931)
Mouldings of the Tudor Period (1931)

Smith, J.T., 'The evolution of the English peasant house to the late seventeenth century: the evidence of buildings', *Journal of the British Archaeological Association* **33** (1970) 122–47

Stratton, A., *The English Interior* (1920)

Summerson, J., *Architecture in Britain 1530–1830* (Harmondsworth, 1953) [Pelican History of Art]

Tipping, H.A., *English Homes. Period III (Late Tudor and Early Stuart)* 2 vols. (1927, 1929)

Turner, T.H. and Parker, J.H., *Some Accounts of the Domestic Architecture in England*, 3 vols. (1851–9) vol. III

Watkin, D., *English Architecture: a Concise History* (1979)

Wayne, D.E., *Penshurst: the Semiotics of Place and the Poetics of History* (1984)

Webb, G., *Architecture in Britain: the Middle Ages* (Harmondsworth, 1956) [Pelican History of Art]

Whiffen, M., *Introduction to Elizabethan and Jacobean Architecture* (1952)

Wight, J.A., *Brick Building in England, from the Middle Ages to 1550* (1972)

Williams, N., *The Royal Residences of Great Britain* (1960)

Wusten, E., *Die Architektur des Manierismus in England* (Leipzig, 1951)

SCOTLAND

Cruden, S., *The Scottish Castle* (Edinburgh, 1960)

Dunbar, J.G., *The Historic Architecture of Scotland* (1966; 2nd edn 1978)

Hay, G., *Architecture in Scotland* (1969; rev. 1977)
The Architecture of Scottish Post-Reformation Churches, 1560–1843 (Oxford, 1957)

MacGibbon, D. and Ross, T., *Castellated and Domestic Architecture of Scotland*, 5 vols. (Edinburgh, 1887–92)

McWilliam, C., *et al*, *The Buildings of Scotland* (Harmondsworth, 1978–)
West, T.W., *A History of Architecture in Scotland* (1967)

WALES

Haslam, R., *et al*, *The Buildings of Wales* (Harmondsworth, 1979–)
Hilling, J.B., *The Historic Architecture of Wales* (Cardiff, 1976)
Smith, P., 'Rural housing in Wales', *The Agrarian History of England and Wales* (gen. ed. H. P. R. Finberg) vol. IV, 1500–1640, ed. J. Thirsk (Cambridge, 1967), chap. 11, 767–813
Smith, P., *Houses of the Welsh Countryside* (1975)

III Crafts and Decorative Arts

1 General and interior decoration

Beard, G., *Decorative Plasterwork in Great Britain* (1976)
Cook, O. and Smith, E., *English Cottages and Farmhouses* (1954)
  The English House through Seven Centuries (1968)
Jourdain, M., *English Decoration and Furniture of the Early Renaissance 1500–1650* (1924)
Wilson, M., *The English Country House and its Furnishings* (1977)
Yarwood, D., *The English Home* (1979)

2 Ceramics

Barton, K.J., *Pottery in England from 3500 BC to AD 1750* (Newton Abbot, 1975)
Brears, P.D., *Collector's Book of English Country Pottery* (Newton Abbot, 1974)
  The English Country Pottery: its History and Techniques (Newton Abbot, 1971)
Charleston, R.J. and Towner, D., *English Ceramics 1580–1830: a Commemorative Catalogue of Ceramics and Enamels to Celebrate the Fiftieth Anniversary of the English Ceramic Circle 1927–1977* (1977)
Cushion, J.P., *Tablewares* (1976)
Eames, E.S., *Medieval Tiles* (1968)
Godden, G.A., *An Illustrated Encyclopedia of British Pottery and Porcelain* (1966)
Honey, W.B., *English Pottery and Porcelain* (1933), 5th edn, rev. R. J. Charleston (1962)
  European Ceramic Art, vol. I: *An Illustrated Historical Survey*, rev. A. Lane (1963); vol. II: *A Dictionary of Factories, Artists and Technical Terms* (1952)

Jewitt, Ll., *The Ceramic Art of Great Britain* [1878], selected and ed. G. A. Godden (1972)
Lewis, G., *Collector's History of English Pottery* (1969)
Mankowitz, W. and Haggar, R.G., *The Concise Encyclopedia of English Pottery and Porcelain* (1957)
Rackham, B., *Medieval English Pottery*, rev. edn, J. G. Hurst (1972)
Rackham, B. and Read, H., *English Pottery. Its Development from Early Times to the End of the Eighteenth Century* (1924; repr. 1973)
Savage, G. and Newman, H., *An Illustrated Dictionary of Ceramics* (1974; rev. 1976)

3 Clocks

Beeson, C.F.C., *English Church Clocks, 1280–1850* (Chichester, 1971)
Dawson, P.G., Drover, C.B. and Parkes, D.W., *Early English Clocks: a Discussion of Clocks up to the Beginning of the Eighteenth Century* (Woodbridge, 1982)
Jagger, C., *Royal Clocks: the British Monarchy and its Time-Keepers, 1300–1900* (1983)
Loomes, B., *The Early Clockmakers of Great Britain* (1981)
Symonds, R.W., *Masterpieces of English Furniture and Clocks* (1940)

4 Furniture

Aronson, J., *Encyclopedia of Furniture* (1966)
Beard, G., *The National Trust Book of English Furniture* (1985)
Cercinsky, C., *English Furniture from Gothic to Sheraton* (NY, 1937)
Cercinsky, H. and Gribble, E.R., *Early English Furniture and Woodwork* (1922)
Chinnery, V., *Oak Furniture. The British Tradition* (1979)
Eames, P., *Medieval Furniture* (1977)
Edwards, R., *The Dictionary of English Furniture*, 3 vols. (rev. 1954)
  English Chairs (1970)
  The Shorter Dictionary of English Furniture (1964)
Fastnedge, R., *English Furniture Styles from 1550 to 1830* (Harmondsworth, 1955)
Gloag, J., *A Guide to Furniture Styles. English and French 1450–1850* (1972)
  A Short Dictionary of Furniture (1951; rev. 1969)
  A Social History of Furniture Design from BC 1300 to AD 1960 (1966)
  The Englishman's Chair (1964)

Jenning, C., *Early Chests in Wood and Iron* (1974)

Jervis, S.S., *Printed Furniture Designs before 1650* (1974)

Jourdain, M., *Decoration and Furniture of the Early Renaissance 1500–1650* (1924)

Joy, E.T., *Furniture: the Connoisseur Illustrated Guides* (1972)

Macquoid, P. and Edwards, R., *A Dictionary of English Furniture*, 3 vols. (1954)

Mercer, E., *Furniture, 700–1700* (1969)

Rogers, J.C., *English Furniture*, rev. M. Jourdain (1959)

Smith, H.C., *Catalogue of English Furniture and Woodwork in the Victoria and Albert Museum. Vol. I: Gothic and early Tudor* (1923)

Sparkes, I.G., *English Domestic Furniture, 1100–1837* (1980)

Symonds, R.W., *Masterpieces of English Furniture and Clocks* (1940)

Tomlin, M., *English Furniture: an Illustrated Handbook* (1972)

Wills, G., *English Furniture 1550–1760* (Enfield, 1971)

Wolsley, S.W. and Luff, R.W.P., *Furniture in England: the Age of the Joiner* (1968)

5 Glass

Ash, D., *A Dictionary of British Antique Glass* (1975)

Brady, D. and Serban, W., *Stained Glass: a Guide to Information Sources* (Detroit, 1980) [Art and Architecture Information Guide Series, vol. X]

Caviness, M.H., *Stained Glass before 1540: an Annotated Bibliography* (Boston, 1983)

Charleston, R.J., *English Glass: and the Glass used in England 400–1940* (1984)

Crompton S. (ed.), *English Glass* (1967)

Cunningham, W., *Alien Immigrants to England* (1969)

Engle, A., *Readings in Glass History 8* (Jerusalem, 1977) [On Elizabethan glassmaking]

Fleming, A., *Scottish and Jacobite Glass* (1977)

Godfrey, E.S., *The Development of English Glass Making, 1560–1640* (Oxford, 1975)

Honey, W.B., *English Glass* (1946)

Hughes, B., *English, Scottish, and Irish Table Glass from the Sixteenth Century to 1820* (1956)

Marson, P., *Glass and Glass Manufacture* (1918)

Newman, H., *An Illustrated Dictionary of Glass* (1977)

Powell, H.J., *Glassmaking in England* (Cambridge, 1923)

Read, H., *English Stained Glass* (1926)

Salzman, L.F., *Building in England down to 1540: a Documentary History* (1952; rev. 1967)

Thorpe, W.A., *English Glass* (3rd edn, 1961)
A History of English and Irish Glass (1929; 1969)

Truman, C., *An Introduction to English Glassware to 1900* (1984)

Westropp, M.S.D., *Irish Glass* (1921)

Winbolt, S.E., *Wealden Glass: the Surrey-Sussex Glass Industry, 1261–1615* (Hove, 1933)

Woodforde, C., *English Stained and Painted Glass* (1954)
Stained Glass in Somerset 1250–1830 (Oxford, 1946)

6 Jewellery

The Cheapside Hoard of Elizabethan and Jacobean Jewellery, London Museum Catalogues no. 2 (1928)

Clayton, M., *The Collector's Dictionary of the Silver and Gold of Great Britain and North America* (1971)

Evans, J., *English Jewellery from the 5th Century AD to 1800* (1921)
A History of Jewellery 1100–1870 (1953; 2nd edn, 1970)

Hackenbroch, Y., *Renaissance Jewellery* (1980)

Heiniger, E. and J., *The Great Book of Jewels* (Lausanne, 1974)

Newman, H., *An Illustrated Dictionary of Jewellery* (1981)

Oman, C.L., *British Rings 800–1914* (1974)
Victoria and Albert Museum. Catalogue of Rings (1974)

Princely Magnificence: Court Jewels of the Renaissance, 1500–1630, exhibition catalogue, Victoria and Albert Museum, 1980

Smith, H. C., *Jewellery* (1908)

Tait, H., *Jewellery through 7,000 Years* (1976)

7 Metalwork

ARMOUR

Aylward, J.D., *The Small Sword in England* (1960)

Blair, C., *European Armour Circa 1066 to Circa 1700* (1958)

Cripps-Day, F.H., *Fragmenta Armamentaria: an Introduction to the Study of Greenwich Armour*, I ii (1934); I iii (1944); I iv (1945)

Drummond, J. and Anderson, J., *Ancient Scottish Weapons* (1881)

Dufty, A.R., *European Armour in the Tower of London* (1968)

Hayward, J.F., 'The armoury of the first Earl of Pembroke', *Connoisseur* (1964)

Laking, Sir G.F., *A Record of European Armour and Arms through Seven Centuries*, 5 vols. (1920–2)

Mann, Sir J., *European Arms and Armour*, 2 vols. (1962) [Wallace Collection catalogue]
An Outline of Arms and Armour in England from the Early Middle Ages to the Civil War (1960; rev. A. R. Dufty, 1969)

Petersen, H.L., *Arms and Armour in Colonial America, 1562–1783* (Harrisburg, Penn., 1956)

BRASS (DOMESTIC)

Curle, A., *Domestic Candlesticks from the Fourteenth to the End of the Eighteenth Century* (Edinburgh, 1926)

Gentle, R. and Field, R., *English Domestic Brass 1680–1810 and the History of its Origins* (1975)

Michaelis, R.F., *Old Domestic Base-metal Candlesticks from the Thirteenth to the Nineteenth century* (1978)

BRASS (MONUMENTAL)

Giuseppi, M.S. and Green, R.A., *An Appendix to a List of Monumental Brasses in the British Isles by Mill Stephenson* (1938)

Le Strange, R., *A Complete Descriptive Guide to British Monumental Brasses* (1972)

Macklin, H.W., *The Brasses of England* (1907)

Norris, M., *Monumental Brasses*, 2 vols. (1978)

Stephenson, M., *A List of Monumental Brasses in the British Isles* (1926; repr. 1964)

CUTLERY

Hayward, J.F., *English Cutlery, Sixteenth to Eighteenth century* (1957)

Welch, C., *History of the Cutlers' Company of London and of the Minor Cutlery Crafts with biographical Notices of Early London Cutlers*, 2 vols. (1916 and 1923)

IRON

Campbell, M., *An Introduction to Ironwork* (1983)

Ffoulkes, C., *Decorative Ironwork from the Eleventh to the Eighteenth Century* (1913)

Gardner, J.S., *Ironwork* (1927; repr. 1978)
Ironwork in the Victoria and Albert Museum (1930)

Lindsay, J.S., *An Anatomy of English Wrought Iron* (1964)
Iron and Brass Implements of the English House (1964)

Schubert, H.R., *History of the British Iron and Steel Industry c. 450 BC – 1775 AD* (1957)

PEWTER

Hatcher, J. and Barker, T.C., *A History of British Pewter* (1974)

Homer, R.F., *Five Centuries of Base Metal Spoons* (1975)

Peal, C.A., *Pewter of Great Britain* (1983)

Wood, L.I., *Scottish Pewter-ware and Pewterers* (Edinburgh, 1905)

SILVER AND GOLD

Ash, D., *Dictionary of British Antique Silver* (1972)

Barrett, G.N., *Norwich Silver and its Marks 1565–1702* (Norwich, 1981)

Chadwick, O., *English Silver* (1976)

Challis, C.E., *The Tudor Coinage* (Manchester, 1978)

Collins, A.J., *Jewels and Plate of Queen Elizabeth I* (1955)

Glanville, P., *Silver in England* (1987)
Tudor and Stuart Silver. Catalogue of the National Collection in the Victoria and Albert Museum (1988)

Hayward, J.F., *Virtuoso Goldsmiths and the Triumph of Mannerism 1540–1620* (1976)

Heal, A., *The London Goldsmith 1200–1800* (1935)

Hernmarck, C., *The Art of the European Goldsmith 1430–1830*, 2 vols. (1977)

How, G.E.P. and J.P., *English and Scottish Silver Spoons*, 3 vols. vol. I (1952); vol. II (1953); vol. III (1957)

Jackson, C.J., *English Goldsmiths and their Marks* (1929; rev. I. Pickford, 1986)
An Illustrated History of English Plate, Ecclesiastical and Secular, 2 vols. (1911; repr., 1967)

Oman, C., *English Church Plate, 597–1830* (Oxford, 1957)
English Domestic Silver (5th edn, 1962)
English Engraved Silver 1150–1900 (1978)

Reddaway, T.F. and Walker, E.M., *Early History of the Goldsmiths' Company, 1327–1509* (1975)

Ridgeway, M.H., *Chester Goldsmiths from Early Times to 1726* (Altrincham, 1968)
Snodin, M., *English Silver Spoons* (1974; rev. 1982)
Watts, W.W., *Old English Silver* (1924)
Wernham, E., *Domestic Silver of Great Britain and Ireland* (Oxford, 1931)

8   Textiles

Arnold, J., *A Handbook of Costume* (1973)
'*Lost from Her Majesties Back*' (1980)
Patterns of Fashion, 1560–1660 (1985)
Queen Elizabeth's Wardrobe Unlocked (1988)
Ashelford, J., *A Visual History of Costume: the Sixteenth Century* (1983)
Baines, B.B., *Fashion Revivals from the Elizabethan Age to the Present Day* (1981)
Barnard, E.A.B. and Wace, A.J.B., 'The Sheldon tapestry weavers and their work', *Archaeologia* **78** (1928) 255–314
Beck, T., *Embroidered Gardens* (1979)
Cunnington, C.W. and P., *Handbook of English Costume in the Sixteenth Century* (1944)
Digby, G.W., *Elizabethan Embroidery* (1963)
Fabric of Nature (Durham, [1980])
Hughes, T., *English Domestic Needlework* (1961)
Kendrick, A.F., *Catalogue of Tapestries in the Victoria and Albert Museum* (1914)
English Decorative Fabrics of the Sixteenth to the Eighteenth Centuries (Benfleet, 1934)
English Needlework (1933; 2nd edn rev. by P. Wardle, 1967)
King, D. (ed.), *British Textile Design in the Victoria and Albert Museum. Vol. I: Medieval to Rococo* (Tokyo, 1980)
Levey, S.M., *Lace: a History* (1983)
Lubell, C. (ed.), *Textile Collections of the World. Vol. II: United Kingdom and Ireland* (1976)
Nevinson, J.L., *Catalogue of English Domestic Embroidery*, Victoria and Albert Museum (1950)
Swain, M., *The Embroideries of Mary Queen of Scots* (1973)
Historical Needlework: a Study of Influences in Scotland and Northern England (1969)
Tattersall, C.E.C., *A History of British Carpets*, rev. S. Reed (Leigh-on-Sea, 1966)
Thomson, W.G., *A History of Tapestry* (1973)
Tapestry Weaving in England (1914)
Verlet, P. *et al.*, *The Book of Tapestry* [tr. from French] (1978)

Wardle, P., *A Guide to English Embroidery* (1970)
Wingfield-Digby, G., *Victoria and Albert Museum: the Tapestry Collections. Medieval to Renaissance* (1980)

IV   Gardens and Parks

Amherst, A., *A History of Gardens in England* (1895)
Comito, T., *The Idea of the Garden in the Renaissance* (New Brunswick, 1978)
Cox, E.H.M., *A History of Gardening in Scotland* (1935)
Crisp, F., *Medieval Gardens. 'Flowery Medes' and Other Arrangements of Herbs, Flowers and Shrubs Grown in the Middle Ages, with some Account of Tudor, Elizabethan and Stuart Gardens*, 2 vols., ed. C.C. Paterson (1924)
Dutton, R., *The English Garden* (1937)
Giamatti, A.B., *The Earthly Paradise and the Renaissance Epic* (Princeton, 1969)
Green, D., *The Gardens and Parks at Hampton Court and Bushy* (1974)
Hadfield, M., *A History of British Gardens* (1969)
Topiary and Ornamental Hedges (1971)
'Trees and their periods: some notes on arboricultural planting in the British Isles', *Garden History* **4** (1976) 23–9
Harris, J. (ed.), *The Garden, a Celebration of One Thousand Years of British Gardening* (Victoria and Albert Museum exhibition catalogue, 1979)
Harvey, J.H., *Early Nurserymen* (1974/5)
Medieval Gardens (1981)
Harvey, J.H., 'The supply of plants in the North-West', *Garden History* **6** (1978) 33–7
Hunt, J.D., *Garden and Grove. The Italian Renaissance Garden in the English Imagination: 1600–1750* (1986)
Hyams, E., *A History of Gardens and Gardening* (1971)
Leith-Ross, P., *The John Tradescants: Gardeners to the Rose and Lily Queen* (1984)
MacGregory A. (ed.), *Tradescant's Rarities: Essays on the Foundation of the Ashmolean Museum 1683* (Oxford, 1983)
McLean, T., *Medieval English Gardens* (1981)
Steane, J.M., 'The Development of Tudor and Stuart garden design in Northamptonshire', *Northamptonshire Past and Present* **5** (1977) 383–406
Strong, R., *The Renaissance Garden in England* (1979)

Taylor, C., *The Archaeology of Gardens*
(Princes Risborough, 1983)
Thacker, C., *The History of Gardens* (1979)
Urwin, A.C.B., *The Houses and Gardens of
Twickenham Park 1227–1805* (Borough
of Twickenham Local History Society
Paper No. 54, 1984)
Wilson, D.R. and Wilson, J., 'The site of
the Elvetham entertainment', *Antiquity*
56 (1982) 46–7

V   Hardwick Hall

Boynton, L. and Thornton, P., 'The
Hardwick Hall inventories of 1601',
Journal of the Furniture History Society
7 (1971)
Durant, D.N., *Bess of Hardwick* (1977)
Durrant, D.N. and Riden, P. (eds.), *The
Building of Hardwick Hall*, Derbyshire
Record Society: Part 1 (1980); Part 2
(1984)
Girouard, M., *Hardwick Hall* (1976)
Life in the English Country House (New
Haven, 1978)
*Robert Smythson and the Elizabethan
Country House* (New Haven, 1983)
Jourdain, M., 'Needlework at Hardwick
Hall', *Country Life* **26**, March 1927
'Some tapestries at Hardwick Hall',
Country Life **26**, March 1927
Nevinson, J., 'An Elizabethan herbarium:
embroideries by Bess of Hardwick after
the woodcuts by Mattioli', *National
Trust Yearbook 1976–77* (1977)
'Embroideries at Hardwick Hall', *Country
Life* **29**, November 1973
Sitwell, S., 'Early memories of Hardwick
Hall and Bolsover Castle', *National
Trust Yearbook 1976–77* (1977)
Strong, R., 'A new heaven, a new earth',
Spirit of the Age (1975)

VI   Literature and Drama

1   General

BIBLIOGRAPHIES AND RESEARCH GUIDES
The various volumes in the Critical
Heritage series published by Routledge &
Kegan Paul are extremely valuable, as are
the Recent Studies series published in
English Literary Renaissance.
(1)   *Annals of English Literature 1475–1960.
The Principal Publications of Each Year
Together with an Alphabetical Index of
Authors with their Works*, compiled by
J.C. Ghosh and E.G. Withycombe,

revised by R.W. Chapman (2nd rev.
edn, Oxford, 1961)
(2)   Beal, P., *Index of English Literary
Manuscripts*, Vol. I: *1450–1625* (Part I,
Andrewes – Donne; Part 2, Douglas –
Wyatt) (1980)
(3)   Case, A.E., *A Bibliography of English
Poetic Miscellanies, 1521–1750* (1935)
(4)   Greg, W.W., *A Bibliography of the
English Printed Drama to the
Restoration*, 4 vols. (1939–59)
(5)   Harner, J.L., *English Renaissance
Prose Fiction, 1500–1660: an Annotated
Bibliography of Criticism* (Boston, 1978)
(6)   Heninger, S.K., Jr, *English Prose,
Prose Fiction, and Criticism to 1660: a
Guide to Information Sources* (Detroit,
1975)
(7)   Horden, J. (ed.), *Halkett and
Laing: a Dictionary of Anonymous and
Pseudonymous Publications in the English
Language*, 3rd rev. and enlarged edn,
1475–1640 (1980)
(8)   Jones, W.M. (ed.), *The Present State
of Scholarship in Sixteenth-Century
Literature* (Columbia, 1978)
(9)   Lievsay, J.L., *The Sixteenth Century:
Skelton through Hooker* (NY, 1968)
[selected bibliography]
(10)   Logan, T.P. and Smith D.S. (eds.),
*The Predecessors of Shakespeare: a
Survey and Bibliography of Recent
Studies in English Renaissance Drama*
(1973)
(11)   Pollard, A.W. and Redgrave, G.R., *A
Short-title Catalogue of Books Printed in
England . . . 1475–1640*, rev. by W.A.
Jackson, F.S. Ferguson, and K.
Panzer; Vol. I (1976); vol. II (1986)
(12)   Rogal, S.J., *A Chronological Outline of
British Literature* (Westport, Conn.,
1980)
(13)   Shaaber, M.A., *Check-list of Works of
British Authors Printed Abroad, in
Languages other than English, to 1641*
(NY, 1975)
(14)   Tilley, M.P., *A Dictionary of the
Proverbs in England in the Sixteenth and
Seventeenth Centuries* (Ann Arbor,
1950)
(15)   Watson, G. (ed.), *The New Cambridge
Bibliography of English Literature*.
Vol. I: *600–1660* (Cambridge, 1974)
(16)   Whiting, B.J. and Whiting, H.W.,
*Proverbs, Sentences and Proverbial
Phrases from English Writings Mainly
before 1500* (Cambridge, Mass., 1968)
See also the annually published
bibliographies, *The Year's Work in
English Studies; the Annual*

Bibliography of English Language and Literature: and *The MLA International Bibliography of Modern Languages and Literature*.

GENERAL HISTORIES

(17) Briggs, J., *This Stage-Play World: English Literature and its Background, 1580–1625* (Oxford, 1983)

(18) Evans, M., *English Poetry in the Sixteenth Century* (1955)

(19) Ford, B. (ed.), *The New Pelican Guide to English Literature*, vol. I: *Medieval Literature* (Harmondsworth, 1982)

(20) Ford, B. (ed.), *The New Pelican Guide to English Literature*, vol. II: *The Age of Shakespeare* (Harmondsworth, 1982)

(21) Ford, B. (ed.), *The New Pelican Guide to English Literature*, vol. III: *From Donne to Marvell* (Harmondsworth, 1982)

(22) Lewis, C.S., *English Literature in the Sixteenth Century, Excluding Drama* (Oxford, 1954)

(23) Ricks, C. (ed.), *Sphere History of Literature*. Vol. II: *English Poetry and Prose, 1540–1674* (1970; rev. 1986)

(24) Roston, M., *Sixteenth-century English Literature* (1982)

(25) Spearing, A.C., *Medieval to Renaissance in English Poetry* (Cambridge, 1985)

(26) Waller, G., *English Poetry of the Sixteenth Century* (1986) [Longman Literature in English Series]

ANTHOLOGIES

(27) Ault N. (ed.), *Elizabethan Lyrics, from the Original Texts* (1925; 3rd edn, repr. 1986)

(28) Bullett, G. (ed.), *Silver Poets of the Sixteenth Century* (1947) [Wyatt, Surrey, Sidney, Raleigh, Sir John Davies]

(29) Chambers, E.K. (ed.), *The Oxford Book of Sixteenth-century Verse* (1932; rev., Oxford, 1970)

(30) Evans, M. (ed.), *Elizabethan Sonnets* (1977)

(31) Hall, J., *The Court of Virtue 1565*, ed. R.A. Fraser (1961)

(32) Hollander, J. and Kermode, F., *The Literature of Renaissance England* (NY, 1973) [The Oxford Anthology of English Literature, vol. II]

(33) Klein, H.M. (ed.), *English and Scottish Sonnet Sequences of the Renaissance*, 2 vols. (Hildesheim, 1984)

(34) Lucie-Smith, E. (ed.), *The Penguin Book of Elizabethan Verse* (Harmondsworth, 1965)

(35) MacQueen, J. (ed.), *Ballatis of Luve: the Scottish Courtly Love Lyric 1400–1570* (Edinburgh, 1970)

(36) Muir, K. (ed.), *Elizabethan Lyrics: a Critical Anthology* (1952)

(37) Reese M.M. (ed.), *Elizabethan Verse Romances* (1968)

LITERARY STUDIES

(38) Aers, D., Hodge, B. and Kress, G., *Literature, Language, and Society in England 1580–1680* (Dublin, 1981)

(39) Aitken, A,.J. (ed.), *Bards and Makers. Scottish Language and Literature: Medieval and Renaissance* (Glasgow, 1977)

(40) Allen, D.C., *Image and Meaning: Metaphoric Traditions in Renaissance Poetry* (Baltimore, 1960)

(41) Allen, D.C., *Mysteriously Meant: the Rediscovery of Pagan Symbolism and Allegorical Interpretation in the Renaissance* (Baltimore, 1970)

(42) Alpers, P., *Elizabethan Poetry: Modern Essays in Criticism* (NY, 1967)

(43) Altman, J.B., *The Tudor Play of Mind* (Berkeley, 1978)

(44) Atkins, J.W.H., *English Literary Criticism: the Renascence* (1947)

(45) Attridge, D., *The Rhythms of English Poetry* (1982) [English Language Series 14]

(46) Attridge, D., *Well-weighed Syllables: Elizabethan Verse in Classical Metres* (Cambridge, 1974)

(47) Auerbach, E., *Mimesis: the Representation of Reality in Western Literature*, tr. W.R. Trask (Princeton, 1953)

(48) Bateson, F.W., *English Poetry and the English Language* (1934; 3rd edn, rev., Oxford, 1973)

(49) Berdan, J.M., *Early Tudor Poetry, 1485–1547* (New York, 1920)

(50) Braden, G., *The Classics and English Renaissance Poetry: Three Case Studies* (New Haven, 1978)

(51) Brown, J.R. and Harris B. (eds.), Stratford-upon-Avon Studies, II: *Elizabethan Poetry* (1960)

(52) Bush, D., *Classical Influences in Renaissance Literature* (Cambridge, Mass., 1952)

(53) Bush, D., *Mythology and the Renaissance Tradition in English Poetry* (1932; rev edn, NY, 1963)

(54) Bush, D., *The Renaissance and English Humanism* (Toronto, 1956)

(55)   Buxton, J., *Sir Philip Sidney and the English Renaissance* (1954)

(56)   Buxton, J., *A Tradition of Poetry* (1967)

(57)   Caspari, F., *Humanism and the Social Order in Tudor England* (Chicago, 1954)

(58)   Chew, S., *The Pilgrimage of Life* (New Haven, 1962)

(59)   Chew, S., *The Virtues Reconciled: an Iconographic Study* (Toronto, 1947)

(60)   Clarke, S., *The Elizabethan Pamphleteers: Popular Moralistic Prose Pamphlets 1580–1640* (Rutherford, 1983)

(61)   Colie, R., *Paradoxia Epidemica: the Renaissance Tradition of Paradox* (Princeton, 1966)

(62)   Colie, R., *The Resources of Kind: Genre Theory in the Renaissance* (Berkeley, 1973)

(63)   Comito, T., *The Idea of the Garden in the Renaissance* (New Brunswick, NJ, 1978)

(64)   Conley, C.H., *The First English Translators of the Classics* (New Haven, 1927)

(65)   Cooper, H., *Pastoral: Medieval into Renaissance* (Ipswich, 1977)

(66)   Craig, H., *The Enchanted Glass: the Elizabethan Mind in Literature* (NY, 1936)

(67)   Cruttwell, P., *The English Sonnet* (1966)

(68)   Crutwell, P., *The Shakespearean Moment* (1954)

(69)   Curtius, E.R., *European Literature and the Latin Middle Ages*, tr. W. Trask (1953)

(70)   Davis, W.R., *Idea and Act in Elizabethan Fiction* (Princeton, 1969)

(71)   van Dorsten, J., *Poets, Patrons, and Professors: Sir Philip Sidney, Daniel Rogers, and the Leiden Humanists* (Leiden, 1962)

(72)   Ferguson, M.W., *Trials of Desire: Renaissance Defenses of Poetry* (New Haven, 1983)

(73)   Ferry, A., *The 'Inward' Language: Sonnets of Wyatt, Sidney, Shakespeare, Donne* (Chicago, 1983)

(74)   Fletcher, A., *Allegory: the Theory of a Symbolic Mode* (Ithaca, 1964)

(75)   Forster, L.W., *The Icy Fire: Five Studies in European Petrarchism* (Cambridge, 1969)

(76)   Fowler, A., *Conceitful Thought: the Interpretation of English Renaissance Poems* (Edinburgh, 1975)

(77)   Fowler, A., *Kinds of Literature: an Introduction to the Theory of Genres and Modes* (Oxford, 1982)

(78)   Fowler, A., *Triumphal Forms: Structural Patterns in Elizabethan Poetry* (Cambridge, 1970)

(79)   Freeman, R., *English Emblem Books* (1948)

(80)   Frye, N., *The Anatomy of Criticism: Four Essays* (Princeton, 1957)

(81)   Giamatti, A.B., *The Earthly Paradise and the Renaissance Epic* (Princeton, 1966)

(82)   Goldberg, J., *James I and the Politics of Literature* (Baltimore, 1983)

(83)   Grabes, H., *The Mutable Glass: Mirror Imagery in Titles and Texts of the Middle Ages and the English Renaissance* (Cambridge, 1982)

(84)   Greaves, M., *The Blazon of Honour: a Study in Renaissance Magnanimity* (1964)

(85)   Greenblatt, S., *Renaissance Self-Fashioning: from More to Shakespeare* (Chicago, 1980)

(86)   Greene, T.M., *The Light in Troy: Imitation and Discovery in Renaissance Poetry* (New Haven, 1982)

(87)   Hannay, M. (ed.), *Silent But for the Word: Tudor Women as Patrons, Translators, and Writers of Religious Works* (Kent, Ohio, 1984)

(88)   Harbison O.B. (ed.), *English Literary Criticism: the Renaissance* (NY, 1967)

(89)   Hardison, O.B., *The Enduring Monument: a Study of the Idea of Praise in Renaissance Literary Theory and Practice* (Chapel Hill, 1962)

(90)   Haydn, H., *The Counter-Renaissance* (NY, 1950)

(91)   Helgerson, R., *The Elizabethan Prodigals* (Berkeley, 1976)

(92)   Helgerson, R., *Self-crowned Laureates: Spenser, Jonson, Milton and the Literary System* (Berkeley, 1983)

(93)   Hogrefe, P., *The Sir Thomas More Circle: a Program of Ideas and their Impact on Secular Drama* (Urbana, 1959)

(94)   Hollander, J., *The Untuning of the Sky: Ideas of Music in English Poetry, 1550–1700* (Princeton, 1961)

(95)   Hollander, J., *Vision and Resonance: Two Senses of Poetic Form* (NY, 1985)

(96)   Hulse, C., *Metamorphic Verse: the Elizabethan Minor Epic* (Princeton, 1981)

(97)   Ing, C., *Elizabethan Lyrics: a Study in the Development of English Metres and their Relation to Poetic Effect* (1951)

(98)   Inglis, F., *The Elizabethan Poets: the*

Making of English Poetry from Wyatt to Ben Jonson (1960)

(99) Javitch, D., *Poetry and Courtliness in Renaissance England* (Princeton, 1978)

(100) Keach, W., *Elizabethan Erotic Narratives: Irony and Pathos in the Ovidian Poetry of Shakespeare, Marlowe, and their Contemporaries* (New Brunswick, 1977)

(101) Kermode, F., *Shakespeare, Spenser, Donne: Renaissance Essays* (1971)

(102) Kermode, F. (ed.), *English Pastoral Poetry, from the Beginnings to Marvell* (NY, 1972)

(103) Kernan, A., *The Cankered Muse: Satire of the English Renaissance* (New Haven, 1959)

(104) King, J.N., *English Reformation Literature: The Tudor Origins of the Protestant Tradition* (Princeton, 1982)

(105) Kinsley, J., *Scottish Poetry: a Critical Survey* (1955)

(106) Kratzmann, G., *Anglo-Scottish Literary Relations 1430–1550* (Cambridge, 1980)

(107) Lever, J.W., *The Elizabethan Sonnet Sequence* (1956)

(108) Levin, H., *The Myth of the Golden Age in the Renaissance* (Bloomington, 1969)

(109) Lewis, C.S., *The Allegory of Life: a Study in Medieval Tradition* (Oxford, 1936)

(110) Lewis, C.S., *English Literature in the Sixteenth Century, Excluding Drama* (Oxford, 1954)

(111) Loughrey, B. (ed.), *The Pastoral Mode: A Casebook* (1984)

(112) Mack, M. and Lord G. de F. (eds.), *Poetic Traditions of the English Renaissance* (New Haven, 1982)

(113) MacQueen, J., *Alexander Scott and Scottish Court Poetry of the Middle Sixteenth Century* (1968)

(114) Manley, L., *Convention, 1500–1750* (Cambridge, Mass., 1980)

(115) Marinelli, P.V., *Pastoral* (1971)

(116) Martindale, J., *English Humanism: Wyatt to Cowley* (1984)

(117) Mason, H.A., *Humanism and Poetry in the Early Tudor Period* (1959)

(118) Matthiessen, F.O., *Translation: an Elizabethan Art* (Cambridge, Mass., 1931)

(119) Maynard, W., *Elizabethan Lyric Poetry and its Music* (Oxford, 1986)

(120) Mazzaro, J., *Transformations in the Renaissance English Lyric* (Ithaca, 1970)

(121) Miller, E.H., *The Professional Writer in Elizabethan England: a Study in Non-Dramatic Literature* (Cambridge, Mass., 1959)

(122) Minta, S., *Petrarch and Petrarchism, the English and French Traditions* (Manchester, 1980)

(123) Miskimin, A.S., *The Renaissance Chaucer* (New Haven, 1975)

(124) Murrin, M., *The Allegorical Epic: Essays in its Rise and Decline* (Chicago, 1980)

(125) Murrin, M., *The Veil of Allegory: Some Notes toward a Theory of Allegorical Rhetoric in the English Renaissance* (Chicago, 1969)

(126) O'Connor, J.J., *'Amadis de Gaule' and its Influence on Elizabethan Literature* (New Brunswick, 1970)

(127) Orgel, S., *The Jonsonian Masque* (Cambridge, Mass., 1965)

(128) Owst, G.R., *Literature and Pulpit in Medieval England: a Neglected Chapter in the History of English Letters and of the English People* (Oxford, 1933)

(129) Parker, P.A., *Inescapable Romance: Studies in the Poetics of a Mode* (Princeton, 1979)

(130) Pattison, B., *Music and Poetry of the English Renaissance* (1948)

(131) Pearcy, L.T., *The Mediated Muse: English Translations of Ovid 1560–1700* (Hamden, Conn. 1984)

(132) Peterson, D.L., *The English Lyric from Wyatt to Donne: a History of the Plain and Eloquent Styles* (Princeton, 1967)

(133) Pomeroy, E.W., *The Elizabethan Miscellanies: their Development and Conventions*, California University Publications English Studies no. 36 (Berkeley, 1973)

(134) Praz, M., *The Flaming Heart: Essays on Crashaw, Machiavelli, and other Studies in the Relations between Italian and English Literature from Chaucer to T.S. Eliot* (Garden City, 1958)

(135) Prescott, A.L., *French Poets and the English Renaissance: Studies in Fame and Transformation* (New Haven, 1978)

(136) Puttenham, G., *The Arte of English Poesie (1589)* ed. G.D. Willcock and A. Walker (Cambridge, 1936)

(137) Quilligan, M., *The Language of Allegory: Defining the Genre* (Ithaca, 1979)

(138) Raspa, A., *The Emotive Image: Jesuit Poetics in the English Renaissance* (Fort Worth, 1983)

(139) Reese, M.M., *The Cease of Majesty* (1961)

(140) Rhodes, N., *Elizabethan Grotesque* (1980)

(141) Roche, T.P., *Petrarch and the English Sonnet Tradition* (NY, 1986)

(142) Schlauch, M., *Antecedents of the English Novel, 1400–1600: from Chaucer to Deloney* (1963)

(143) Selden, R., *English Verse Satire, 1590–1765* (1978)

(144) Simpson, C.M., *The British Broadside Ballad and its Music* (New Brunswick, 1966)

(145) Sinfield, A., *Literature in Protestant England: Religious Anxiety and Literature from Sidney to Milton* (Brighton, 1983)

(146) Smith, G.G. (ed.), *Elizabethan Critical Essays*, 2 vols. (1904)

(147) Smith, H., *Elizabethan Poetry: a Study in Conventions, Meaning, and Expression* (Cambridge, Mass., 1952)

(148) Southall, R., *The Courtly Maker: an Essay on the Poetry of Wyatt and his Contemporaries* (Oxford, 1964)

(149) Spearing, A.C., *Medieval Dream Poetry* (Cambridge, 1976)

(150) Spiers, J.H., *The Scots Literary Tradition: an Essay in Criticism* (1940; 2nd ed., 1962)

(151) Spingarn, J.E., *A History of Literary Criticism in the Renaissance with Specific Reference to the Influence of Italy in the Formation and Development of Modern Classicism* (1899; enlarged edn., NY, 1952)

(152) Starnes, D.T. and Talbort, E.W., *Classical Myth and Legend in Renaissance Dictionaries. A Study of Renaissance Dictionaries in their Relation to Classical Learning of Contemporary English Writers* (Chapel Hill, 1955)

(153) Stevens, J., *Music and Poetry in the Early Tudor Court* (1961)

(154) Stevens, J., *The Old Sound and the New* (Cambridge, 1982)

(155) Tayler, E.W., *Nature and Art in Renaissance Literature* (NY, 1964)

(156) Thompson, J., *The Founding of English Metre* (1961)

(157) Tuve, R., *Allegorical Imagery: some Medieval Books and their Posterity*, ed. T.P. Roche (Princeton, 1966)

(158) Tuve, R., *Elizabethan and Metaphysical Imagery: Renaissance Poetic and Twentieth-Century Critics* (Chicago, 1947)

(159) Whingham, F., *Ambition and Privilege: the Social Tropes of Elizabethan Courtesy Theory* (Berkeley, 1984)

(160) Wilson, F.P., *Elizabethan and Jacobean* (Oxford, 1944)

(161) Wilson, J., *Entertainments for Elizabeth I* (Cambridge, 1980)

(162) Winters, Y., 'The sixteenth-century lyric in England: a critical and historical reinterpretation', *Poetry*, **53** (1939) 258–72; **54** (1939) 35–51

2   Drama

GENERAL STUDIES

(163) Adams, H.A., *English Domestic or Homiletic Tragedy, 1575–1642* (NY, 1943)

(164) Alexander P. (ed.), *Studies in Shakespeare: British Academy Lectures* (1964)

(165) Anderson, M.J. (ed.), *Classical Drama and its Influence* (1965)

(167) Axton, M. and Williams, R. (eds.), *English Drama: Forms and Development. Essays in Honour of Muriel Clara Bradbrook* (Cambridge, 1977)

(166) Axton, M., *The Queen's Two Bodies: Drama and the Elizabethan Succession* (1977)

(168) Baker, H., *Induction to Tragedy: a Study in a Development of Form in 'Gorboduc', 'The Spanish Tragedy', and 'Titus Andronicus'* (Baton Rouge, 1939)

(169) Baskerville, C.R., *The Elizabethan jig and related song drama* (Chicago, 1929)

(170) Bentley, G.E., *The Profession of Dramatist in Shakespeare's Time, 1590–1642* (Princeton, 1971)

(171) Bernard, J.E. Jr, *The Prosody of the Tudor Interlude* (New Haven, 1936)

(172) Bethell, S.L., *Shakespeare and the Popular Dramatic Tradition* (1944)

(173) Bevington, D., *From 'Mankind' to Marlowe: Growth of Structure in the Popular Drama of Tudor England* (Cambridge, Mass., 1962)

(174) Bevington, D., *Tudor Drama and Politics: a Critical Approach to Topical Meaning* (Cambridge, Mass., 1968)

(175) Boas, F.S., *University Drama in the Tudor Age* (Oxford, 1914)

(176) Bond, R.W., *Early Plays from the Italian* (Oxford, 1911)

(177) Boughner, D.C., *The Braggart in Renaissance Comedy: a Study in Comparative Drama from Aristophanes to Shakespeare* (Minneapolis, 1954)

(178) Bowers, F., *The Elizabethan Revenge Tradition, 1587–1642* (Princeton, 1940)

(179) Bradbrook, M.C., *English Dramatic*

Form: a History of its Development
(1965)

(180) Bradbrook, M.C., *The Growth and Structure of Elizabethan Comedy* (1955)

(181) Bradbrook, M.C., *The Rise of the Common Player* (1962)

(182) Bradbrook, M.C., *Themes and Conventions of Elizabethan Tragedy* (Cambridge, 1935)

(183) Braden, G., *Renaissance Tragedy and the Senecan Tradition: Anger's Privilege* (New Haven, 1985)

(184) Brody, A., *The English Mummers and their Plays: Traces of Ancient Mystery* (n.d.)

(185) Brown, J.R. and Harris, B. (eds.), *Elizabethan Theatre* (1966) Stratford-upon-Avon Studies

(186) Brown, J.R. and Harris, B. (eds.), Studies: *Jacobean Theatre* (1960) Stratford-upon-Avon Studies

(187) Campbell, L.B., *Divine Poetry and Drama in Sixteenth-Century England* (Berkeley, 1959)

(188) Chambers, E.K., *The English Folk Play* (Oxford, 1933)

(189) Chambers, E.K., *English Literature at the Close of the Middle Ages* (Oxford, 1945)

(190) Chambers, E.K., *The Medieval Stage*, 2 vols. (Oxford, 1903)

(191) Charlton, H.B.C., *The Senecan Tradition in Renaissance Tragedy* (Manchester, 1946)

(192) Clemen, W., *English Tragedy Before Shakespeare: the Development of Dramatic Speech*, tr. T.S. Dorsch (1961)

(193) Cope, J.I., *The Theatre and the Dream: from Metaphor to Form in Renaissance Drama* (Baltimore, 1973)

(194) Craik, T.W., *The Tudor Interlude: Stage, Costume, and Acting* (Leicester, 1958)

(195) Cunliffe, J.W. (ed.), *Early English Classical Tragedies* (Oxford, 1912)

(196) Denny, N. (ed.), *Medieval Drama* (1973) Stratford-upon-Avon Studies

(197) Dessen, A.C., *Elizabethan Drama and the Viewer's Eye* (Chapel Hill, 1977)

(198) Dessen, A.C., *Elizabethan Stage Conventions and Modern Interpreters* (Cambridge, 1984)

(199) Dollimore, J., *Radical Tragedy: Religion, Ideology, and Power in the Drama of Shakespeare and his Contemporaries* (1983)

(200) Doran, M., *Endeavors of Art: a Study of Form in Elizabethan Drama* (Madison, 1963)

(201) Edwards, P., *Threshold of a Nation: a Study of English and Irish Drama* (Cambridge, 1979)

(202) Eliot, T.S., *Elizabethan Essays* (1934)

(203) Ellis-Fermor, U., *The Jacobean Drama* (1936)

(204) Farnham, W., *The Medieval Heritage of Elizabethan Tragedy* (Oxford, 1956)

(205) Gardiner, H.C., *Mysteries' End: an Investigation of the Last Days of the Medieval Religious Stage* (New Haven, 1946)

(206) Green, A.W., *The Inns of Court and Early English Drama* (New Haven, 1931)

(207) Greenfield, *The Induction in Elizabethan Drama* (Eugene, Ore., 1969)

(208) Harbage, A., *Shakespeare and the Rival Traditions* (NY, 1952)

(209) Hattaway, M., *Elizabethan Popular Theatre: Plays in Performance* (1982)

(210) Herford, C.H., *Studies in the Literary Relations of England and Germany in the Sixteenth Century* (Cambridge, 1886)

(211) Herrick, M.T., *Comic Theory in the Sixteenth Century* (Urbana, 1950)

(212) Herrick M.T., *Italian Tragedy in the Renaissance* (Urbana, 1965)

(213) Herrick, M.T., *Tragicomedy: its Origin and Development in Italy, France, and England* (Urbana, 1955)

(214) Hillebrand, H.N., *The Child Actors: a Chapter in Elizabethan Stage History* (Urbana, 1926)

(215) Holmes, M., *Shakespeare and his Players* (1972)

(216) Hotson, L., *Shakespeare's Motley* (1952)

(217) Jacquot, J. (ed.), *Fêtes de la Renaissance*, 2 vols. (Paris, 1956); *Le Lieu théâtral à la Renaissance* (Paris, 1964); *Dramaturge et société . . . aux 16e et 17e siecles* (Paris, 1968)

(218) Jacquot, J. (ed.), *Les Tragédies de Sénèque et le Théâtre de la Renaissance* (Paris, 1973)

(219) Kahrl, J., *Traditions of Medieval English Drama* (1974)

(220) Kantorowicz, E., *The King's Two Bodies: a Study in Medieval Political Theory* (Princeton, 1957)

(221) Kernodle, G.R., *From Art to Theatre: Form and Convention in the Renaissance* (Chicago, 1944)

(222) Klein, D., *Milestones to Shakespeare: a Study of the Dramatic Forms and Pageantry that were a Prelude to Shakespeare* (1970)

(223) Leech, C. and Craik, T.W. (ed.), *The Revels History of Drama in English, vol. III: 1576–1613* (1975)

(224) Leggatt, A., *Citizen Comedy in the Age of Shakespeare* (Toronto, 1973)

(225) Levin, R., *The Multiple Plot in English Renaissance Drama* (Chicago, 1971)

(226) Lindley, D. (ed.), *The Court Masque* (Manchester, 1984) [Revels Plays Companion Library]

(227) Lucas, F.L., *Seneca and Elizabethan Tragedy* (Cambridge, 1922)

(228) Manifold, J.S., *Music in English Drama* (1956)

(229) Margeson, J.M.R., *The Origins of English Tragedy* (1967)

(230) Mehl, D., *The Elizabethan Dumb Show: the History of a Dramatic Convention* (1966)

(231) Mill, A.J., *Medieval Plays in Scotland* (Edinburgh, 1927)

(232) Motter, T.H.V., *The School Drama in England* (1929)

(233) Muir, K. and Schoenbaum, S. (eds.), *A New Companion to Shakespeare Studies* (Cambridge, 1971)

(234) Orgel, S., *The Illusion of Power: Political Theater in the English Renaissance* (Berkeley, 1975)

(235) Potter, R., *The English Morality Play: Origins, History and Influence of a Dramatic Tradition* (1975)

(236) Prior, M., *The Language of Tragedy* (NY, 1947)

(237) Reed, A.W., *Early Tudor Drama* (1926)

(238) Reiss, T.J., *Tragedy and Truth: Studies in the Development of a Renaissance and Neoclassical Discourse* (New Haven, 1979)

(239) Ribner, I., *The English History Play in the Age of Shakespeare* (1957)

(240) Ricks, C. (ed.), *English Drama to 1710* (1971) [vol. III, Sphere History of English Literature]

(241) Rossiter, A.P., *English Drama from Early Times to the Elizabethans: its Background, Origins and Development* (1950; repr., 1958)

(242) Salingar, L., *Dramatic Form in Shakespeare and the Jacobeans* (Cambridge, 1986)

(243) Salinger, L., *Shakespeare and the Traditions of Comedy* (Cambridge, 1974)

(244) Sanders, N., Southern, R., Craik, T.W. and Potter, L., *The Revels History of Drama in English, vol. II: 1500–76* (1980)

(245) Sanders, W., *The Dramatist and the Received Idea* (Cambridge, 1968)

(246) Smith, G.C.M., *College Plays Performed in the University of Cambridge* (Cambridge, 1923)

(247) Spivack, B., *Shakespeare and the Allegory of Evil: the History of a Metaphor in Relation to his Major Villains* (NY, 1958)

(248) Stamm, R., *The Mirror Technique in Senecan and Pre-Shakespearean Tragedy* (Berne, 1975) [Cooper Monographs 23]

(249) Taylor, J. and Nelson, A.H. (eds), *Medieval English Drama, Essays Contextual and Critical* (Chicago, 1972)

(250) Thompson, E.N.S., *The English Moral Plays* (New Haven, 1910) [Transcriptions of the Connecticut Academy of the Arts and Sciences]

(251) Thomson, P., *Shakespeare's Theatre* (1983)

(252) Ure, P. (ed. J.C. Maxwell), *Elizabeth and Jacobean Drama* (Liverpool, 1974)

(253) Waith, E., *Ideas of Greatness: Heroic Drama in England* (1971)

(254) Weimann, R., *Shakespeare and the Popular Tradition in the Theatre*, ed. R. Schwartz (Baltimore, 1978)

(255) Wells, S. (ed.), *English Drama (excluding Shakespeare): Select Bibliographical Guides* (Oxford, 1975)

(256) Welsford, E., *The Court Masque: a Study of the Relationship between Poetry and the Revels* (Cambridge, 1927)

(257) Welsford, E., *The Fool, his Social and Literary History* (1935)

(258) Wickham, G., *Shakespeare's Dramatic Heritage: Collected Studies in Medieval, Tudor and Shakespearean Drama* (1969)

(259) Wilson, F.P., *The English Drama, 1485–1642* (Oxford, 1969)

(260) Withington, R., *English Pageantry*, 2 vols. (Cambridge, Mass., 1918–20)

THEATRE HISTORY

(261) Armstrong, W.A., *The Elizabethan Private Playhouses: Facts and Problems* (1958)

(262) Baldwin, T.W., *The Organization and Personnel of the Shakespearean Company* (Princeton, 1927)

(263) Gentley, G.E., *The Seventeenth-Century Stage*, 7 vols. (Oxford, 1941–68)

(264) Berry, H. (ed.), *The First Public Playhouse: the Theatre in Shoreditch, 1576–1598* (Montreal, 1979)

(265) Campbell, L.B., *Scenes and Machines*

on the English Stage during the Renaissance (Cambridge, 1923)

(266) Chambers, E.K., *The Elizabethan Stage*, 4 vols. (Oxford, 1923)

(267) Cook, A.J., *The Privileged Playgoers of Shakespeare's London, 1576–1642* (Princeton, 1981)

(268) Edwards C. (ed.), *The London Theatre Guide, 1576–1642* (Foxton, Herts., 1979)

(269) Feuillerat, A. (ed.), *Documents Relating to the Office of the Revels at Court in the Time of Queen Elizabeth* (Louvain, 1908) [Materialen zur Kunde des alteren englischen Dramas **24**, ed. W. Bang]

(270) Feuillerat A. (ed.), *Documents Relating to the Revels at Court in the Time of King Edward VI and Queen Mary* (Louvain, 1914) [Materialen zur Kunde des alteren englischen Dramas **21**, ed. W. Bang]

(271) Foakes, R.A., *Illustrations of the London Stage, 1580–1642* (1985)

(272) Foakes, R.A. and Rickert, R.T. (eds), *Henslowe's Diary* (Cambridge, 1961)

(273) Gair, W.R., *The Children of Paul's: the Story of a Theatre Company 1553–1608* (Cambridge, 1982)

(274) Gildersleeve, V.C., *Government Regulation of the Elizabethan Drama* (NY, 1908)

(275) Greg, W.W., *Dramatic Documents from the Elizabethan Playhouses*, 2 vols. (Oxford, 1931)

(276) Gurr, A., *Playgoing in Shakespeare's London* (Cambridge, 1987)

(277) Gurr, A., *The Shakespearean Stage, 1574–1642* (1970; 2nd edn, Cambridge, 1980)

(278) Harbage, A., *Annals of English Drama 975–1700*, rev. S. Schoenbaum (1964)

(279) Harbage, A., *Shakespeare's Audience* (NY, 1941)

(280) Hodges, C.W., *The Globe Restored: a Study of the Elizabethan Theatre* (1953; 2nd edn, 1968)

(281) Hodges, C.W., *Shakespeare's Second Globe* (1973)

(282) Joseph, B., *Elizabethan Acting* (Oxford, 1951)

(283) King, T.J., *Shakespearean Staging, 1599–1642* (Cambridge, Mass., 1971)

(284) Linnell, R., *The Curtain Playhouse* (1977)

(285) Linthicum, M.C., *Costume in the Drama of Shakespeare and his Contemporaries* (Oxford, 1936)

(286) Murray, J.T., *English Dramatic Companies 1558–1642*, 2 vols. (1910)

(287) Nagler, A.M., *Shakespeare's Stage*, tr. R. Mannheim (New Haven, 1978)

(288) Nungezer, E., *A Dictionary of Actors and of Other Personages Associated with the Public Presentation of Plays in England Before 1642* (New Haven, 1929)

(289) Orrell, J., *The Quest for Shakespeare's Globe* (Cambridge, 1983)

(290) Reynolds, G.F., *On Shakespeare's Stage* (Boulder, Col., 1967)

(291) Reynolds, G.F., *The Staging of Elizabethan Plays at the Red Bull Theater, 1605–25* (New York, 1940)

(292) Rhodes, E.L., *Henslowe's Rose: the Stage and Staging* (Lexington, 1976)

(293) Southern, R., *The Staging of Plays Before Shakespeare* (1973)

(294) Stopes, C.C., *William Hunnis and the Revels of the Chapel Royal* (Louvain, 1910) [Materialen zur Kunde des alteren englischen Dramas **29**, ed. W. Bang]

(295) Wickham, G., *Early English Stages, 1300–1660*, 3 vols. (1959–72)

3 Authors

Ascham, Roger (1515–68)
Humanist and tutor to Elizabeth I. Educated St John's, Cambridge. *Toxophilus* (1545), *The Scholemaster* (1570).
English Works, ed. W.A. Wright (1904) *The Schoolmaster*, ed. J.E.B. Mayor (1863; NY, 1868); R.J. Schoek (Ontario, 1966); L.V. Ryan (Ithaca, 1967)

Ryan, L.V., *Roger Ascham* (Stanford, 1963) See VI. 57

Bale, John (1495–1563)
Dramatist, polemicist, and cleric. Bishop of Ossory. *King John*. *The Dramatic Writings of John Bale*, ed. J.S. Farmer (1907)

Blatt, T.B., *The Plays of John Bale: a Study of Ideas, Technique and Style* (Copenhagen, 1968) See VI. 219

Campion, Thomas: see VII. 2

Chapman, George (*c.* 1559–1634)
Poet, dramatist, and translator. Educated ?Oxford. Travelled abroad. *Ovid's Banquet of Sense* (1595). Completed Marlowe's 'Hero and Leander' (1598); translated *Iliad* (1598–1608) and *Odyssey* (1616). Individual plays are published in the

New Mermaids and Revels series.
Works, 3 vols., ed. R.H. Shepherd
(1874–5)
*The Plays of George Chapman: the
Comedies*, ed. A. Holaday and M.
Kiernan (Urbana, 1970–   )
Chapman's Homer, 2 vols., ed. A.
Nicholl (1957)

Jacquot, J., *George Chapman, sa vie, sa
    poésie, son théâtre, sa pensée* (Paris,
    1951)
Lord, G. de F., *Homeric Renaissance: the
    'Odyssey' of G. Chapman* (New Haven,
    1956)
MacLure, M., *George Chapman, a Critical
    Study* (Toronto, 1966)
Rees, E., *The Tragedies of George Chapman:
    Renaissance Ethics in Action*
    (Cambridge, Mass., 1954)
Waddington, R.B., *The Mind's Empire.
    Myth and Form in George Chapman's
    Narrative Poems* (Baltimore, 1974)

Daniel, Samuel (1562–1619)
Poet. Educated Magdalene Hall,
Oxford. Travelled in Europe.
Sixteenth-century works include *Delia*
(1592) and *Musophilus* (1599).
Associated with Queen's Revels
Children.
Complete Works, ed. A.B. Grosart
(1885–96; NY, 1963)
Civil Wars, ed. L. Michel (New
Haven, 1958)
Poems and 'A defence of ryme', ed. A.C.
Sprague (Cambridge, Mass., 1930)

Harner, J.L., *Samuel Daniel and Michael
    Drayton, a Reference Guide* (Boston,
    1980)
Svensson, L.-H., *Silent Art: Rhetorical and
    Thematic Patterns in Samuel Daniel's
    'Delia'* (Lund, 1980)
Rees, J., *Samuel Daniel: a Critical and
    Biographical Study* (Liverpool, 1964)
Seronsy, C., *Samuel Daniel* (NY, 1967)
Spriet, P., *Samuel Daniel, 1563–1619: sa vie
    – son oeuvre* (Paris, 1968)

Davies, Sir John (1569–1626)
Poet, civil servant, and jurist. Educated
Winchester, Queen's, Oxford, and
Middle Temple. *Orchestra* (1596),
Nosce Tiepsum (1599).
Kreuger, R. (ed.), *The Poems of Sir John
    Davies* with intro by Kreuger and R.
    Nemser (Oxford, 1975)
Sanderson, J.L., *Sir John Davies* (Boston,
    1975)

Deloney, Thomas (*c.* 1560–1600)
Writer of ballads and prose fiction.

Jack of Newberie (1597), *The Gentle
Craft* (1598). *The Gentle Craft, the
Second Part* (1599), and *Thomas of
Reading* (1600).
Thomas Deloney: the novels, ed. M.E.
Lawlis (Bloomington, 1961)
Works, ed. F.O. Mann (Oxford, 1912;
1967)

Howarth, R.G., *Two Elizabethan Writers of
    Fiction: Thomas Nashe and Thomas
    Deloney* (Cape Town, 1950)
Lawlis, M.E., *Apology for the Middle Class:
    the Dramatic Novels of Thomas Deloney*
    (Bloomington, 1960)
Wright, E.P., *Thomas Deloney* (Boston,
    1981)
See VI. 142

Donne, John (1572–1631)
Poet and cleric. Born a Roman
Catholic. Educated Hart Hall, Oxford
and Inns of Court. Secular poetry in
the 1590s. 'Holy sonnets' early in
seventeenth century. Ordained in
Church of England, 1614; Dean of St
Paul's, 1621.
The Poetry of John Donne, ed. H.J.C.
Grierson (1912)
The English Poems of John Donne, ed.
A.J. Smith (Harmondsworth, 1971)
*The Complete English Poems of John
Donne*, ed. C.A. Patrides (1985)
Selected Prose, ed. Neil Rhodes
(Harmondsworth, 1987)
The Divine Poems, ed. H. Gardner
(Oxford, 1952)
Satires, Epigrams, and Verse Letters, ed.
W. Milgate (Oxford, 1967)
The Elegies and 'Songs and Sonnets', ed.
H. Gardner (Oxford, 1965)

Carey, J., *John Donne: Life, Mind and Art*
    (1981)
Leishman, J.B., *The Monarch of Wit: an
    Analytical and Comparative Study of
    the Poetry of John Donne* (1951)
Roston, M., *The Soul of Wit: a Study of
    John Donne* (Oxford, 1974)
Sanders, W., *John Donne's Poetry*
    (Cambridge, 1971)
Smith, A.J. (ed.), *John Donne: Essays in
    Celebration* (1972)
Stein, A., *John Donne's Lyrics: the
    Eloquence of Action* (Minneapolis, 1962)
Webber, J., *Contrary Music: the Prose Style
    of John Donne* (Madison, 1963)
See VI. 68, 102, 134

Douglas, Gavin (*c.* 1475–1522)
Cleric, poet, and translator. Educated
St Andrews and ?Paris. Bishop of
Dunkeld. Author of *The Palice of*

Honour and a translation of the *Aeneid*.
The Poetical Works of Gavin Douglas, 4
vols., ed. S. Small (Edinburgh, 1874)
The Shorter Poems of Gavin Douglas,
ed. P.J. Bawcutt (Edinburgh, 1967)
'*The Aeneid*', 4 vols., ed. D.F.C.
Coldwell (1957–64) [Scottish Text
Society]
Selections from Gavin Douglas, ed.
D.F.C. Caldwell (Oxford, 1964)

Bawcutt, P., *Gavin Douglas: a Critical
Study* (Edinburgh, 1976)

Drayton, Michael (1563–1631)
Poet and dramatist. Sixteenth-century
works include *Idea* (1593), *Ideas
Mirrour* (1594); *Piers Gaveston*
(*c*. 1593), *Matilda* (1594), *Endymion and
Phoebe* (1595), *Robert, Duke of
Normandy* (1596), *Mortimeriados*
(1596), *Englands Heroicall Epistles*
(1597).
Works 4 vols., ed. J.W. Hebel (1931–5);
5th vol. ed. K. Tillotson and B.H.
Newdigate (1941) Complete rev. edn,
Oxford, 1961
Poems [selected] 2 vols., ed. J. Buxton
(1953)

Berthelot, J.A., *Michael Drayton* (NY, 1967)
Hardin, R.F., *Michael Drayton and the
Passing of Elizabethan England*
(Lawrence, Ka, 1973)
Harner, J.L., *Samuel Daniel and Michael
Drayton, a Reference Guide* (1980)
de Nagy, N.C., *Michael Drayton's
'England's Heroical Epistles': a Study in
Themes and Compositional Devices*
(Bern, 1968)
Newdigate, B.H., *Michael Drayton and his
Circle* (Oxford, 1941)
Wrestling, L.H., *The Evolution of Michael
Drayton's 'Idea'* (Salzburg, 1974)

Elyot, Sir Thomas (*c*. 1490–1546)
Prose writer, diplomat, and civil
servant. *The Boke Named the
Governour* (1531); *Dictionary* (1538).
The Boke Named the Governor, 2 vols.,
ed. H.H.S. Croft (1880); ed. S.E.
Lehmberg (1962)

Dees, J.S., *Sir Thomas Elyot and Roger
Ascham, a Reference Guide* (Boston,
1980)
Kelso, R., *The Doctrine of the English
Gentleman in the Sixteenth Century*
(Urbana, 1929)
Major, J.M., *Sir Thomas Elyot and
Renaissance Humanism* (Lincoln, Neb.,
1964)
See VI. 57

Gascoigne, George (1525?–77)
Poet, dramatist, prose writer; soldier;
civil servant. Educated Trinity,
Cambridge and Gray's Inn. Travelled
in Netherlands. *A Hundreth Sundrie
Flowres* (1573) and *The Posies of George
Gascoigne* (1575) contain his innovatory
work.
Works, 2 vols., ed. J.W. Cunliffe
(Cambridge, 1907)
*The Green Knight: Selected Poetry and
Prose*, ed. R. Pooley (Manchester,
1982)
A Hundreth Sundrie Flowres, ed. C.T.
Prouty (Columbia, 1942) [University of
Missouri Studies, vol. XVII, no. 2]

Johnson, R.C., *George Gascoigne* (NY,
1972)
Prouty, C.T., *George Gascoigne: Elizabethan
Courtier, Soldier, and Poet* (NY, 1942)

Greene, Robert (*c*. 1558–92)
Dramatist and prose writer. Educated
St John's and Clare Hall, Cambridge.
Among many works are the prose
works *Pandosto* (1588); *Menaphon*
(1589); and *Greene's Groats-worth of
Witte* (1592). Plays include *Orlando
Furioso*, *Frier Bacon and Frier Bungay*,
and *James the Fourth*.

Complete Works, 15 vols., ed. A.B.
Grosart (1881–6; NY, 1964)

Hayashi, T., *A Textual Study of Robert
Greene's 'Orlando Furioso', with an
Elizabethan Text* (Muncie, Ind., 1973)
See VI. 121, 142

Greville, Fulke, Lord Brooke
(1554–1628)
Poet, prose writer, and civil servant.
Educated Shrewsbury and Jesus,
Cambridge. Friend of Sir Philip
Sidney. *Caelica; Mustapha* (pub. 1609);
Life of Sir Philip Sidney (1610).
Works, 4 vols., ed. A.B. Grosart (1870)
Poems and Dramas, 2 vols., ed. G.
Bullough (1939, 1969)
Selected Writings of Fulke Greville, ed.
J. Rees (1973)

Larsen, C., *Fulke Greville* (Boston, 1980)
Rebholz, R.A., *The Life of Fulke Greville,
First Lord Brooke* (Oxford, 1971)
Rees, J., *Fulke Greville, Lord Brooke,
1554–1628. A Critical Biography* (1971)
Waswo, R., *The Fatal Mirror: Themes and
Techniques in the Poetry of Fulke
Greville* (Charlottesville, 1972)

Hall, Joseph (1574–1656)
Satirist and clergyman. Educated

Emmanuel, Cambridge. *Virgidemiarum Sex Libri* (1597–8); contributes to the *Parnassus* plays. Later Bishop of Exeter and Norwich.
Poems, ed. A. Davenport (Liverpool, 1949)

Huntley, F.L., *Bishop Joseph Hall, 1574–1656: a Bibliographical and Critical Study* (Cambridge, 1979)
McCabe, R.A., *Joseph Hall, a Study in Satire and Meditation* (Oxford, 1982)
See VI. 143

Hawes, Stephen (1475?–1523)
Poet, courtier, and civil servant. Educated Oxford. *Passetyme of Pleasure* (1509).
The Works of Stephen Hawes [in facsimile], ed. J.F. Spang (Delmar, NY, 1975)
The Minor Poetry of Stephen Hawes, eds. F.W. Gluck and A.B. Morgan (1974) [EETS OS **271**]
The Pastime of Pleasure, ed. W.E. Mead (1928) [EETS OS **173**]

Edwards, A.S.G., *Stephen Hawes* (Boston, 1982)

Herbert, Mary (*née* Sidney), *Countess of Pembroke* (1564–1621)
Poet, translator, and major literary patron (at Wilton). Translated *Psalms* (with Sir Philip Sidney). Du Plessis Mornay's *Discourse of Life and Death*, Garnier's *Antonius*, and Petrarch's *Trionfo della Morte*.
The Psalms of Sir Philip Sidney and the Countess of Pembroke, ed. J.C.A. Rathmell (NY, 1963)
'*The Triumph of Death' and other Unpublished and Uncollected Poems*, ed. G.F. Waller (Salzburg, 1977)

Waller, G.F., *Mary Sidney, Countess of Pembroke* (Salzburg, 1979)

Heywood, John (*c.* 1497–*c.* 1580)
Dramatist and musician. Maries into family of Sir Thomas More; prominent under Mary I and exiled as Roman Catholic under Elizabeth I. Plays include *The Play of the Wether* (1533) and *The four P's* (?1545).
The Dramatic Writings, ed. J.S. Farmer (1905)
The Proverbs, Epigrammes, and Miscellanies, ed. J.S. Farmer (1906)
The Foure P's; The Play of the Wether in *The Chief pre-Shakespearean Dramas*, ed. J.Q. Adams (Boston, 1924)

Johnson, R.C., *John Heywood* (NY, 1970)

Hooker, Richard (*c.* 1553–1600)
Clergyman, scholar, and theologian. Educated Corpus Christi, Oxford. Master of the Temple, 1585. *Laws of Ecclesiastical Politie*, I-IV (1593), V (1597).
Works, 8 vols., ed. W.S. Hill *et al.* (Cambridge, Mass., 1977–   )
Laws of Ecclesiastical Polity, 3 vols., ed. J. Keble, rev. R.W. Church and F. Paget (Oxford, 1888); abridged edn, eds. A.S. McGrade and B.W. Vickers (1976)

Hill, W.S. (ed.), *Studies in Richard Hooker* (Cleveland, Ohio, 1972)
Marshall, J.S., *Hooker and the Anglican Tradition: an Historical and Theological Study of Hooker's 'Ecclesiastical Polity'* (1963)
Morris, C., *Political Thought in England: Tyndale to Hooker* (1953)

Kyd, Thomas (1558–94)
Dramatist. Educated Merchant Taylors' School. *Spanish Tragedy* (*c.*1589, printed 1592). Kyd may have written a lost precursor of Shakespeare's *Hamlet*.
Works, ed. F.S. Boas (1901; rev. Oxford, 1955)
The Spanish Tragedy, ed. P. Edwards (1959); ed. B.L. Joseph (1964); ed. A.S. Cairncross (1967); ed. T.W. Roos (Edinburgh, 1968); ed. J.R. Mulryne (1970)

Edwards, P., *Thomas Kyd and Early Elizabethan Tragedy* (1966)
Freeman, A., *Thomas Kyd: Facts and Problems* (1967)
Murray, P.B., *Thomas Kyd* (NY, 1970)
See VI. 168, 178

Lodge, Thomas (*c.* 1558–1625)
Poet, dramatist, translator, and prose writer. Educated Merchant Taylors' School, Trinity, Oxford, and Lincoln's Inn; later studied medicine in Avignon and converted to Roman Catholicism. Travelled to South America. *Forbonius and Prisceria* (1584); *Scillaes Metamorphosis* (1589); *Rosalynde* (1590); *Phillis* (1593); *Wounds of Civill War* (1594); *A Fig for Momus* (1595); *A Margarite of America* (1596). Translator of Josephus and Seneca.
Complete works, 4 vols., ed. E. Gosse (1875–83; NY, 1963)

Paradise, N.B., *Thomas Lodge: the History of an Elizabethan* (New Haven, 1931)

Rae, W.D., *Thomas Lodge* (NY, 1967)

Ryan, M. Jr, *Thomas Lodge, Gentleman* (Hamden, Conn., 1959)

Sisson, C.J., *Thomas Lodge and other Elizabethans* (Cambridge, Mass., 1933)

Tenney, E.A., *Thomas Lodge* (Ithaca, 1935)

Lyly, John (*c.* 1554–1606)

Poet, dramatist, prose writer, and controversialist. Educated Merchant Taylors' School and Magdalene, Oxford. Entered Marprelate controversy. Prose works include *Euphues* (1578) and *Euphues and his England* (1580). Plays include *Campaspe* (1584), *Sapho and Phao* (1584), *Endymion* (1591), *Midas* (1592).

Complete works, 3 vols., ed. R.W. Bond (Oxford, 1902; 1967)

Euphues, ed. M.W. Croll and H. Clemons (1916; NY, 1964)

Galatea and *Midas*, ed. A. Lancashire (1970)

Houppert, J.W., *John Lyly* (Boston, 1975)

Hunter, G.K., *John Lyly. The Humanist as Courtier* (1962)

Jeffrey, V.M., *John Lyly and the Italian Renaissance* (Paris, 1929; NY, 1969)

Saccio, P., *The Court Comedies of John Lyly: a Study in Allegorical Dramaturgy* (Princeton, 1969)

Lyndsay, Sir David (*c.* 1485–*c.* 1555)

Scottish poet, courtier, and diplomat. *The Dreme* (1528); *Complaynt to the King* (1529); *Testament, and Complaynt, of our Soverane Lordis Papyngo* (1530); *Ane Pleasant Satyre of the Thrie Estaitis* (1540); *History of Squyer Meldrum*.

Works, 4 vols., ed. D. Hamer (STS, 1931–6)

Ane Satyre of the Thrie Estatis, ed. J. Kinsley (1954)

Squyer Meldrum, ed. J. Kinsley (1959)

Kantrowitz, J.S., *Dramatic Allegory: Lindsay's 'Ane Satyre of the Thrie Estatis* (Nebraska, 1975)

Marlowe, Christopher (1564–93)

Poet, dramatist, and government agent. Educated King's School, Canterbury and Corpus Christi, Cambridge, from which after government intervention he gained an MA. Dates of his works uncertain: *Dido, Queene of Carthage* (*c.* 1587); *Tamburlaine* Pt 1 (*c.* 1587). Pt 2 (1588); *Jew of Malta, Edward II, Massacre at Paris, Dr Faustus* in following years. Non-dramatic work includes the incomplete *Hero and Leander* and translations of Ovid's *Amores*. Died in brawl.

The Complete Works of Christopher Marlowe, ed. Roma Gill., vol. I: *Translations* (Oxford, 1987)

Complete Works, 2 vols., ed. F.T. Bowers (Cambridge, 1973)

Complete Plays and Poems, ed. E.D. Pendry and J.C. Maxwell (1976)

Complete Poems and Translations, ed. S. Orgel (Harmondsworth, 1971)

Plays, ed. L. Kirschbaum (NY, 1962); ed. I. Ribner (NY, 1964); ed. J.B. Steane (Harmondsworth, 1969); ed. R. Gill (1971)

Cutts, J.P., *The Left-Hand of God: a Critical Interpretation of the Plays of Christopher Marlowe* (1973)

Godshalk, W.L., *The Marlovian World Picture* (The Hague, 1974)

Knoll, R.E., *Christopher Marlowe* (NY, 1969)

Leech, C., *Christopher Marlowe: Poet of the Stage* (NY, 1986)

Masinton, C.G., *Christopher Marlowe's Tragic Vision: a Study in Damnation* (Athens, Ohio, 1972)

Sanders, W., *The Dramatist and the Received Idea: Studies in the Plays of Marlowe and Shakespeare* (Cambridge, 1968)

Shepherd, S., *Marlowe and the Politics of Elizabethan Theater* (NY, 1986)

Steane, J.B., *Marlowe: a Critical Study* (Cambridge, 1964)

Summers, C.J., *Christopher Marlowe and the Politics of Power* (Salzburg, 1974)

Waith, E.M., *Ideas of Greatness: Heroic Drama in England* (NY, 1971)

Weil, J., *Christopher Marlowe: Merlin's Prophet* (Cambridge, 1977)

Zucker, D.H., *Stage and Image in the Plays of Christopher Marlowe* (Salzburg, 1972)

See: VI. 85, 100, 173

More, Sir Thomas (1478–1535)

Lawyer, civil servant, MP, writer and controversialist. Educated in household of Cardinal Morton, at Canterbury College, Oxford, and Inns of Court. Friend of English and foreign scholars and humanists, including Erasmus, and patron of Holbein. Early prose works include the *Lyfe of Johan Picus Erle of Mirandula* and *History of Richard III*. *Utopia* (1516). *Dialogue* (1528) opens his public campaign against Protestantism. Lord Chancellor (1529), resigned 1532. Imprisoned and executed for refusing Oath of Supremacy.

Sylvester, R.S. and Miller, C.H. (eds.), *Yale Edition of the Complete Works of Sir Thomas More* (1965–)
Utopia, tr. P. Turner (Harmondsworth, 1965)

Davies, J.C., *Utopia and the Ideal Society: English Utopian Writing 1516–1700* (Cambridge, 1981)

Fox, D. and Leech, P. (eds.), *Thomas More: the Rhetoric of Character* (Otago, 1979)

Guy, J., *The Public Career of Thomas More* (Brighton, 1980)

Hexter, J.H., *More's 'Utopia': the Biography of an Idea* (Princeton, 1952)

Johnson, R.S., *More's 'Utopia': Ideal and Illusion* (New Haven, 1969)

Jones, J.P., *Sir Thomas More* (1979)

Marius, R., *Thomas More: a Biography* (1984)

Schoeck, R.J., *The Achievement of Thomas More: Aspects of his Life and Works* (1976)

Surtz, E., *The Praise of Pleasure: Philosophy, Education, and Communism in More's 'Utopia'* (Harvard, 1957)
The Praise of Wisdom: a Commentary on the Religious and Moral Backgrounds of St Thomas More's 'Utopia' (Chicago, 1957)

Sylvester, R.S. (ed.), *St Thomas More: Action and Contemplation* (New Haven, 1972)

Sylvester, R.S. and Marc'hadour, G.P. (eds.), *Essential Articles for the Study of Thomas More* (1977)
See VI. 85, 117

Nashe, Thomas (1567–1601)
Pamphleteer, satirist, polemicist. Educated at St John's, Cambridge. Participated in Marprelate controversy and famous satirical battle with Richard and Gabriel Harvey, terminated by the bishops' ban and the burning of their books in 1599. Besides his satires, major works include *The Unfortunate Traveller* (1594).

McKerrow, R.B. (ed.), *The Works of Thomas Nashe* (1904–10; repr. with add. notes by F.P. Wilson, 1958)

Steane, J.B. (ed.), *Thomas Nashe: 'The Unfortunate Traveller' and Other Works* (Harmondsworth, 1972)

Hibbard, G.R., *Thomas Nashe: a Critical Introduction* (1962)

Nicholl, C., *A Cup of News: the Life of Thomas Nashe* (1984)

Schrickx, W., *Shakespeare's Early Contemporaries: the Background of the Harvey-Nashe Polemic and 'Loves Labours Lost'* (Antwerp, 1956)

Peele, George (*c.* 1558–96)
Actor, dramatist, and poet. Educated Christ's Hospital, Pembroke, and Christ Church, Oxford. Major plays include *Araygnement of Paris* (1584); *Edward I* (1593); *Battle of Alcazar* (1594); *The Old Wives' Tale* (*c.*1595?); *David and Fair Bethsabe* (1599).
Life and Works, 3 vols., gen. ed. C.T. Prouty (New Haven, 1952–70)

Ashley, L.R., *George Peele* (NY, 1970)

Raleigh, Sir Walter (?1552–1618)
Courtier, soldier, explorer, poet, and historian. Educated at Oriel, Oxford; expedition to Virginia, 1584; Guiana, 1595. Lyric poetry of uncertain date; *Discoverie of Guiana* (1596). Turbulent political career terminated by James I's distrust. Imprisoned in Tower 1603–16. *The History of the World* (1614). Failure of Orinoco expedition led to execution.
The works of Sir Walter Ralegh, Kt., now First Collected; to Which are Prefixed the Lives of the Author, 8 vols., eds. W. Oldys and T. Birch (1829; repr. 1965 and 1968)
The Poems of Sir Walter Ralegh, ed. A. Latham (1929; rev. 1951)
Selected Writings, ed. G. Hammond (Manchester, 1984)
History of the World, abridged and ed. C.A. Patrides (1971)

Adamson, J.H. and Folland, H.F., *The Shepherd of the Ocean* (1969)

Bradbrook, M.C., *The School of Night: a Study in the Literary Relationships of Sir Walter Raleigh* (Cambridge, 1936)

Edwards, P., *Sir Walter Ralegh* (1953)

Greenblatt, S.J., *Sir Walter Ralegh: the Renaissance Man and his Roles* (New Haven, 1973)

Lefranc, P., *Sir Walter Ralegh, ecrivain: l'oeuvre et les idées* (Paris, 1968)

Oakeshott, W., *The Queen and the Poet* (1960)

Racin, J., *Sir Walter Ralegh as Historian: an Analysis of the 'History of the World'* (Salzburg, 1974)

Winton, J. [Pratt, J.], *Sir Walter Ralegh* (1975)

Sackville, Thomas, Earl of Dorset (1536–1608)
Poet, dramatist, and statesman. Educated ?Oxford, Inner Temple. *Gorboduc* with Thomas Norton;

contributed to *Mirror for Magistrates*. *Gorboduc*, ed. J.W. Cunliffe in *Early English Classical Tragedies* (Oxford, 1912); in *Five Elizabethan Tragedies*, ed. A.K. McIlwraith (1959); ed. I.B. Cauthen, Jr (1970)

The Mirror for Magistrates, ed. L.B. Campbell (Cambridge, 1938, 1946; NY, 1960)

Bacquet, P., *Un contemporain d'Elisabeth I: Thomas Sackville. L'homme et l'oeuvre* (Geneva, 1966)

Berlin, N., *Thomas Sackville* (NY, 1974)

See VI. 168, 204

Sidney, Sir Philip (1554–86)
Courtier, soldier, author. Close family ties with leading nobles. Educated Shrewsbury and Christ Church, Oxford. Travelled extensively in France, Germany, and Italy (1572–5) and became famous among statesman and scholars throughout Europe. Lost favour of Elizabeth for tactless militant protestantism. Knighted 1582 for diplomatic reasons. No literary work published in his lifetime: *The Lady of May* (1578 or 1579); first version of the *Arcadia*, 1580; *Astrophel and Stella* and *Defence of Poetry* (*c.* 1581); began revising the *Arcadia*, 1584. Governor of Flushing 1585. Died of wounds received at Zutphen. Given one of the sixteenth century's most lavish funerals and quickly assumed mythic status. *New Arcadia* published in three versions in 1590, 1593, and 1598; *Astrophel and Stella* (1591); *Defence of Poetry* (1595).

The Poems, ed. W.A. Ringler, Jr, (Oxford, 1962)

The Countess of Pembroke's Arcadia (the Old Arcadia), ed. J. Robertson (Oxford, 1973)

The Old Arcadia, ed. K. Duncan-Jones (Oxford, 1985)

The Countess of Pembroke's Arcadia [*the New Arcadia*], ed. Maurice Evans (Harmondsworth, 1977)

An Apology for Poetry, ed. G. Shepherd (1965)

Miscellaneous Prose, ed. K. Duncan-Jones and J. van Dorsten (Oxford, 1973)

Kalstone, D., *Sir Philip Sidney: Selected Poetry and Prose* (1970)

Buxton, J., *Sir Philip Sidney and the English Renaissance* (1954)

Connell, D., *Sir Philip Sidney: the Maker's Mind* (Oxford, 1977)

Davis, W.R., and Lanham, R.A., *Sidney's Arcadia. A Map of Arcadia: Sidney's Romance in its Tradition. The Old Arcadia* (New Haven, 1965)

van Dorsten, J.A., Baker-Smith, D. and Kinney, A. (eds.), *Sir Philip Sidney: 1586 and the Creation of a Legend* (Leiden, 1986)

Hamilton, A.C., *Sir Philip Sidney: a Study of his Life and Works* (Cambridge, 1977)

Howell, R., *Sir Philip Sidney. The Shepherd Knight* (1968)

Kalstone, D., *Sidney's Poetry: Contexts and Interpretations* (Cambridge, Mass., 1965)

Kimbrough, R., *Sir Philip Sidney* (1971)

McCoy, R.C., *Sir Philip Sidney: Rebellion in Arcadia* (New Brunswick, 1979)

Myrick, K.O., *Sir Philip Sidney as a Literary Craftsman* (Cambridge, Mass., 1935) [Harvard Studies in English, vol. XIV]

Osborn, J.M., *Young Philip Sidney, 1572–1577* (New Haven, 1972)

Raitiere, M.N., *Faire Bitts: Sir Philip Sidney and Renaissance Political Theory* (Pittsburg, 1984) [Duquesne Studies: Language and Literature Series 4]

Robinson, F.G., *The Shape of Things Known: Sidney's 'Apology' in its Philosophical Tradition* (Cambridge, Mass., 1972)

Waller, G.F. and Moore, M.D. (eds.), *Sir Philip Sidney and the Interpretation of Renaissance Culture: the Poet in his Time and Ours. A Collection of Critical and Scholarly Essays* (1984)

Weiner, A.D., *Sir Philip Sidney and the Poetics of Protestantism: a Study of Contexts* (Minneapolis, 1978)

Sidney's sister and brother followed in his footsteps to form the most glittering literary family of the century:

Sidney, Robert (1563–1626)
Governor of Flushing, 1588. Baron Sidney (1603). Viscount Lisle (1605). Earl of Leicester (1618). Poetry probably written in 1590s.

The Poems, ed. P.J. Croft (Oxford, 1984)

Skelton, John (*c.* 1460–1529)
Poet and cleric. Educated at ?Peterhouse, Cambridge. Laureate, Oxford, 1489; Louvain, 1492; Cambridge, 1493. Tutor to Prince Henry (Henry VIII), ?1496–1501. Ordained 1498. Poetry – especially satire – profoundly concerned with

competing interest groups at court.
Works include *The Bowge of Court*
(1498), pub. 1499. *The Garlande of
Laurell* (?1495); *Phillyp Sparowe*
(?1505); *Speke Parott and Collyn Clout
(?1521–2); The Tunnying of Elynour
Rummynge* (?1517) and the play
Magnyfycence (?1515–16).

The Complete English Poems, ed. J.
Scattergood (Harmondsworth, 1983)
Magnificence, ed. P. Neuss
(Manchester, 1980)
Kinsman, R.S. (ed.), *John Skelton: Poems*
(Oxford, 1969) [selection]

Carpenter, N.C., *John Skelton* (NY, 1968)
Edwards, H.L.R., *Skelton: the Life and
Times of an Early Tudor Poet* (1949)
Fish, S.E., *John Skelton's Poetry* (New
Haven, 1965)
Gordon, I.A., *John Skelton, Poet Laureate*
(Melbourne, 1943)
Harris, W.O., *Skelton's 'Magnyfycence' and
the Cardinal Virtue Tradition* (Chapel
Hill, 1965)
Heiserman, A.R., *Skelton and Satire*
(Chicago, 1961)
Kinsman, R.S. (ed.), *John Skelton, Early
Tudor Laureate: an Annotated
Bibliography c. 1488–1977* (Boston,
1979)
Nelson, W., *John Skelton, Laureate* (NY,
1939) [Columbia University Studies in
English and Comparative Literature,
No. 139]
Pollet, M., *John Skelton, Poet of Tudor
England*, tr. J. Warrington (1962)
See VI. 85, 117, 148

Spenser, Edmund (?1552–99)
Civil servant and poet. Educated
Merchant Taylors' School. Contributed
translations to Jan van der Noodt's
Theatre for Voluptuous Worldlings.
Pembroke College, Cambridge: MA
1576; close friend of Gabriel Harvey.
Secretary to John Young, Bishop of
Rochester, 1578. In Earl of Leicester's
employ, 1579. *Shepheardes Calender*,
1579. Secretary to Lord Grey de
Wilton, Lord Deputy of Ireland, 1580.
Remained in Ireland as civil servant
and planter. *The Faerie Queene*, I–III,
1590. Granted royal pension, 1591.
*Amoretti and Epithalamium, Colin
Clout's come home Againe*, 1595. *The
Faerie Queene*, I–VI, *Fowre Hymnes,
Prothalamion*, 1596. Sherrif of Cork,
1598. *A Viewe of the Present State of
Ireland*, 1598. Left Ireland following
sack of his home, Kilcolman, during

Tyrone rebellion; died in London,
1599. 'Cantos of Mutability', 1609.
*Variorum Edition of the Works of
Edmund Spenser*, 10 vols., ed. E.
Greenlaw *et al.* (Baltimore, 1932–58,
1966)
Poetical Works, 3 vols., eds. J.C. Smith
and E. de Selincourt (Oxford,
1909–10). Single volume edition, 1912.
The Faerie Queene, ed. A.C. Hamilton
(1977); ed. T.P. Roche
(Harmondsworth, 1981)

Alpers, P.J., *The Poetry of 'The Faerie
Queene'* (Princeton, NJ, 1967)
Alpers, P.J. (ed.), *Edmund Spenser: a
Critical Anthology* (Harmondsworth,
1969)
Aptekar, J., *Icons of Justice: Iconography
and Thematic Imagery in Book V of
'The Faerie Queene'* (NY, 1969)
Arthos, J., *On the Poetry of Spenser and the
Form of the Romances* (1956)
Bender, J., *Spenser and Literary Pictorialism*
(Princeton, NJ, 1972)
Bennett, J.W., *The Evolution of 'The Faerie
Queene'* (Chicago, 1942)
Berger, H. Jr, *The Allegorical Temper:
Vision and Reality in Book II of
Spenser's 'Faerie Queene'* (New Haven,
1957)
Brooks-Davies, D., *Spenser's 'Faerie
Queene': a Critical Commentary on
Books I and II* (Manchester, 1977)
Cain, T., *Praise in 'The Faerie Queene'*
(Lincoln, Nebraska, 1978)
Cheney, D., *Spenser's Image of Nature:
Wild Man and Shepherd in 'The Faerie
Queene'* (New Haven, Connecticut,
1966)
Cullen, P., *Infernal Triad: the Flesh, the
World, and the Devil in Spenser and
Milton* (Princeton, NJ, 1974)
*Spenser, Marvell, and the Renaissance
Pastoral* (Cambridge, Mass., 1970)
Dunseath, T.K., *Spenser's Allegory of
Justice in Book Five of 'The Faerie
Queene'* (Princeton, NJ, 1968)
Ellrodt, R., *Neoplatonism in the Poetry of
Spenser* (Geneva, 1960)
Evans, M., *Spenser's Anatomy of Heroism:
a Commentary on 'The Faerie Queene'*
(Cambridge, 1970)
Fletcher, A., *The Prophetic Moment: an
Essay on Spenser* (Chicago, 1971)
Fowler, A., *Edmund Spenser* (Longmans for
British Council, 1978)
Fowler, A.D.S., *Spenser and the Numbers of
Time* (1964)
Freeman, R., *'The Faerie Queene': a
Companion for Readers* (1970)

Hamilton, A.C., *The Structure of Allegory in 'The Faerie Queene'* (Oxford, 1961)

Hamilton, A.C. (ed.), *Essential Articles for the Study of Edmund Spenser* (Hamden, Conn., 1972)

Hankins, J., *Source and Meaning in Spenser's Allegory: a Study of 'The Faerie Queene'* (Oxford, 1971)

Hieatt, A.K., *Chaucer, Spenser, Milton: Mythopoeic Continuities and transformations* (Montreal, 1975)

Short Times Endless Monument: the Symbolism of the numbers in Spenser's 'Epithalamion' (NY, 1960)

Hoffman, N., *Spenser's Pastorals: 'The Shepheardes Calender' and 'Colin Clouts Come Home Again'* (Baltimore, 1977)

Hough, G., *A Preface to 'The Faerie Queene'* (1962)

Leslie, M., *'Fierce Warres and Faithfull Loves': Martial and Chivalric Symbolism in 'The Faerie Queene'* (Cambridge, 1983)

Lewis, C.S., *Spenser's Images of Life*, ed. A. Fowler (Cambridge, 1967)

MacCaffrey, I.G., *Spenser's Allegory: the Anatomy of Imagination* (Princeton, NJ, 1976)

McLane, P., *Spenser's 'Shepheardes Calender': a Study in Elizabethan Pastoral* (Notre Dame, Ind., 1961)

Nelson, W., *The poetry of Edmund Spenser: a Study* (NY, 1963)

Nohrnberg, J., *The Analogy of 'The Faerie Queene'* (Princeton, NJ, 1976)

O'Connell, M., *Mirror and Veil: the Historical Dimension of Spenser's 'Faerie Queene'* (Chapel Hill, 1977)

Renwick, W.L., *Edmund Spenser: an Essay on Renaissance Poetry* (1925; repr., 1961)

Roche, T.P., *The Kindly Flame: a Study of the Third and Fourth Books of Spenser's 'Faerie Queene'* (Princeton, NJ, 1964)

Rose, M., *Heroic Love: Studies in Sidney and Spenser* (Cambridge, Mass., 1968)

Sale, R., *Reading Spenser: an Introduction to 'The Faerie Queene'* (NY, 1968)

Shire, H., *A Preface to Spenser* (1978)

Shore, D.R., *Spenser and the Poetics of Pastoral: a Study of the World of Colin Clout* (Kingston, 1983)

Tonkin, H., *Spenser's Courteous Pastoral: Book VI of the 'Faerie Queene'* (Oxford, 1972)

Welsford, E., *Spenser's 'Fowre Hymnes' and 'Epithalamion': a Study of Spenser's Doctrine of Love* (Oxford, 1967)

Williams, K., *Spenser's 'Faerie Queene': the World of Glass* (1966)

See VI. 74, 76, 78, 85, 102, 109, 157

Surrey, Henry Howard, Earl of

(1518–47)

Poet; member of leading political dynasty, soldier, courtier. Lyric poetry, imitated from Petrarch and other Italians, as well as translation of part of *The Aeneid*. Executed for treason. His poetry has its principal effect through bastardised versions in *Tottel's Miscellany* (1557), and he became a literary topic in his own right later in the century.

The Poems of Henry Howard, Earl of Surrey, ed. F.M. Padelford (1920; rev. 1928, repr. 1966)

The 'Aeneid' of Henry Howard, Earl of Surrey, ed. F. Ridley (1963) [University of California Publications **26**]

Henry Howard, Earl of Surrey: Poems, ed. E. Jones (Oxford, 1964) [selection]

Henry Howard, Earl of Surrey: Selected Poems, ed. D. Keene (Manchester, 1985)

See VI. 117, 156

Turberville, George (*c.* 1540–1610)

Poet, translator, and diplomat. Educated Winchester, New College, Oxford, and Inns of Court. Travelled to Russia. *Epitaphes, Epigrams, Songs, and Sonets* (1567); *The Books of Faulconrie. The Noble Art of Venerie or Hunting* (attributed), 1575.

Sheidley, W.A., *George Turberville* (NY, 1981)

Watson, Thomas (1555–92)

Poet, dramatist, and translator. Educated ?Oxford and Inns of Court. Translated Sophocles' *Antigone* (1581). *Hekatompathia* (1582). Tr. Tasso's *Aminta* (1585). *The First Sett of Italian Madrigalls Englished* (1590). *Poems*, ed. E. Arbor (1870)

The Hekatompathia or Passionate Centurie of Love, ed. S.K. Heninger, Jr (Gainesville, 1964)

Wyatt, Sir Thomas (1503–42)

Poet and diplomat. Educated St John's, Cambridge. Travelled in France, Spain, and Italy; 1536 imprisoned in wake of Anne Boleyn's disgrace but returned to royal favour. With Surrey introduced sonnet to England, translating the lyric poetry of Petrarch and other Italian masters. Influential in bastardised form through *Tottel's Miscellany*.

Collected Poems of Sir Thomas Wyatt, eds. K. Muir and P. Thomson (Liverpool, 1969)
Sir Thomas Wyatt: the Complete Poems, ed. R.J. Rebholz (Harmondsworth, 1978)
Sir Thomas Wyatt: Collected Poems, ed. J. Daalder (1975)

Baldi, S., *Sir Thomas Wyatt*, tr. F.T. Prince (1961)
Jentoft, C.W., *Sir Thomas Wyatt and Henry Howard, Earl of Surrey, a Reference Guide* (1980)
Kamholtz, J.Z., 'Thomas Wyatt's Poetry: the Politics of Love', *Criticism* **20** (1978) 349–65
Muir, K., *Life and Letters of Sir Thomas Wyatt* (Liverpool, 1963)
Thompson, P., *Sir Thomas Wyatt and his Background* (1964)
See VI. 25, 85, 117, 148

MINOR WRITERS
W.E. Shieldey, *Barnabe Goode*, (Boston, 1981)
Gorges, Sir Arthur, *Poems*, ed. H.E. Sandison (Oxford, 1953)
V.F. Sterne, *Gabriel Harvey: his Life, Marginalia, and Library*, (Oxford, 1979)
R.R. Cowley, *Henry Peacham, his contribution to English Poetry*, (1971)
Alan R. Young, *Henry Peacham*, (Boston, 1979)

4   William Shakespeare (1564–1616)

Born Stratford-upon-Avon, educated King's New School, Stratford. By 1592 established in London theatrical world. *Venus and Adonis* (1593); *Rape of Lucrece* (1594). Leading member of Lord Chamberlain's company (King's company from 1603) by 1594. *Sonnets* (1609). Plays published 1623.

EDITIONS
The *Complete works*, ed. S. Wells and G. Taylor (Oxford, 1986)
Individual plays are best read in the New Arden, Oxford, Penguin, Sygnet, or Cambridge series.
Kerrigan, J. (ed.), *The 'Sonnets' and 'A Lover's Complaint'* (Harmondsworth, 1986)

Secondary bibliography
To provide an adequate introduction to the vast literature on Shakespeare would

overwhelm this bibliography. The following selection lists more comprehensive guides; some of the indispensable texts, chiefly reference; and then concentrates on recent Shakespeare criticism, omitting commentaries on individual plays or genres unless these stand as major statements relating to the wider reading of Shakespeare.

BIBLIOGRAPHICAL GUIDES
Muir, K. and Schoenbaum, S. (eds.), *A new Companion to Shakespeare Studies* (Cambridge, 1971)
Wells, S., *Shakespeare: a Reading Guide* (1969)
Wells, S. (ed.), *The Cambridge Companion to Shakespeare Studies* (Cambridge, 1986)
Shakespeare: Select Bibliographical Guides (1973)

BIOGRAPHY
Bentley, G.E., *Shakespeare: a Biographical Handbook* (New Haven, 1961)
Chambers, E.K., *William Shakespeare: a Study of Facts and Problems*, 2 vols. (Oxford, 1930)
Honigman, E.A.J., *Shakespeare: the 'Lost' Years* (1985)
Schoenbaum, S., *Shakespeare's Lives* (1970)
William Shakespeare: a Documentary Life (Oxford, 1975)
William Shakespeare: Records and Images (1981)

TEXT
Bowers, F., *On Editing Shakespeare* (Charlottesville, 1966)
On Editing Shakespeare and the Elizabethan Dramatists (Philadelphia, 1955)
Greg, W.W., *The Editorial Problem in Shakespeare: a Survey of the Foundations of the Text* (3rd edn, Oxford, 1954)
The Shakespeare First Folio: its Bibliographical and Textual History (Oxford, 1955)
Hinman, C., *The Printing and Proof-reading of the First Folio of Shakespeare* (Oxford, 1963)
Hinman, C. (ed.), *The Norton Facsimile: the First Folio of Shakespeare* (NY, 1968)
Honigman, E.A.J., *The Stability of Shakespeare's Text* (1965)
Howard-Hill, T.H., *Shakespearean Bibliography and Textual Criticism: a Bibliography* (Oxford, 1971)

McKerrow, R.B., *Prolegomena for the Oxford Shakespeare: a Study in Editorial Method* (Oxford, 1939)

NON-DRAMATIC POETRY

Booth, S., *An Essay on Shakespeare's Sonnets* (New Haven, 1969)

Colie, R., *Shakespeare's Living Art* (Princeton, 1974)

Landry H. (ed.), *New Essays on Shakespeare's Sonnets* (NY, 1976)

Melchiori, G., *Shakespeare's Dramatic Meditations* (Oxford, 1976)

See also VI. 96, 100

DRAMATIC WORKS

Alvis, J. and West, T.G. (eds), *Shakespeare as Political Thinker* (Durham, NC, 1986)

Axton, M., *The Queen's Two Bodies: Drama and the Elizabethan Succession* (1977)

Bamber, L., *Comic Women, Tragic Men: a Study of Gender and Genre in Shakespeare* (Stanford, 1982)

Baquet, P., *Les Pièces Historiques de Shakespeare II: La Deuxième Tetralogie et 'Henry VIII'* (Paris, 1979)

Barber, C.L., *Shakespeare's Festive Comedy: a Study of Dramatic Form and its Relation to Social Custom* (Princeton, 1959)

Barton, J., *Playing Shakespeare* (1984)

Bayley, J., *Shakespeare and Tragedy* (1981)

Beckerman, B., *Shakespeare at the Globe 1599–1609* (NY, 1962)

Bergeron, D.M. (ed.), *Pageantry in the Shakespearean Theater* (Athens, Georgia, 1984)

Bevington, D., *Action is Eloquence: Shakespeare's Language of Gesture* (Cambridge, Mass., 1984)

Berry, R., *The Shakespearean Metaphor: Studies in Language and Form* (1978)

Booth, S., *'King Lear', 'Macbeth', Indefinition and Tragedy* (New Haven, 1983)

Bradbrook, M.C., *The Living Monument: Shakespeare and the Theatre of his Time* (Cambridge, 1979)

Shakespeare the Craftsman (1969)

Bradbury, M. and Palmer, D. (eds), *Shakespearean Comedy* (1957)

Bradley, A.C., *Shakespearean Tragedy* (1905)

Brennan, A., *Shakespeare's Dramatic Structures* (1986)

Brissenden, A., *Shakespeare and the Dance* (1981)

Brook, G.L., *The Language of Shakespeare* (1976)

Brooke, N., *Shakespeare's Early Tragedies* (1968)

Brown, J.R., *Discovering Shakespeare: a New Guide to the Plays* (1982)

Shakespeare's Plays in Performance (1966)

Brown, J.R. and Harris, B. (eds), *Early Shakespeare* (1961) Stratford-upon-Avon Studies

Later Shakespeare (1966) Stratford-upon-Avon Studies

Bullough, G., *Narrative and Dramatic Sources of Shakespeare*, 8 vols. (1957–75)

Campbell, L.B., *Shakespeare's Histories: Mirrors of Elizabethan Policy* (San Marino, 1947)

Carroll, W.C., *The Great Feast of Language in 'Loves Labours Lost'* (Princeton, 1976)

Chaudhuri, S., *Infirm Glory: Shakespeare and the Renaissance Image of Man* (1981)

Clemen, W., *The Development of Shakespeare's Imagery* (1951)

Coghill, N., *Shakespeare's Professional Skills* (1964)

Colie, R., *Shakespeare's Living Art* (Princeton, 1974)

David, R., *Shakespeare in the Theatre* (Cambridge, 1981)

Dollimore, J. and Sinfield, A. (eds), *Political Shakespeare: New Essays in Cultural Materialism* (Manchester, 1985)

Donawerth, J., *Shakespeare and the Sixteenth-Century Study of Language* (Urbana, 1984)

Drakakis, J. (ed.), *Alternative Shakespeares* (1985)

Dusinberre, J., *Shakespeare and the Nature of Women* (1975)

Eagleton, T., *William Shakespeare* (Oxford, 1986)

Edwards, P., *Shakespeare and the Confines of Art* (1968)

Edwards, P., Ewbank, I.-S. and Hunter, G.K. (eds), *Shakespeare's Styles: Essays in Honour of Kenneth Muir* (Cambridge, 1980)

Elam, K., *Shakespeare's Universe of Discourse: Language-Games in the Comedies* (Cambridge, 1984)

Empson, W., *Essays on Shakespeare*, ed. D. Pirie (Cambridge, 1986)

Evans, B., *Shakespeare's Tragic Practice* (Oxford, 1979)

Evans, M., *Signifying Nothing: Truth's True Contents in Shakespeare's Text* (Brighton, 1986)

Faas, E., *Shakespeare's Poetics* (Cambridge, 1986)

Ferguson, J., *The Man behind 'Macbeth'* (1969)

Fiedler, L., *The Stranger in Shakespeare* (1973)

Frye, N., *The Myth of Deliverance: Reflections on Shakespeare's Problem Comedies* (Brighton, 1983)

A Natural Perspective: the development of Shakespeare's Comedy and Romance (NY, 1965)

Frye, R.M., *The Renaissance Hamlet: Issues and Responses in 1600* (Princeton, 1984)

Garber, M., *Coming of Age in Shakespeare* (1981)

Garber, M.B., *Dream in Shakespeare: From Metaphor to Metamorphosis* (New Haven, 1974)

Goodwin, J., *A Short Guide to Shakespeare's Plays* (1979)

Granville-Barker, H., *Prefaces to Shakespeare* (1927–48; 1958)

Hammond, G., *The Reader and Shakespeare's Young Man Sonnets* (1981)

Hawkins, H., *The Devil's Party: Critical Counter-Interpretations of Shakespearean Drama* (Oxford, 1985)

Hibbard, G.R., *The Making of Shakespeare's Dramatic Poetry* (Toronto, 1981)

Homan, S., *Shakespeare's More Words than Words can Witness: Essays on Visual and Nonverbal Enactment in the Plays* (Lewisburg, 1980)

Honigmann, E.A.J., *Shakespeare's Seven Tragedies: the Dramatist's Manipulation of Response* (1976)

Hulme, H.M., *Explorations in Shakespeare's Language: some Problems of Lexical Meaning in the Dramatic Text* (1962)

Hunter, G.K., *Dramatic Identities and Cultural Tradition: Studies in Shakespeare and his Contemporaries* (Liverpool, 1978)

Hussey, S.S., *The Literary Language of Shakespeare* (1982)

Huston, J.D., *Shakespeare's Comedies of Play* (1981)

Jardine, L., *Still Harping on Daughters: Women and Drama in the Age of Shakespeare* (Brighton, 1983)

Jones, E., *The Origins of Shakespeare* (Oxford, 1978)

Scenic Form in Shakespeare (Oxford, 1971)

Joseph, B.L., *Shakespeare's Eden* (1971)

Joseph, Sister M., *Shakespeare's Use of the Arts of Language* (1947; repr. NY, 1966)

Kahn, C., *Man's Estate: Masculine Identity in Shakespeare* (Berkeley, 1981)

Kastan, D.S., *Shakespeare and the Shapes of Time* (1982)

Knight, G. Wilson, *The Crown of Life: Essays in Interpretation of Shakespeare's Final Plays* (1959)

The Imperial Theme (1931)

The Wheel of Fire: Interpretations of Shakespearean Tragedy (1930; 4th edn, 1959)

Kott, J., *Shakespeare our Contemporary*, tr. B. Taborski (1964; 2nd rev. edn, 1967)

Krieger, E., *A Marxist Study of Shakespeare's Comedies* (1979)

Leggatt, A., *Shakespeare's Comedy of Love* (1974)

Lenz, C.R.S. *et al.* (eds), *The Woman's Part: Feminist Criticism of Shakespeare* (Urbana, 1980)

Long, M., *The Unnatural Scene: a Study in Shakespearean Tragedy* (1976)

McGuire, P.C. and Samuelson, D.A. (eds), *Shakespeare, the Theatrical Dimension* (NY, 1979)

Mahood, M.M., *Shakespeare's Wordplay* (1957)

Miola, R.S., *Shakespeare's Rome* (Cambridge, 1983)

Muir, K., *Shakespeare's Comic Sequence* (Liverpool, 1979)

Shakespeare's Sources (1957; rev. 1977)

Nevo, R., *Comic Transformations in Shakespeare* (1980)

Nicholl, C., *The Chemical Theatre* (1979)

Nuttall, A.D., *A New Mimesis: Shakespeare and the Representation of Reality* (1983)

Onions, C.T., *A Shakespeare Glossary*, enlarged and rev. R.D. Eagleson (Oxford, 1986)

Parker, P. and Hartman, G. (eds), *Shakespeare and the Question of Theory* (1985)

Pettet, E.C., *Shakespeare and the Romance Tradition* (1949)

Platt, M., *Rome and Romans According to Shakespeare* (Washington, 1983)

Porter, J.A., *The Drama of Speech Acts: Shakespeare's Lancastrian Tetralogy* (Berkeley, 1979)

Rabkin, N., *Shakespeare and the Problem of Meaning* (1982)

Reese, M.M., *The Cease of Majesty: a Study of Shakespeare's History Plays* (1961)

Shakespeare: his World and his Work (1953)

Riemer, A.P., *Antic Fables: Patterns of Evasion in Shakespeare's Comedies* (Manchester, 1980)

Righter, A. [Barton], *Shakespeare and the Idea of the Play* (1962)

Rossiter, A.P., *Angel with Horns: and other*

Shakespeare Lectures, ed. G. Storey (1961)

Salingar, L., *Dramatic Form in Shakespeare and the Jacobeans* (Cambridge, 1986)
Shakespeare and the Traditions of Comedy: a Study of Dramatic Form and its Relationship to Social Custom (Cambridge, 1974)

Schanzer, E., *The Problem Plays of Shakespeare*

Schoenbaum, S., *Shakespeare: the Globe and the World* (NY, 1979)

Snyder, S., *The Comic Matrix of Shakespeare's Tragedies* (Princeton, 1979)

Spivack, B., *Shakespeare and the Allegory of Evil* (1958)

Summers, J.M., *Dreams of Love and Power: on Shakespeare's Plays* (Oxford, 1984)

Taylor, G. and Warren, M. (eds), *The Division of the Kingdoms: Shakespeare's Two Versions of 'King Lear'* (Oxford, 1983)

Thomson, A., *Shakespeare's Chaucer: a Study in Literary Origins* (Liverpool, 1978)

Thomson, P., *Shakespeare's Theatre* (1983)

Tillyard, E.M.W., *Shakespeare's History Plays* (1944)

Traversi, D., *An Approach to Shakespeare* (1938, rev. edn, 1968)

Trewin, J.C., *Going to Shakespeare* (1978)

Trousdale, M., *Shakespeare and the Rhetoricians* (1982)

Urkowitz, S., *Shakespeare's Revision of 'King Lear'* (Princeton, 1980)

Vickers, B., *The Artistry of Shakespeare's Prose* (1968)

Weiman, R., *Shakespeare and the Popular Dramatic Tradition in the Theatre* (Baltimore, 1978)

Wilders, J., *The Lost Garden: a View of Shakespeare's English and Roman History Plays* (1975)

Wilson, J.D., *The Fortunes of Falstaff* (Cambridge, 1944)

See also VI. 257

VII Music

1 *General*

An encyclopedic introduction to all aspects of music is offered by

(1)   Sadie, S. (ed.), *The New Grove Dictionary of Music and Musicians*, 20 vols. (1980). This contains authoritative articles on the major topics relating to music in this period, as well as biographical entries for the leading composers. Excellent bibliographies are included.

(2)   Abraham, G. and Hughes, A. (eds), *The New Oxford History of Music*. III: *Ars Nova and the Renaissance* (1960)

(3)   *The New Oxford History of Music*. IV: *The Age of Humanism, 1540–1630* (1968)

(4)   Anglo, S., *Spectacle, Pageantry and Early Tudor Policy* (1969)

(5)   Baskerville, C.R., *The Elizabethan Jig and Related Song Drama* (1929)

(6)   Benham, H., *Latin Church Music in England 1460–1575* (1977)

(7)   Van den Borren, C., *Les Origines de la musique de clavier en Angleterre* (Brussels, 1912; English tr., 1914)

(8)   Boyd, M.C., *Elizabethan Music and Musical Criticism* (1940; rev. 1962)

(9)   Caldwell, J., *English Keyboard Music before the Nineteenth Century* (1973)

(10)   Carpenter, N.C., *Music in the Medieval and Renaissance Universities* (Norman, 1958)

(11)   Doughtie, E., *Lyrics from English Airs 1596–1622* (Cambridge, Mass., 1970)

(12)   Elliott, K. and Rimmer, F., *A History of Scottish Music* (1973)

(13)   Farmer, H.G., *A History of Music in Scotland* (1947)

(14)   Fellowes, E.H., *English Cathedral Music from Edward VI to Edward VII* (1941; rev. 1969)

(15)   Fellowes, E.H., *English Madrigal Composers* (1921)

(16)   Fellowes, E.H., *English Madrigal Verse 1588–1632* (1929; rev. 1967)

(17)   Finney, L., *Musical Backgrounds for English Literature: 1580–1650* (1961)

(18)   Frost, M., *English and Scottish Psalm and Hymn Tunes, c. 1545–1677* (1953)

(19)   Gibbon, J.M., *Melody and the Lyric Form, Chaucer to the Cavaliers* (1930)

(20)   Harrison, F.Ll., *Music in Medieval Britain* (1958; rev. 1963)

(21)   Hollander, J., *The Untuning of the Sky: Ideas of Music in English Poetry, 1500–1700* (Princeton, 1961)

(22)   Kerman, J., *The English Madrigal: a Comparative Study* (NY, 1962)

(23)   Krummel, D.W., *English Music Printing 1553–1700* (1975)

(24)   le Huray, P., *Music and the Reformation in England, 1549–1660* (1967; rev. edn, Cambridge, 1978)

(25)   le Huray, P., *The Treasury of English Church Music, 1540–1650* (1965)

(26)   Mackerness, E.D., *A Social History of English Music* (1964)

(27)   Maynard, W., *Elizabethan Lyric Poetry and its Music* (Oxford, 1986)

(28) McGee, T.J., *Medieval and Renaissance Music: a Performer's Guide* (Toronto, 1985)

(29) Mellers, W., *Music and Society* (1946)

(30) Meyer, E.H., *Early English Chamber Music* (rev. 1982)

(31) Monson, C.A., *Voices and Viols in England, 1600–1650: The Sources and the Music* (1982)

(32) Munrow, D., *Instruments of the Middle Ages and Renaissance* (1976)

(33) Montagu, J., *The World of Medieval and Renaissance Musical Instruments* (Newton Abbot, London and Vancouver, 1976)

(34) Obertello, A., *Madrigali italiani in Inghilterra* (Milan, 1949)

(35) Osborn, J.M. (ed.), *The Autobiography of Thomas Whythorne* (1961)

(36) Pattison, B., *Music and Poetry of the English Renaissance* (1948; 2nd edn, 1970)

(37) Pomeroy, E.W., *The Elizabethan Miscellanies: their Development and Conventions* (Berkeley, 1973)

(38) Price, D.C., *Patrons and Musicians of the English Renaissance* (Cambridge, 1981)

(39) Reese, G., *Music in the Renaissance* (1954; rev. 1959)

(40) Remnant, M., *English Bowed Instruments from Anglo-Saxon Times to Tudor Times* (Oxford, 1986)

(41) Rimbault, E.F. (ed.), *The Old Cheque-book, or Book of Remembrance of the Chapel Royal* (1872, rev. 1966) [Campden Society, NS 3]

(42) Rogers, C.C., *The History of the Chapel Royal of Scotland* (Edinburgh, 1882)

(43) Routh, F., *Early English Organ Music, from the Middle Ages to 1837* (1973)

(44) Seng, P.J., *The Vocal Songs in the Plays of Shakespeare: a Critical History* (1967)

(45) Shire, H.M., *Song, Dance and Poetry of the Court of Scotland under King James VI* (1969)

(46) Simpson, C.M., *The English Broadside Ballad and its Music* (New Brunswick, 1966)

(47) Steele, R., *The Earliest English Music Printing* (1903)

(48) Sternfeld, F.W., *Music in Shakespearean Tragedy* (1963; rev. 1967)

(49) Sternfeld, F.W. (ed.), *A History of Western Music*, vol. I: *Music from the Middle Ages to the Renaissance* (NY, 1973)

(50) Stevens, D., *The Mulliner Book: a Commentary* (1952)

(51) Stevens, D., *Tudor Church Music* (NY, 1955; rev. 1966)

(52) Stevens, J., *Music and Poetry in the Early Tudor Court* (1961; 2nd edn, Cambridge, 1979)

(53) Temperley, N., *The Music of the English Parish Church* (1979)

(54) Walker, E., *A History of Music in England*, ed. J.A. Westrup (1907; 3rd edn, Oxford, 1952)

(55) Warlock, P., *The English Ayre* (1926)

(56) Woodfill, W., *Musicians in English Society from Elizabeth I to Charles I* (Princeton, 1948)

(57) Wulstan, D., *Tudor Music* (1985)

EDITIONS OF MUSIC

The Collected Lute Music of John Dowland, ed. D. Poulton and B. Lam (1974)

The Collected Works of William Byrd (1937–50); rev. as *The Byrd Edition* (1973– .). Complete edition.

Early English Church Music (1963–   ) [Series includes volumes of liturgical and sacred music by Dering, Gibbons, Giles, William Mundy, Ramsey, Sheppard, Tallis, Taverner, Tomkins, Tye, and White; also collections of masses, magnificats, and organ music.]

The English Madrigal School (1913–24); rev. as *The English Magrigalists* (1956–   ). Complete edition.

The English School of Lutenists (1920–32); rev. as *The English Lute-Songs* (1959–   ). Complete edition.

Musica Britannica (1951–   )
[includes:
    1 The Mulliner Book
    5 Tomkins, keyboard music
    6 Dowland, ayres for four voices
   14 and 19 Bull, keyboard music I/II
   15 Music of Scotland 1500–1700
   18 Music at the court of Henry VIII
   20 Gibbons, keyboard music
   22 Consort songs
   23 Weelkes, anthems
   24 Giles and Richard Farnaby, keyboard music
   25 Dering, secular vocal music
   27 and 28 Byrd, keyboard music I/II
   36 Early Tudor songs and carols
   40 Music for mixed consort
   44 Elizabethan consort music I
   48 Gibbons, consort music]

The Oxford Book of Anthems, compiled by C. Morris (1978)

The Oxford Book of Madrigals, ed. P. Ledger (1978)

The Treasury of English Church Music 1545–1650, ed. P. le Huray (rev. 1982)

Tudor Church Music (1922–9) [Series includes liturgical and sacred music by Aston, Byrd, Gibbons, Merbecke, Parsley, Tallis, Taverner, Tomkins, White]

2   Composers and musicians

Byrd, William

b. ?Lincoln, 1543; d. Stondon Massey, Essex, 4 July 1623.

Composer. Father, ?Thomas Byrd, Gentleman of Chapel Royal. 25 March 1563: Organist and Master of Choristers at Lincoln Cathedral. February 1570, succeeded Parsons as Gentleman of Chapel Royal. Earl of Worcester, Petre family, special patrons. Tutor to Earl of Northumberland's daughter. 1575 Byrd and Tallis issued, *Cantiones, Quae ab Argumento Sacrae Vocantur*, dedicated to Elizabeth I. 1588, *Psalmes, Sonets and Songs*. 1589, *Songs of Sundrie Natures*. 1590 contributed to Thomas Watson's *First Sett of Italian Madrigalls Englished*. 1591, 'My Ladye Nevells Book'. Three masses published *c.* 1593–*c.* 1595. 1605 *Gradualia*, 2nd vol. 1607; both vols., 1610. 1611, *Psalmes, Songs and Sonnets*. Contributed to *Parthenia* with Bull and Gibbons, *c.* 1612–13. 1614, contributed to Leighton's *Teares or Lamentations of a Sorrowful Soule*.

Andrews, H.K., 'The printed part-books of Byrd's vocal music', *The Library*, 5th series, **19** (1964)

The Technique of Byrd's Vocal Polyphony (1966)

Clulow, P., 'Publication dates for Byrd's Latin masses', *Music and Letters* **47** (1966), 1–9

Fellowes, E.H., *William Byrd* (1936; 2nd edn, 1948)

William Byrd: a Short Account of his life and Work (1923)

Kerman, J., *The Masses and Motets of William Byrd* (1981)

Neighbour, O.W., *The Consort and Keyboard Music of William Byrd* (1978)

Noble, J. *et al.*, *High Renaissance Masters: Josquin, Palestrina, Lassus, Byrd, Victoria* (1984)

Campion, Thomas

b. London 1567; d. London, buried 1 March 1620.

Physician, poet, and composer.

Educated Peterhouse, Cambridge, and Gray's Inn. Verse circulating in early 1590s. Collection of twenty-one songs in Rosseter's *A Booke of Ayres* (1601). Published *Observations on the Art of English Poesie* (1602). Composed masques during 1600s and 1610s. Published *A New Way of Making Fowre Parts in Counter-point, by a most Familiar, and Infallible Rule*, 1613 or 1614; same years, *Two Bookes of Ayres*; 1617–18?, *Third and Fourth Booke of Ayres. Tho. Campiani Epigrammatum Libri II* (1619).

Davis, W.R. (ed.), *The Works of Thomas Campion: Complete Songs, Masques and Treatises, with a Selection of the Latin Verse* (NY, 1967)

Lindley, D., *Thomas Campion* (Leiden, 1986)

Lowbury, E., Salter, T. and Young, A., *Thomas Campion: Poet, Composer, Physician* (1970)

Kastendieck, M.M., *England's Musical Poet: Thomas Campion* (NY, 1938)

Sabol, A.J. (ed.), *Songs and Dances for the Stuart Masque* (1959; rev. Providence, 1968)

Vivian, P. (ed.), *Campion's Works* (Oxford, 1909)

Cornysh, William

b. *c.* 1465; d. 1523.

From a musical family, composer, poet, actor, and dramatist. From 29 September 1509, Master of the Children of the Chapel Royal.

Chambers, E.K., *The Elizabethan Stage* (Oxford, 1923)

Pulver, J., *A Biographical Dictionary of Old English Music* (1927; rev. 1973)

Wallace, C.W., *The Evolution of English Drama up to Shakespeare* (Berlin, 1912)

See also VII. 52

Dowland, John

b. ?London, 1563; d. London, buried 20 February 1626.

8 July 1588: BMus, Christ Church, Oxford. 1590, composed Accession Day Tournament music. 1592, contributed to Thomas East's *The Whole Booke of Psalmes*. 1584, refused position of Queen's lutenist; went abroad, Italy, Germany. Returned 1596 or 1597. 1597, *The First Booke of Songes or Ayres of Foure Partes with Tableture for the Lute*. 1598, lutenist of Christian IV of Denmark. 1600, *The Second Booke of Songs or Ayres*. 1603, *The Third and Last Booke of Songs*.

The Collected Lute Music of John Dowland,
    ed. D. Poulton and B. Lam (1974)
Poulton, D., *John Dowland* (1972; rev.
    1982)
Spink, I., *English Song: Dowland to Purcell*
    (1974)
See also VII. 11, 16

Fayrfax, Robert
    b. Deeping Gate, Lincs., 23 April 1464;
    d. ? St Albans, ?24 October 1521.
    1497, Gentleman of Chapel Royal;
    1501 MusB Cambridge. 1504, MusD
    Cambridge. 1511, DMus Oxford.

Warren, E.B., *Life and Works of Robert
    Fayrfax, 1464–1521, Musicological
    Studies and Documents* **22**, ed. A.
    Carapetyan (Rome, 1969)
See also VII. 20

Ferrabosco, Alfonso I
    b. Bologna, 1543; d. Bologna, 12 August
    1588.
    Musical family. Worked variously in
    Bologna, Rome, Turin, Paris; in
    England *c.* 1562, *c.* 1567, 1572–8 and
    received Pension from Elizabeth I.
    Influenced many, incl. Morley and
    Byrd.
Arkwright, G.E.P., *Arkwright Transcripts*
See also VII. 34, 56, 57

Ferrabosco, Alfonso II
    b. ?Greenwich, before 1578;
    d. Greenwich, buried 11 March 1628.
    Annuity from Elizabeth I, employed by
    James I. Instructor of Henry Prince of
    Wales. 1609 *Book of Ayres*. 7 and 8
    July 1626, Composer of Music in
    Ordinary and Composer of Music to
    the King.
Cunningham, P. (ed.), *Extracts from the
    Accounts of the Revels at Court*
    Shakespeare Society (1842)
Sabol, A.J. (ed.), *Songs and Dances for the
    Stuart Masque* (1959; rev. Providence,
    1968)
See also VII. 67

Gibbons, Orlando
    b. Oxford 1583, d. Canterbury 5 June
    1625.
    Composer and organist. 1596–8,
    chorister at King's College. 1599, sizar
    of King's. Chapel Royal by 19 May,
    1603 as Organist. 1606, MusB
    Cambridge. 1619, musician of Privy
    chamber. 1622, DMus Oxford. 1623,
    Organist of Westminster Abbey.
Fellowes, E.H., *Orlando Gibbons and his
    Family* (rev. 1970)
See also VII. 9, 22, 24, 30, 41, 43

Ludford, Nicholas
    b. *c.* 1485; d. ?Westminster in or after
    1557.
    Composer. 1521, Fraternity of St
    Nicholas, Guild of the Parish Clerks of
    the City of London. Royal Free Chapel
    of St Stephen's; Westminster.
See VII. 20

Morley, Thomas
    b. Norwich 1557 or 1558; d. London
    early October 1602.
    Composer, editor, theorist, organist.
    Pupil of Byrd. 1583, Master of the
    Choristers, Norwich Cathedral. 1588,
    BMus Oxford. Organist at St Paul's by
    1591. 1592, Gentleman of Chapel
    Royal. 1593, *Canzonets*. 1594,
    Madrigalls to Foure Voyces. 1595,
    Canzonets, *Ballets*. 1597, *Plaine and
    Easie Introduction to Practicall Musicke*.
    1598, patent of monopoly of printed
    music. 1599, *First Booke of Consort
    Lessons*. 1600, *First Booke of Ayres;
    Second Booke of Songs*. 1603, *Third and
    Last Booke of Songs*.
Morley, T., *A Plain and Easy Introduction
    to Practical Music* (1597), ed. R.A.
    Harman (1952)
Murphy, T.A., *Thomas Morley's Editions of
    Italian Canzonets and Madrigals*
    (Tallahassee, Fla, 1964)
See also VII. 15, 16, 22, 53, 65

Sheppard, John
    b. *c.* 1515; d. ?1559 or 1560.
    Composer. Magdalen, Oxford before
    1548. 1552, Gentleman of Chapel
    Royal.
See VII. 14, 20, 24, 50, 51

Tallis, Thomas
    b. *c.* 1505; d. Greenwich, 23 November
    1585.
    Composer. 1532, Organist at
    Benedictine Priory of Dover. 1537 and
    1538, ?organist at St Mary-at-Hill,
    London. 1541 and 1542, Lay Clerk
    Canterbury Cathedral. ?1543 onwards,
    Gentleman of Chapel Royal. 1575,
    granted with Byrd patent of monopoly
    of printed music.
Doe, P., *Tallis* (1968; rev. 1976)
See also VII. 9, 14, 18, 20, 22, 24, 30, 36,
    50, 51, 52

Taverner, John
    b. South Lincolnshire, *c.* 1490;
    d. Boston, Lincolnshire, 18 October
    1545.
    Composer. 1524–5, Lay Clerk

Tattershall Collegiate Church. 1526, instructor of the choristers, Cardinal's College, Oxford. 1530s, Lay Clerk St Botolph's, Boston.

Hand, C., *John Taverner: his Life and Music* (1978)
Josephson, D.S., *John Taverner, Tudor Composer* (Ann Arbor, 1979)
See also VII. 20, 50, 51, 52

Tye, Christopher
  b. *c.* 1505; d. ?1572.
  Composer. 1536, BMus Cambridge. 1537, Lay clerk, King's College. 1543, Master of the Choristers, Ely Cathedral. 1545, DMus Cambridge. 1560, Holy orders.
See VII. 6, 14, 20, 24, 30, 51

Weelkes, Thomas
  b. ?Elsted, Sussex, ?baptised 25 October 1576; d. London, buried 1 December 1623.
  Composer. *Madrigals to 3, 4, 5, & 6 Voyces* (1597). 1598, Organist at Winchester College. *Balletts and Madrigals to Five Voyces, with One to 6 voyces* (1598). *Madrigals of 5. and 6. Parts, apt for the Viols and Voices* (1600). Contributed to *The Triumphes of Oriana*, 1601. By 1602 Organist and *informator choristarum* at Chichester Cathedral. 1602, BMus Oxford. *Ayres of Phantasticke Spirites for Three Voyces* (1608). By 1608, Gentleman of the Chapel Royal. 16 January 1617, dismissed as *informator choristarum* and Organist.

Brown, D., *Thomas Weelkes: a Biographical and Critical Study* (1969)
Mellers, W., *Harmonious Meeting: a Study of the Relationship between English Music, Poetry and Theatre, c. 1600–1900* (1965)
Welch, C.E., *Two Cathedral Organists. Thomas Weelkes (1601–1623) and Thomas Kelway (1720–1744)*, The Chichester Papers, **8** (Chichester, 1957)
See also VII. 16, 22, 24

White, Robert
  b. *c.* 1538; d. London November 1574.
  Composer. 13 December 1560, BMus Cambridge. Michaelmas 1562, Master of the Choristers, Ely Cathedral. Annunciation 1567, Master of the Choristers, Chester Cathedral. By 3 February 1570 Master of the Choristers, Westminster Abbey.

Neighbour, O., *The Consort and Keyboard Music of William Byrd* (1978)
See also VII. 8, 30

Wilbye, John
  b. Diss, baptised 7 March 1574; d. Colchester, between September and November 1638.
  Composer. Working for the Kytsons at Hengrave Hall by 1598. *First Set of Madrigals*, 1598. Contributor to *Triumphes of Oriana*, 1601. *Second Set of Madrigals*, 1609.

Brown, D., *Thomas Weelkes: a Biographical and Critical Study* (1969)
Brown, D., *John Wilbye* (1974)
See also VII. 16, 22

VII   Shrewsbury

Champion, W.A., *Population Change in Shrewsbury 1400–1700* (1983) Shrewsbury Local Studies Library MS **6821**]
  'The Shrewsbury lay subsidy of 1525', *Shropshire Archaeological Society Transactions* **64** (1985) 35–46
  Shrewsbury Tolls and Commerce (1986) [Shrewsbury Local Studies Library MS **6855**]
Forrest, H.E., *The Old Houses of Shrewsbury: their History and Associations* (1911; 3rd edn, Shrewsbury, 1932)
Mendenhall, T.S., *The Shrewsbury Drapers and the Welsh Wool Trade in the Sixteenth and Seventeenth Centuries* (Oxford, 1953)
Owen, H., *Ancient and Present State of Shrewsbury* (Shrewsbury, 1808)
Owen, H. and Blakeway, J.B., *History of Shrewsbury*, 2 vols. (1825)
Phillips, T., *The History and Antiquities of Shrewsbury* (Shrewsbury, 1779)
Smith, J.T., 'The domestic architecture of Shrewsbury', *Archaeological Journal* **113** (1956) 186–7
  Shrewsbury: Topography and Domestic Architecture to the Middle of the Seventeenth Century (Birmingham University MA thesis, 1953)
Victoria County History, *Shropshire* III, 54–89; 232–49

IX   The Visual Arts

1   General
Cook, O., *The English House Through Seven Centuries* (1968)

Croft-Murray, E., *Decorative Painting in England 1537–1837*, vol. I: *Early Tudor to Sir James Thornhill* (1962)

Cunningham, W., *Alien Immigrants to England* (1969)

Edwards, R. and Ramsey, L.G.G. (eds), *The Connoisseur Period Guides: the Tudor Period, 1500–1603* (1956)

Girouard, M., *Life in the English Country House* (1978)

Jourdain, M., *English Interior Decoration 1500–1830* (1950)

Pevsner, N. *et al.*, *The Buildings of England* (Harmondsworth, 1951–74)

2   Engraving

Barkley, H., *Likenesses in Line: an Anthology of Tudor and Stuart Engraved Portraits* (1982)

Bartsch, A., *Le Peintre graveur* (1803–21)

Corbett, M. and Lightbown, R., *The Comely Frontispiece: the Emblematic Titlepage in England 1550–1660* (1969)

Herbert, A.S., *Historical Catalogue of Printed Editions of the English Bible 1525–1961* (1968)

Hake, H.M. and O'Donoghue, F.M., *Catalogue of Engraved British Portraits . . . in the British Museum*, 6 vols. (1908–28)

Hind, A.M., *Engraving in England in the Sixteenth and Seventeenth Centuries: Part I, The Tudor Period* (Cambridge, 1952)

Johnson, A.F., *A Catalogue of Engraved and Etched English Title-pages . . .* (1934)

McKerrow, R.B., *Dictionary of Printers and Booksellers . . . 1557–1640* (1910)

McKerrow, R.B. and Ferguson, F.S., *Title-page Borders used in England and Scotland, 1485–1640* (1932)

3   Painters

Bennick, Simon (*c.* 1480–1561)
Illuminator. Of Flemish artist family, from Bruges and Ghent, and father of Levina Teerlinc, bringing her with him when he entered the service of Henry VIII. At some point returned to Bruges.
See IX. 5

Bettes, John I (*fl.* 1531–70; already dead by latter date).
Miniaturist, oil painter, and wood engraver. Worked on coronation of Henry VIII.

Dodgeson, C., 'The portrait of Franz Burchard', *BM* 12 (1907), 39–40
See IX. 5, 58

Bettes, John II (*fl.* 1578 /9–99)
Oil painter and ?miniaturist. Single signed portrait known. Perhaps pupil of Nicholas Hilliard.
See IX. 4, 5, 15, 58

Brounckhorst, Arnold van (*fl.* 1565 /6–80)
Oil painter. Flemish. Partner of Nicholas Hilliard in gold prospecting in Scotland. Principal painter to James VI of Scotland.
See IX. 4, 5, 58

Critz, John De (1555–1641)
Oil painter and decorative painter. Flemish, brought to England in 1568. Travels to France and ?Italy. Painter to the Navy. 1603. Sergeant Painter, 1605.

Leith-Ross, P., *The John Tradescants: Gardeners to the Rose and Lily Queen* (1984)

MacGregor, A., 'The Tradescants: Gardeners and Botanists' and 'The Tradescants as collectors of rarities' in A. MacGregory (ed.), *Tradescant's Rarities: Essays on the Foundation of the Ashmolean Museum 1683* (Oxford, 1983)

Piper, D., 'Some portraits by Marcus Gheeraerts II and John De Critz reconsidered', *Proceedings of the Huguenot Society* 20 (1960), 210–19

Poole, R.L., 'The De Critz family of painters', *Walpole Society* 2 (1913), 45–68
See IX. 5, 11, 15, 58

Custodis, Hieronimo (*fl.* 1589–93)
Oil painter. Flemish exile from Antwerp.
See IX. 5, 6, 58, 59

Eworth, Hans (*fl.* 1540–73)
Oil painter and designer. Flemish, from Antwerp. Official portraitist to Mary I. Out of favour with Elizabeth I until 1572.
See IX. 19, 58, 62

Flicke, Gerlach (*fl.* 1545, d. 1558)
Painter. From Osnabruck. Imprisoned 1554.

Hervey, M., 'Notes on a Tudor painter; Gerlach Flicke', *BM*, **17** (1910), 71–9, 147–8
See IX. 5, 58

Gheeraerts, Marcus the Elder (?1525–?1599)
Etcher. Flemish, from Bruges. Brought family to England, 1567–8. Etched

procession of the Order of the Garter, 1576.

See IX. 15

Gheeraerts, Marcus the Younger
(*c.* 1561–1635)
Painter. Flemish; brought to England from Bruges, 1567–8. Married sister of John De Critz. His sister marries Isaac Oliver. Fashionable court painter from 1590s to 1620s.

Cust, L., 'Marcus Gheeraerts', *WS* **3** (1914)
Piper, D., 'Some portraits by Marcus Gheeraerts II and John De Critz reconsidered', *Proceedings of the Huguenot Society* **20** (1960), 210–19
Poole, R.L., 'Marcus Gheeraerts, father and son, painters', *WS* **3** (1914) 1–8
Millar, O., 'Marcus Gheeraerts the Younger, a sequel through inscriptions', *BM*, **105** (1963), 533–41
See IX. 5, 14, 15, 58, 61, 65

Gower, George (1540?–d. 1596)
Oil painter and decorative painter. Fashionable court painter by 1573. Sergeant Painter, 1581. Attempts, with Nicholas Hilliard, a monopoly on royal portraits, 1584. Painter to the Navy by 1593.

Goodison, J.W., 'George Gower. Serjeant-Painter to Queen Elizabeth' *BM*, **90** (1948), 261–5
Strong, Roy, 'A portrait by Queen Elizabeth I's Serjeant-Painter', *Art Association of Indianapolis Bulletin*, December 1963, 52–8
Waterhouse, E.K., 'A note on George Gower's self-portrait at Milton Park', *BM* **90** (1948), 267
See IX. 5, 11, 15, 58, 61, 70

Heere, Lucas de (1534–84)
Illuminator and painter. Flemish, from Ghent. In England 1567–77.

Yates, F.A., *The Valois Tapestries* (1959) [p. 133 n. 2]
See IX. 58, 61

Hilliard, Lawrence (1581/2–1647/8)
Miniaturist and goldsmith. Son and pupil of Nicholas Hilliard.
See IX. 14, 15, 42

Hilliard, Nicholas (*c.* 1547–1619)
Miniaturist, oil painter, designer, goldsmith, jeweller, wood engraver. Son of a goldsmith. Taken to Geneva during reign of Mary I. Apprenticed as a goldsmith to Robert Brandon, 1562; Freeman of the Goldsmiths Company,

1569. Travelled to France in train of ambassador, Sir Amyas Paulet, 1576–8; in service of Duc d'Alencon, 1577; met Francois Gaultier, Ronsard, and other artists of the French court. Recalled to England by Elizabeth I. Teacher of Isaac Oliver, Rowland Lockey, Laurence Hilliard, and others. Jointly designed and made Great Seal of England, 1584–6. Involved in various monopoly bids and schemes, including (with George Gower) an attempt to impose monopoly on royal portraits, 1584; financial problems. Between 1598 and 1603 wrote *A Treatise Concerning the Arte of Limning*, probably at the request of Richard Haydocke. Style lost favour under James I.

A Treatise Concerning the Arte of Limning, eds, R.K. Thornton and T.G.S. Cain (Ashington, 1981); eds, A.F. Kinney and L.B. Salamon (Boston, 1983)

Auerbach, E., 'More light on Nicholas Hilliard', *BM* **91** (1949), 166–8
Blakiston, N., 'Nicholas Hilliard and Bordeaux', *TLS*, 28 July 1950
'Nicholas Hilliard and Queen Elizabeth's third Great Seal', *BM* **90** (1948), 101–7
'Nicholas Hilliard as a traveller', *BM* **91** (1949), 169
'Nicholas Hilliard at court', *BM* **96** (1954), 17–8
'Nicholas Hilliard: some unpublished documents', *BM* **89** (1947), 187–9
Goldschmidt, E.P., 'Nicholas Hilliard as wood engraver', *TLS*, 9 August 1947
Pope-Hennessy, J., *A Lecture on Nicholas Hilliard* (1949)
Strong, R., *Nicholas Hilliard* (1975)
'Nicholas Hilliard's miniature of Francis Bacon rediscovered and other minutiae', *BM* **106** (1964), 337
See IX. 4, 5, 14, 15, 42, 44, 48, 50, 51, 52, 53, 56, 57, 58, 62, 64, 65, 66, 67, 70, 73, 74

Holbein, Hans, 'the younger'
(*c.* 1497–1543)
Oil painter, miniaturist, designer. Born Augsburg, of a family of artists. In Basle by 1515. Friend of Erasmus, who recommended him to Sir Thomas More. In consequence of Reformation hostility to images in Basle, travelled to England, 1526–8. Returned to Basle, 1528–32. In England once more from 1532, patronised by Thomas Cromwell, and became leading court artist. Participated in Henry VIII's marriage

negotiations through portraits of prospective brides. Learned the art of the miniature from Lucas Hornebolte. Holbein profoundly influenced Hilliard and others; but was perhaps even more influential in the long term by virtue of his stimulus to English connoisseurship; the volume of his drawings passed through the hands of many of the chief sixteenth- and seventeenth-century collectors and remains in the royal collection.

Ganz, P., *The Paintings of Hans Holbein: First Complete Edition* (1950)

Grossman, F., 'Holbein, Torrigiani, and some portraits of Dean Colet', *JWCI* **13** (1950), 211–13

Holbein and the court of Henry VIII, exhibition catalogue, Queen's Gallery, Buckingham Palace (1978–9)

Parker, K.T., *The Drawings of Hans Holbein in the Collection of HM the King at Windsor Castle* (1945)

Rowlands, J., *Holbein: the Paintings of Hans Holbein the Younger. Complete Edition* (Oxford, 1985)

See IX. 5, 34, 40, 42, 50, 53, 56, 70

Hornebolte, Gerard (*fl.* 1510–31)
Illuminator and miniaturist. Flemish, from Ghent. Court painter to Margaret of Austria, Regent of the Netherlands. Brought family to England *c.* 1525. No longer active in England after early 1530s.

Holbein and the Court of Henry VIII, exhibition catalogue Queen's Gallery, Buckingham Palace (1978–9)

See IX. 5, 10, 42, 45

Hornebolte, Lucas (1490/5–44)
Illuminator, miniaturist, perhaps oil painter, decorative painter, and designer. Flemish, from Ghent. Son of Gerard and brother of Susanna Hornebolte, one of the leading Burgundian artistic families. In England by 1525, King's Painter by 1531. Taught Holbein the art of the miniature.

See IX. 5, 10, 42, 45, 66, 67

Hornebolte, Susanna (d. before 1557)
Member of Hornebolte family of Burgundian artists. Works admired by Dürer. Brought to England *c.* 1525. Married twice in England.

See references under Gerard and Lucas above

Ketel, Cornelius (1548–1616)
Painter. Native of Gouda. Worked at Fontainebleau. In England, 1573–81.

See IX. 5, 6, 59, 61, 70

Lockey, Rowland (*fl.* 1581–1616)
Miniaturist, goldsmith, designer, and oil painter. Apprenticed to Nicholas Hilliard, 1581

Kurz, O., 'Rowland Lockey', *BM* **99** (1957), 13–16

See IX. 4, 15, 42, 56, 58, 59

Meulen, Steven van der (*fl.* 1543–1568)
Painter. Flemish, from Antwerp. In London by 1560. Travelled to paint Erik VI of Sweden as prospective husband for Elizabeth I. Noted as 'famous' in Lumley Inventory.

Hill, G.F., 'Two Netherlandish artists in England, Steven van Herwijck and Steven van der Meulen', *WS* **11** (1923), 29–32

Constable, W.G., 'A new work by "the famous paynter Steven"', *BM* **67** (1935), 135–6

See IX. 5, 58

Modena, Nicholas da (d. 1568/9)
Decorative painter, sculptor, and carver. Italian. Worked at Fontainebleau. In England from 1537. Works for Office of the Revels and on royal tombs.

See IX. 5

Moro, Antonio (1517/20–1576/7)
Oil painter. Flemish. Court painter in Netherlands and Spain. In England, 1553–5.

Hymans, H., *Antonio Moro, son oeuvre et son temps* (Brussels, 1910)

See IX. 5, 58

Oliver, Isaac (1565/7–1617)
Miniaturist. French, born Rouen. Son of goldsmith. In England by 1568. Trained artist before becoming pupil of Nicholas Hilliard. Visited Italy, 1596. Married sister of Marcus Gheeraerts the Younger, 1602.

Edmond, M., 'An Isaac Oliver sitter identified', *BM* **124** (1982), 496–501

See IX. 4, 14, 42, 50, 58, 59, 61, 67

Peake, Robert (*c.* 1551–1619)
Oil painter, decorative painter, and goldsmith. Employed by Office of the Revels by 1576. Principal Painter to Henry Prince of Wales. Sergeant Painter, 1607.

Finberg, A.J., 'An authentic portrait by Robert Peake', *WS* **9** (1921), 89–95

See IX. 5, 11, 14, 15, 16, 65

Scrots, William (*fl.* 1537–54)
Painter. Court painter to Mary of
Hungary, Regent of the Netherlands.
In England, 1545. Succeeded Holbein
as Sergeant Painter.
See IX. 4, 5, 58, 70

Segar, Sir William (*fl. c.* 1580 /5–d. 1633)
Painter and herald. Probably painting
by 1580s. Heraldic career from 1585;
Garter King of Arms, 1603. Knighted,
1617.

Grossman, F., 'Holbein, Torrigiani, and
some portraits of Dean Colet', *JWCI*
13 (1950), 211–13
Piper, D.T., 'The 1590 Lumley inventory:
Hilliard, Segar and the Earl of Essex',
BM **99** (1957), 224–31, 299–303
See IX. 4, 58, 61

Shute, John (d. 1563)
Painter-stainer, miniaturist, and
architect. In Italy, *c.* 1550. *The First
and Chief Grounds of Architecture*
(1563).

Teerlinc, Levina (1510 /20–76)
Illuminator, miniaturist, and designer.
Flemish, from Bruges. Daughter of
Simon Benninck, and thus member of
famous Burgundian artist family. In
England from 1545. Married George
Teerlinc. In service of Henry VIII as
'paintrix', 1546. Presented series of
miniatures as New Year gifts to
monarch, 1553–76. Few identified
works extant.
See IX. 5, 14, 15, 16, 42, 59, 60, 66, 67

Zuccaro, Federigo (1540 /3–1609)
Painter. Roman. Visited England, 1575.
Collaborated with brother Taddeo at
heart of Roman Mannerist art.
See IX. 58, 61

4 Painting

PRIMARY WORKS

*A Very Proper Treatise, Wherein is Briefly
Set Forth the Arte of Limning* (1573)
Haydocke, R., *A Tracte Containing the
Artes of Curious Paintings, Carvings and
Buildings*, tr. of G.P. Lomazzo
(Oxford, 1598)
Hilliard, Nicholas, *A Treatise Concerning
the Arte of Limning*, eds. R.K.
Thornton and T.G.S. Cain (Ashington,
1981); eds. A.F. Kinney and L.B.
Salamon (Boston, 1983)
Shute, J., *The First and Chief Groundes of
Architecture* (1563)

SECONDARY WORKS

(1)   Adler, D., 'The riddle of the sieve:
the Sieve Portrait of Queen Elizabeth'
in *Renaissance Papers, 1978*, ed. A.L.
Deneef and M. T. Hester (Durham.
NC: Southwestern Renaissance
Conference, 1979), 1–10.
(2)   Anglo, S., *The Great Tournament Roll
of Westminster* (Oxford, 1968)
(3)   Arnold, J., 'The "Coronation"
portrait of Queen Elizabeth I', *BM* **120**
(1978) 727–41
(4)   Auerbach, E., *Nicholas Hilliard* (1961)
(5)   Auerbach, E., *Tudor Artists: a Study
of Painters in the Royal Service and of
Portraiture on Illuminated Documents
from the Accession of Henry VIII to the
Death of Elizabeth I* (1954)
(6)   Collins Baker, C.H. and Constable,
W.G., *English Painting of the Sixteenth
and Seventeenth Centuries* (Florence
and Paris, 1930)
(7)   Benesch, O., *The Renaissance in
Northern Europe* (Harvard, 1945)
(8)   Bergeron, D., *English Civic Pageantry
1558–1642* (1971)
(9)   Buxton, J., *Sir Philip Sidney and the
English Renaissance* (1954)
(10)   Colding, T.H., *Aspects of Miniature
Painting: its Origins and Development*
(Copenhagen, 1953)
(11)   Croft-Murray, E., *Decorative Painting
in England 1537–1837*. Vol. I: *Early
Tudor to Sir James Thornhill* (1962)
(12)   Cust, L., *Notes on the Authentic
Portraits of Queen Mary of Scots* (1903)
(13)   Cust, L., 'The painter HE', *Walpole
Society* **2** (1913)
(14)   Edmond, M., *Hilliard and Oliver: the
Lives and Works of Two Great
Miniaturists* (1983)
(15)   Edmond, M., 'Limners and
picturemakers: new light on the lives of
miniaturists and large-scale portrait-
painters working in London in the
sixteenth and seventeenth centuries',
WS **47** (1980), 60–242
(16)   Edmond, M., 'New light on Jacobean
painters', *BM* **118** (1976) 74–83
(17)   Einstein, L., *The Italian Renaissance
in England* (NY, 1902)
(18)   Englefield, W.A.D., *History of the
Painter-Stainers' Company Of London*
(1923)
(19)   *Hans Eworth: a Tudor Painter and his
Circle*, catalogue of an exhibition at
Leicester Museum and Art Gallery and
the National Portrait Gallery by R.
Strong (Leicester, 1965)
(20)   Foister, S., 'Paintings and other

works of art in sixteenth-century inventories', *BM* **123** (1981) 273–82

(21) Foskett, D., *Collecting Miniatures* (Woodbridge, 1979)

(22) Foskett, D., *A Dictionary of British Miniature Painters*, 2 vols. (1972)

(23) Goulding, R.W., 'The Welbeck Abbey miniatures: a catalogue raisonné', *WS* **4** (1916) 1–224

(24) Graziani, R., 'The *Rainbow Portrait* of Queen Elizabeth I and its religious symbolism', *JWCI* **35** (1972), 250–4

(25) Hazard, M.E., 'The anatomy of "liveliness" as a concept in renaissance aesthetics', *Journal of Aesthetics and Art Criticism*, **33** (1975) 407–18

(26) Hill, G.F., 'Two Netherlandish artists in England, Steven van Herwijck and Steven van der Meulen', *WS* **11** (1923) 29–32

(27) *Hilliard and Oliver*, exhibition catalogue by Graham Reynolds, Victoria and Albert Museum (1947; revised and expanded, 1971)

(28) Hotson, L., *Mr W H* (1964)

(29) Hotson, L., 'Queen Elizabeth's Master Painter', *Sunday Times* colour supplement, 22 March 1970

(30) Hotson, L., *Shakespeare by Hilliard* (1977)

(31) Hulton, P., *America 1585: the Complete Drawings of John White* (London, 1985)

(32) Earl of Ilchester, 'Cameos of Queen Elizabeth', *Connoisseur* **63** (1922)

(33) *A Kind of Gentle Painting: an Exhibition of Miniatures by the Elizabethan Court Artists Nicholas Hilliard and Isaac Oliver*, catalogue by E. Brett (Edinburgh, 1975)

(34) 'The King's Good servant', Sir Thomas More, exhibition catalogue by J.B. Trapp and H.S. Herbruggen (1977)

(35) Kipling, G., *Triumph of Honour: Burgundian Origins of the Elizabethan Renaissance* (Leiden, 1977)

(36) Lees-Milne, J., *Tudor Renaissance* (1951)

(37) Long, B.S., *British Miniaturists* (1929)

(38) Long, B.S., 'Miniaturists, their desks and boxes', *Connoisseur* **83** (1929) 323–7

(39) Mercer, E., *English Art 1553–1625*, Oxford History of English Art, vol. VII (Oxford, 1962)

(40) Millar, O., *The Tudor, Stuart, and early Georgian Pictures in the Collection of Her Majesty the Queen* (1963)

(41) Morison, S. and Barker, N., *The Likeness of Sir Thomas More* (1963)

(42) Murdoch, J., Murrell, J., Noon, P.J. and Strong, R., *The English Miniature* (New Haven, 1981)

(43) Murrell, J., *The Waye Howe to Lymne: Tudor Miniatures Observed* (1983)

(44) O'Donoghue, F.M., *A Descriptive and Classified Catalogue of Portraits of Queen Elizabeth* (1894)

(45) Paget, H., 'Gerard and Lucas Hornebolt in England', *BM* **101** (1959) 396–402

(46) Parry, G., *The Golden Age Restor'd* (Manchester, 1981)

(47) Phillips, J., *The Reformation of Images: Destruction of Art in England 1535–1660* (Berkeley, 1973)

(48) Piper, D., 'The 1590 Lumley inventory: Hilliard, Segar and the Earl of Essex', *BM* **99** (1957) Part 1, 224–31; Part 2, 299–303

(49) *The Renaissance at Sutton Place*, exhibition catalogue (Guildford, 1983)

(50) Reynolds, G., *English Portrait Miniatures* (1952)

(51) Reynolds, G., *Nicholas Hilliard and Isaac Oliver*, Victoria and Albert Handbook (1947)

(52) Reynolds, G., 'The painter plays the spider', *Apollo*, April 1964, 279–84

(53) Reynolds, G., 'Portrait miniatures from Holbein to Augustin', *Apollo*, October 1976, 274–81

(54) Reynolds, G., *Wallace Collection: Catalogue of Miniatures* (1980)

(55) Strong, R., *Art and Power: Renaissance Festivals 1450–1650* (1984)

(56) Strong, R., *The Cult of Elizabeth* (1977)

(57) Strong, R., *The Elizabethan Image: Painting in England 1540–1620*, Tate Gallery exhibition catalogue (1969)

(58) Strong, R., *The English Icon: Elizabethan and Jacobean Portraiture* (1969)

(59) Strong, R., *The English Renaissance Miniature* (1983)

(60) Strong, R., 'Federigo Zuccaro's visit to England in 1575', *JWCI* **22** (1959) 359–60

(61) Strong, R., *Gloriana: the Portraits of Queen Elizabeth I* (1987) [This is a revision of (65), but each has independent value]

(62) Strong, R., 'Hans Eworth reconsidered', *BM* **108** (1966) 225–33

(63) Strong, R., 'The Leicester House miniatures: Robert Sidney, 1st Earl of Leicester and his circle', *BM* **127** (1985), 694–701

(64) Strong, R., 'Queen Elizabeth, the Earl of Essex and Nicholas Hilliard', *BM* 101 (1959), 145–9

(65) Strong, R., *The Portraits of Queen Elizabeth I* (Oxford, 1963)

(66) Strong, R., *Tudor and Jacobean Portraits*, 2 vols. (1969)

(67) Strong, R. and Murrell, V.J., *Artists of the Tudor Court: the Portrait Miniature Rediscovered, 1520–1620* (1983)

(68) Vallance, A., *Art in England during the Elizabethan and Stuart periods* (1908)

(69) Walpole, H., *Anecdotes of Painting*, ed. R.N. Wornum, 3 vols. (1888)

(70) Waterhouse, E., *Painting in Britain 1530 to 1790*, Pelican History of Art (1954; 4th edn, Harmondsworth, 1978)

(71) Williamson, G.C., *The Art of the Miniature Painter* (1905)

(72) Williamson, G.C., *Catalogue of the Miniatures in the Possession of J. Pierpoint Morgan* (1906)

(73) Winter, C., *Elizabethan Miniatures* (1943)

(74) Winter, C., 'Hilliard and Elizabethan miniatures', *BM* **89** (1947) 175–83

(75) Woodward, J., *Tudor and Stuart Drawings* (1951)

(76) Yuasa, N., 'She is all eyes and ears: a study of the Rainbow Portrait of Queen Elizabeth', in *Poetry and Drama in the Age of Shakespeare: Essays in Honour of Professor Shonosuke Ishii's Seventieth Birthday*, ed. P. Milward and T. Anzai, Renaissance Monographs, no. 9 (Tokyo, 1982)

5   Sculpture

Crossley, F.W., *English Church Monuments, 1150–1550* (1921)

Esdaile, K.A., *English Church Monuments, 1510–1840* (1946)

English Monumental Sculpture since the Renaissance (1927)

Gardner, A., *Albaster Tombs of the pre-Reformation Period in England* (Cambridge, 1940)

Stone, L., *Sculpture in Britain: the Middle Ages* (Harmondsworth, 1958) [Pelican History of Art]

Whinney, M., *Sculpture in Britain 1530–1830* (Harmondsworth, 1964) [Pelican History of Art]

See IX. 39

Sources of Illustrations

Colour Plates

Index

Major entries are shown in capital letters. Literary works are listed under the author where known. Page numbers of illustrations are shown in italics.